Stranger Among Friends

STRANGER AMONG FRIENDS

DAVID MIXNER

Bantam Books
New York • Toronto • London • Sydney • Auckland

STRANGER AMONG FRIENDS
A Bantam Book/August 1996

Grateful acknowledgment for permission to reprint the following: "Your Laughter" by Pablo Neruda, from *The Captain's Verses*. Copyright © 1972 by Pablo Neruda and Donald D. Walsh. Reprinted by permission of New Directions Publishing Corp. "Arrival in Madrid of the International Brigade" by Pablo Neruda, from *Residence on Earth*. Copyright © 1973 by Pablo Neruda and Donald D. Walsh. Reprinted by permission of New Directions Publishing Corp.

BOOK DESIGN BY JAMES SINCLAIR

Library of Congress Cataloging-in-Publication Data

Mixner, David B.
Stranger among friends / David B. Mixner.
p.   cm.
Includes index.
ISBN 0-553-10073-4
1. Mixner, David B.   2. Gay activists—United States—Biography.
3. Gay rights—United States. I. Title.
HQ75.8.M59A3   1996
305.9′0664′092—dc20
[B]   96-24542
CIP

Published simultaneously in the United States and Canada

Bantam Books are published by Bantam Books, a division of Bantam Doubleday Dell Publishing Group, Inc. Its trademark, consisting of the words "Bantam Books" and the portrayal of a rooster, is Registered in U.S. Patent and Trademark Office and in other countries. Marca Registrada. Bantam Books, 1540 Broadway, New York, New York 10036.

PRINTED IN THE UNITED STATES OF AMERICA
BVG   10 9 8 7 6 5 4 3 2 1

For Patsy

A Personal Note

This book is one man's journey through a great movement of the last few decades. It is not meant to be an historical record of the gay and lesbian community in the United States. There are thousands upon thousands of brave men and women who contributed to this movement who are not recorded in these pages but whose courage and accomplishments have been immense. In a few instances, names and particulars have been changed in order to respect the privacy and wishes of those portrayed, but I have endeavored to honor their brave struggle faithfully.

Contents

"Three passions, simple but overwhelmingly strong, have governed my life; the longing for love, the search for knowledge, and unbearable pity for the suffering of mankind."

—*Bertrand Russell*

Prologue

THE President and I were born three days apart. We both dreamed of serving our country. There was one difference. He could pursue his dreams while I felt I could not. Bill Clinton was born straight and I was born gay.

We were children in a special time. We thought anything was possible. There were heroes—Rosa Parks, Martin Luther King, Jr.—who made us believe one person with courage could truly make a difference. John F. Kennedy's inaugural address inspired us to service. No aspiration—to soar to the moon and beyond, to change the world, to be president when you grew up—seemed too great.

In the early seventies Clinton and I reminisced about the similarities of our childhoods. We had both grown up in small-town America with strong mothers who dreamed with us. We were both ambitious, and we loved to impress adults. We were constantly engaged in the politics of approval. We sought the acceptance and admiration of our peers and our families and our neighbors. We had both taken lonely walks down country roads in those early years and fantasized not only about seeing the world but having the world see us. We both loved the world of politics. We had both been in the wilderness, longing to break away, yearning to reach a place where at last we would not be outsiders.

That yearning is with me still. Bill Clinton found his dream. But our separate journeys overlapped decades later, and then, suddenly, each became crucial to the other's dream. This is the story of my journey.

PART ONE

The Journey

"Precious father, loving mother,
Fly across the lonely years,
And old home scenes of my childhood
In fond memory appears."
—*Old Hymn*

The Awakening

It was the morning of July 19, 1993. In our one-room office in my home in West Hollywood, California, I and my two staffers, Tony Leonhardt and Jeremy Bernard, sat facing the television set. Covering the walls of the office were campaign posters, souvenirs from the Democratic National Convention that had nominated Bill Clinton the previous July, mementos from his inauguration, and photographs of the President and me. They symbolized years of work for which the moment we now awaited was the climax. We hoped it would be a moment of triumph. I wondered whether before the next hour was over I would want to take them all down.

In just a few minutes the President of the United States was scheduled to speak to the nation on the issue of gays and lesbians in the military. We were swamped with apprehensiveness. We had heard from sources within the White House that Clinton was preparing to make an announcement we would view as a disastrous retreat from all that we had fought for for so long. That morning White House presidential adviser

George Stephanopoulos had called to inform us of the President's final decision. He had greeted me warmly, then said, "David, the President asked me to call and to seek your support for his policy."

"I don't know what it is yet," I answered. "No one has told me."

"Well, we have been busy putting the finishing touches on it—even as late as last night."

I did not find this very encouraging. "George, I wish I could have assisted in the process," I said. "If the policy is the rumored 'Don't Ask, Don't Tell,' I won't be able to support it. In fact, I will actively oppose it."

"Don't make any quick judgments, David," Stephanopoulos protested. "I think you will be pleased and surprised with the speech. We have had to make some compromises, but we believe this to be a big step forward."

I told him I hoped he was right. "There is nothing I would like to do more than to support the President on this one," I said. "Let's talk after the speech."

"Okay, David," he answered. "Just give it careful thought."

I was a tangle of emotions as I hung up the phone. I wanted to be optimistic, but "compromises"? What was meant by "compromises"? And I was angry. After years of friendship, and after working so hard for his election and raising millions of dollars for his campaign, I thought the least Clinton could have done was to call me personally to tell me what he had decided. It wasn't easy to put aside my sense of having been treated discourteously—I knew that when he was ready to make other major announcements he had personally called those who were involved beforehand. But forget my bruised ego. It was the substance that would matter. I sat there waiting and tried to be hopeful.

Then came the standard announcement that CNN was interrupting its regularly scheduled program. We watched the President of the United States proceed to the podium, making his way along a stage surrounded by flags and filled with military personnel, with the Joint Chiefs of Staff seated in the center. On the occasion of this heralded "historic announcement" we could not see a single gay or lesbian leader in the group on the stage or visible in the audience.

The first parts of the speech were encouraging. Clinton spoke with eloquence of his abhorrence of discrimination against gays and lesbians and of the contributions our community makes to society. Despite Stephanopoulos's hedging, my spirits began to rise. Then Clinton began to outline his policy. We listened to the nation's commander in chief, our political hero, yield to his subordinates in the military and set back our struggle for freedom with an uncompromising "Don't Ask, Don't Tell" policy. Supposedly it would make it safer for us to serve in the military; actually it still forced us to stay in the closet and live in fear. We sat there stunned.

This was not supposed to happen. He had promised the leaders of the battle for the rights of homosexuals that when he had achieved the White House, he would issue an executive order that with the stroke of his pen would end decades of oppression against lesbians and gays who wanted to serve their country. This was the moment he promised, and he had betrayed us.

I knew Bill Clinton well enough to realize he had convinced himself that he had done his best—that he had, in fact, paid a political price for supporting us. I felt differently. Through decades of political struggle, I had waited for a president like Clinton—one of my own generation, one whom I knew and had worked with, one who would finally set the gay and lesbian community free. On November 3, 1992, the waiting had ended. We had that president and I had access to him. I could move easily in and out of the White House. I knew many of his staff personally and most members of his cabinet. As I watched his inauguration on January 20, I had believed with all my heart that the next four years would be years of opportunity—and fulfillment.

Listening to my President on this day nearly half a year later, I realized the dream was over. I had a crucial decision to make: whether to support the policy he had just announced and keep my access to him alive but not be able to live with my conscience, or to reject it. The choice I made would determine my future course, professionally and personally. Everything I had done in my life was preparation for this decision. I had had a long and difficult journey. Now I had to declare who I was—not only to others but to myself.

The journey began with my parents. Ben and Mary Mixner's life was about their children. Patsy was their oldest, Melvin three years younger, and myself three years behind him. We lived in a rural area near the town of Elmer in southern New Jersey, where Dad worked for a corporate farm and in the summer was in the fields eighteen hours a day. For a while Mom did shift work in the local glass factory, and later got a job as bookkeeper at the local John Deere tractor dealership. They both worked terribly hard. Money was always short. My parents kept very little for themselves. Caring for their children was what mattered.

My mother's closet said everything about their sacrifice, although sacrifice was the last way they would have perceived their lives. Inside the cavernous space hung two dresses and a worn winter coat—nothing more. She would return from her shift at the factory, prepare dinner, and do the endless laundry for a household with three active youngsters. I remember the old-fashioned washer, and the way she had to feed every piece of clothing, every sheet and towel, through the wringer, then rinse them by hand in a big tub behind the washer and put them through the wringer again. I can still smell the sweet fresh scent of sheets and towels that had been dried on the clotheslines in the sun.

Mom and Dad did everything they could to mute the harshness of our lives. Summers were especially wonderful. Crops fresh from the fields and our garden kept us fed during those months. We ate tomato sandwiches for lunch and baked stuffed tomatoes and corn on the cob at suppertime. On weekends and paydays we had special treats—hamburger gravy over white bread or Mrs. Paul's fish sticks. I remember accompanying my father around the fields. I loved the smell of the clean air, the freshly plowed fields, and the grass after a thunderstorm. At night Dad would sometimes take me with him and let me watch him supervise the Jamaican migrant workers as they pitched just-harvested pea vines into the mechanical viners and sang the songs of their homeland as they worked.

Our rural setting was a vast playground for us kids. As the youngest, I had more space for freedom and exploration than Patsy and Melvin but we all wandered in the woods behind our large white farmhouse. Melvin and I would sneak off and skinny-dip in the irrigation ponds behind the barn. Since Mom and Dad both worked, my Grandfather Grove lived with us when I was a young child and looked after me. The glorious garden behind the house was his and it was the pride of the family; it not only fed us, it glowed with the hundreds of flowers he planted. He would lean up against the cinder-block cesspool and give me instructions on how to plant, hoe, and care for the garden. Gardening was hot, hard work and I dreaded it, but he let me take rest breaks and I'd listen eagerly to his stories about the Seven Mountains in Pennsylvania where he grew up, his work with Roosevelt's Civilian Conservation Corps—the CCC—and the hard times of the Depression.

At twilight on those summer nights, as I walked down our narrow country road to meet Mom as she drove home from work, I would dream of faraway places and try to imagine what lay beyond the horizon where the violent purple thunderstorms formed. Sometimes I'd venture into the fields to catch fireflies, miss the ride with Mom, and have to walk all the way back to the house. Even on the nights when he had to work late in the fields Dad always came home for dinner, and the whole family sat around the table in the kitchen and talked as we ate. Mom thought it important that we discuss what was going on in the world outside. Afterward there would be ice cream on the screened front porch and then Dad would go back to work.

When I was small we could not afford a television set, and our information about that outside world came from *The Philadelphia Inquirer* delivered by the mailman, Mr. Schaffer. He'd honk the horn of his 1938 Dodge as he stuffed our mailbox with word from elsewhere and I would run down the lane to get to the newspaper first. Of course, there was other "news" as well—local talk you'd garner by listening to the neighbors gossiping about each other on our party-line telephone. We kids were adept at lifting the receiver without being detected. At the country store in Shirley owned by Mr. Ale, where we went to buy the bare necessities we couldn't sew or grow ourselves, we'd hear the local farmers talking about their work and their problems, and if Dad was feeling flush I would get a five-cent ice cream cone.

Winters were severe and dark. We knew the cold was on the way when the air filled with the smell of burning leaves. We took turns shoveling coal into the furnace to keep the house warm. There was no farmwork, of course, and Dad spent the winter months fixing tractors and trucks in preparation for spring planting. Vicious northeasters buried the land in snow and stranded us in our homes, but Dad drove a snowplow and it was fun to ride with him. Sometimes a storm would catch us by surprise, and he'd load his pickup with cinder blocks, chain the school bus to the truck, and pull it through the snowdrifts to get all the kids home safely. Melvin and I would build tunnels through the snowbanks and Mom would have hot chocolate and cinnamon toast for us when we came back to the house.

Winters also meant we got to spend more time together as a family. Dad's workdays were shorter and Mom didn't have to work such long hours at the tractor dealer. Holidays were special, and we looked forward to them all year. We'd head into the woods looking for our Christmas tree, and when we hauled it home it filled the living room with the sharp scent of pine. Mom would inspect it for bare spaces and Dad would string the lights, and then we'd all hang the decorations on the tree while Mom told us the history of each and every ball—"That one came from Grandma Hartman," "We got this one when your father and I first got married." On Christmas Day a host of relatives would arrive from the neighboring towns. My mother's brothers and sisters and their children filled our house. My Uncle Bob and Aunt Ann Grove, my Aunt

Evelyn and Uncle Don, would be laughing around the festive table as we kids eagerly opened our presents. We waited impatiently while Dad said grace and then we dug into the wonderful turkey, its filling (we didn't call it stuffing) always enriched with a little bit of Grandpa Grove's cigar ashes for good luck. There was lemon butter and pickled eggs and spiced peaches, and a whole feast of desserts, and the spread was always the same every Christmas. We looked forward to it all year long.

My folks were realists. They made sure we kids had the skills to cope in what they saw as a difficult world. They didn't believe in "protecting" us from the harsh realities of their lives or the crises that struck them or those around them. We learned that whatever the problem, it could be handled with dignity and honor. Over and over throughout my childhood, we were taught how to adjust to change. Money problems were endless. I remember the time when without forewarning the corporate farm for which my father worked failed to pay its workers the usual end-of-the-year bonus—money my parents had counted on to buy us next year's clothes. For a bit Mom couldn't handle it, and from my upstairs bedroom window I watched her walk back through the fields and fling herself down in a hedgerow crying tears of fear. Then she picked herself up, came back to the house, brushed her hair, turned to us with a smile, and said, "We'll just make do with what we have. Who wants some homemade cookies?" Some years later, when after thirty years of working for the farm my father was laid off with two weeks notice, we all pitched in to make ends meet. It was simply expected of us. I picked beans and moved irrigation pipe that summer and turned the money over to Dad. Patsy, grown by then, sent checks from where she was working in Baltimore, and Melvin got a job and took out loans so he could stay in college. There was no sense of failure. You just made do and moved on.

The same attitude prevailed around death. You faced it. When a neighboring farm wife died at an early age, ten-year-old Patsy was sent over to stay at the house to help out. When our sixteen-year-old cousin Bobby was killed in an automobile accident in 1955, all of us were expected to help. We stayed with his brothers and sisters, we did the washing and ironing for the family, and I cleaned their house. We were taken to the funeral and taught how to cope with grief—theirs and ours—by helping and serving others. Three and four decades later, in the age of AIDS, I was to find these coping skills all too grievously valuable. It was the great wisdom of my parents to know there was no kindness to be found in sheltering their children from a world that had pain as well as love.

They set an example by their own lives. In truth, my father's life was about service. He was a volunteer fireman and always the first on the scene to help a neighbor. One evening in 1956 the phone rang in the middle of the night, always a sign of bad news. It was our neighbor, Mr. Sickler, calling to say that my sister and her boyfriend had been in a bad automobile accident just a mile away from our house. I remember standing in the hallway as my parents frantically pulled on their clothes. Mom kissed me. "You boys have to be here alone," she said. "Something has happened to Patsy. She'll be all right. Be brave and we'll be home soon."

They raced out of our driveway and turned down the same country road that was always such a place of joy to me. As they drove around the bend, their headlights picked out the mass of mangled steel that had been Richie's car. Dad slammed on the brakes, leaped out, and came on my sister bleeding badly in a drainage ditch, her head cradled in the lap of Mrs. Elwell, an elderly widow neighbor, who had heard the crash and found her.

Another neighbor called the nearby town for an ambulance but there was none available to service the people in our rural area. Richie wasn't badly hurt so he was placed in the front seat of our old Ford. Then Dad bent down into the ditch, picked up his daughter in his arms, placed her in the back seat of our old Ford, and sped to the local hospital. As Patsy recovered, Dad vowed that no other father would have to gather his child into the back seat of a car to get medical help.

When local officials told him there was no money to service the rural areas, this didn't stop him. He was on a mission. We had to take care of our own. He called his friends and neighbors together and organized them into the Upper Deerfield Volunteer Ambulance Association. They held turkey shoots and cake sales to raise money to buy our own ambulance, and found an old 1941 Cadillac ambulance in a nearby town. They cleaned it, stocked it with supplies, took first aid classes, and started service to the country areas. Today the association has multiple vehicles and is a major volunteer rescue unit in the region. The lesson wasn't lost on us kids. When there's a problem, take care of it. Don't be deterred, don't waste energy complaining, just do it.

Mom was the great protector of us all; nothing was going to harm her family. She was gentle and loving and she had a fine sense of humor but she could be tough as nails in a crisis. One bright fall morning when I was fourteen, Mom and I set off for town to deliver some homemade cakes for a Red Cross bake sale. On our way was my "Aunt" Millie Crispin's country store, where we'd stop in the early morning hours to help her set out her baskets of local tomatoes, fresh corn, and peaches to sell to the tourists on their way along Route 40 to the Jersey shore. It was a small white cinder-block building barely twenty feet square, with woods behind it. Aunt Millie also stocked the local papers and a few necessities inside, but most of her business came from selling the farm-fresh produce. She had called the night before; she had just gotten in her first pumpkins and hoped I could help set them out.

Mom and I were in a great mood that morning. It was a fine crisp day and the leaves on the trees had turned brilliant red and gold. We were puzzled as we turned into the dirt drive in front of the store. "That's strange," Mom said. "The produce doors are still closed. Run to the door, David, and see if Aunt Millie's there yet."

When I turned the knob the door opened readily. I gaped in horror. It was a bloodbath inside. Aunt Millie lay on the floor covered in blood, near a sodden stack of newspapers and knocked-over displays. I vomited. Mom bolted to my side. As we tried to grasp the sight before us, we heard the slam of the door in the back and the sound of running feet.

Aunt Millie had been stabbed repeatedly. We rushed to a nearby house to summon help, telephoned the police and Dad, and came back to our car with the neighbor, his gun in hand to protect us, to wait for them. Dad got there first and Mom fell weeping into his arms. Then the police arrived, followed by the coroner and, before long, the press. Word had spread quickly, and even the Philadelphia papers, an hour and a half away, came down to cover the murder. Some of the photographers tried to take pictures of Mom and me, but my father towered over them and told them bitingly that wasn't how we did it down here and if he were they, he'd put those cameras away. To my amazement, they did.

It was a long, sad, strenuous day. The police and neighboring farmers searched the woods to no avail. The police warned us that the killer might think Mom and I could identify him, so we might be at risk, and the first thing Dad did when we got home was check the outside lights. Some of them didn't work and it was getting dark. He got out his gun and phoned our neighbors, and they were there in minutes, lighting up the area around the house with their headlights to protect us until the outdoor lights were fixed. I can still see him as he sat up the whole night long, keeping watch with his gun at the ready. In the morning after church, he packed us into the car and we drove to a remote area called the Pine Barrens for a picnic lunch. We all needed to distance ourselves from the slaughter.

By Monday our parents decided it was time for us to get back to normal and they sent me off to school. Three days later the police came to the school and arrested "Joe Robinson," a boy who sat right behind me in history class, for the murder of Aunt Millie. I was dumbfounded. I couldn't believe it. There he had been three days running, sitting just behind me. I scarcely knew him—only that he came from a desperately poor black family of migrant workers—because we local kids didn't mix with the few black children in our classes, all of them from families like the Robinsons. They would show up at the start of the school year in the fall, disappear when their families followed the crops south, and return in the spring to be ready for the summer harvest. Most of us, teachers and students alike, ignored them. It never occurred to us not to.

We found out that there were more than a dozen children in the Robinson family, all living in a house with no heat, not much food, and no indoor plumbing. His father had beaten Joe. Mom sat me down a few days after the arrest and told me I had to pray for the ability to forgive him. "Coming out of such a cruel and awful background, there's no way he could think straight," she told me. "We're so lucky, David. We have so much when so many have so little."

I was stunned. I could not believe what I was hearing. She had seen Aunt Millie lying slaughtered in all that blood just as I had. How could she say that? She did want Joe punished but she resolutely refused to condemn him. I still remember the moment, a few weeks after the arrest, when she turned to me and said, "I think I have it hard, but I simply can't imagine not having heat, food, and water for my children. I think I would kill too."

Over the months she forced me to look beyond my own anger. Eventually I did come to see Aunt Millie's death in a different way; but I don't think I fully appreciated the gift that she gave me until much, much later.

In terms of facilities, Daretown Elementary School was primitive. There were four classrooms on each side of the old building, with a wood-floored auditorium between them. In the dark basement was our lunchroom, a large room furnished with homemade wooden tables and benches. My mother and her friends held turkey dinners to raise money for a kitchen so that the kids could have one hot meal a day. Except for textbooks there were few resources—no library or visual aids or music and art teachers. A twenty-year-old encyclopedia was our only reference work. You had to be dedicated to teach there for the pittance you were paid. Many of our teachers were farmers' wives who had taken a few education courses at Glassboro State College and who desperately needed the extra income.

The assumption throughout the school and the community was that when they grew up, the boys would take over their fathers' farms and the girls would find husbands, tend their homes, raise the children, and settle down into Grange and church work. You went to school to learn to read and to know enough arithmetic to be able to balance the books. Our teachers' expectations were no different. They never taught us to embrace change, to aspire to greatness, or to dream. Just as certain as the cycle of the seasons and the backbreaking labor of farming was the presumption that the life we were born into was the life we would go on living.

But this was not my parents' presumption. Around that dinner table and every time we were together, they pushed us to discover more about the world outside our isolated community. Almost every Saturday Mom drove me into Woodstown to the public library. She taught me to revere books and to value what lay inside them. I loved stories of faraway places and biography and politically oriented books, and I borrowed John Kennedy's *Profiles in Courage* so many times that I nearly wore out the binding.

In fact, the entire family followed politics. On election day Mom would take me into the voting booth with her and tell me all about the candidates beforehand. My first political memory is when I was ten. Tennessee populist Estes Kefauver wanted the Democratic nomination for president in 1956, and I thought his Davy Crockett coonskin hat was terrific. The whole family loved his antics and his championship of the workingman; and we all watched the Democratic National Convention that summer to see our hero, who ended up being Adlai Stevenson's running mate. I spotted a new hero that night: young Senator John F. Kennedy, who was seeking the vice presidential slot and whose youth and sparkle dazzled me. I thought it would be terrific to be part of that world. Four years later I papered the walls of my bedroom with Kennedy campaign posters and handed out bumper stickers around town. My mother thought it was great. Billy Graham or the President of the United States—that was what she aspired to for me. Her hopes were boundless.

My parents' plans for their children were firm: We were to get an education, go on to college, and become professionals in whatever field we chose. They never swerved from these goals even when times were bleakest.

Woodstown High School was my first real step into a broader world—and a shock. Although Woodstown served the needs of the nearby farming communities, it was also home to some of the employees at the huge Du Pont plant located near Wilmington, Delaware. Many of the students came from these more "sophisticated" Du Pont families, and they made those of us bused in from the rural areas each morning feel inferior and dumb. We had a tough time competing academically. When we got to Woodstown we were already behind the town kids, whose elementary school years had been much richer than ours, and it didn't get any easier because Woodstown High made more rigorous academic demands than we were used to. Most of my Daretown friends retreated to the Future Farmers of America or secretarial classes and chose not to compete with the townies.

But for me, not to compete was never an option. Not to make it to college would have been a devastating blow to my parents; I would have failed them as a son. I felt like a fish out of water, caught between two worlds and belonging to neither. My old world of the farm, the woods, and the FFA did not conform to the road I had to take. Yet the lives of the town kids were utterly foreign to me. I didn't know how to act. I had no confidence I could measure up academically. But I was a quick study and I deliberately developed a style that charmed the teachers into giving me good grades. I was just "bad" enough in high school to attract attention and respect from the students but not so bad as to alienate their parents or my teachers. It worked. I had friends, I was a "good guy," I became one of the gang, I brought home acceptable report cards, I was meeting my parents' expectations.

Nonetheless, from the day I entered high school I wanted out of it. It was a way station I had to endure but I hated it. It was intolerably hard to live a facade. Now I know why. Then I thought I was the only person in the school like myself. In the midst of my gang of friends I was alone.

From my earliest awareness of sexuality—and long before I could recognize these feelings for what they were, much less had a word for them—I knew I was gay. What is striking to me is not this awareness but that I always knew I could not speak of it to a soul. I always had the bone-deep security of my parents' love. Their decency and integrity and forthrightness were a living model of what was expected of us. How does a child of such a home, a child who always talked freely about whatever else was on his mind, know instinctively to be silent about this most crucial part of his self?

Even in early childhood, my fantasies were about men. I was fascinated by the men who worked in the fields, my sister's boyfriends, my brother's buddies. I remember that when I was small, I used to like to run naked through the yard in a kind of declaration of liberation. My mother's response was to get her famous "long wooden spoon" and spank me for it. A few years later, when Patsy was in high school and her dates picked her up, I would retreat to my room thinking of what it would be like to be going out with her boyfriends. I developed crushes on male television stars and never missed an episode of *Route 66* with George Maharis. Some of my teachers became objects of my fantasies. After school I used to shoplift nudist publications from the local news store in town and cherish them in the privacy of my bedroom. When I was done with them, I tucked them away in a secret hiding place under the floorboards, safe from discovery.

And from the very first moment that I knew I was "different," I believed I was bad. I was convinced it was only a matter of time before everyone would know my evil thoughts. I hadn't the slightest doubt that they went far beyond the kind of misbehaviors that provoked the wooden spoon. They would be the worst thing my family could ever know about me. I thought about suicide at an early age. The summer that I was eight, in the midday heat when my folks were at work, I would gather all the blankets in the house, go into my closet or creep under my bed, and wrap the heavy blankets around me hoping that I would suffocate for being bad. Sometimes I climbed high into a tree back in the woods and dangled from the topmost limb, only to lack the nerve to release my grip and smash to the ground. At moments like that, death was the only solution that I could see.

Back then there was no storefront literature, no *Time* cover stories, no movie of the week, no special section in the bookstore that even acknowledged the existence of homosexuality. There was nothing I could read, no one to talk to. My only "knowledge" came from fag jokes, occasional reports in our local newspaper about men who were arrested in the town park for acts alluded to in vague terms, and implications that people like that were sick or depraved. One day in high school I went into the library and took down a copy of Webster's dictionary. As I leafed through to the H's I was absolutely convinced that everyone in the library knew what I was looking up. My face grew hot as my shaking hands searched down the columns for the word. Finally I found it. The definition was full of terms like "pervert," "mental disorder," and "social misfit."

Wherever I was, I listened and watched in an effort to gather more information from the people and institutions closest to me: family, friends, my school and church. I discovered none of them knew any more about it than I did; those who did mention it used the degrading terms or cracked crude and hurtful jokes. Every such remark reinforced just how horrible my secret was. I lived in intense fear of my gayness. I knew my family would abandon me if they discovered it. I cannot remember a single time in my childhood when I was not in fear of discovery.

It got much worse when I entered high school and began to realize just how insular my hometown community really was. Our neighbors felt passionately about "preserving their way of life" for their families. Any difference, like any change, was a threat. My acutely attuned ear heard the harsh judgments they pronounced on those in the neighborhood who had not met their narrowly defined morality. I saw a local girl in my high school forced to drop out and be sent away because she was pregnant. Another bright sweet teenager was shunned because she dated a black student. There was no way in God's world that these people would understand and accept me.

Ultimately, living where I did, knowing its nature, I realized that if I was to go on with my life, I would have to work out my own path and modify my dreams. If it meant dishonesty or deceit, so be it. This was more than a matter of personal survival—it was essential to protecting my family from a shame that I knew would destroy them. I hadn't the slightest doubt about it. Living the truth was impossible. My parents needed my lies. And so I began the serious game of avoiding discovery at all costs.

I had started my long, silent creation of a David who was acceptable to others back in grade school. Even then I was always on guard against a misstep that would reveal my true nature. I went in for all the right male activities, playing football, building forts in the woods, joining the Boy Scouts, talking about girls, and participating in "mischief night" at Halloween by stealing a neighbor's outdoor privy and setting it down in the center of town. When I was a little older and the guys got involved in the usual adolescent games like strip poker, I wanted it to never stop, then was swallowed by the fear that they would realize I was enjoying it too much.

I was brutally reminded of what would happen if I was discovered to be a homosexual by what happened to "Freddy Jones." He was a tall, blond, handsome, masculine boy in my hometown who was several years older than I was. I had a crush on him from a very early age, although I assumed he was a "regular" guy, and I was ashamed of my feelings. But as I got older, it became known among the boys that Freddy was the town queer, and that he would "take care of you." As they joked and ridiculed him I was frantic that I not be thought "like Freddy," so I vigorously joined the mocking chorus. It made me feel ashamed and at the same time it made me feel safer, yet I still wanted desperately to talk to him—the first person I actually knew who was a homosexual.

Freddy's family finally sent him away to a private school, but my attraction was as strong as ever and I missed seeing him on the streets. Then came the day when my mother walked into the house after work and said to my father, "Ben, did you hear about the Jones boy? He committed suicide at his school."

"Hell, Mary," Dad answered, "given what he was, he's better off dead."

"Oh, Ben, don't say that," my mother protested. "Think how hard this is for his parents, and all the pain he caused them in their lives."

I can hear them today. Dad and Mom weren't mourning for Freddy. They were mourning for the parents who had such a terrible son. They were the victims, not the boy who had been tormented by his peers into killing himself. Despite my shock and my guilt—I could not forget how I had tried to prove my manhood by joining in with the mob—I knew what the real message was. If I too was discovered, it could only bring shame and death.

To this day, I wish I could take back my hateful words and my willingness to join in the mob.

The conservatism of our area was not confined to "moral" sexual behaviors. For all their genuine commitment to service to others, and their eagerness that the world outside be open to us, my parents shared many of the community's attitudes. Ours was a closed society. I found myself in direct conflict with Mom and Dad in my high school years. In the late fifties and early sixties the civil rights movement began to impinge on the awareness of even our isolated area. When I was in grade school, I had never questioned the separation we children kept between ourselves and the black migrant youngsters who were in our classes during the growing and harvest seasons—it was the way things were. But I was old enough now to register the intolerance toward blacks that I saw in my family and neighbors. The news in the papers and on television brought the movement to the fore. Clearly, those around me saw it as a threat.

For Mom and Dad, as with most of those we knew, segregation was a given. Salem County was a hotbed of distrust and isolation between the races. Just as in the Deep South, whites expected blacks to remain in their "proper place"—in fact the area was sometimes called "Little

Dixie." It frightened them when the unspoken rules started to break down. Although state laws officially barred segregation in New Jersey, everyone "knew" that the blacks didn't eat in our restaurants, that they sat in a special section in the movies, that they certainly did not interact with us socially. The black community in my hometown kept to itself, either in its own section of town called Yorktown or in the countryside, where the poverty was unspeakable and the houses no more than unheated shacks without running water or electricity, like that of the Robinson family. I remember as a child looking at the walls of a broken-down house just across the field from us and seeing the large gaps between the planks. I kept thinking how freezing cold it must have been in winter.

My parents' belief in helping others extended to the poor blacks in the area. They took blankets to the family in the shack across the field. They brought clothes to many others. But they also had a deep-rooted belief that separation of the races was essential to a stable society. They never articulated this to us kids, but that was because they assumed they didn't need to. They thought we knew it. We didn't. When we saw them help people regardless of race, we thought that was what we were supposed to do. We were. Similarly, when we heard Martin Luther King call upon all people of goodwill to respond in the fight against injustice, we thought that was what we were also supposed to do. Not so. As our parents witnessed their children's efforts to work for the equality of people of all races, not just whites, they were not only baffled—they were appalled.

I became increasingly involved in the civil rights movement in high school, not only picketing but even sending money urgently needed at home to Dr. King in Atlanta. My folks were livid. My involvement with "them" embarrassed them in front of their neighbors. My junior year, 1963, was the year of the Birmingham demonstrations, when the nation watched on its television sets the sight of the police turning fire hoses and dogs on young demonstrators fighting for their freedom. I told my parents I wanted to go south that summer and join them in the fight. They were furious. They forbade me even to think of it. We argued for hours one night and ended up screaming at each other. My father went into a rage, hit me repeatedly, and ordered me to my room "until you get that bullshit out of your head."

Shaken, I called my sister Patsy in Baltimore. During my high school years Patsy had increasingly become my anchor. I knew that although she had been popular when she was in high school, and had played women's basketball, become a local beauty queen, was a good student,

and had dated nearly all the handsome men in her class, she'd experienced many of the same feelings of not belonging that I did. Patsy had
left home when I was still in grade school to attend the Johns Hopkins
School of Nursing in Baltimore, but our closeness did not change and by
the time I moved on to Woodstown High she had become my phone
buddy. Whenever I had a problem I shared it with her. I talked about my
struggles with my parents, my feelings of loneliness, and my growing
hunger to make a difference in the world. Patsy told me of her own
experiences with segregation at Hopkins, and her own commitment to
the civil rights movement. I can still remember her outrage the first time
she had to take a body to the hospital morgue and was faced with two
doors: one marked "Whites," the other "Colored."

I don't think I could have endured the battles over my activism without Patsy. She was a crucial buffer between me and my parents every
time, and this night she urged me to be patient. I was too distraught to
listen. "I can't stand it any longer, Patsy!" I yelled into the phone. "I've
got to get out of here. I can't take it anymore!"

Again, Patsy counseled patience. "David, you've only got one more
year to go," she reminded me. "Finish it and you can do anything you
want after that. I know it's hard. I felt that way too. But it *is* Mom and
Dad's home and they've got to live with their neighbors. They're wrong
on this one, David, but you have to wait it out."

Once again she saved me. I calmed down at last, put aside the summer
trip, and served out my last year in high school, playing my accustomed
role of being a good guy but not abandoning my activism. When we
went on our senior class trip to Washington, a restaurant refused to serve
the black kids in our group. Our teachers let the white kids go in for a
snack but several of us joined the black students outside and stood there
shouting, "Freedom! Freedom! Freedom now!" The teachers couldn't
get us away from there fast enough.

To this day, Dr. King remains as important a role model for me as he
was back in the 1960s, but when I think about it now, I realize that his
words in those days carried a second message, one special to me. When
he railed against injustice, I knew that he understood the pain of being
different. By working for the liberation of blacks, I intuitively knew I was
fighting for my own liberation. I had only one goal: to graduate from
high school and escape before I was discovered and destroyed.

With graduation night came freedom. As my fellow students shared
nostalgia and tears, I could not stop laughing. I remember walking off
the stage in the football field after receiving my diploma and wanting to

leap with joy. I watched the people in the stands laugh at my laughter as I walked past them. No one knew I was laughing at being free of them— and free to leave home at last. I thought that I would leave all the pain and deceit behind me. Surely, I believed, the world out there had to be a better place.

CHAPTER TWO

Into Politics

Lᴵᴷᴱ many of my generation, I saw college as the bridge that would connect my dream of seeing the world with actually moving into that world. But I invested far more in my dream than that. To be free of the constricted morality of my hometown opened the possibility of finding the happiness and peace I had never really known. How that might happen I had no idea—I certainly knew I still had to conceal my sexuality—but at least there was possibility, reason for hope. I came to Arizona State University in Tempe alive with eagerness.

I ended up in Tempe chiefly because of its climate; all through childhood I had suffered from recurrent bronchitis and the family doctor thought the desert air would have a healing effect. It was a large school. The campus was a curious mixture of traditional southwestern adobe architecture and stark modern structures. In the center was the massive white-columned glass library, surrounded by traditional older sandstone buildings. Palm trees swayed in the desert winds, creating a seductive calmness. Together with the other students in the large freshman class, I filled out endless forms and registered for courses. English literature was my choice of major. Reading had been my great pleasure as well as my chief refuge throughout my childhood and poetry my special delight; now it would become the center of my academic life and introduce me to the great classics, ancient and modern, that I had missed. I knew I had a lot to learn. I saw college as a place where I could build an intellectual base to reexamine and fortify the values and principles I had already developed at home. Yet within weeks of my arrival there in the fall of 1964, my energy was not devoted to my studies but to a whirlwind exploration of activism, politics, and sexuality. When I reflect back on my time at college, it is not the academics that I remember most vividly, but my baptism into activism.

It was a tumultuous time. In the "Freedom Summer" before I got to Tempe, northern students had joined southern black activists in a drive to register black voters throughout Mississippi, and in June, as the effort got under way, three civil rights workers, two white and one black, disappeared. Their murdered bodies were found several weeks later. That same August, at Lyndon Johnson's instigation, Congress had passed the Tonkin Gulf Resolution that gave the President a free hand to expand the war in Vietnam, and increasing numbers of American troops were being sent there. For many of the nation's young, the time was fast approaching when they would have to make a choice: to remain on the sidelines or to decide to commit to the fight for freedom—and if they chose that, as their uneasy parents warned, to put their future at risk by opposing the government's policies.

I had no doubt about my choice. We might be embarked on a hazardous course by taking our unpopular message to a divided nation, but what did that matter when injustices were everywhere? I quickly found myself invested in myriad acts of political protest. I boycotted grapes to support Cesar Chavez in the Delano farmworkers' strike. I turned out to cheer activist Tom Hayden when he spoke at the university, helped establish picket lines to protest a speech by Vietnam War architect General William Westmoreland, engaged in a sit-in to oppose Sheriff Jim Clark of Selma, Alabama, who had beaten civil rights protesters on a freedom march. There never was enough time to fight for all the urgent causes. After all those years of being unable to act out my feelings at home, I was determined not to miss any opportunity to demonstrate my exploding sense of political commitment.

And in a way I could recognize only years later, my activism was also a refuge. Unlike those who form long-lasting friendships in their college days, my university years were devoid of close personal relationships. That kind of closeness is rooted in shared, spontaneous intimacy. My fear of my homosexuality didn't allow me to become too close to anyone. All my personal life was directly related to my activism. My friends were those I'd have dinner with after an organizing meeting and then argue with into the early morning hours over the latest terrible headlines. Arizona was Goldwater country then—Barry Goldwater had been chosen as the Republicans' presidential nominee in the August 1964 convention and was defeated by Lyndon Johnson in November—and very conservative. The number of activists on the campus was small, and we tended to band together both socially and politically. When activists and political organizers from other states drifted through Tempe on their way to the West Coast, we would sit with them for hours on end and share convictions and ideas on actions. I was diligent about staying in touch with them through phone calls and letters after they left, following up on what we had talked about, and reporting on what we were doing. Although I certainly didn't realize it at the time, in many ways this was my initial effort at creating a "network" of like minds all over the country, one that would serve me well in the coming years. I became expert at being a friend to others but not allowing them into my life. My life in Tempe was filled with activity and people—yet today I am hard put to remember most of them.

One day in the fall of 1966 I read a story in *The Arizona Republic* about city garbage workers who had gone on strike demanding the right to form a union. The workers were mostly Hispanic and they were earning wages so shamefully low that it was virtually impossible for them to support their families. The city's response had been to fire any of the strikers who supported the union. By the time I became aware of the strike, over one hundred had already been ousted. Their plight and their courage moved me to action.

After my Thursday classes, I went down to the picket line in front of Tempe City Hall to join the pickets. They were clearly startled by the appearance of this buzz-cut student in their picket line. As I walked with them shouting organizing slogans in broken Spanish, one of the workers inserted himself by my side.

Hector was a man in his fifties, dressed in dirty Levi's and a straw hat. His face looked like the map of the world, evidence of his rough journey. He had startling blue eyes, jet-black hair, and a Zapata-like mustache. As we marched, he kept staring at me. I grew more and more uncomfortable. Finally he asked bluntly, in heavily accented English, "Why are you here?"

"I read about the strike in the newspaper and I wanted to show my support. Is it okay that I'm here?"

He laughed. "Sure. What do you know about us?"

I recited the facts about their low wages from that morning's *Arizona Republic.*

"No, no," he said. "What do you know about *us?*"

I was puzzled.

"About my life," he explained, "what it is like to live like we do, about fears for my family. That is what I mean."

I admitted I really didn't know anything about it at all.

"That is what I thought. I have six children and I can't buy enough food to feed them on these wages. They go without decent clothes and I can't buy them books so they don't have to lift garbage like their father. I walk into my home each night and feel that I have failed them. I can't buy medicine and take them to a doctor. I feel hopeless and powerless. This is what this line is about, *mi amigo.*"

I was stunned into silence. We kept on circling and then he asked me, "Where are the rest of the students?"

Not wanting to admit that as far as I knew, most of them didn't know or care about the strike, I lied. "We are going to have a meeting and plan ways to help," I told him.

His eyes grew wide. "Really?"

"Yes, of course."

Hector turned to the other strikers in the picket line and called out loudly, "My friends, the students at the university are going to help us. This fine young man says there is going to be a meeting."

Hector's story and his courage—and my lie—led to the first organizing project I would be responsible for from start to finish.

Back in my campus apartment, I sat in my beanbag chair and wondered how to proceed. It was one thing to join a sit-in or demonstrate against the war or spend hours brainstorming issues with others who thought as I did. It was another to originate action.

Almost instinctively I went to my desk and started writing down the names of every student and professor I knew to be progressive in their views. Pulling out my phone book, I started dialing their numbers and asking them to come to a meeting in my apartment. Ten of them showed up that night. They looked to me to provide direction. I told them about my conversation with Hector. I come from a family of storytellers, although this was so bred in the bone that I'd never been conscious of it, and I brought his plight alive. By evening's end we had agreed to constitute ourselves a "committee" to support the strikers and to hold a rally on campus and a march to the Tempe City Hall. Before the meeting, I had made a list of tasks we'd need to do—get permission to hold the rally, create flyers, make posters to be placed around campus, and create a "phone tree" to contact other faculty and students to urge them to attend. Before they left, I assigned each person in the room a job and told them I'd call them the next night to see how they were doing with it.

Hector's story of his struggle had moved me deeply and I was fearful of letting him down. These workers were fighting for justice in our own backyard. By the time the day of the rally and march arrived, I had come to know many of the strikers personally and to witness their profound poverty. But the best intentions in the world would be meaningless if the effort failed. I was dissolved in nerves.

We gathered together in the middle of the large desert campus, the library looming above us, set up our signs calling for justice for the workers, and started using our bullhorn to gather a crowd. There were no more than a hundred of us at first—students, workers, and professors. My heart sank at the turnout.

It was time for me to speak. I kept looking at the ground and pushing a pebble around with the tip of my cowboy boot, but there was nothing for it but to go ahead. I mounted a low white stucco wall, bullhorn in hand, to champion the cause of my new friends. Just as I was beginning, a commotion broke out across the campus. I stood on my toes to see what was happening. Approaching our small rally were several dozen police dressed in full riot gear, with menacing blue helmets and Plexiglas shields across their faces. They marched in formation, their wood batons beating in unison against the palms of their gloved hands. They positioned themselves directly behind the rally, on watch across from where I was standing.

Then, suddenly, the crowd swelled. Students by the hundreds abandoned their way to class and joined us in protest against this invasion of our campus home by an overreacting police force. As I started speaking again, I remembered my mother's advice. She always told me that if I had something important to say, to say it from the heart. I dropped the notes I had prepared the night before. I looked out over the crowd of students and workers and starting speaking from the heart. I knew exactly what I had to tell them—Hector's own story of poverty and fear and injustice. My voice took on a life of its own as I spoke of the hunger of the workers' children. I could see empathy and concern on the faces of those who moments before had been too busy to care.

I urged them not to be afraid of blue helmets and nightsticks and to join us on the march on City Hall. I watched awestruck as hundreds of students were moved to come with us. As the march formed the uniformed riot police circled around us and followed us to downtown Tempe.

Bolstered by the crowd, I felt of value and needed. It was an exultant day. I had not only made a difference; I also learned never to be too fast in proclaiming a failure. The students discovered there was a whole world they had never even noticed before, and the workers found that others cared about their plight. We were all enriched, and while the city managed to break the strike, eventually the workers did succeed in joining a union.

By then, the Vietnam War was starting to surpass all other issues on campuses nationwide. Reports of fierce battles and growing death tolls aired on the nightly news. In the early years of the war many Americans felt it was extremely unpatriotic, even traitorous, to resist their country's policy while soldiers were overseas fighting to implement it. Appealing to their patriotism had been an effective way to silence dissent, especially in conservative places like Arizona State. But that was beginning to change now. In early 1965 came the first large marches against the war in San Francisco and Washington. My network of campus activists raised money to pay for buses to these marches by holding folk concerts at the local coffee shop. A year later we were skipping classes to gather around the television sets in our dormitory recreation rooms to watch the hearings on the conduct of the Vietnam War led by Senator J. William Fulbright, chairman of the Senate Foreign Relations Committee. Witness after witness pointed out the folly of our effort. For his courage in speaking out Fulbright became a new hero on college campuses everywhere.

As my antiwar activism grew, I grew even closer to Patsy. She was even more vehemently opposed to the war than I was. When we needed money to send buses to that first march in Washington, it was Patsy who sent a check. I shared everything with her: what we were doing, what had worked, what hadn't, my excitements, my fears of failure. I trusted her absolutely. I couldn't wait to tell her of every new adventure. As the counterculture reared its head even in Tempe, I acknowledged that I was experimenting with drugs. By March of 1967 I had started using marijuana and LSD on a regular basis with my activist friends. Instead of arguing into the night about a new issue, we'd leave our organizing meetings and crowd into someone's small campus apartment, light up a joint, put on Janis Joplin or The Beatles, and drift off into another world. Sometimes the participants would engage in heterosexual group sex and I would sit on the sidelines, a desperately lonely voyeur.

That spring an activist friend named Joanna called to say that the Arizona hippie community had announced the state's first "love-in," to be held in a local park in Tempe. We had heard about these outdoor gatherings of music, dancing, drugs, nudity, and chanting ever since they began in San Francisco's Haight-Ashbury, and I was certainly not about to miss so historic an event. The morning of the love-in I woke up early, put on my tie-dyed T-shirt, wrapped a red bandanna around my still short hair for a headband, and opened the door for Joanna and her friends. She was tie-dyed too, dressed for the occasion in a long robe with her flowing blond hair spread over her shoulders, and she promptly sat herself down cross-legged on the floor and started rolling joints on my Woolworth coffee table. We lit up and simultaneously dropped some red dragon LSD. Joanna's boyfriend had brought along a special pair of glasses with prisms for lenses. When we put them on we saw a kaleidoscope of brilliant shifting colors, and we walked to the park so drugged out that how we ever found it is beyond me.

Maybe by sound rather than sight. There were hundreds gathered there, some in vivid clothing and others naked, dancing in circles or by themselves to the beat of drums and the sound of flutes. People went about hugging everyone around them, hands raised in the V-for-peace sign. Children with wreaths of flowers in their hair played amid the dancers.

It was an ecstatic moment. To see such freedom and open joy gave me permission to join in and feel myself belonging to something at last. I refused to surrender the prism glasses to Joanna, and amid the flashing colors lost myself in the celebration. I danced alone, hugged men and women alike, and ripped off my T-shirt so I could paint my chest in vivid colors. I laughed aloud at the antics around me. I found a young child with flowers in her hair and I lifted her up, threw her up toward the heavens, and caught her in my arms. Then we twirled around until we were both so dizzy we fell to the ground in laughter.

I felt so free that for a moment I almost believed I could be open with those around me about who I was, my homosexuality. But "almost" it remained. For all the release of drugs, the feeling of love that surrounded me, the astounding abandon I felt, I knew I had to keep my secret. I knew a great sense of belonging as we danced in the park, but I was not free.

Nor despite my openness with Patsy could I confide in her. She never discouraged me and she never passed judgment, but the truth was too frightening to reveal even to her. As much as I loved and trusted her, I was afraid I would lose her love if she knew who I really was.

So I went back to my activism. The more visible and daring I became in my organizing work, the more invisible I became in my personal life. In many ways, my efforts to create a better world became my hiding place, where I could control the dark forces of my sexual self. As I worked beside my fellow warriors for the causes we believed in, I did not doubt that with few if any exceptions, they would have totally rejected me if they knew of my homosexuality.

The pain of harboring my secret intensified when I met "Kit." (I have changed his name because his family never knew he was gay.) When he walked into the Arizona State locker room clad only in a towel, he literally took my breath away. I fell instantly and utterly in love. I watched him as he talked with the coach, looking so out of place, it seemed to me, in this poorly lit room reeking of male sweat, its floor covered with cracked paint and its walls lined with battered lockers. I could not stop staring at him. He was astoundingly handsome, with a perfect body, dark Italian features, closely cropped black hair, and vivid green eyes. His smile lit up his face. His body language told of his confidence, even of a slight hint of arrogance.

I sat there on the narrow wooden locker-room bench transfixed. Then Kit and the coach parted and he came down the narrow passage between the lockers. "Hi," he said as he brushed past me, "how's it going?" I was mute. Then I realized others might see me staring after him and somehow discover my feelings. I dressed quickly, gathered my equipment, and fled.

Over the next several days, I could barely function. I had never felt this way before. All I could think about was Kit. I replayed the locker-room encounter over and over in my head. I heard him say, "Hi, how's it going?" a thousand times. I looked for him everywhere on campus. My excitement was matched by my shame at the powerful sexual feelings I harbored. There was no way that a person like Kit could have the same terrible secret. He was forbidden territory. I was still convinced that I was one of the few people in the world who was gay. It became a relief not to encounter him again.

"Mind if I join you?" asked a voice above me as I was eating lunch in the sunlit cafeteria of Sahuaro Hall. I knew instantly it was Kit. He sat his large frame in the chair facing me and my gut spasmed. He smiled his astonishing smile and I could no longer push away my feelings. As we chatted casually about college life, we discovered a mutual love of poetry.

"I want to be a writer," he offered, sounding embarrassed by the admission.

"I've got a special love for poetry," I answered, wanting to put him at ease. "Especially Yeats and Neruda. And I write some Japanese haiku for my own pleasure."

He was delighted. "God, it's such a relief to find someone who loves sports *and* poetry. I'd love to see some of your work and share some of mine."

"Well, why don't we get together sometime?" I said. "I'll show you mine if you show me yours."

He laughed out loud. "Let's have dinner tonight at my place," he said. "We can read to each other and celebrate a new friendship."

He gave me his address, picked up the tray of food he had hardly touched, and gave me a thumbs-up sign as he headed for the cafeteria doors.

I don't think I have ever in my life spent a more confusing few hours than between lunch and dinner that day. All he had really offered was a casual dinner to talk about our writings—but in that case, what did he mean by "celebrate our new friendship"? Why was he so suddenly interested in me? So quick to set up dinner? I couldn't sit still. I cleaned my apartment half a dozen times and then walked in the park across the street for what seemed like forever. Could I handle being so in love with this handsome man yet stay only a friend to him? Confused and afraid, I kept reaching for the telephone to cancel dinner, then let my hand drop.

I arrived early at his off-campus apartment building. The exterior looked like an early Holiday Inn converted to apartments, with outside corridors running the length of each floor giving access to the apartment doors. It was a seedy place for a great romance. I walked up to the second-story corridor and knocked on Kit's door. He was waiting for me, dressed in cowboy boots, Levi's, and a white shirt with rolled-up sleeves. As I came inside, our momentary awkwardness passed. It was a warm and inviting place. Candles were lit around the room, the folksinger Odetta sounded from the stereo on the floor, two framed pictures—of Bob Dylan and football player Bart Starr—hung above his sofa bed, and two beanbag chairs were placed against the wall.

I had brought some grass as a host gift and we sat at his handmade dining table and rolled a joint. Kit ordered out for Chinese food and we ate and sat and talked for hours. Eventually we moved to the sofa and read to each other from our writings. His was of a quality that made me feel shy about sharing mine. Yet somewhere in that space of time, I knew in my bones he felt the same way I did. Finally he looked over at me, lifted his hand, and brushed it gently against my face. "What are we going to do about this?" he asked me. It was one of those rare times in my life that I was speechless. I could only give an affirmative nod. As we sat there trembling, Kit reached over and kissed me passionately. We made love. We were the first for each other, and to this day I recall those hours as the most romantic and innocent night of my life.

Kit and I fell head over heels in love. Yet as much as we wanted to celebrate our feelings for each other, they had to be secret. We stayed buddies with our other friends, carefully choosing where we would meet and how often in order not to arouse suspicion. To create an air of casualness, we hung out with the guys and went to the movies and sporting events with them. They kept trying to fix each of us up with dates. We laughed at the way we developed these dates into an art form that avoided sex with the women we took out. I remember the time that a friend joked, "Gee, you guys spend so much time together, you'd think you are married!" We didn't see each other for two weeks after that, fearful that our friend had figured out our relationship.

But once we were behind the closed doors of Kit's apartment, our life took on a different dimension. We shared joyous sex, read poetry aloud, and dreamed of a future where we could be together as a couple. Someday we would have a ranch where we could write, surround ourselves with pets, and live together in safety. We laughed a lot and played silly innocent tricks on each other, short-sheeting the bed or hiding the razor so that we couldn't shave in the morning.

But outside, the campus increasingly became our prison. We had to keep up the charade until we graduated and could find a safe place. Whether there was such a place we had no idea, but finding it was our dream. Neither of us knew anything at all about gay life—or even another gay or lesbian person. Not only were we the first for each other sexually, we were the first for each other in sharing our secret with another human being. And like everyone who loves for the first time, sometimes we didn't know quite how to act with each other and fumbled in awkwardness.

One thing we both knew without a doubt, however: At last we were not alone. Now we had someone to love in our life and we planned to be together for always. If we were careful, we thought, no one would ever know. We spent hours discussing how to structure our lives to keep our secret. We were young and in love, and when we found a way, we thought, there would be no end to our feelings for each other.

Late one afternoon a year or so after we met, Kit called to say he had to get some groceries and would be by later to pick me up. I sat on the grass outside my dorm waiting for him. Evening turned into night; no Kit. I paced back and forth, looking at my watch every few minutes. Maybe his car had broken down. He'd probably be home soon. I kept calling his apartment on the pay phone inside the dorm, but his phone rang and rang, unanswered. Finally, as midnight neared, I pulled myself together and raced the couple of miles to his home. As I was mounting the steps to his darkened second-floor unit, the manager came along and stopped me. He knew me as a frequent visitor. "David, I had a call from Kit's parents about an hour ago," he said. "Kit was killed in an automobile accident. They asked me to seal his apartment. You have to give me your key. I'm really sorry, man . . ."

I collapsed on the cold concrete steps. Numbly, I gave him the key and then I walked back to my dorm in a trance. I remember sitting outside under a palm tree sobbing. I wrapped my arms around my legs in a fetal position and rocked back and forth. I didn't even have Kit's parents' number. They knew nothing about me, and in many ways had never even gotten to know their son. I wasn't asked to the funeral. I never saw him again.

Kit's death left me devastated. I truly believed that I had somehow killed him by loving him. As I grieved, I knew without any doubt that God was punishing us for our love. There was no one with whom I could share my grief. I wept silently in solitude and walked around the campus as if in a stupor. Everyone knew I had lost a friend, and some assumed that a girl I had been dating had died in an accident. Let it be, I thought. They can think what they want. I could see no future without Kit.

In the years that followed Kit's death, I would not allow myself to open up to another man, and I sought out brief, anonymous physical encounters, one after another. I would meet men in parks, rest rooms, and other dark and dirty places. On the few occasions I actually returned to someone's home, I faked a name and fabricated my background to avoid discovery. I wanted no possibility of intimacy, yet these hectic exchanges of sex offered no relief. I thought of Kit constantly, but the memory served only to remind me of shame and forbidden love. All I knew was that I was alone again, as I had always been.

But after a while in Tempe, inevitably, I began to come back to awareness, and as I did I realized Arizona State had become an impossible
place for me. Wherever I turned familiar landmarks reminded me of Kit
and what we had shared. I had no interest in my classes, and when I
began to resume my customary activism, I saw that despite what we had
done, Arizona's extreme conservativism was fundamentally unchanged. I
had started reading the newspapers again and the escalating Vietnam
War was tormenting me. I needed to be where the action was. I had to
work harder to oppose it but this was not a place where I could have an
effect—the major organizing efforts against the war were coming from
the East and West Coasts. In the fall of 1967 I left Arizona State and
headed east to the University of Maryland. Washington, D.C., was right
next door.

I made an initial effort to integrate into university life at Maryland. I
found a one-room basement apartment, enrolled in courses, and tried to
be a student. But the truth was that the only hunger I felt was for the
antiwar movement. For a few months I turned up in my classes, made a
dutiful effort to work, hung out at the local coffee house, went to Peter,
Paul and Mary concerts, and tried to find the right place for me to
express my outrage in useful ways. Patsy's friends in Baltimore had given
me some local names in the movement, but I wanted to do more than
these groups were able to accomplish. Life in College Park grew more
and more confining. The only reason for remaining there was to satisfy
my parents' dream that all three of their children would graduate from
college, although like many young people I thought the best education
lay outside academics. In essence the University of Maryland was soon
no more than a place to hang my hat.

My first real effort on the East Coast was to help at the grassroots
level in organizing the 1967 march on the Pentagon so vividly captured
by Norman Mailer in his book *Armies of the Night*. I had read of the
pending march in *The Washington Post* and tracked down the phone
number and address of the headquarters in Washington. One Saturday I
took the bus into the District and walked to the office to volunteer my
services. Chaos is not an adequate word to describe the pandemonium I
found there. The walls were covered with posters for every cause imaginable. Long handwritten charts and lists were tacked to the spaces between the posters. The place was shrill with voices screaming out orders
to no one in particular. The battered furniture had obviously been bor-

rowed for the cause, and in one room long tables were stacked high with materials for mailings that had to be hand-addressed, stuffed, and sent out.

I was assigned a chair at one of the long tables and joined the assembly line. We were a companionable bunch, so each weekend we tried to gather at the same table for the mailing of the week. From my vantage point I was able to see what was going on in the rest of the office, and I watched carefully to see how it was all done. When I broke for coffee, I would wander around the rest of the headquarters and unobtrusively ask different people about the lists, charts, and procedures in their areas. I learned an enormous amount about how an operation of this magnitude was organized on those breaks. On campus on weekdays I began to skip my classes so I could hand out leaflets to the students urging them to attend the march. When I got back to my apartment at night I would get on the phone to my network of contacts around the country, ask them to suggest additional names, and beg everyone I reached to drive or take a bus to Washington.

I kept my parents posted about what I was doing. By then all around the country politics, families, and neighborhoods were beginning to be defined by their positions on the war, and for many of us of draft age, decisions regarding military service and the war had become a choice between conscience and country, life and death. Mom and Dad tended to oppose the war, although his feelings about it were stronger than hers. One time when I was home Mom had suggested over dinner that I might have to serve. Dad shot back, "Mary, he'll go fight in that damn war when the Rockefellers go fight in it—and not until then!" The table fell silent; he had the final word.

Throughout these years I had shared my agony in coming to terms with the war with my mother in letters similar in tone to those that Bill Clinton was to write from Oxford, and which were later to become an issue in his presidential campaign. There was no middle ground left in the debate—you were either for the war or against it. Back in Tempe we had argued violently about whether to serve, flee to Canada, or resist the draft and face a possible prison sentence of five years. As the war escalated so, somewhat to my surprise, had my invective and my tactics. I was willing to attempt sit-ins, stop troop trains, block draft boards, and drive recruiters for the Dow Chemical Company, who made the terrible weapon napalm, off campus. While tactics like these may not seem unusual today, the risk associated with them back then was made real when General Lewis Hershey, the Selective Service director, announced that he was going to start drafting all the students who were protesting the

Southeast Asia conflict. I decided to stay, face the risk, and if drafted go to prison for five years because, as I wrote my mother, "I believe if our soldiers have to fight in Vietnam, then I should fight here at home for my beliefs."

What is incredible in retrospect, of course, is that all I had to do was reveal that I was a homosexual and I would have automatically been forbidden from serving in the armed forces. Yet never in all my self-searching over the draft issue did I once consider this an option. It would have been far more frightening, and damaging, to confess my sexuality than to spend five years of my life in prison. I never doubted that history would prove those of us opposed to the war to have been right, or that my future would be jeopardized for that opposition. But if my homosexuality became public, it was clear to me that I would never work again. Many of my family and neighbors would support my refusing to serve but would drive me out of their lives if they knew I was gay. Whenever I question whether my perception about the extent of oppression against gays and lesbians in those years was correct, I think back to my readiness to go to prison for five years rather than acknowledge my homosexuality.

The October weekend of the march was bright and clear and the leaves were just starting to change. On Friday night friends began arriving from around the country to crash at my one-room apartment in College Park. One brought his guitar and we spent the small hours of the night sitting around, smoking grass, and singing our favorite folk and antiwar songs. When weariness finally set in, there were fourteen sleeping bags crammed together on the floor.

On Saturday morning the collective excitement was palpable. We rolled up the sleeping bags, produced an enormous breakfast from my tiny kitchen, filled our backpacks with snacks and water, and headed down the street to the local bus stop. Dozens of others were already waiting for the bus into Washington. As we rode into the city, a caravan of buses from all over the Northeast was clogging the roads. Leaning out our bus windows, we waved and shouted to the other buses, gave motorists the peace sign, and sang all the way to our drop-off site at the march. From there, we headed as a group to the trees around the reflecting pool in front of the Lincoln Memorial, where we joined the thousands of others who had come from all over the country to protest the war.

The crowd was vast, enormous beyond expectation or belief. The sense of common cause was contagious. From the back came a great roar; then the cheering moved closer and closer. At last I could see them—the veterans of the Spanish Civil War's Abraham Lincoln Brigade, marching to the front of the crowd with a banner aloft. These aging writers, artists, scholars, and ordinary citizens had fought in Spain in the 1930s to risk their lives for what they perceived to be a greater good. Now they were with us here to share in our protests against another unjust, murderous war. As we gave them a hero's welcome I climbed up a tree to witness their passage, as if in some way, however remotely, I could be part of their story.

The speakers at the rally were endless and predictable. They droned on about the injustices of the war, many using the opportunity to push their favorite ideology or cause. The crowd grew restless under the rhetoric, and turned to visiting with friends or buying buttons or banners. But everyone came alive when there was music and sang along with the musicians when familiar folk songs filled the air.

Toward the end of the rally I remember a speaker who started to chant, "Hell No! We Won't Go!" and within seconds tens of thousands of people were shouting "Hell No! We Won't Go!" in powerful unison, as if we wanted the whole country to hear us. Then slowly the march on the Pentagon began, crossing a bridge over the Potomac, winding along the riverside to the great dull stone building that housed the operations center for the Vietnam War. Surrounding it were solid lines of federal troops with fixed bayonets. They herded us into a huge parking lot, and my friends and I plunked down on the ground. Rumors were rife. Word came from the front of the march that some of the marchers had "stormed" the front of the Pentagon and were being pushed back by the troops. The flashing lights of the armada of police vehicles warned us the situation was deteriorating. Apprehensiveness grew. Then a strange calm took over. In measured tones we began to chant, "Hell No! We Won't Go!" and song filled the air—a great choir of voices singing "We Will Not Be Moved." In fact, where we were there was no real danger of being arrested. An elderly woman dressed in black with vivid silver hair moved slowly through the crowd handing out loaves of French bread. As the marchers broke off pieces of bread the scene took on the air of a holy communion. A radiant soprano voice pierced the air singing the old gospel song "Let Us Break Bread Together."

We sat on for a while, then walked back across the ornately beautiful Memorial Bridge to catch our bus home. It had been a moving and significant day.

By the fall of 1967 attention was focusing on the presidential election of the following year. The probable choices were dismal: two fervent supporters of the war, President Lyndon Johnson and Richard Nixon.

Young, intense, articulate campus organizer Allard Lowenstein, a veteran of the civil rights movement who was among the first to oppose the war, was traveling around the country seeking an alternative to Johnson for 1968. Student organizations such as College Young Democrats and the National Student Association, whose membership included college students all around the country, became battlegrounds between supporters of the current administration and those opposed to the war.

In mid-November, the antiwar forces decided to try to seize control of the College Young Democrats at their upcoming convention in Boston by electing an antiwar slate to replace the organization leadership. If we succeeded, we would deal a huge setback to President Johnson's efforts to quiet dissent in the Democratic Party. As a member of the University of Maryland Young Democrats, I decided to attend the convention and push for the antiwar slate. Then we heard that Senator Eugene McCarthy of Minnesota would be in Boston at the same time, and that he was seriously considering challenging Johnson in the Democratic primaries as a pro-peace candidate. McCarthy was a long-time liberal, a distinguished senator, a published poet, a quiet man who in no way fitted the standard political mode. Now, almost overnight, he was elevated to hero status. Here was someone of national stature willing to bring the issue of Vietnam to the voters.

My role in the Boston convention was minor but it was a great opportunity to watch firsthand the organizing of a floor operation, the creation of a command post to direct the floor fight, and the development of a whip system to keep our delegates on the floor in line. I volunteered my services to the leaders of the effort so I could gain access to the inner workings of the operation. I noted every detail. Late at night the team leadership would gather in a hotel room to do delegate counts and make assignments. I'd lean up against the wall of the room, watching and waiting, and volunteer for any responsible task that might open new doors for me. I listened to them argue angrily about strategy, finally arrive at a consensus, and straggle off at last for a few hours of sleep.

On Saturday morning Arlene Popkins, a complete stranger to me who was in charge of logistics for the convention, grabbed me by my coattail, pulled me off the convention floor, and said, "I need your body at the airport to greet Senator McCarthy and I need it *now!*" Arguing with Arlene, I discovered, was not an option. I followed her outside where she threw me into a car filled with strangers, hit the hood of the car, and yelled to the driver, "You have a load—get moving." Off we went to Logan, where some 150 of us stood watching as McCarthy's plane landed. The door opened and there he stood, silver-haired and smiling.

We went wild, cheering "On to New Hampshire!" I realized that for the first time I was no longer shouting in despair. I was cheering in support of a man of courage, decency, and conscience. He was delivering hope to a whole generation.

For those of us once inspired by John Kennedy's passion and eloquence, Senator McCarthy's austere intellectual style took some getting used to. But it was soon evident that he was articulating our deepest feelings about Vietnam. He made us listen. He commanded respect for his ideas. Later, in his presidential campaign, there was a poster that captured his essence perfectly. It read, "He Stood Alone and Something Happened."

I came back to my apartment in College Park with a new sense of commitment, energy, and purpose: to work for the election of Eugene McCarthy as the next President of the United States. On November 30, the snowy day when he formally announced his candidacy, a group of us went outside on the campus and made snow sculptures of our hero and surrounded them with peace symbols. In the crisp air we sensed a new beginning.

But back home a little later the ringing phone shattered my feeling of hope. It was my mother.

"I have bad news, David," she told me. "Russell Garrison was killed in Vietnam. His helicopter was shot down." Her voice broke in tears.

Russell had lived with his large farm family just across the fields from us. We had been childhood playmates and friends. We went through elementary and high school together. I had always respected and admired him for his strength and his determination, like mine, to break out of our hometown. The army was his way to escape, and now he was dead.

I started crying, for Russell, for myself, for my parents' support of me, for this terrible war. The day of Russell's funeral my Dad went out to our family car and put on a bumper sticker that said, "End the War." I knew what I had to do.

The only possibility for peace was a candidate who would implement it. I took a bus in from College Park to present myself as a volunteer at the national McCarthy for President campaign headquarters in Washington. I expected, as a twenty-one-year-old aspiring to a political career would, that I'd find a smooth professional operation under way. Certainly the march offices had been chaotic, but that was an impromptu effort of the young. This was a presidential candidacy. In my mind's eye I saw serious people sitting at their desks discussing deep issues with other serious people. I was so nervous about being out of place among them that I nearly turned around and caught the next bus back.

The Seventeenth Street headquarters was a mess. Banged-up furniture that looked as if it had been scrounged up from a junkpile, hospital-colored walls in need of a paint job, grimy blinds, not a receptionist in sight. The place was a din of heated exchanges, barked orders, and shouts for help from people looking for supplies. As I stood there Genie Gans, who was one of the campaign organizers, came storming out of national campaign manager Blair Clark's office, kicked the file cabinet, and shouted, "This fucking campaign is never going to get off the ground!"

She saw me standing there blushing. "Hi, sorry about that," she said. "Who are you? If you're going to be around you might as well get used to it."

"That's okay," I answered. "I'm David Mixner. I just came down to help."

She got right down to business. "Do you have any experience in organizing?" she asked.

I described my involvement thus far and she seemed pleased to have someone with any experience at all. I liked her instantly. She seemed to care about making me feel welcome.

"Let me show you around the place and then we'll get you busy with something."

As Genie and I walked from office to office, she introduced me to everyone there, among them a number of people who would later play a major part in my life as political allies, lifelong friends, or both. In the first office, deep in planning the McCarthy student operation, were Marge Sklencar, who was president of the student body at Mundelein College, a Jesuit women's college outside of Chicago; student activist Sam Brown; and Annie Hart, the daughter of Senator Phil Hart, who got up and gave me a big welcoming hug. In the next office, staffing the press operation and at that moment heatedly debating a welfare rights issue, were journalist and future Pulitzer Prize winner Sy Hersh and Marylouise Oates, who had been a young working journalist in New Jersey and was to become the most important and long-lasting friend in my life. By the time Genie had completed the tour of the office, my nervousness had vanished. This shabby headquarters was no different from all those places I knew in the antiwar movement. I felt at home.

From that first day on, the McCarthy for President campaign became a full-time crusade. With my parents' approval, I left college, never to finish my degree. I was brought aboard the campaign at the munificent wage of $320 a month. As long as I could pay my rent and eat—barely— it didn't matter. Here I was actually doing what I'd dreamed of. I could hardly believe it.

Within a day I was at work recruiting students from around the country to go to New Hampshire to canvass for McCarthy in the first of the primaries. For the first time in my life I had a desk of my own. Each morning I would put on my best sports jacket and tie, go to the headquarters, sit proudly behind my desk, lists laid out before me, and work the phones. I had never known anything so heady.

The National Student Association had provided us with lists of key contacts on each campus in the country. "Hey, this is David Mixner from the national McCarthy for President campaign," I'd announce. "We are asking students to go to New Hampshire to canvass for McCarthy. We were given your name as someone who might be willing to organize a busload from your campus. We already have commitments from Harvard, Yale, the University of Pennsylvania. Can we count on you delivering the bodies from your school?"

Without exception the answer was "yes." I'd enter the name on our key organizers list and put together a packet with details on how to organize a busload, the names of our contacts in New Hampshire who would direct them to the appropriate town, and McCarthy for President literature. Then I was on to the next call. I discovered to my pleasure that I was very good at what I was doing. My enthusiasm about our cause was contagious; it made those on the other end of the phone eager to be part of a greater effort. I was off and running.

I never got to New Hampshire myself to see the outcome of the work that we were doing in Washington, but within a short time, our operation had organized dozens of campuses for our "children's crusade" there. One of our tasks when we recruited was to persuade the kids to become "Clean for Gene" by cutting off their long hair and wearing conventional clothing while campaigning. This sounds odd today but it made a lot of sense. Hippiedom carried a decidedly bad aura for many hometown Americans. The message was greeted with reluctance or outright protests at first, but almost always the students got the point. McCarthy was our best hope of ending the war, and we could only achieve his candidacy if we reached a maximum of voters.

Every weekend the students would be driven to New Hampshire, disembark from the buses in their designated town, and report to the local headquarters. Each was assigned a precinct, and they would go off in pairs to canvass voters door to door, soliciting their opinions and urging them to cast their vote for peace. Back in the area headquarters, their findings would be integrated into master lists identifying those who supported McCarthy, were undecided, or endorsed the war. Some of the volunteers became so committed that they stayed in New Hampshire full-time until the primary.

As the campaign gathered momentum, an exhilarating spirit of family grew among the staff at the Washington headquarters. I moved from College Park into a row-house apartment that Sam Brown, the unofficial head of the youth for McCarthy movement and our student coordinator, had rented at 1635 Massachusetts Avenue. It was on the fourth floor, the living room and kitchen floors covered with linoleum, the view a blur through the dirty windows. Sam had the bedroom, not much bigger than a walk-in closet, and my bed was a beat-up foldout couch in the living room. It was ample for two young guys high on a cause, but there never were just the two of us. The place was always full of student volunteers and organizers camping out on our floor and eating the refrigerator bare. When Sam and I were off on assignments it turned into a hotel for anyone who was in town and needed to crash. When we were around, we took back our beds from whoever had preempted them.

Within a few weeks, several of us had not only become close friends but created a miniature political alliance within the campaign. Sam, Annie Hart, Marge Sklencar, and I started spending a lot of time together. Marge would cook us a huge dinner and we'd wind up with bull sessions lasting late into the night, and sometimes others would join us. I became a leader in many ways—encouraging the camaraderie, leading discussions about our stance on the war, pressing for the importance of preserving the grassroots nature of our organizing, planning shared activities from charades to a movie, setting off laughter with wisecracks and off-color jokes.

"Good old Dave" was the persona I adopted, the way everyone I worked with saw me—and my chief defense. In this group of healthy, vigorous young people it wasn't long before dating, affairs, and pairings took over among the staff. More and more, I felt myself an outsider. Friends would try to set me up with this young woman or that and I'd tell them I wasn't ready to start dating; I'd recently lost my fiancée in an automobile accident in Arizona and it was too soon after "her" death. Every time I feminized Kit, I felt I was denying his existence. Increasingly, I took to drugs and alcohol to combat my loneliness. My only outlet for my hard work and sexual abstinence was to spend the weekend with my friends drunk or on acid, coping with the world through blurred unseeing eyes. When I used drugs, I could deceive myself into feeling I was part of their community despite my secret.

For I knew there was no way I could share the truth with them. They were warmhearted and decent people and they would have been generous in their support of me—but just as surely, as an openly gay man, I would not have received any major assignments in the campaign. The emptiness inside of me grew. All I could see to fill it was to throw myself even further into my work, to be good old Dave in group settings, and to drown it with drugs when it became intolerable.

However, my sexuality was not the only source of that sense of isolation. Around me in the campaign in growing numbers were the sons and daughters of Harvard and Yale. There was a truth underlying my facade; I *was* a country boy. They came from Boston and Manhattan; they'd traveled in Europe; they summered on Long Island and Cape Cod; they skied in Vermont. My life until Arizona had been South New Jersey, and Tempe was insular too. Many of their parents' names awed me: Barbara Tuchman, Arthur Schlesinger, the Saltonstalls of Massachusetts. So did their articulateness and confidence, and their knowledge of art, literature, music. That last I could address more easily than my social ineptitude—I read hungrily to start catching up. But when I was in company, mortified by my mispronunciations and shaky grammar, I laughingly claimed that English was my second language and hillbilly my first. I became panicky in social situations that required experience beyond the rudimentary knife, fork, and spoon, and turned down invitations because I was afraid I wouldn't know how to conduct myself properly. Sometimes I'd find myself in such situations in spite of myself, and then I'd use the same brand of humor to deflect attention, put on my country-boy act: "Golly, look at this equipment around my plate—must be expecting the whole family to eat at this setting!" But if I wanted to build the career I sought, I realized I couldn't continue to cop out. So slowly, gradually, I began to try to cope with this too; Sam Brown, whom I could trust, offered help on the proper etiquette when I sought it. It was harder than the intellectual catching-up, however. I knew I had a long way to go.

One evening, as we were sitting around the office talking about the various busloads of students heading north to New Hampshire, Curtis Gans, the national political director of the campaign, came in, joined our semicircle around Sam's desk, and started issuing directives. He told Sam and Annie they would be heading to New Hampshire until after the primary. Marge was to stay in Washington and keep the students flowing north. I waited for my assignment. None was forth-coming.

Then Curtis began to lament that no one in the campaign had experi-ence in precinct caucuses. I perked up—I had participated in the process while at Arizona State.

"I worked in precinct caucuses for several years," I told him, "espe-cially when I was in Arizona."

Curtis looked surprised and skeptical. "How much experience?" he asked.

Feeling challenged, I fired back, "More than anyone here."

Sam burst out laughing. It was a commentary on the youthful nature of the campaign that my sparse experience made me the expert on caucuses.

But so I was. Without missing a beat, Curtis said, "Be on a plane for Minnesota tomorrow. We have to make a good showing in McCarthy's home state—it's Vice President Humphrey's backyard too. Besides, the Minnesota caucuses are just a week before New Hampshire. They could be helpful to us there."

All of a sudden my brashness gave way to nerves. "Curtis, wouldn't it be better to send someone from the senator's Minnesota staff to his home state?"

"They'll be there too, David, but I want one of my own people there." That was the point at which I realized Curtis was building his own influence within the campaign—another useful lesson for me in the realities of political organizing.

In fact, I didn't leave for several days. I spent them in hectic prepara-tion for the trip, asking everyone in headquarters if they knew anyone in Minnesota, making lists, calling up cold turkey people who might know some particulars about the political situation in the state. I milked Sena-tor McCarthy's Capitol Hill staff for valuable information and names. I divided my notebook into sections, one for lists of names, another with the backgrounds of the major political players in Minnesota, one high-lighting important aspects of the state's political history, one noting re-gional voting patterns. Then I tucked the notebook into my briefcase, boarded a plane to Minneapolis, and took off on my first political field assignment.

The McCarthy headquarters in Minnesota made the Washington of-fices look corporate. They were in an abandoned grocery store. The walls were covered with posters imploring America to "Resist!" and "End the War!" I was greeted at the door by a University of Minnesota student named Jock, wearing a shirt and tie but still sporting flowing

Sergeant Pepper hair and a beard that he clearly hadn't been able to bring himself to cut off. He looked mystified at the sight of me. National headquarters had forgotten to tell the locals that I was on the way. Here was this unknown young man, hair cropped, dressed in a suit and tie, holding a battered old briefcase in his hand. I could see what they were thinking: "What in hell do we do with *him*?"

It didn't take long to find out. The operation badly needed phone lines for canvassing. This was my chance to prove myself. With the assistance of Don Green back at the headquarters in Washington and help from my sister Patsy, I launched into my first political fund-raising. I called personal friends and acquaintances around the country, pointing out what a boost it would be nationwide for McCarthy to do well in the Minnesota caucuses. Patsy raised money in Baltimore. Don wrested an additional thousand dollars out of national. In short order, we produced over six thousand dollars and got the phones in place. Just as important—or more so—I was now part of the team.

Hundreds of students, parents, professors from the university, and union members jammed into the headquarters to staff the phones. Peace was their thrust, McCarthy the candidate to implement it, Minnesota the place to give him that crucial boost before New Hampshire. We sensed that the intensive canvassing was having an impact but we were becoming too exhausted to tell. Then, like a nightmare, the war exploded. On January 30, the start of the Vietnamese New Year, the Vietcong launched its infamous Tet offensive against major South Vietnamese cities and U.S. bases and outposts. American casualties soared to record numbers. The country was stunned. General Westmoreland went on television to proclaim that the enemy's plans had gone "afoul," but this was one lie too many. In this first televised war America had known, the carnage was laid out before us on every night's news. Opposition to the war swelled. Our weariness evaporated.

In the last weeks before the caucuses, the headquarters was open twenty-four hours a day. Shifts of volunteers collected canvassing kits and precinct maps so they could walk their territories. Others staffed the phones for those precincts where we had no one to walk them. After sunset a fresh shift came in to work through the night preparing packets for the next day's canvassers, developing new lists, and assembling a card file of those who had committed to McCarthy the previous day. The ancient mimeograph machine cranked out releases.

Meanwhile I was on some ventures of my own. I borrowed a car, and with draft resister Gary Hart (who was to become a California state senator, not the future Democratic presidential aspirant), we went from campus to campus across the state mobilizing students and asking them to recruit others in turn who would commit to voting in the caucuses. I also worked hard to persuade the more Catholic wards in the state to vote for McCarthy. Three of us at headquarters decided to mobilize "Nuns Against the War," using the know-how of a hot young organizer named Jim Goff who knew every Catholic order in the state. We contacted the orders one by one, pressed them to attend the caucuses, and asked them to bring others with them. It was the first time I had ever done recruiting at convents. Before long our crowded headquarters was full of nuns in full habit collecting their packets so they could go door to door to work the Catholic precincts. On the night of the caucuses, some of the nuns were themselves elected delegates to the national convention and became the new ward leaders. It made for terrific newspaper coverage too photographs of our nuns capturing the Catholic wards for McCarthy were spread across the front pages of the Minneapolis papers the next morning.

March 5 was the day. In precincts across the state, much as in the old New England town meetings, people came together in school auditoriums, private homes, and veterans halls to vote on a variety of resolutions and to express their choice for president by choosing local representatives who had committed to a particular candidate. It was the first stage in the state electoral process, which continued through the ward level and culminated in the state convention. The turnout was astounding. Over the years, the average turnout for a precinct caucus had been around fifty-five. This time they came in in the hundreds, debating the war and voting their conscience.

In early evening we sat around a table in headquarters covered with phones, waiting for the calls reporting the returns. At first we couldn't believe them. They were overwhelmingly for McCarthy representatives. "Well, we still haven't heard from the rural areas," we kept warning one another. But as the hours passed it was clear. Minnesota had trounced Lyndon Johnson and given Eugene McCarthy his first victory in the campaign.

We broke out champagne, hugged each other, wiped away exultant tears, and cheered the announcement of each new precinct return. We had truly seen democracy in action. That night we all believed that peace was a little closer.

One week later, on March 12, McCarthy scored impressively in New Hampshire, with Johnson, a sitting president, coming out ahead by a

scant 230 votes. But our exultation was short-lived. On March 16, Senator Robert Kennedy, a hero to most of us for his articulate and passionate advocacy for the poor and powerless, announced he was entering the
race. Only a few months earlier he would have been our first choice to
challenge President Johnson for the nomination. But McCarthy had
committed first, and coming after his Minnesota and New Hampshire
achievements, Kennedy's announcement was a bitter blow. He had failed
to stand up when most needed. Now the antiwar forces were split.

I wrestled with the pain of decision. President Kennedy was my hero.
It was his call to make a better world that had directed me toward politics. When he was murdered I had transferred my loyalty to his brother,
and Robert Kennedy's battle against injustice had been inspiring. But it
was Eugene McCarthy who had dared to challenge a sitting president on
an overwhelming issue of principle. I was growing much less naive about
the tough realities of politics by now, but neither could I forget McCarthy's valor. The day Kennedy announced I shared my anguish with Patsy
and walked for hours trying to decide. But I could not desert the man
who had joined our cause when no one else was ready to take a stand.
My loyalty belonged to him. I would stay with the McCarthy campaign.

Immediately after the Minnesota victory, I had had a call from Curtis
Gans anointing me as the campaign's field organizer in the states that
did not hold primaries. For the most part, the Democratic Party in these
states was controlled by long-entrenched political bosses fervently committed to Johnson's reelection. Their patronage opportunities and thus
their political futures depended on their delivering their handpicked delegates to the President and crushing any antiwar tendencies in the delegate selection process. As I was to find out, the battles in these states
could be bitter and ugly. In rapid succession Don Green, the nonprimary
states coordinator, sent me to Texas, Oklahoma, North Carolina, Kan-
sas, Connecticut, North Dakota—all over the place—each state yielding
a different and often frustrating challenge.

But it was sometimes inspiring as well. I met individuals of very great
courage. In Alabama, articulate African-American John Cashin ignored
threats to his life and organized a delegation of blacks and whites to
challenge the old-boy delegation of his state. In Lyndon Johnson's home
state of Texas, I saw prominent civil libertarian Maury Maverick fighting
for delegates and ignoring the threats to his law practice. North Carolina
was where I met for the first time at the university a freckled, redheaded
student named Taylor Branch. He turned up at a campus rally for
McCarthy eager to help. The North Carolina caucuses were imminent
and he pitched right in, joining those trying to build the first black/white

political coalition between the Kennedy and McCarthy forces. This was one of Taylor's first involvements in the civil rights arena (he was to go on to win a Pulitzer Prize in 1989 for his history of the Martin Luther King years, *Parting the Waters*), and he carried on this same work later in the campaign in his home state of Georgia.

No one impressed me as much as the energetic, charismatic, and determined Connecticut housewife Anne Wexler, who later became a White House adviser to Jimmy Carter. She took on almost singlehandedly the political machine of one of the nation's most powerful political bosses, John Bailey. We sat in the capacious kitchen of her handsome Westport home looking out at the sweep of lawn and I asked her what made her spend day after day on the road fighting so tough a battle.

"You can't ignore injustice by surrounding yourself with beauty, David," she said. "I have two sons. I can't conceive of them dying in that war. I can't bear the thought of mothers burying their young."

"But you're getting pounded daily. They keep attacking you for being disloyal to the party. Doesn't it get to you after a while?"

"Sure. But then I look at the pictures of my sons and my fear vanishes. My boys are going to know their mother left this world a better place."

She was not afraid to articulate her idealism. It was from Anne that I learned to take complex issues and give them a human face.

I went to Oklahoma with Eli Segal, who was to become Clinton's campaign manager in 1992. He was a warmhearted, intellectual, intense man who looked more like a professor than the bright young lawyer he was, and he had always impressed me because he was the most prepared person in the entire headquarters. We shared a cab to National Airport from the office and boarded the plane to Oklahoma City, but I couldn't figure out why he seemed so nervous. You could feel his tension and hear it in his voice. It was utterly out of character.

"Eli," I asked at last, "why in hell are you so fidgety?"

"Nothing. Just haven't been to Oklahoma before or really that much in the South, and I'm a little nervous."

That didn't make much sense. "It's no big deal," I told him. "Southerners are just like everyone else. Just more conservative."

"Yeah, David, sure. You aren't Jewish though."

"*What?*"

"You aren't Jewish," he repeated. "I can't help but wonder if I'm going to face anti-Semitism from them. A New York Jew heading into Oklahoma to tell them what to do. It makes me nervous. There's a large Klan there and a history of segregation. With a last name like Segal, how do you think I'm going to be greeted by the locals?"

"Don't worry," I reassured him, "I wear size thirteen E cowboy boots. I won't let them fuck with you."

We both broke into laughter and he seemed to relax a little; but what struck me most, of course, was that he too had his secret fear. I learned an important lesson that day, though one I could not always hold to—recognizing Eli as a man who courageously moved through his fear to do the work that had to be done.

On March 31 I was in our large Pennsylvania headquarters working on the write-in campaign for McCarthy. It had been announced that Johnson would address the nation on Vietnam, and over a hundred of us gathered around the television sets desperately hoping that the President would declare a moratorium on the bombing of the North. We heard him say there would be no more bombing above the twentieth parallel. We heard him say he would not authorize the sending of another two hundred thousand troops to the war zone, as the military had requested. And then came the words we had never even dreamed of: "I shall not seek, and will not accept, the nomination of my party for another term as your president."

The stunned silence erupted into an explosion of cheers. We had toppled a president. We danced celebrating into the streets and found hundreds of exuberant students from the University of Pennsylvania marching to Independence Hall. In the Wisconsin primary two days later, where Johnson was of course still on the ballot, McCarthy supporters outvoted his almost two to one. Everything seemed possible.

The euphoria was short-lived. On April 4 Martin Luther King was assassinated in Memphis. I heard the news in the Philadelphia railroad station when I was changing trains on my way to Pittsburgh from Washington. Next to me a black woman began to pray. On the other side a man swore, over and over. Numbness and grief swamped us all. I collapsed on a bench in the station and remember wondering dumbly what sense nonviolence actually made—whether it was really possible for good people to survive in an ugly world. I must have gotten on my train, but the journey to Pittsburgh is a blank.

The days that followed are not. Riots broke out in the city's black community and from my hotel window I watched the flames. On television I saw report after report of cities burning in rage, of National Guardsmen wielding machine guns posted on the steps of the United States Capitol. And I remember the police escorting me and several other McCarthy campaign staffers through the rioting to the Pittsburgh airport, where we flew in silence to Tennessee. My old organizing buddies from Arizona had asked that I represent them at the memorial march in Memphis and at the funeral in Atlanta because they knew how deeply I revered King, and to be there helped me to mourn. But what I remember above all are the hundreds of thousands as they followed the mule-drawn caisson bearing his body. We were as one in our grief. The world was bleaker after April 4.

And more was to come. In June 1968 almost the entire McCarthy campaign went to California to work in the crucial primary there. By then Kennedy had won states like Indiana and Nebraska, while McCarthy had scored an upset victory in Oregon. California was going to be pivotal in deciding who would carry the mantle of the peace movement into the Democratic Convention in Chicago in August. From Pacific Palisades matrons to UCLA hippies, our Westwood headquarters teemed with an energy I have rarely known in any campaign. The cars on the freeways sported Kennedy bumper stickers or "McCarthy Flowers," and by primary night on June 4, the race was too close to call. We were in the hotel ballroom as the returns began coming in; Kennedy was winning but McCarthy was only a few points behind. And then someone shouted, "Kennedy's been shot!" and the enormous room broke into screams and sobs. I fled to my room, and all night long, like so many others, sat fixed to the television set waiting for news of his condition. All through the next day we kept the vigil; then, still not knowing, I flew back to Washington on the red-eye. We learned he had died as we stepped off the plane.

I went straight to Patsy's in Baltimore—my refuge as always. Together we watched the funeral in New York City on television. When we learned that the funeral train was to go from there to Washington, where he would be laid to rest in Arlington National Cemetery, we walked down to the Baltimore station to join the throngs standing by the tracks, singing freedom songs as they waited. In the distance came the sound of the train. The crowd fell silent. Then a young black man raised his powerful voice in "The Battle Hymn of the Republic," and as the train bearing the body of Robert Kennedy passed by, we all joined hands and sang with him.

We all lost heart after June 4; it had been too murderous a year. McCarthy basically stopped campaigning after the assassination. But the war and the dying went on. Drained of passion though we were, the Chicago convention was only weeks ahead and it was as urgent as ever to secure him the nomination.

So my next assignment was Georgia, where a complex civil rights battle was under way. Its militant segregationist governor, Lester Maddox, had handpicked all the delegates to the convention. Out of the 117 he chose, there were only 7 blacks. An insurgent group of brave blacks and white liberals in the Georgia Democratic Party Forum decided to hold its own convention in Macon on August 10 to select an alternative Freedom delegation to the one Maddox had engineered. It would be open to everyone and the delegation it chose would be half black, half white. The McCarthy campaign went all out in support, committing major resources and participation. We had a bright young man already on the scene there, Charlie Negaro, who had laid important groundwork among the insurgents with the assistance of Taylor Branch and Branch's classmate from the University of North Carolina, Parker Hudson. The national campaign sent Sam Brown, Ivanhoe Donaldson, Curtis Gans, and me to Georgia. Sam and Curtis worked on building coalitions. They also had to wrestle with the tricky political problem of Vice President Humphrey's own campaign for the nomination. He had entered the race on April 27 and had support from many civil rights advocates; and we could not let the Freedom delegation be turned into a McCarthy political ploy. If Macon succeeded, it would be a huge embarrassment to Humphrey in Chicago—but we did not want to estrange his supporters now.

I was assigned to make a three-day swing through southwest Georgia, hitting cities and towns that had earned their place in the history books because of their virulent opposition to civil rights. When I left the Atlanta headquarters in my rental car, I realized it was a good thing I had Georgia license plates on my car. Segregationists looked askance at out-of-town cars driven by young white student types. The farther I saw the lights of Atlanta recede in my rearview mirror, the edgier I became. This region had been a battleground, marked by shootings, police harassment, firebombings, and bitter street fights. I had heard too many stories of cars full of rowdy young whites out to chase down strangers driving through their towns, and sheriffs stopping cars they didn't like the sight of late at night and roughing up their occupants.

My job was to meet with people in this part of Georgia who had indicated they were going to the convention in Macon. This area was key to our strategy of taking a challenge delegation to Chicago. The cities of Americus and Albany had been the site of brutal confrontations over civil rights. Albany had haunted Dr. King because it was one of the few places where he had not been able to crack the power of the segregationists. We needed delegates from these areas in Chicago. They would bring a poignant and powerful human face to the challenge delegation.

I stayed in motels. That way, I would not jeopardize the safety or livelihoods of those I visited. For blacks and whites alike, participating in Macon was risk enough. It was their governor, after all, who had used an ax handle to chase blacks from his Atlanta restaurant.

Inside the room of my small roadside motel the first night, I locked the door and pulled the curtains, wondering if I was being melodramatic. Was I an idiot to have made the trip alone? Was I overreacting? I blew a fortune in quarters activating my "massage bed," but it didn't relieve my tension a whit. I have never been so glad to see daylight as that morning when I woke from a ragged sleep to see a dart of sunlight poking through a tiny opening in the curtains. I am of a mind to believe that evil does not occur in the light of day. It is cowards who need the darkness to practice their hatred.

I was going to a meeting in Americus that morning. Most of the work had already been done by others; my job was simply to explain what would happen at the Macon convention and to answer any questions. The more information we could give the courageous people who had decided to go to Macon, the less likely they would be to decide at the last minute that the risk to their jobs or their safety was too great.

The semirural area I drove through was dotted with broken-down houses—shacks, many of them—with privies at the side. The children playing in the yards were visibly suffering from malnutrition. The depth of the poverty stunned me. I pulled up in front of a worn, unpainted house with a front porch crowded with overstuffed furniture. A black woman came out and enveloped me in her arms. "We have been waiting for you!" she cried. "The folks are out back. Come on around."

I followed her around the side to the backyard. Half a dozen people, all black, were talking energetically. They saw me, fell silent, and stared. I was wearing a suit and found myself wishing I'd put on jeans. But I remembered a piece of advice my mother had given me: "If you have something important to say, dress well to show respect to the people you want to listen to you. Dress as if you have something important to say." I respected these people. Their courage had inspired me.

I took off my jacket, hooked it on a piece of wood jutting out of the side of the house, and sat down.

I thanked them for coming and outlined the procedures for the convention. I assured them that those who were elected delegates in Macon would have their finances covered for the trip to Chicago. Then I said, "I know you place yourselves in jeopardy by attending . . ."

My host held up her hand.

"Stop right there, honey. We live here. We know what it's like. I don't need to hear from you how dangerous it is. You are getting in that car to head back to Atlanta. We're staying. Don't get me wrong, honey—we're glad you're here. This is helpful. But we have fought for a long time. Many of us have gone to jail. We can take it from here, baby."

My face turned red. I wondered if I had been insensitive. I said, "I understand, ma'am. What else do you need from me?"

They asked me a batch of logistical questions, we drank iced tea, and I left. They'd been impressive: blunt, realistic, committed, dignified.

Albany was my next destination, where there was a meeting that evening at Albany State College. They were mostly students and professors, a different kind of group—all business. They wanted to get to the facts and get home. I stayed in a nearby motel room afterward and found the fear was virtually gone. The courage of the kind people I had met that morning had erased it. As they had said, they lived here. I was going back. I understood what they were telling me.

I spent the next two days in a series of small, brisk meetings in the towns of South Georgia: Sylvester, Sumer, Tifton, Millwood, Waycross. My message and the brave individuals I met in each place were much the same. But the hopelessness on the children's faces has never stopped haunting me. I still see them today.

On August 10, more than six hundred delegates from all over Georgia gathered in Macon. Blacks and whites held up homemade standards blazoning the names of their counties. Ministers in clerical collars leaned over into the rows of chairs arguing for this point or that. Black students in dashikis walked around with lists, counting the votes on various resolutions. Prospective delegates stood at the podium and spoke of the significance of their being there; Georgia, they proclaimed, would never be the same.

Congressman John Conyers from Detroit had come south to keynote the convention and he fired it up by denouncing the deal Humphrey had made that allowed Lester Maddox to handpick the members of the "official" delegation. But in truth, Conyers was only the warm-up speaker. The convention was waiting for one of its own to ascend to the podium—Julian Bond.

Bond was a hero to them before he spoke—this handsome young man with piercing eyes had been the first black elected to the Georgia legislature, had been refused his seat, and had gone to court to win the right to represent his own constituents. He was soft-spoken, but his message was not. He challenged the evils of a system that would allow a segregationist governor to choose the delegates to the party's national convention. "We will not be denied our rightful place in Chicago," he charged. "We have fought too long, too hard to be denied it." The convention went wild. That day Bond became a spokesperson for their courage, their dignity, and their freedom—and a presence on the national scene.

The voting for the delegates who would go to Chicago began. Many had tears in their eyes. Some of those for whom they were casting their votes had served time in jail for their cause. It was everyone's cause. This was a radiant day.

Georgia was a victory for McCarthy, and as Laurence Stern of *The Washington Post* wrote, it "was a clear triumph of organization." For those of us young white students who had participated in this historical moment, it was probably the most glorious moment of the campaign. I felt the glory but I was torn by conflict. My homosexuality had me churning. I had sat in Macon witnessing the bravery of black Americans risking their lives fighting for what they believed. I did not have their courage. I was afraid to fight my fight. Those around me were ready to court rejection and danger. I could not risk either. This great moment of healing was only for others.

CHAPTER THREE

Building a Future

CHICAGO. In 1968 the very name came to symbolize the battle for the heart and soul of a nation. The violence and anger surrounding the Chicago convention revealed a nation intensely divided over one of the great moral questions of this century. Democracy failed in the convention hall, and the brutality that erupted in the streets around it brought the war home to America as never before.

But I was full of eagerness when I arrived. This was my first national convention. I had spent the last year preparing for this moment. I had dreamed of it ever since I was ten and had seen my first convention on television and imagined myself parading around the floor of the hall to the rousing music of the band. Never in my dreams of glory did I imagine the reality would be a display of raw, abusive political power, or troops with bayonets chasing me and my colleagues down the streets of the convention city.

Chicago looked like an armed camp. In addition to the thousands of police mobilized by Mayor Richard Daley, there were nearly six thousand National Guardsmen and over seven thousand federal troops. Throughout the summer the left had been promising massive demonstrations, including civil disobedience, to protest the war. Hard-liners on both sides escalated the rhetoric all summer until there seemed to be no middle ground. By convention time Daley had whipped his city into a frenzy of fear over the tens of thousands of invading "Yippies" who would place every citizen in jeopardy. The Yippies—a new left fringe group given to deliberately provocative threats—inflamed the fear with a barrage of outrageous warnings: They would put LSD into the water supply, they would burn the city to the ground. Chicago was a battle waiting to happen.

Police in riot gear were everywhere we turned. There had already been clashes between the police and protesters in Lincoln Park, on the city's North Side. The political forces of McCarthy, George McGovern (who had entered the race to provide a place for Robert Kennedy supporters), and Humphrey were arriving to hold a convention in which it was a foregone conclusion that the Vice President would be nominated. Our hopes rested in reaching enough progressive Humphrey delegates to pass an antiwar plank and to challenge the Maddox delegation from Georgia.

Hubert Humphrey, long-time champion of civil rights, was now Lyndon Johnson's handpicked successor, the candidate of the bosses and the pro-war delegates and the defender of the status quo. Humphrey's supporters were not interested in an open convention. They intended to crush dissent, endorse the war, roll over their opponents, and nominate their man. Watching the people with real power in action, I realized my political experience had been no more than kindergarten level.

It was as disheartening inside the Amphitheater where the convention was held as on the streets. Almost at once, the Humphrey forces began to strip their opponents not only of power but dignity. They moved up the vote on the challenge to the Maddox delegation from Tuesday to Monday night in a speedy effort to diffuse a potentially explosive situation. Using every ticket we could lay our hands on, we packed the galleries with Macon delegation supporters. Throughout the evening the antiwar delegates on the floor and the observers in the galleries joined in chants of "Julian Bond! Julian Bond!" But they were no match for those in charge. Their plan was to seat both delegations, giving each person a half vote, and they delayed the vote on the Georgia challenge until after 2:00 A.M., when all of America would have gone to bed and the cameras had shut down for the night. The roll call made it clear it was going to be close. At the end, the Humphrey compromise won by fewer than four hundred votes. Cries of outrage filled the hall.

I joined the protesters in the street the next morning. I could not return to the hall after that.

On Tuesday night the Humphrey forces tried the same tactic, conducting the debate around the peace plank in the platform at an hour that would avoid public scrutiny. This time it didn't end as intended. The antiwar delegates refused to be silenced and the chair finally had to adjourn the session in the early morning hour.

Just as determined were the protesters, who night after night had been beaten in Lincoln Park, out of the public eye. That Tuesday night, for the first time, they marched to Grant Park, across from the Hilton, the hotel where the delegates were staying, and into the glare of the cameras and the national press. It was too much for Mayor Daley. He brought in National Guard troops, in full riot gear with bayonets fixed to the end of their guns. Jeeps with their radiators covered with barbed wire were arrayed behind the Guardsmen, set to run into the protesters and disperse them when a signal was given.

The troops were visibly nervous, the protesters livid. Then, as the imminence of confrontation mounted, several young women moved along the line of troops and placed flowers in the barrels of their bayoneted guns. Peter Yarrow and Mary Travers of Peter, Paul and Mary began to sing "Where Have All the Flowers Gone?" and the tension eased dramatically. Daley decided that for the moment it was better to let us be and spend the night in the park, and for the first time since our arrival there was relative calm.

It did not last. On Wednesday afternoon, the debate on the war finally took place. Although 80 percent of those who voted in the primaries had cast their ballots for antiwar candidates, Humphrey's forces prevailed. The antiwar plank lost by five hundred votes. That evening blood flowed in the streets of Chicago.

As dusk fell and the convention prepared to nominate Hubert Humphrey, a mule train arrived from Dr. King's Poor People's Campaign, his last organizing effort to awaken the nation to the plight of the poor. Many of us joined the procession behind the wagon in tribute to his memory. The police blocked it from proceeding to the front of the Hilton, then surrounded us on all four sides so that no one could leave their human corral. Without provocation, they waded into us, swinging their clubs against every living target in their reach, whipping us out of our shoes, beating us to the ground, forcing us against the walls of the hotel itself. Some of us were thrown through the window of the Hilton bar, and the police followed with their nightsticks, jumping through the shattered glass and beating us without mercy. I remember going into a fetal position and feeling the blows of the billy club on my legs. The chant of the police: "Kill! Kill! Kill!" still resounds in my nightmares.

When the violence finally subsided, I pulled myself out through the glass and into the street. It was littered with shoes, pocketbooks, and twisted eyeglasses. City street sweepers were already at work, attempting to hide away the debris of destroyed dreams. I hurt all over and my right leg was badly bruised and battered—I was to be on and off crutches over the next several years. As always, I found a phone and called Patsy for solace, then limped back into the park to join the growing army of defiant protesters. In the white glare of the television lights, an Episcopal bishop in full ritual garb gave communion to the protesters while the Guard stood in array around them. When those inside the convention heard of the bloodbath at Balboa and Michigan, hundreds of delegates left the hall and walked to the park bearing candles and singing "We Shall Overcome." As they reached us, we wept.

If only that had been the end of it. Daley and the police, it turned out, were not done. On the next night, as Humphrey gave his acceptance speech, the Chicago police invaded the sixteenth-floor headquarters of the McCarthy campaign in the Hilton and went systematically from room to room beating the young McCarthy workers bloody. This time there was no national television to catch their rampage. Only David Douglas Duncan's photographs for *Life* magazine recorded the horror of an event that most of the nation never knew happened. Violence had become an old story.

Nonetheless, the country's future, as well as my own, was changed by the batons of Chicago. Knowing the horror of what even our democratic nation could be capable of is a legacy we still live with today.

I left the next day and headed back to my family to heal. Home for them was now Parma, Ohio, where they had moved to find work after I left home. Although the house felt somewhat distant to me—"home" is always the place of one's childhood—they and their love were unchanged. My father picked me up at the airport. Mom opened the door, clad in her full-length apron, and hugged me as I hobbled inside on my injured leg. My favorite chicken pot pie was waiting for me on top of the stove. She prodded me to share what had happened in Chicago as we ate dinner, knowing that to talk about it would help. Dad played with his food in silence, then couldn't stand it and blew. "So help me God, son," he shouted, "if I ever run across any of those sons of bitches I'll kill them!" I wept, and Mom wrapped me in her arms.

Soon afterward, McCarthy staffer John O'Sullivan, a very bright law student and organizer in New York, suggested that the youthful campaign staff meet for a weekend retreat at his family's home on Martha's Vineyard to decide how to proceed with the November elections. The tourists had left the island by then so the Vineyard was peaceful and the weather chilly but glorious. The O'Sullivan home was a two-story gray shingled house that sat on an inlet. A deck wrapped around the back of the house, extending out over the water. We met in the living room. The tall windows overlooked the deck and the marsh beyond, where we watched the birds swoop and circle and felt a healing tranquillity after the brutality of Chicago. The leaders of a defeated "tribe" were gathering in the wilderness to plan for their next journey. It was not an easy task. We were all struggling over the question of supporting Humphrey, despite knowing his Republican opponent, the supposedly "new" Richard Nixon, was an impossible alternative.

Yale student John Shattuck was there, and Sam Brown, Eli Segal, Tony Podesta, and Michael Driver—good friends all. It was an impressive group, and the truth was we were quite taken with ourselves. In a sense, we believed the press clippings that described us as the nation's future leaders. (In my parents' living room they had hung framed clippings from the campaign in which political reporters for *The New York Times* and *The New Republic* quoted me.) We were also all male. The movement in the late sixties was still very sexist, and only men had been invited to this retreat. There was much arrogant male bonding—slapping backs, talking about different women, sharing the visions we had of our own futures. I was uncomfortable every time the conversation shifted to dating, love interests, and conquests, hoping that no one would try to involve me in the give-and-take. Nobody did. They were having too good a time telling their own stories to notice.

We were all very bitter about Chicago and it was hard to stop talking about it, but we had to face the problem of November. Some were too discouraged to want to involve themselves in the political process at all. Some argued strongly about the importance of stopping Nixon. Others could not bring themselves to support a Democratic Party committed to pursuing the war in Vietnam. When the argument got too heated, one of us would take the angry person out on the deck or for a long walk to cool off.

I was in the group that wanted to support Humphrey but felt he had to make some gesture to end the war. He would be giving a major Vietnam speech in the near future and we were hoping he would open the door to our support. I think we all knew, however, that no matter what he said it would be hard for us to work for him with any passion.

There was plenty of passion, however, when we turned to the elections for the Senate. Many of our most vocal antiwar supporters were running for reelection or for new seats. We plotted ways to raise money and provide staff for the candidacies of Harold Hughes of Iowa and Paul O'Dwyer of New York, and to work for the reelection of our heroes, McGovern of South Dakota and Wayne Morse of Oregon. But the real purpose of the retreat was to heal ourselves of a brutal political year and to find a future. We knew we needed each other if we were to continue to have the influence to bring about change. We were not ready to check out of the system. We had dreamed too long about being a part of it to give up now.

Nor did we. It wasn't only the press that had tabbed us as future leaders. The liberal establishment in Washington—the media, progressive business leaders, and the remnants of President Kennedy's administration—was eager to harness the energy of this new generation and bring it into the mainstream of American politics. And we were eager to join it. It was intoxicating to be invited in by those elders who had been only names to us.

One of them was John Gardner, who had been Johnson's Secretary of Health, Education and Welfare, and was now chairman of the National Urban Coalition, an organization of corporate leaders determined to rebuild the cities after the urban riots of the late 1960s. Gardner was working with Robert Kennedy campaign aides David Borden and Adam Walinsky on the possibility of creating a National Action Corps, a private venture that would harness the passion of American students opposed to the war and direct it toward helping to solve the country's urban problems. Borden and Walinsky had conceived the idea after the assassination, and Gardner commissioned a study to determine its feasibility. The three of them thought that my background—straitened and rural—was a useful credential for leading the survey, and Gardner approached me.

I took the assignment and utilized the same outreach that had been so valuable before. By phone, mail, and in one-on-one meetings, my staff canvassed student leaders, political activists, and young elected officials across the country for their input on the idea of the Corps. Having the blessing of the highly regarded John Gardner opened the doors to many gifted younger politicians, such as Jay Rockefeller, now a Democratic senator from West Virginia; John Danforth, who was to become a Republican senator from Missouri; and Donald Graham, who was then a policeman and is now publisher of *The Washington Post*.

The survey concluded that a National Action Corps funded by private resources was unlikely to work. It was not a surprise. It did not seem possible to institutionalize the passion and energy that American students were demonstrating around the issue of the war. If you separated out the war, the diversity in background, geography, and ideology was too great. But the project did enable those of us on the survey staff to continue building our network and our efforts to reform the Democratic Party. Eli Segal, Don Green, and I used our time in the Action Corps project to coordinate the former McCarthy/Kennedy campaign teams to plan the next steps in our opposition to the war.

The project had another enduring benefit for me; in the course of the survey I met two remarkable people who were to be very important in my life. Tim Wirth, who went on to become a United States senator and is currently at the State Department, and Doris Kearns Goodwin, the Pulitzer Prize–winning historian and writer, both helped me immeasurably during this time. Although I had proved to be an excellent organizer, I had very few skills when it came to functioning successfully in a more institutionalized world.

Tim was Gardner's deputy, and he was assigned to watch over the Action Corps project. I was to report to him daily on our progress and to seek his advice as the study progressed. Tim took me under his wing and proceeded to smooth out my rough edges. He wound up being an across-the-board mentor, from teaching me how to write a good memo to providing me with road maps on how to venture around the Washington establishment.

He was a former White House Fellow, a tall, Gary Cooperish figure with an engaging smile and a sharp, decisive mind that had made him a star on the Washington scene very early. He called me into his office one morning shortly after I had sent him my first progress report.

"David, what do you think of this report?" he asked me.

"What do *I* think? I'm not sure I understand the question."

"Let me cut to it," he said. "It is one of the worst-written reports I have ever seen." He proceeded to outline the serious flaws in substance and in style. I sat there stricken, frozen in chagrin. Every last one of my old insecurities about my ignorance and my Ivy League colleagues' competence came flooding back.

Tim took a look at my face and stopped. "David, relax," he said gently. "You are one of the best organizers in the country. No one said you also had to be the best memo and/or report writer." Then he smiled at me and went on: "But I *am* going to see that you're good at this work. You have so much to offer and I want to help you—if you'll let me."

"Tim, I don't know what to say or even what to do," I told him. "I feel in over my head. I'm sorry if I let you down."

"No one has let anyone down. You just haven't had some of the advantages the rest of us have had and it's up to me to insure that you do. You have too much talent not to be competitive in this world. Let me help you."

I was swept with gratitude and I said so. "Just tell me how to proceed and I'm yours," I said, and meant it.

Tim gave me an instant crash course on how to structure a report and the kind of substance required. With my draft before me, I stayed up all that night rewriting it. I brought it in to him the next morning, sat across from his desk, and tried not to fidget in my chair as he read. Then he looked up and flashed that extraordinary smile. "Damn it, you're good, Mixner. This is excellent. I am impressed." I could have wept with joy.

Tim's wife was as kind and thoughtful to me as he was. Wren Wirth was a stately and beautiful woman with black hair, riveting eyes, and the greatest elegance even in jeans and a sweatshirt. I wasn't exactly a fashion plate in those days, but because of my work with the Urban Coalition I was starting to receive invitations to some Washington dinner parties. Wren would say, "David, I saw a great suit that was just perfect for you at Garfinkel's. You ought to go down now and pick it up before they sell it. Remember, no cuffs, honey."

She took me in hand with the greatest tact. I'd be invited to their house and asked to come a little early so we could talk. We did talk, but somehow in the course of the conversation there would also be those instructive moments about Washington etiquette. "Can you believe in this busy city it's really important to get thank-you notes out so quickly? It drives me crazy. Notes for every little thing. Where do we get the time?" I knew what she was doing, of course—the kindest instructions imaginable on how to function properly in Washington—and I was very grateful. Like Tim, she cared about me.

Doris Kearns was just as caring. She was a White House Fellow at the time, assigned to the White House during the remaining months of

President Johnson's term. I met her at a dinner party at Tim and Wren's house and we hit it off. She had classic Irish good looks—sandy red hair and all—and a strong, clear voice; I kept expecting her to burst into an Irish folk song any minute. She was passionate about the Boston Red Sox and we could talk baseball all night long: which was the better team, the Philadelphia Phillies or the Red Sox. We were quickly friends.

Doris shared Tim's assessment of my skills and potential, though I never quite understood why, and she was the one who helped me make the transition from support staffer to substantive participant. Given her Boston background and her reputation in Washington as brilliant and a comer, she was close to Senator Edward Kennedy. In the late fall of 1968, at Doris's urging, the senator asked her to invite me to a round-table at his home about possible legislative and political priorities for the next year. I realized this was an acknowledgment of Doris's belief in me, and an indication as well that others in the Washington establishment respected my opinion and my skills. At the age of twenty-three, it is very heady to have an invitation to brief one of America's foremost political figures.

I rode out to the senator's home with Doris, terrified at what was expected of me. She was full of reassurances; everyone was nervous before a meeting with Ted Kennedy. This did not make the butterflies in my stomach disappear.

When we walked into his spacious McLean home, the senator gave Doris a big hug and greeted me with a hearty handshake and a pat on the back. I was starstruck. He was far warmer in person than on the television screen; the Kennedy good looks and charm put me at ease at once. The house was welcoming too, the rooms filled with cheerfully patterned sofas and chairs and the tables and shelves covered with family photographs. Now and then as we talked I'd glimpse a football or other memento of a happier time. Homey as it was, there was no way not to realize you were in a dynastic house.

The senator opened the meeting by outlining his goals for the next couple of months, before Nixon took office. There were a dozen or so of us, and we all knew he was the leading contender for the Democratic presidential nomination in 1972, but he kept control of the agenda, asking our opinion of what we thought should be his legislative priorities in the next session of Congress. The party had to rebuild itself after the brutal convention in Chicago and he wanted to help set that new course in Congress.

Then he went around the room one by one asking for our thoughts. Those before me spoke of protecting the Great Society programs from incursions by the new president, of pending labor legislation and new civil rights housing legislation. I was seated about halfway along the circle and I thought I'd have a heart attack by the time he got to me. Here was a Kennedy seeking my advice and I had no idea what I was going to say. I certainly believed opposition to the war had to be a priority, but when he got to me I felt my presentation was a tired and boring rehash of campaign rhetoric. I searched the faces of the others to see if I could read their reactions and decided this was probably the last such meeting I'd ever be asked to.

Finally, Kennedy came to Doris. She was sitting on a folding chair to his left, with a yellow pad on her lap. She had been taking notes as each person shared his views. She looked around the circle, smiled at us all, and then with impressive articulateness gave a brilliant point-by-point analysis of possible options for the senator. She was substantive and concise, presenting not only her views but a summary of everyone else's.

I was still in a state of awe as Doris drove me back to my apartment after the meeting. Finally, I turned to her and asked, "How in the hell do you do that? Your summation at the end was unbelievable. I felt I bombed."

She laughed out loud. "Thanks. You didn't bomb but you weren't prepared. In a meeting like this, know the three or four points you want to be sure to get across before you enter the door. Then be concise and to the point. Don't waste time on a lot of rhetoric that they've all heard before."

"I blew it, didn't I?"

"Come on, Dave, you were fine. Another thing I've learned is to take notes of what everyone else is saying and keep reviewing them. At the end you can summarize the meeting for others, and if you're lucky you will be able to find the consensus position in it all."

We drove silently for a while. I knew what I wanted. I wanted to be like Doris Kearns and earn the respect of people in future meetings by doing exactly what she told me: having the best information and presenting it clearly. I valued her support immeasurably.

The election that year would be dramatic. At Johnson's insistence, his vice president had defended the war throughout the campaign. Many liberals, disgusted by Chicago, planned to vote for minor third parties or stay home. But in late September, Humphrey finally broke free of the shadow of the President and advocated a quick end to the war. From the moment of this Vietnam speech until election day he gathered steam, and many progressives chose to return to the party. On November 5 Nixon won, but the popular vote was startlingly close: 43.4 percent for Nixon, 42.7 percent for Humphrey. Humphrey simply ran out of time to present himself as his own man.

The Democratic Party had to mend its fences. Although it retained control of both houses of Congress, to lose the presidency was devastating. One of the major issues throughout the 1968 elections had been the consistent abuse of the democratic process by a few political bosses who wrote the delegate selection rules that enabled them to pick their own people regardless of what the people wanted. Despite all our defeats on the convention floor, we did manage to achieve one victory—and it was one that would forever change the face of the party. In a barely noticed effort, Governor Harold Hughes of Iowa, Connecticut activist Anne Wexler, and Eli Segal wrote and shepherded through the convention a rules plank that established two commissions: one to examine the process of selecting delegates and the other to review the party's rules and to make them fairer. The two commissions were charged with making their recommendations in time for the 1972 national convention. Political wizard Lawrence O'Brien, then the chairman of the Democratic National Committee, interviewed by *The National Journal* about the impact of these commissions, said, "It's the greatest goddam change since [the advent of] the two-party system."

The chairman of the national party is picked by the party's presidential nominee, and Humphrey's choice was Senator Fred Harris of Oklahoma, who was empowered to make the appointments to these two commissions. Every leading Democrat in the country wanted to be on them. The Commission on Delegate Selection was the power appointment since its decisions would affect the choice of the next Democratic nominee. Throughout late 1968 and early 1969, labor, the reformers, the bosses, and other constituencies lobbied fiercely for their choices. At the beginning of February Harris announced that Senator George McGovern would head the Delegate Selection Commission and Congressman James O'Hara of Michigan the Rules Commission. He also announced the appointments to each commission. It was then that Harris made the mistake that would dramatically affect my life.

February 8 in Washington was cold and rainy, so I decided to stay put at home. Early that morning the phone rang. Eli Segal and Curtis Gans were calling to offer their congratulations. Confused, I asked, "For what?" Harris, they told me, had just announced that I was one of his appointments to the new Rules Commission. I was stunned. I hadn't the faintest idea I was under consideration. Shortly thereafter, the doorbell rang and Western Union delivered a telegram from Senator Harris. It was supposed to inform me of my appointment to the Rules Commission but a staffer had mixed up the two messages. The telegram announced my appointment to the more powerful McGovern Commission on Delegate Selection. I talked to Eli, Anne, and Sam Brown, and we decided to take advantage of the slipup. I fired back a return telegram to Harris stating my delight in accepting his appointment to the Delegate Selection Commission and contacted the press, which printed the tale of the wrong message.

Senator Harris accepted his error with good grace and I was placed on the McGovern Commission. Suddenly I was in a whole new world of politics. Among the twenty-eight members of the new commission were influential Los Angeles attorney Warren Christopher, Maine Democratic Committeeman George Mitchell, Senator Birch Bayh of Indiana, Harold Hughes, the newly elected senator from Iowa, Senator Adlai Stevenson III of Illinois, son of the presidential candidate, and George McGovern. Christopher, Mitchell, and Stevenson represented the established party. Hughes and McGovern championed reform. Bayh was often to be the swing vote between the two camps.

I was exultant and I was scared. I worried whether my abilities could rise to the occasion. This was the heart of the Democratic Party establishment. Being one of the very few reformers appointed to the commission, I knew that the aspirations of others hinged on my effectiveness. Harris scheduled the first public meeting of the commission for April. With Doris Kearns's advice firmly in mind, I began to prepare for my debut on the public scene. I called activists across the country to seek their opinion of what our priorities should be, read briefing memos circulated by Eli and Anne and reformer Ken Bode, and sought out those who had firsthand experience of the abuse of power in the last selection process. The commission would be holding hearings all over the country to solicit information such as this and the staff would prepare the final report. But I wanted to walk into those rooms with my Doris Kearns points in hand and know what the hell I was talking about once I was inside.

Washington in April is stunningly beautiful, but I saw none of it as I headed to the first meeting of the McGovern Commission. Patsy had traveled down from Baltimore to share the big moment and to be a calming influence. Our good friend Judy Green, Don's wife, joined us as we entered the Old Senate Office Building. Judy had a tranquillity that all of us envied. She would put her hand on your arm and you'd feel safe and protected. I would go to her and Don's house for dinner just to feel safe; I could relax there with gossip and laughter as nowhere else. I needed Patsy and Judy that day because fear controlled me. When I was dressing that morning I couldn't even find my cuff links, so there were safety pins instead in my only white shirt.

The caucus room was intimidating. It was here, amid the dark wood paneling and huge crystal chandeliers, that John F. Kennedy had announced his candidacy. At one end was a huge conference table with twenty-eight large chairs, and the other end was packed with lights, cameras, reporters, and spectators. I stopped in the doorway, stunned by the sight before me, and felt a tap on my shoulder.

"Excuse me, sir. My name is Mudd, Roger Mudd. Could we interview you for CBS News?"

I knew who Roger Mudd was—who didn't?—and moved to get out of his way. Then I realized he was speaking to me. One of America's most prominent reporters wanted to interview *me*? His camera crew moved in behind him. Mudd thrust the microphone into my face and asked whether, given that this was the first gathering of the Democratic Party since the bloody Chicago convention, I intended to raise the issue of the violence in these hearings.

I couldn't believe what was happening. I couldn't understand why Mudd wanted my opinion. But I acted as if it were entirely appropriate and said that yes, I did indeed intend to bring up the issue of violence. After all, Mayor Daley was still pressing charges against many of the demonstrators, making it impossible for the party to heal.

As I looked over his shoulder I could see Patsy and Judy Green giggling at the sight. The interview was as unreal to them as it was to me. But it sent a signal to other political correspondents in the room that I might be worth talking to, and within minutes I was besieged by reporters. With that one interview, I became a spokesperson for the reformers.

The first major gathering of Democratic Party decision-makers since the Chicago convention was about to begin. Hughes, Wexler, and Segal had called a prior meeting of the reformers to determine our priorities for this hearing. We all agreed that proportional representation, the role of women in the party, adequate representation of minorities, and direct election of delegates were crucial issues. I knew that the young whom I represented on the commission would be insistent that the subject of the Chicago violence should be heard at this hearing. It had a "Remember the Alamo" ring for many of the nation's students. If I were to maintain any credibility with the people I represented and those I worked with, it was essential that I raise this issue in the most visible way possible in this hearing, with all the media covering it. If I didn't, I would have a hard time mobilizing the political force essential if the commission was to endorse substantive reforms. I was beginning to learn what was necessary and what warranted compromise in order to effect change.

Fred Harris, Humphrey's running mate Edmund Muskie, and a host of other party dignitaries testified that day. But the most dramatic moment came when presidential front-runner Ted Kennedy entered the room. You knew someone powerful had arrived because all the television cameras swung to the doorway and the discarded flashbulbs made the floor of the hearing room look like a war zone. Kennedy took his place behind the witness table and the room buzzed with excitement. People in the back of the ornate chamber climbed on their chairs to catch a glimpse of the heir apparent. His testimony was eloquent and stirring, calling for reform and healing and pleading with the party to move forward on issues of concern to the poor and powerless.

This was going to be the most visible moment of the hearing, and now was the time for me to act on my obligations to those I represented. I knew that Kennedy and his family were close friends of Mayor Daley, who had played so important a part in John Kennedy's election, and I was going to put him in a difficult position. But there it was.

I forged ahead: "Senator, hoping to avoid in the future the police-state tactics that took place in Chicago with the sanction of the Democratic mayor, will you publicly condemn those tactics and the involvement of the mayor?"

As Kennedy's smile froze, the room blazed with flashbulbs. Kennedy shot me an angry look. He fidgeted with his papers on the witness table, then answered very astutely that by pushing for reforms, the party would be able to avoid future Chicagos. He ignored my question about Mayor Daley. The regulars were disappointed at his failure to support the mayor and the reformers were equally disappointed at his failure to condemn him.

Shortly thereafter, two commission members invited me to lunch to offer some "friendly advice." Katherine Peden, one of Kentucky's most prominent Democrats, was upset by my "performance" at the first public hearing. A very elegant woman with silver hair, she sat very straight and addressed me with condemnation in her voice. "My dear, why did you bring up Chicago? That's a dead horse."

I looked at her, smiled, and said, "I almost was too." She was taken back. The other commission member, Patti Knox, a Michigan national committeewoman who had close ties to labor, broke out laughing. Ms. Peden was not amused.

Senator Harold Hughes of Iowa was a burly former truck driver, a recovering alcoholic, and one of the great orators of our time. Because he had supported McCarthy and was the major force behind the rules plank creating the commissions, the reformers assumed that he would be a leading contender for the second slot on a 1972 presidential ticket that almost certainly would be headed by Ted Kennedy. As we traveled around the country to commission hearings, Hughes and I became good friends. In New Orleans in July of 1969, Patti Knox and I were in his suite planning our next moves on the commission. The phone rang. The senator picked it up and we saw his face pale. "Ted Kennedy has been in an accident," he told us. "He wasn't injured but a young woman was killed. Teddy didn't call the police right away and it looks very messy."

We sat in shock. Hughes talked with great admiration about Kennedy and the tribulations of his family. You could feel his pain and grief for a friend and a colleague. Then, as the night went on, the conversation shifted from the incident in Chappaquiddick to the 1972 presidential race that lay ahead. Inevitably—and as always—one individual's personal tragedy became a political opportunity for others. Suddenly Hughes, McGovern, and Muskie were front-runners for President of the United States. In politics, those who hesitate lose valuable time they may never make up. The senator, Patti, and I started planning for his presidential bid. Patti made lists of party and labor people the he should call; I made lists of McCarthy and Kennedy types whose support he should seek; and by morning he was reaching for the phone.

Hughes was a champion of the labor unions and therefore one of the few candidates who could actually unite the reformers and the more conservative AFL-CIO. I sat in his office several months later as he agonized over whether or not he could actually run. He had lived a hard life. His alcoholism had led to public drunkenness. He was almost in tears as he spoke of the impact of a campaign on his wife and daughter, knowing that he had already put them through so much pain. Before me was a frightened man who knew exactly what the Nixon people would do with his past. Finally, he looked up, and with tears said, "David, I just can't do it."

Sitting across from me was a man who saw his past haunt his future. I understood. It was enormously frustrating because that past could actually have brought much-needed insight to the office of President. His harsh journey had not made him bitter; indeed he was compassionate and caring. I knew he had made the right decision for himself but I also knew the country had lost the opportunity to choose a humane and powerful leader.

Once again, I was in a cab heading into Chicago. This time I saw no troops on my ride to the center of the city. The McGovern Commission had come here for a public hearing and our first witness was to be Mayor Daley. The party regulars did not want me at this hearing. Adlai Stevenson called other commission members urging that I not be allowed to attend. Chicago politicians kept telephoning McGovern to ask that I be banned from the hearing panel there because the mayor did not want the violence in Chicago to be a part of the proceedings. Finally McGovern called me and asked me to stay home because he was concerned that my appearance would "reopen the old wounds that the party is attempting to heal."

I refused. I would be returning to Chicago, I said, and there had better be a chair for me at the commission table. Because of his enormous power, no one had held Mayor Daley accountable for the police riot that destroyed not only lives but the integrity of the Democratic Party. Many of those arrested were still facing charges. The mayor was taking a hard line and no one in the party was willing to take him on. What he had done to us in this city was outrageous and immoral. My allies, my friends, would never forgive me, nor would I forgive myself, if I did not take this opportunity to confront those responsible for the bloodshed.

I woke up very early on the morning of the day of the hearing, riddled with nerves and having second thoughts about attending. The pressure brought on me had been so intense that I was beginning to question my own judgment. Perhaps it *was* time to let the convention fade into the past. Maybe my actions were exacerbating the wounds. I took a long hot bath and closed my eyes in reflection. I kept seeing the bodies of the beaten, the forlorn twisted eyeglasses lying on the battleground. I knew what I had to do. I put on my one dark blue suit and my trademark cowboy boots, and left for the hearing.

It was in yet another bland hotel ballroom. Green baize cloths were draped over the panel table in front of the room and a massive bank of television cameras was set to record the mayor's appearance. A perky young Democratic Party volunteer directed me to a side room where the panel was to meet before the hearing. By the time I got there, most of the other members were in session. The room fell silent as I entered. I could feel the tension and anger directed at me. I took a seat across the table from Senator Stevenson. He glared at me.

He was the first to speak, and he addressed McGovern: "Senator, I would like to make it a policy of this hearing that only those commission members specifically assigned to this hearing be allowed on the platform and to ask questions."

McGovern responded decisively. "Senator Stevenson, I appreciate your concern," he said, "but the rules of the commission are clear. Any commission member may attend and participate in any function of the commission. David has every right to be here today."

Following the usual procedure at these pre-hearing meetings, McGovern then went around the room and asked the panel members what questions they intended to pursue. When he reached me, he said, "David, what questions would you like to ask the witnesses today?"

"I intend to ask Mayor Daley to apologize for the violence by the police at the convention and to support amnesty for all those arrested by his police, including The Chicago Seven."

Stevenson turned red in the face and I saw his hand clench into a fist. He began to pound the table. "You . . . you . . . you are exactly the kind of people who are going to destroy the Democratic Party." He leaned over the table and shook his finger at me. "That question is so out of line it is unbelievable. How dare you bring this crap into our backyard?"

I was taken aback by the vehemence of his attack. I pushed my chair back from the table to create some distance between us. There was chaos in the room as everyone tried to get McGovern's attention. The uproar scared me, but I was determined not to be intimidated. An hour later, after intense and angry debate, they recognized that I would not budge. Finally, Bill Dodds, the soft-spoken liberal UAW representative on the commission, turned to me and said, "David, to have you ask that question of the mayor might make it more difficult for the mayor to hear what you are attempting to say. Would you be comfortable if that question was asked by someone else on the commission?"

I knew that Bill, whom I greatly respected, was concerned about my anger. "As long as it is that question," I said, "I will have no problem if it is asked by someone else."

McGovern turned to me. "If I ask the question for you, will you out of respect for Senator Stevenson remain silent during the whole hearing?"

Knowing that McGovern needed my cooperation now and that his presenting the question to Mayor Daley would be a thousand times more effective than my asking it, I said, "Senator, of course I will agree to that."

We entered the ballroom together. Several reporters grabbed me and asked what I intended to ask the mayor. I remained silent. As we took our assigned seats, I looked out over the ballroom. There wasn't an empty seat in the place.

Daley entered the ballroom surrounded by his aides. Flashbulbs popped as he took his seat at the witness table. McGovern greeted him and Daley responded by reading a statement welcoming the commission to Chicago.

Several panel members asked the mayor a polite question or two. I passed when McGovern came to me. I could see the startled faces of the reporters. They thought they had just lost a good story. Then McGovern kept his word and asked my question about the demonstrators and amnesty. Daley's face turned purple. He erupted into a tirade against the demonstrators who had attempted to wreck the Democratic Party at *his* convention. He would never offer them amnesty, he proclaimed, and with that gathered his papers, mobilized his entourage, and stormed out of the ballroom.

I felt at last that the mayor had been confronted with his actions, and had in his arrogance shown the world what we had faced in that terrible August week. I could finally close the book on Chicago and move on.

The McGovern Commission finally made its historic recommendations to the Democratic National Committee. The reformers lost on the important issue of proportional representation, but we were able to change the face of our party forever. We insisted on new guidelines that let it look like the society it represented and be inclusive of minorities. Patti Knox and I pushed hard for women to be 50 percent of the delegates at the next convention. All delegates from now on would have to be directly elected by the people, undercutting the power of the political bosses to handpick them.

With these and other changes the doors of the Democratic Party were opened to minorities and women, to the young and the old. No longer would the power of the bosses prevail over the vote of the American people.

The commission reforms enabled Senator McGovern himself to become the next nominee of the Democratic Party. I benefited too. My

very visible participation in the hearings and my involvement in drafting
the report brought me new political influence at the national level.

On January 20, 1969, Richard Nixon was inaugurated as President of
the United States. He was anxious to find an approach that would calm
the forces of youthful dissent so he could pursue his Vietnam policies.
Through my involvement with John Gardner at the National Action
Corps, in the early months of his administration I became an unofficial
liaison between the young Nixon people in the White House and the
McCarthy youth. I had met White House staffers Richard Blumenthal
and John Campbell at the Executive Office Building when I was seeking
opinions on how to proceed with the Action Corps, and had some initial
discussions with them and Jay Wilkinson, son of the famous Oklahoma
coach, about opening a dialogue between us and Nixon youth. I naively
believed that the new administration might be ready to hear our views
on the war, that talking with them would have an effect.

Wilkinson and Campbell convinced the senior staff that it would be
beneficial to hold a retreat with some of them and a few students to
exchange ideas. They shifted through hundreds of names to find the
right mix and be sure the retreat went smoothly. They chose Airlie
House, an old Virginia estate, for the location, and picked the end of
April for the date. Jay asked whether I would be willing to participate
too. If it helped the staff to understand the views of those opposed to the
war, I said, I would be delighted to attend. Five carefully chosen students
would be coming.

It was spring in Washington and the White House was surrounded by
blossoming trees. I was in awe of being allowed into the Nixon White
House with such ease. A military escort greeted me at the gate and
ushered me through the West Wing to a helicopter waiting to take us to
Airlie House. For the first time in my life I felt the intoxicatingly seductive power of this building. Once you are in it you never want to be left
outside again. At the helicopter, formally dressed military guards helped
me board. We fastened our seat belts and lifted off the south lawn. I
looked down at the tourists outside the fence and remembered all the
times I had stood there taking pictures of a departing helicopter, wondering if the President was inside. I couldn't believe that I was finally
inside that helicopter. I stifled a giggle as we flew over the river into
Virginia.

We landed within minutes near the main house of the estate. Airlie
House is a classic Virginia country manor with vast green lawns, white

fences set amid the fields, ponds here and there, and forest. Among the youthful participants were a bright student leader named Xandra Kayden and an articulate African-American, Joe Rhodes. Inside the house we were met by top Nixon aide John Ehrlichman, Communications Director Herb Klein, Ray Price, Peter Flanigan, and Jay Wilkinson. I was the only one there with a history of actively opposing the war.

I looked at the senior staff members and it struck me that they had come because they could then tell the press they had met with students against the war. I suddenly felt like window dressing. Nothing useful was going to be decided at this meeting. We sat around a big conference table in a room that looked out over the beautiful grounds. A fire glowed in the fireplace. We went around the table introducing ourselves. Ehrlichman promptly took control of the meeting and said the administration would "not tolerate the violence on campus and the attacks on public property." I thought: So much for dialogue. Xandra, Joe, and I tried repeatedly to make them confront the issue of the war that was dividing the nation. We said that to equate the breaking of a few windows in a campus ROTC building with the violence of Vietnam was absurd.

But they seemed more interested in our personal lives than our views on the war. Did we believe in God? they asked. Didn't we want successful careers? Wasn't having money and family important to us? At one point, I found myself wondering how they would react if they knew I was a homosexual. They were smug and condescending. Not once in the day-long session did we make progress. Clearly, the helicopter ride was the highlight.

Given that fruitless day, I was surprised when in early May Wilkerson and Campbell suggested that perhaps it would be wise to meet with the young McCarthy leadership on a more informal level. I offered to host a gathering in my apartment. They were delighted at the idea and suggested that Tricia Nixon might even attend. I smiled to myself. There was no way that Tricia Nixon was going to be a draw to the McCarthy youth. Just as clearly, they had no idea of my living conditions.

I was still living in the fourth-floor walk-up apartment at 1635 Massachusetts Avenue NW that I'd moved into when it was Sam Brown's. It had not improved with time. The only word for it was a dump.

So I called Patsy and she agreed to come down from Baltimore the day of the party and help set it up. She went into shock when she walked in. I can still see her standing there in the middle of the living room, turning around in a circle and moaning, "Oh, my God! Oh, my God!" The walls were painted what had once been yellow and were dirty with fingerprints, the venetian blinds were broken, the cracked linoleum was caked with dirt, and the only real piece of furniture was a bright purple couch with torn upholstery. She grabbed her purse and yelled at me to get moving. We went shopping with her credit cards, desperately look-ing for anything that could make the apartment presentable within the next several hours. She bought curtains to cover the windows, a spread to put over the couch, a bedspread, a bath mat, towels, sheets, and dishes and glasses. Back home we rolled up our sleeves and got to work. Patsy went through the bathroom shaking Comet all over it, then continued into the living room. She put ammonia on the floors while I washed windows and the bathtub. Just as we were ready to go through the whole apartment and scrub, the water and power went off. The guests were due to arrive in less than six hours. We couldn't stop laughing. "Well, it can't get any worse," Patsy said. At that very moment the doorbell rang. We looked at each other, terrified. I went to the door, unlocked my multi-tude of deadbolt locks, and opened it to see two proper-looking men in blue suits standing in the dingy hallway.

"Mr. Mixner?"

"Yes."

"We are from the Secret Service." They showed their badges. "We are here to scout this location for a possible visit by Ms. Tricia Nixon tonight."

I stifled my laughter and shouted over my shoulder, "Patsy, the Secret Service is here!"

"You're kidding—I hope," she shouted back.

The two agents walked into the apartment, which was strewn with packages from our shopping trip. Ammonia and Comet were all over the floors. They glanced at each other and went into the bedroom. Patsy and I burst out laughing again. They came out with their faces unbelieving.

"Well, thank you, sir. We have seen what we need to see."

"I bet you have," said Patsy.

There would be no visit by the daughter of the President of the United States that night. The power and water came on an hour later and we scrubbed the whole place. New curtains hung from the windows to cover the dirty blinds, an ironing board with a colorful sheet over it served as the bar, and a new shower curtain hid the impossible tub.

That evening twenty-five young McCarthy activists, half a dozen younger Nixon staff, Senator McCarthy, *The Washington Star*'s colum-nist Mary McGrory, *The New Republic*'s Paul Wieck, and several others mingled and talked. It was easy to distinguish between the two groups. The Nixon people wore Brooks Brothers suits. Our antiwar activists wore paisley ties with blue work shirts. Their hair was clipped; ours was long, with sideburns that reached down the sides of our faces. But if the Nixonites felt uncomfortable, they didn't show it. They were polite and engaging. In fact, they couldn't seem to discover enough about us. We were people of the same age but from two different worlds. Both sides thought they would be the nation's future leaders. Their group worked inside the White House while ours surrounded it in the streets outside. They loved meeting McCarthy and he loved having a new audience. Mary McGrory actively attempted to convert "these nice young people" to the cause of peace. My sister held her breath in the hope that the makeshift curtains would not come tumbling down. At 1:00 A.M., bushed from the running around and scrubbing of the day, I handed everyone their coats and sent them on their separate ways.

Never again would the two sides meet in so relaxed an atmosphere. The war made that impossible. Instead, each prepared for battle.

CHAPTER FOUR

The Vietnam Moratorium

MARY McGrory's apartment overlooking Rock Creek Park served as a gathering place for lively minds to articulate their convictions while they sat relishing her unbelievable meat loaf. Tall, stately Mary is a Washington institution. Her columns have championed the liberal cause since the 1950s, and in the Kennedy administration were the richest and most textured commentary anyone wrote. We all cheered when she won a Pulitzer Prize in 1975; it was a tribute to an extraordinary career and her unswerving commitment to justice.

I first met Mary when she was covering the McCarthy campaign. She had known the senator since the 1950s, when he was campaigning for Adlai Stevenson for President. They shared a common passion for poets, liberal politics, and Irish humor. Passionately committed to peace, she was enchanted and encouraged by the students converging into New Hampshire to work for her dear friend Eugene McCarthy.

As one of those students, I joined her group of favorites and won a coveted invitation to her home. It was a welcoming place, with sofas and chairs in soft prints and a Kennedy-style rocking chair she loved to sit in. There were books everywhere—on shelves, stacked on the end tables, in the kitchen. Many evenings, over one of her home-cooked meals, I listened to McCarthy recite Yeats, or heard Secretary of Defense Clark Clifford expound on his efforts for peace inside the Johnson White House. Mary worked her way around the room like an intellectual coach, encouraging each person to speak up about his and her ideas. You weren't allowed to be a slacker, and she was a tough taskmaster with those she thought mentally lazy or lacking in conviction. She had a reporter's ear for sharp and witty dialogue and she deliberately brought people of opposing views together to insure a lively evening.

I do not have that closeness with her anymore, and it is my loss. When I came out of the closet in 1977, Mary was one of those who had a great deal of difficulty with it. Her working-class background and her devout Catholicism made it very difficult for her to understand or accept my homosexuality. We made efforts to sustain our friendship but we couldn't. For a while I continued to come to evenings at her home when I was visiting Washington and she was always the gracious hostess. But we could not go on as if there had been no change, for the barrier between us was too great. She is one of a number of people who drifted out of my life. She is also one of those people whom I miss the most.

But we had strong bonds until then, and one was our passionate opposition to the continuing slaughter in Vietnam. We were driven to do anything possible to stop the killing. In March of 1969, in the early days of the Nixon administration (and before I went to the meeting at Airlie House), Mary was convinced that if someone from the White House could meet with some of her "students," they would surely see the folly of their policies. She convinced John Ehrlichman to come to her apartment to meet off the record with Sam Brown, John O'Sullivan, and me. Mary wanted Ehrlichman to hear directly from the youth of America that there would be no political peace in the country as long as there was no peace in Vietnam.

Sam, Johnny O, and I arrived at Mary's Woodley Avenue apartment dressed in our best suits. We weren't sure that we could make any progress but knew that we had to give it our best—for peace and for Mary. As we entered the foyer, Mary took a look at Sam's long and unkempt hair and said, "No, no, no . . . this won't do. We have to deal with that now."

Sam laughed. Then he realized Mary meant it. He gave me a panicky "do something" look. "Come on, Mary, it's fine," he protested. "He's seen longer hair than this."

"Sam, this meeting is about the war, not your hair. I won't have it become an issue."

With that, she took his hand and led him into her bedroom. Johnny O and I followed them, grateful that we were not to be the victim of her shears. She took off Sam's jacket, put a towel around his shoulders, and got to work. Sam looked stricken. We heard him moan with each snip. I am certain the only reason he was saved from a crew cut was the ringing doorbell that heralded Ehrlichman's arrival.

We exchanged greetings with Ehrlichman, who kept an assured smile on his face and made small talk until Mary invited us into her very small dining area just off the kitchen and sat us down for a feast of meat loaf and cheesecake. The conversation over dinner began with politenesses but it turned tense as soon as we began to discuss our differences. At first Ehrlichman avoided the subject of the war and attempted to make us feel we were not a part of a greater America. He asked us if we had ever been in the service, what we had contributed to our communities, whether our parents approved of our activities.

But like people around most of the dining-room tables in America, this group could not avoid the war for long. We were unrelenting in articulating our opposition to it. Sam made it clear that the campuses would become places of great unrest if the war continued. Johnny O talked about the political price that the Democrats had already paid for pursuing the war and warned Ehrlichman that the Republicans could pay the same price the next time.

It had no effect on him. We moved into the living room for coffee and sat in Mary's comfortable chairs. He made it clear that this administration was not going to be intimidated by a bunch of long-haired students (Sam's haircut had proven fruitless!) and that it would take all measures necessary to keep the peace.

I shot back: "Sir, there are thousands of us ready to be arrested because we will not serve in this war."

Ehrlichman leaned forward in his chair. "You *will* go!" he ordered.

Johnny O said, "Never!"

In all seriousness, and with his voice rising in anger, Ehrlichman answered, "Then we will put you all in jail for a long time."

Sam shouted back, "There aren't enough jails to hold us all."

Then, in a truly terrifying moment, this top aide to the President of the United States pointed his finger at each of us in succession and said in a fake German accent, "Then we will build the wall of our stockades higher and higher."

Mary, pale and shaken now, spoke up. "Sir, that is uncalled for in this home. These are substantive people who believe deeply in peace. I will not have my guests threatened with prison."

The evening ended after that. As the door closed behind Ehrlichman we all looked at one another, speechless. It was Sam who spoke up at last. "And for that I cut my hair?" he asked. Laughter was a release.

Despite Nixon's long-standing flirtations with the right and his witch-hunting of the left, some liberals had hoped that when he took office he would decide it was politically advantageous to end the war. We drove away from Mary's that night sick with apprehension. "They're going to keep at it," Sam said. "The caskets are still going to keep coming home. I can't stand it."

Our divided nation would grow even more divided. Those in power would use the war to turn parents against their children, neighbor against neighbor, and workers against their bosses. We had just heard tough talk from a man who seemed to find satisfaction in creating fear. This administration could well play for keeps. If we continued our active dissent against the war, it now seemed possible we would face character assassination, harassment, and even indictments for conspiring against the government. We did not doubt that John Ehrlichman was capable of all those things.

The next night the three of us with a group of friends gathered around a television set to watch the evening news. The lead story was vivid film of battles in Vietnam. Before our eyes lay wounded GIs and terrified or dead Vietnamese. We looked at one another and knew we had no choice. We had to bring all our resources together to convince America of the insanity of this war. We proceeded to do just that.

Jerome Grossman, a Massachusetts businessman active in the peace movement, was the person who suggested a nationwide strike against the war. Jerry proposed to Sam Brown that there be a day in the fall of 1969 where "business as usual" would come to a halt in protest. Immediately Sam set up initial discussions with some of his Harvard friends and confidants to refine the proposal. Rather than "strike," he suggested the word "moratorium"; it would be less threatening to the great American middle class that was the battleground between the pro- and antiwar forces.

Sam got to work building a team to implement the idea. He received commitments from California businessman Harold Willens and Boston area intellectual and millionaire Martin Peretz for financial backing of the initial organizing stages. He asked champion swimmer David Hawk to join him in the leadership. David looked like a Hollywood leading man acting the part of a young revolutionary, but he was already widely known as a forceful, articulate advocate in the draft resistance movement and was facing charges himself for refusing to serve in the war. His resistance credentials were a valuable counterpart to Sam's political skills.

I was next on Sam's list. He flew down from Boston and sat on the old purple sofa in my apartment outlining the plans. On October 15, 1969, the nation would come to a halt to discuss the war. Universities would put aside regular classes, workers would meet in union halls, and vigils would be held in local communities to protest the slaughter. I was skeptical. It was hard for me to believe that in just six months time, a few individuals with limited funds could bring the entire nation to a halt.

But Sam persuaded me. He needed someone with experience in politics who understood politics, could lobby Capitol Hill on the war, and could reach into the labor movement to be a cofounder and coordinator. I had never lobbied a legislative body, but the contacts I had developed with members of Congress and with labor in the McGovern Commission would be invaluable. I listened to him, asked some questions, and said yes. No other antiwar effort then going on could have as much impact as this vision—if we brought it off. And if it didn't work, I would have the peace of mind that comes from knowing I had given it my best. "Count me in," I told him.

Sam, Hawk, and I decided the first priority was to find an excellent field organizer. We thought immediately of McCarthy field organizer Marge Sklencar, who'd gone back to Mundelein College after the campaign. She'd be terrific—a gifted and experienced organizer who'd be a lively member of the group, sometimes big sister to it, at other times brash and as tough as nails. Just what we needed. All three of us got on the phone to urge her to join us as one of the four coordinators of the Moratorium. She was reluctant at first. She didn't want to leave college again for yet another crusade. But we kept calling her and she changed her mind. "I must be crazy," she said, "but I'll be there next week."

We set up tiny offices that spring at 1029 Vermont Avenue NW in Washington. Each of us had a single phone line, a desk, and a chair. That was it. On the first day there, we sat on the floor eating sandwiches from the downstairs deli. Hawk grinned at the sight. "We must be out of our minds," he said, echoing Marge. "October fifteenth is just a few months away and we don't even have a phone system."

Marge agreed. "What a way to go broke. We'll never see a paycheck."

Sam, always the realist, corrected her. "That's not true, Marge—we have enough money to meet our payroll for at least a month."

I joined in the laughter. The absurdity was obvious: four young people in their early twenties, with almost no money, believing they could bring the nation to a halt. I leaned back against the wall and looked at my new soulmates. They were wonderful. In no time we had become one another's support system and family. I swallowed a surge of sadness. Here I was again, an intimate part of a venture with powerful bonds of connectedness—and only I knew the truth that I was an outsider. I didn't want to be straight—I just wanted to be free. I wanted to have what my friends had, to live my life as they did, openly and honestly. I was lonely. I wanted relief from my self-imposed celibacy, and I could not have it. I needed them and they needed me, but the truth would estrange us.

We had a lot of work to do before announcing the Moratorium to the press. It was conceived as an ongoing operation, not a onetime event, with the halt on October 15, but the protests escalating each month thereafter until the war came to an end. But we had to make that first day work or there would be none to follow.

If we were to have credibility with the media, it was important that the first announcement include specific commitments. Marge contacted the National Student Association and together they drafted a statement, to be signed by hundreds of student body presidents, calling on their colleges and universities to "cease business as usual" on October 15 to engage in serious discussions about the war. Hawk secured the support of other antiwar organizations and the endorsements of major religious leaders and groups. Sam became our spokesperson and fund-raiser. He met with potential contributors to raise desperately needed funds, and with journalists to give them advance briefings to lay the groundwork for announcement day. My job was to work the political establishment for the endorsements of national, state, and local officials. It was essential that we firm up our natural base before branching out into more non-traditional communities.

Hawk had numerous one-on-one meetings with the "peace establishment." He patiently explained that we were committed to total withdrawal of American troops, not only to a halt of the bombing of the North. He repeated that our goals were the same as theirs. He told them we had raised significant funds to take the antiwar movement to a new level and expected more. Although the movement leaders remained uneasy about our more political operation, they agreed to endorse us and we pledged to cooperate with them.

Overall, we had spectacular success in organizing the support we needed for this first stage. Over the next month, as Sam brought in more money, we added a few additional staffers and increased our office space. By the end of June, we felt we were ready to present the Vietnam Moratorium Committee to the media.

We called a press conference in a hotel meeting room just down the street from the office. The four of us walked down the street with stacks of press releases in our arms. Hawk repeated his familiar theme: "This is really crazy. Four kids are about to enter a room and tell the national press that we're going to bring the nation to a halt."

"Well, it's our turn," I answered. "All the last two presidents have done is succeed in ripping the nation apart. What the hell—we can't do any worse."

"We're going to kick their asses today," Sam announced.

"Let's hope they don't kick ours," said Marge.

We were all trying to cover up our nervousness. Holding the press releases with their thousands of endorsements in front of us, we walked into the room. It was wall-to-wall with TV reporters, cameras, lights, and the print press sitting there with pads and pencils waiting for us to begin.

We had agreed that Sam would read the release. It began: "On October 15, 1969, this nation will cease 'business as usual' to protest the war in Vietnam and to force the Nixon administration to bring the troops home," and it ended: "Since the goal of the action is to get massive and diverse sectors of American society to cease to do 'business as usual,' it is important to employ actions and rhetoric that will maintain the broadest possible opposition to the war."

Questions followed, the cameras kept working, and the large turnout insured nationwide coverage of our plans. That night Marge made dinner for the ever-growing Moratorium staff to celebrate the success of the conference. Sam and Hawk had dates afterward, and I went on home. It had been a day of triumph and historical significance, but as I walked into my apartment I felt empty. I longed for someone to be there with me and for me, to share a glass of wine, to talk, to love. I knelt by the bed and prayed to God to take away my homosexuality, then got in bed alone.

•   •   •

The summer of 1969 was a time of hope. The response to the vision of the Moratorium was astonishing—we had clearly reached those millions of Americans hungry for a way to express their opposition to the war without being perceived as disloyal to the country they loved. Blue-collar workers, war veterans, centrist religious leaders, ordinary citizens—all responded.

We were working together wonderfully well. I was at ease with my three buddies and with our growing staff. In fact, I realized, I was equally at ease with the senators and congresspersons from whom I solicited support. It dawned on me that thanks to people like Tim and Wren Wirth and Doris Kearns and my Moratorium family, I had lost a lot of my discomfort about my background and education. The people I was working with came from homes that were rich, poor, and in-between; they had gone to every kind of school; and what we were doing was what mattered, not our pasts. I no longer seemed to need my good old Dave facade. It pleased me a lot.

Sam, old friend and organizer Mike Driver, Susan Werbe, who was our press person, and I took an old row house on Eighteenth Street NW and created a community for our expanding Moratorium crew. We held Sunday brunches for the staff, journalists, and prominent antiwar personalities and turned the place into a social center for us and our supporters. Sometimes, CBS correspondents John Hart or Bruce Morton came to these Sundays. We'd find newspaperman Jules Witcover or columnist Mary McGrory in vigorous conversation with Senator McGovern or Michigan Congressperson Don Riegle. These were companionable, lively get-togethers and everyone relished them.

One of our strong supporters was then-Congressman Richard Ottinger of New York. Betty Anne Ottinger, who was then his wife, ended up not only doing volunteer work at the Moratorium but taking us under her protective wing. She was determined to make our living conditions a little less primitive, made sure we had a working refrigerator and kept it stocked with food, and was always there to listen to our fears and triumphs.

Shirley MacLaine was another formidable supporter. These were the years when Shirley was politically very active; she had been an antiwar McGovern delegate to the 1968 convention and called to volunteer her help with the October 15 protest when it was first announced. She'd arrive at the Sunday brunches bearing bags of groceries—enough to feed the entire staff for the coming week—challenge the politicians around the table to do more to end the war, and argue ideas and policy with all of us. When the mood got too serious or tempers flared, Shirley's infec-

tious laugh would calm everyone down. Those Sundays were the start of
a long, warm friendship between Shirley and me, and I remember them
with delight.

By July it was time to broaden our base more directly. Activist Rick
Stearns, student organizer Dan MacIntosh, and I headed across the
country in an old convertible VW beetle stickered with peace symbols.
Rick and Dan were heading home to California, and I was on my way to
do some organizing for the Moratorium on the West Coast. The three
of us looked like Haight-Ashbury hippies. Rick had long sideburns and
wore a French beret. Dan alternated between the organizer's classic
work shirt and his tie-dyed T-shirts. I wore a work shirt and now and
then a headband. We had just seen *Easy Rider* and driving along in our
convertible we felt as if we were on a similar adventure. Once we pulled
in for gas at a truck stop in rural Missouri. The truck drivers were clearly
not happy to see us and Dan said, "I think we ought to leave these
gentlemen to themselves and get our asses out of here." We paid for the
gas, but in backing up to swing out of the gas line, Rick accidentally
tapped the bumper of the car behind us. We got out to check and the
paint wasn't even touched, but this was an alarm bell for the truckers and
they all headed for our tiny car. Rick hit the accelerator and we shot the
hell out of there. It made for great storytelling when we got to the West
Coast.

In San Francisco I did the organizing I had come for and then went to
see my good friend Marylouise Oates, with whom I'd worked in the
McCarthy campaign, and who had become a key player in the antiwar
movement. Marylouise was a combination of Auntie Mame and a reporter from *The Front Page*—tall, powerful, sensitive, and tough—and
was now living in Berkeley with her future husband, student body president Charlie Palmer. I know no one who has the capacity to be a more
loyal friend than Marylouise and no one who is a fiercer fighter against
injustice.

I saw Marylouise and Charlie, and then made a pilgrimage to People's
Park in Berkeley. This little plot of land had become a battlefield between National Guard troops and students back in May. Originally a
garbage-strewn lot owned by the university (which had torn down the
old houses on it when it bought the land), in a dramatic communal effort
the month before, activists, students, neighbors, and local merchants had
moved in on the site and planted grass, trees, and flowers. It had become
an urban oasis, but Governor Ronald Reagan viewed it as a seizure of
public land and ordered a crackdown.

On May 15 the bulldozers arrived and the police sealed off the area around the park. Sheriff's deputies fired into the crowd of students and kept up the barrage for hours. That night Reagan sent in the Guard, turning Berkeley into an occupied zone for days, drawing national attention and resulting in hundreds of arrests, many injuries, one blinding, and a death.

Marylouise had called me in Washington asking for funds to treat the injured and continue the battle, and I had staffed telephones for several days, urging key antiwar contributors to send money and working the East Coast press to cover the story.

For my efforts she wrote a tribute that still moves me to tears. It spoke of a tree that stood in the park:

> "That tree is a friend to you and me," [the old man] told the
> little girl. "It provides shade and sweet-smelling branches. It
> gives help against the rains and, underground, its roots hold
> our land together. It stands straight and tall, no matter what
> the weather. It is firm and warm and strong.
> "It is a friend to you and me and to all people who want parks
> and flowers and sunshine and gentle rain. And it is named for
> an old and dear friend of our park.
> "It is called the Mixner Tree."

I went to People's Park and found that Reagan had surrounded it with an eight-foot chain-link fence to keep people out. Inside the fence was a beautiful green space with flowers and trees held prisoner to one man's ideology. But I saw my tree, and I moved on, determined to plant more of them around the country.

When I got back to Washington, we were facing an emerging crisis in the Moratorium Committee. Allard Lowenstein was a hero to many in the antiwar movement. In the November election he had won a seat in Congress from his Long Island district, aided by the support of thousands of students, many of whom decided they could not in good conscience work for Vice President Humphrey and had poured into his congressional district to canvass for him. His oratory, frantic pace, and boundless energy were legendary. He had a remarkable ability for finding the best and brightest among the students and directing their energies into activism. His life had been about social justice, and he was passionate about the Democratic Party. Until his election Allard had been on the road almost full-time urging students to fight injustice and inequality by getting involved. Now the Congress was his life, but his intensity and convictions had not changed.

Sam, David Hawk, and Marge had worked closely with Allard, aided his election campaign, and were friends. My relationship with him was more removed, consisting of chance encounters when our paths crossed in organizing around the country.

When we started the Moratorium, we went to visit Allard in his congressional office. It was not a pleasant meeting. He was visibly upset that those he considered his protégés were moving forward with plans to oppose the war without his input or consent.

"I wish you had consulted me before embarking on this venture," he said irritably. "I could have saved you a lot of trouble. These plans will never work. You have it all wrong."

I saw Sam's and David's backs stiffen but Sam kept his cool. "Allard, I don't think we have it wrong. We've talked to hundreds of people and there is a great deal of excitement. We want your support."

"Well, you might have talked to hundreds but you haven't talked to me. I know this field better than any of you. Let's be honest, Sam—you not only want my support but you *need* my support."

By now Sam too had an edge to his voice. "We are going to proceed, if necessary without your support," he answered, "but we would like to have it. October fifteenth will work one way or another."

Allard ignored him. "Here is what I believe this protest should be. I want a July fourth march on Washington, similar to the 1963 civil rights march, with tens of thousands of people walking up Pennsylvania Avenue carrying American flags. At the march we must also condemn the anarchy of the left and the violence taking place on campuses. All violence must be condemned."

David lost it. "Allard, I won't be part of anything that divides the movement. Yes, there has been violence on our side, but dropping bombs on cities in Vietnam is not the same as broken windows on campus. I won't be part of comparing the two."

Allard's voice was rising: "If you don't take on the left in the movement, I will not only not support the Moratorium, I will actively oppose it and urge others to stay away."

Sam wanted to get out of the office. "Allard, we'll discuss it among the four of us and get back to you," he said to calm the air. I had remained quiet through most of the meeting. This was Sam's and Hawk's good friend and I didn't want to interfere where friendship was involved.

But when we got back to the office, we all felt strongly that equating spasmodic violence by some segments of the antiwar movement with the brutal devastation of Vietnam was ridiculous. That strategy would play right into Nixon's hand. We knew a patriotic Fourth of July march would never get off the ground. Lowenstein was furious when we turned down his proposal. He made a brief attempt to create a committee for his own march but activists gave it a chilly reception.

By early summer his anger had turned into direct hostility toward the Moratorium and he was creating huge problems for us among the moderate voices on Capitol Hill. He "left-baited" us, passing along word on the Hill that we were extremists supportive of violence and that anyone who endorsed us would be hurt politically. Sam and David felt betrayed by their hero. Capitol Hill was my job, and I went door-to-door patiently explaining to members of Congress the true vision of the Moratorium. I showed respect for Allard and his extraordinary work by downplaying our disagreements but being emphatic that we would not divide the movement at this crucial stage. The Moratorium and Allard shared a common goal: to withdraw American troops from Vietnam. The only differences between them were on how that point should be made on the home front.

My approach worked. I was able to build a block of moderates in the Congress who endorsed the Moratorium and successfully undercut Allard. We then planted several stories in the press about his attempts to left-bait us to clear away any such perceptions. That finally got his attention. He called and asked if I would come to his office to discuss "the unfortunate situation."

There was plenty of tension when we met. I was forthright about our differences and the increasing bitterness between him and the Moratorium. He couldn't resist one last attempt at control, offering me a position on his staff to be "trained politically," which he assured me would make me more powerful than anything I could hope to accomplish at the Moratorium. I did not find his offer of interest or his legendary charisma persuasive, but we managed to reach our own "peace agreement." Later, when it became clear that October 15 would be successful, Allard started taking credit for organizing it. On the day he spoke at numerous rallies and claimed that its peaceful nature was the result of the demands he had made on us, we simply ignored him.

Just as important as our Hill work were our efforts to convince labor to join forces with us in opposing the war. With the exception of some traditional progressive labor unions and labor locals, most of the internationally known labor leadership had either not taken a stand on the war or were supporting administration policies. The Moratorium's priority target was Walter Reuther, head of the United Automobile Workers (UAW) and a Humphrey Democrat. We knew he was personally very troubled by the war but was concerned about the reaction he would face among his rank and file members if he went on record opposing it. Many union members were veterans of World War II or Korea. For them it was unpatriotic not to support their government when it was sending American boys overseas. Moreover, what had been a liberal base among blue-collar workers was growing increasingly more conservative. Reuther was caught in a classic moral dilemma: the difference between his personal beliefs and those of the constituency that provided him with his power.

His UAW office in Washington was headed by an extraordinary man named Bill Dodds. Bill was quiet on the surface, with a serenity that made you trust him, an Irish twinkle in his eye, and a dry wit, but his commitment to issues of social justice and peace was intense. His convictions were evident the moment we entered his office. Ben Shahn's portrait of Gandhi hung on the wall behind his desk.

Dodds was vehemently opposed to the war and eager to bring the UAW into the antiwar coalition, but he was not optimistic about the chances of our receiving the support of the UAW or Mr. Reuther personally. Nonetheless, he took charge of the effort. His office became the operations center and I in effect became his staff. Under his direction we mapped out a strategy that would provide the safest path for Reuther and the union's endorsement. Bill would set up meetings with key UAW officials from around the country to enlist them in our effort. He would go first, explaining why the UAW should get involved, and then I would talk about our plans for October 15 to reassure them they would feel comfortable participating in the events.

To provide a solid base of factual data, Sam called on his Harvard contacts to get the input of economists. These data were to be given to the key union members Bill had chosen to draft a position paper on the economic cost of the war to working people. Many of the Great Society programs of President Johnson were being gutted because of these costs. Documenting this was important if union members were to understand how the war was destroying many of the priorities of the union movement. Each time we finished a draft position paper, Bill would submit it to Reuther. Then he'd bring it back to the operations center heavily marked with revisions, many of them simplifying too academic a thrust so that the paper would be cast in terms that the workers would understand. Then we'd tackle it all over again.

But the day finally came when Sam and I walked into Bill's office and the smile on his face told us the good news. Reuther and the UAW would be endorsing the Moratorium and coming out against the war in Vietnam. But first Mr. Reuther wanted to meet with us to take the measure of his new political allies. This was to take place in Bill's office. I was certain Gandhi would be looking over us to insure that it went well.

Meeting Walter Reuther was like meeting a legend. His courageous exploits in organizing the United Automobile Workers were renowned. I was struck by how short he was, although his compact body had the feel of a prizefighter. He was on guard like a fighter too. But he could not have been more cordial. He extended his hand, flashed a smile, and told us how grateful he was for our work against the war. Despite the charm, however, he was all business. You could actually see him take our measure. He asked us focused questions about our plans for October 15 and a bit about our backgrounds, and made sure we understood that he had a lot at stake.

Our brief meeting ended with lots of mutual congratulations and a story. As Sam and I were about to leave, Reuther told us about the man who hated going to the dentist more than anything else in the world. Finally, when his toothache became unbearable, he had no choice but to seek relief. As he sat in the chair and the dentist warmed up his drill, the patient grabbed him by his private parts and said, "We aren't going to hurt each other, are we, Doctor?"

I had no doubt what Reuther meant by telling that story and we did not violate his trust.

During the summer, the Moratorium grew and grew. The idea had taken on a life of its own. Our offices expanded to two floors, we had regional offices around the country, our staff had grown to dozens, and thousands of small contributions arrived in each day's mail. Marylouise Oates joined us in August to handle the press for the Moratorium. Susan Werbe and Joan Libby, our researchers, were printing our own newspaper, the *Peace Times*, which went out to all our supporters around the country. It contained substantive articles related to the war and gave its readers the latest news of the activities planned for Moratorium Day.

It was almost a year since our Martha Vineyard's retreat, and the participants decided it was time to get together again. This time we extended our invitations to include some other young men committed to social change. We called a few women too, at the last minute, but there was no question we still viewed the future as the domain of straight white males.

In September a group of us took the ferry over to the Vineyard from the mainland and headed for John O'Sullivan's home. Coming up the dirt driveway, we could see some early arrivals already gathered in front, and Rick Stearns and Taylor Branch got up to greet us. So did a tall, rather lanky, good-looking man I didn't know. He had wiry hair that grew out like an afro and wore a tattered, baggy sweater over his jeans. "Hello," he said, extending his hand. "I'm Bill Clinton, a friend of Rick's."

We all went inside to lots of greetings and good-natured kidding; it was old-time week and we were glad to be together again. We sat in the kitchen drinking coffee and bringing each other up-to-date on what we'd been up to. We had gone back to our various lives after the 1968 election, mostly school or jobs, and we were all still involved in opposing the war. But this weekend was to be more about networking than dealing with bigtime issues. We had no great differences about substance or tactics. When we gathered in the living room overlooking the marsh, Sam and I reported on the Vietnam Moratorium and asked for their help, but it was already a given that everyone would be supporting it. Others described their own political or activist efforts, again in the same low-key style. But our sessions were much more relaxed this time, and the real work that weekend was the bonding that evolved as we took long walks together or sat in the sun on the deck outside and talked.

Rick Stearns was at Oxford and he had invited his fellow Rhodes Scholars Strobe Talbott and Bill Clinton to the retreat. Some knew Talbott but Clinton was new to most of us. Although he looked like a 1960s hippie, he had not really been a player in the antiwar movement. By then, it was rare to find a politically active young person in America who had not been a participant on one side or the other of this long, anguishing debate. Clinton had left his home in Hope, Arkansas, to attend Georgetown University and work part-time for Arkansas Senator William Fulbright, the Senate's most vocal opponent of the war, so his nonparticipation seemed even more surprising. In fact, this retreat was to be his first real exposure to the antiwar activists of his generation.

Clinton was smooth and initially that generated some distrust. I watched him make each person feel he was the most important and wisest one there, a gift he is blessed with to this day. He'd ask about their lives and tell them how much they mattered, put his arm around their shoulders as they walked. It seemed to me he was focusing on those he felt were most important, whether because of visibility or connections. You suspected that at least some of what he was doing was calculated. Yet before long, you forgot about it. It simply didn't matter. His extraordinary talent for "connecting" was irresistible.

The people in this room were hardened by their struggle against the war in Vietnam. Many had been in the forefront of the civil rights movement. Some had gone to jail in order to desegregate America. Others had placed their promising careers in jeopardy to fight for their beliefs. Now in their midst was this charismatic young man who had been at most a spectator and fringe player in the great moral arena that consumed his generation. Although Arkansas had been a battleground for freedom for American blacks, Clinton had not been a real participant in their struggle. He was a man whose involvement had consisted of befriending those who were making change, but avoiding that which might place him at risk. He had strong political ambitions. He intended to run for office. He did not walk the picket lines, sit in at segregated lunch counters, leave school to work for McCarthy or Kennedy. He was radical in thought but not in action.

Some of this I learned that weekend, and some I was to discover later. But as I came to know Bill Clinton those few days, I realized I already understood a great deal about him through my own journey. I saw that obtaining the approval and trust of these bright young minds was critical to his own self-esteem. He needed their validation to justify his long journey from Hope. When we finally got to spend time with each other, we found that we were connected not only by our ambitions for the future but by the similarities of our pasts. Small-town America had given us our ethical values and been a cocoon of security in our early years but we both knew that it had also been our prison. In childish stories with a moral attached to them, privation is said to strengthen the spirit, but the reality is otherwise. Romanticizing hardship is a legend best abandoned.

Clinton and I took a long walk along a Vineyard beach. His warmth invited confidences. There was no fear of being judged. He had an astonishing capacity to invite your trust and make you feel close to him. At first we talked of our childhoods. We recalled our hometowns, our families, the ceaseless worries about money, our struggle to make it to the outside world, and our dreams. We shared the sense of isolation that had permeated us, of feeling out of place with our contemporaries and knowing there simply had to be more for us elsewhere. Both of our mothers had worked hard and struggled so that we could make it, and we talked of how we had missed them when they were not at home. We found a special connection when we spoke of those small-town values of caring and compassion that had helped shape our politics.

Bill was forthcoming about his life. At first, I felt awkward talking about myself but his ease made that pass. We were like reformed prisoners in our determination to make the most of our escape from the suffocation of the world we had grown up in. We had dreams to fulfill, not only for ourselves but for those who had never made it out.

We also had differences in background. Bill was able to go to Georgetown and excel academically, which was not the course I had taken. I wondered to myself how he had attended inadequate rural schools like mine, yet been able to end up achieving such academic distinction. His Rhodes scholarship awed me. I both admired and envied it. I knew firsthand how difficult that journey must have been. And I asked myself what might have happened if I hadn't assumed so many paths were closed to me—if I hadn't been gay.

As we strolled down the beach arm in arm that day, I experienced for the first time a genuine desire to tell another person about my homosexuality. Clinton's openness about himself and his warm, easy intimacy made me feel safe. But common sense prevailed. I only revealed to him about myself what he had already experienced in his own life.

I felt the closeness between us. I felt I understood the motivating factors that were driving him to succeed. I thought: I know so much about him and he knows so little about me. In some sense, I guess, I was hoping that this man so similar to myself would be able to fulfill some of the dreams I would never be allowed to realize.

We sat down on a dune for a while and looked out at the sea. Finally Bill asked, "With your visibility in opposing the war, are you ever embarrassed about returning home and seeing families who have lost their sons to the war?"

I knew what he was asking. From the hometowns of America had come some of the war's bravest recruits.

"Yes," I told him. "It can be very painful. I had a really hard time seeing my friend Russell Garrison's parents after he was killed in Vietnam. We'd been kids together, classmates right through high school. It was awful."

"It's real hard coming from those small towns and being against the war. After your friend died and you went home, didn't you feel that you had let them down? How did you deal with it?"

"I don't really know, Bill. I just sort of plowed through the visit. I guess what I really want is not to have any more wooden boxes with the remains of my high school buddies coming back home."

He was silent for a bit. I could see he was struggling. "Oh, God, it's so difficult," he said at last. "I've had to fight so hard for the approval of people from my area. I just don't want to give it up."

I told him I knew what he meant. "But sometimes," I said, "we aren't given any choice."

I was struck by his sincerity and his frankness. We both came from places of fierce, elemental patriotism, where most of the people we loved and respected were strong proponents of the war. I realized that in many ways I had more freedom than Clinton. He had to wrestle not only with his personal beliefs about the war but also with the impact his actions might have on his determination to run for office. My homosexuality removed such options from my life, so I had no constraints to prevent me from acting on my opposition. We sat on those Vineyard dunes, coming from the same place and offering each other mutual support, but he could be open about his indecision and his pain. I hid mine.

After the retreat, Bill was going home to Arkansas for a while, but we agreed to meet again at the Moratorium, on his way back to Oxford. On the sand dunes of Martha's Vineyard we knew we had become friends.

By late September thousands of schools, churches, universities, and businesses were planning to participate in discussions about the war on October 15. Over seven thousand people had signed on to organize events in their neighborhoods. *Time*, *Life*, and *Newsweek* were preparing cover stories. Our offices could not handle the volume of phone calls and mail. Hundreds of volunteers crowded into the regional offices as well as our Washington headquarters. The working press jammed our briefings. Belatedly, the White House realized the impact we were having, and floundered—for a while—on how to respond. Rallies, candlelight marches, and teach-ins were being organized in hundreds of cities, suburbs, and small towns across the country. As a *Newsweek* reporter wrote, "Originally, October 15 was to have been a campus-oriented protest involving a Moratorium on normal academic activities. But it has quickly spread beyond the campus. And, if everything goes according to the evolving plans, the combination of scheduled events could well turn into the broadest and most spectacular antiwar protest in American history."

The day Bill Clinton came through Washington on his way back to Oxford, I was frantically juggling phone calls while opening envelopes and helping count the checks from the day's mail. I heard a voice from behind me: "You have time to speak to an old country boy?" Bill seemed a little lost amid the extraordinary energy around him. I took him on a tour of the operation and Sam joined us for lunch. We talked about our astonishment at the dimensions the Moratorium had grown to and the way it had captured the nation's imagination. Then we went back to the office and Bill volunteered to work. He sat down with our field organization and gave them the names of key contacts in the South who might help us in an area where we were especially weak. For a bit he joined a group collating a press release, but he was too fidgety to stay there long. Finally, he surrendered to his restlessness and simply roamed the offices taking everything in. He was an astute observer, and kept asking people what they were doing and why. We had little time to visit. There was too much for me to deal with to take a break.

But we made up for it that night. Bill slept on the old purple couch and we sat up into the early morning talking. He was clearly moved by what he had seen that day. "You know, it's hard to go back to Oxford with all of this happening over here," he said. "I feel as though I should stay and help."

I realized that in a way he was seeking my approval for him to go back there. "Very few of us get to Oxford," I told him "You can go there for me and I'll do this for you."

We broke up in laughter and agreed to be each other's proxies. "Maybe I can organize a protest at Oxford this fall with some of my friends," he said.

He did. He helped set up a Moratorium event of about a thousand people who gathered in front of the American embassy in London. He called his friends who were overseas with him to urge them to attend, and on the day of the demonstration he served as a marshal, keeping people in the line of march and directing them to the right location. Ironically, that one protest would be used by George Bush in the presidential campaign years later, when he attempted to portray Clinton as a militant antiwar activist and draft dodger. In an interview on CNN, Bush said, "Maybe I'm old-fashioned, but to go to a foreign country and demonstrate against your own country when your sons and daughters are dying halfway around the world—I am sorry but I think that is wrong."

The day before a climactic event there is nothing left to do. You've prepared for it for months, invested half your life in it, everything is in place, it's too late now, and it will either work or it will fail. When I went into the Moratorium offices, all I could think about was whether or not we would be able to meet all the hype. October 14 was the longest day of my life.

Edie Wilkie, who worked for a California congressperson, had joined with a group of Hill staffers urging their bosses to kick off the Moratorium by keeping the House of Representatives open all through the night of the fourteenth to debate the war. Conservatives had vowed to shut down any such attempt. Our plan was to have several hundred people sit on the Capitol steps in support of the debate going on inside. This would be our first event of the Moratorium. That evening, as I headed to the Capitol, I looked up at the light on the top of the dome. It stays lit when Congress is in session. Long ago, when the light went out, it let families know that the members were on their way home. Tonight we hoped to keep it lit to let a nation know about the horrors of a brutal war. The light was on.

As I rounded the east side of the Capitol, I saw before my eyes on the steps thousands of people sitting there to acknowledge the debate within. I made my way into the center of the throng to sit with Edie. The crowd kept growing. I finally let myself begin to believe the Moratorium was going to work.

The participants began reading the names of those who had died in Vietnam. The names of the war dead ricocheted off the side of the Capitol into the night. Inside, our congressional supporters were using every parliamentary procedure imaginable to keep the debate alive. It was long after midnight before the pro-war forces were able to muster enough votes to stop it. Slowly the crowd dispersed into the night. With only a couple of hours to sunrise, I sat on the steps and waited. Then the sun rose and the city lay shining under its glow. As tears ran down my face, I felt alive.

I went home, showered, and went to the Moratorium offices. The place was already packed with reporters and camera crews looking for one more angle, one more interview. Marylouise Oates had set up a spectacular press operation for the day itself, and everything was going smoothly when I arrived. Marylouise ran a tight ship, and she had orchestrated exactly what would happen and when. The press briefing later in the day was to be the big event. We were to postpone any interviews until then.

Mary McGrory, always the smart reporter, showed up at our offices with a basket of food, including my favorite meat loaf. Mary knew two things: that there was no way that I was going to miss her meat loaf and that I understood that she was an important and terrific reporter. I escorted her past the other journalists and into our inner offices where the four of us were waiting out the day. As she was setting out the food in her basket and collecting her exclusive interview of what it was like on the "inside" of the Moratorium, Marylouise came to the door.

"David, may I see you a minute?" Her voice was chilly.

I went out into the hallway and she was livid. "Just what in the hell am I supposed to tell the other reporters now that you've let Mary inside?" she demanded. "They're furious and I have to deal with them."

I did feel guilty about putting Marylouise in so difficult a spot and tried to cover my tracks. "I'm sorry, Marylouise—I just didn't think. She brought us lunch."

"Lunch, hell! She just got an exclusive. Now I have to go in there and get her and I'll be the bad apple in her eyes."

I did learn a lesson. For me, it was my good friend Mary and she had her meat loaf. For the others, it was a very different story.

By noon the phones were ringing off the hook and our staff could barely handle the flow of reports from around the country. Susan Werbe and Joan Libby brought in fresh word every few minutes. It was happening. Literally millions of Americans had stopped what they were doing this day to protest the war.

In place after place, people were reading the names of every soldier who had died in Vietnam. In some cities church bells were rung more than forty thousand times, once for each of the dead. In El Paso, Texas, thousands carried "luminaries" to mourn the dead. High school students wore black armbands to school, and there were armbands on the sleeves of stockbrokers all over Wall Street. Churches and synagogues held services and all-day prayer vigils to pray for the end of the war. Colleges and universities across the land canceled their classes and devoted the entire day to studying Vietnam. Even soldiers on patrol in Vietnam, who heard about the Moratorium in the press and in letters from home, wore black armbands. During the day the major cities started reporting in with numbers—over 100,000 in Boston, 2,700 in Lexington, Kentucky, 50,000 at Bryant Park in New York City, 15,000 in Baltimore, 5,000 in Tucson, 75,000 in Cleveland, 15,000 in Chicago, 100,000 in San Francisco—and the totals kept growing as the day went on. We got word that the next day's editions of *The Cleveland Plain Dealer* would headline its front page "Millions Protest War!"

We sat stunned, scarcely able to believe the enormous reservoir of concern and emotion we had tapped. Late in the afternoon we held our press briefing for the hundreds of reporters and camera crews that filled the room. But the real story was in the many hundreds of thousands who carried the candles, tolled the bells, and read the names of the dead.

We capped off the day with a massive candlelight rally and march at the Washington Monument. Michael Driver had been organizing the event for weeks. Mrs. Martin Luther King led it off with a speech that echoed her husband's eloquent commitment to end the war. Then a candlelight procession of fifty thousand marchers made its way to the White House. I waited a little while, and from the monument grounds watched the moving sea of candles as a chorus swelled into "All we are saying is give peace a chance." In front of the White House a large "candle for peace" had been placed before the iron fence. Coretta King said a silent prayer, then lit the candle. On and on the marchers came, candles in their hands as they softly sang the anthem for peace.

After the march ended I returned to the offices. It was quiet by then; most of our people had gone off to the vigils that were to last through the night. Sam, Marge, and Hawk had all agreed to do television interview shows. I had declined. I had given some press interviews and made a few speeches, but turned down major shows like *Face the Nation*. I thought I should keep a low profile because of my gayness. It puzzled some of my friends, but most still thought me enough of a maverick for it not to seem out of place.

Throughout the day I had worn my only suit. Back in the office I changed into jeans, a denim jacket, and my cowboy boots, and put on a cowboy hat. Now that the day was over, I didn't know what to do. I lay back on one of the office sofas, took out my harmonica, and began to play "We Shall Overcome."

CHAPTER FIVE

The November March

WE were not the only show in town, nor our Moratorium the only large-scale antiwar protest. The National Mobilization Against the War—popularly known as the New Mobe—had also scheduled a March on Washington, and our success suggested that there could be hundreds of thousands converging on the capital on November 15.

Like a number of other antiwar organizations, the New Mobe was to the left of the Moratorium both politically and ideologically. As Francine du Plessix Gray characterized us both in *The New Yorker*, "It has been said that the New Mobe leaders have the arrogance of prophets and the Moratorium leaders have the cautiousness of politicians."

In many respects she was right. Although our goals were identical, we differed dramatically in style and process. The Mobe had been one of the first groups to organize against the war, and was a broad coalition of long-standing peace groups such as the Quakers, SANE, and Women Strike for Peace. It was wary of electoral politics. Maintaining the "ideological purity" of its opposition to the war was crucial. As we saw it, the

Mobe found compromise a dirty word; it couldn't imagine conducting a dialogue with someone like Robert McNamara, for example, who had been Kennedy and Johnson's Secretary of Defense, because it viewed him as a war criminal, while we believed that the more people we could talk to, the greater the possibility of changing at least some minds.

The Moratorium was organized more like a political campaign, with a clear goal and a well-defined message. Like the New Mobe, we wanted the troops out of Vietnam and wanted them out now. But the Mobe felt that only a mass expression of disgust by the populace against the war would end it; and while we agreed with that, we thought it very important that the form this expression took not generate the kind of political backlash that would make ending the war all the harder.

On paper the differences seemed minor, but the tensions between us were real. The truth was, we needed each other—and we both resented it. The New Mobe was in need of our organizing and funding skills, and we needed a way to follow up on our October achievement. We recognized that the November March was going to happen, with or without us.

Delicate negotiations ensued. We wanted the March to have a broad enough appeal to sustain our support among the Middle Americans we had worked so hard to bring into the antiwar movement. The New Mobe insisted that no one who wanted to be part of the March be excluded, including the American Communist Party and those who openly sympathized with the Vietcong. Left-wing extremists were likely to alienate the moderates and our new supporters.

All of us got angrier and angrier. Ironically, the New Mobe offices were only a few floors above us in the same Vermont Avenue building. We might as well have been ten miles apart. It was convinced that the new kid on the block was trying to take over its March, and we were not only worried about keeping our support base, we were appalled when we discovered how little it had done about critical logistics. There was less than a month to go, and they didn't know what the hell they were doing.

It was David Hawk, who stayed calm and deliberate even when tempers flared, who was the key figure in keeping the two sides together. His credentials helped. A guy with a pending indictment for draft evasion and a history of active involvement in the resistance was someone the Mobe could accept. He'd sit in crowded, smoky, windowless rooms for hours and mediate a hostility that at times was more intense than the anger about the war itself. He'd listen, and then repeat what became his mantra: We had to iron out our differences because we could not afford to go into November fifteenth divided. Slowly, skillfully, he saw to it that the main issues were worked out. We would both collaborate on the choice of speakers, and both agreed to insure that the tone presented to the nation would be a positive one, yet not one that would compromise the strong beliefs of the New Mobe. The Moratorium was to take charge of the massive logistical problems. As we had discovered, there were hardly any preparations for the enormous masses of people who would be descending on Washington in three short weeks. Almost no housing was available for the marchers. There were no plans for the thousands of buses, no sanitation systems, and no permit for the March itself. The Mobe hadn't even begun to coordinate the March with the city or the White House.

We announced on October 20 that the Moratorium was endorsing the March. After some very strenuous sessions we had managed to come to an agreement on speakers. The New Mobe reluctantly acceded to George McGovern, whose long and early denunciations of the war they admired, but insisted that Eugene McCarthy was too "political" and couldn't speak from the stage—he would only be allowed to address the marchers at the assembly point before it left the Capitol.

Sam and I asked John O'Sullivan and Tony Podesta, our McCarthy colleagues who were two of the best organizers in the country, to come to Washington to coordinate a team to handle the logistical nightmare. John Shattuck came down from Yale to handle the marshals; Arlene Popkins, who'd thrown me into the car to greet McCarthy in Boston, came to handle sanitation and affectionately became known as "the shit lady" for her efforts; Taylor Branch worked on the buses; and Washington activist Maggie Morton took over housing. They were among the dozens of others camped out all over town bringing structure to the operation.

Even though the White House was publicly taking a very hard-line stance against the March—refusing to even issue a permit—it knew that it had to work out a relationship with us because at least half a million people were going to be converging on Washington whether the administration liked it or not. So behind the scenes, John and Tony worked with domestic affairs adviser Richard Blumenthal to set up an official liaison with the White House. They established a "command post" linking the White House, the city, the New Mobe, and the Moratorium.

The command post was a sight to behold. There in a room full of tables covered with phones, half-eaten sandwiches, empty coffee cups, stacks of papers, and maps of the city sat blue-suited, short-haired White House Republican staffers side by side with the New Mobe in their jeans, their long hair a tangle. Thanks to John's uproarious humor and

Tony's good-natured but firm get-down-to-business approach, both sides worked hard but with a genuine camaraderie. In the spirit of things, the young White House staffers even arranged for the White House Mess to deliver food to everyone working in the command post.

The October Moratorium had generated an antiwar momentum that even the President could no longer ignore, and on November 3, in an effort to thwart the swell, Nixon made a televised appeal to the nation. It was an ugly, belligerent speech. He refused to wind down America's involvement. He pledged to crack down on dissent and advocated more extensive bombings if the North Vietnamese did not agree to American terms. "I appeal to you, the great Silent Majority of my fellow Americans," he proclaimed to an already divided nation, dividing it further. That night we all knew the March would be enormous. That night the war became Nixon's war.

And that night the fierceness of his speech moved many of us in the Moratorium closer to the hard-line positions and rhetoric of the New Mobe. I was one of them. Sam was not. It was the first time we had differed. He was adamant that we keep the course we had originally charted; we could not allow Nixon to dictate our direction. Hawk and Marge felt even more strongly than I did and were ready to charge the barricades, and I found myself mediating between them and Sam. There was an even wider gap between the Moratorium and more moderate antiwar figures such as Adam Walinsky, Robert Kennedy's aide, who had been enormously helpful to the Moratorium with legal advice, especially in dealing with the Department of Justice. Adam and those who believed as he did had little tolerance for the strident, often violent rhetoric of the left. They abhorred it in itself and because they believed it would alienate that "Silent Majority" whose ultimate support the antiwar movement needed. The divisions were no longer confined to the Mobe and the Moratorium. We were becoming divided among ourselves.

The most serious problem the Moratorium had to deal with was the permit; the March could not take place without it. The administration had assigned Deputy Attorney General Richard Kleindienst and White House Counsel John Dean, of subsequent Watergate fame, to be its negotiators, and they had been regularly turning down the requests. I was certain this was a deliberate effort to heighten tensions and increase the risk of confrontation and violence. If a bloody chaos was the prevailing image on the country's television sets on November 15, the White House would be able to make a more persuasive case that we were radical, anarchic, and unpatriotic. According to du Plessix Gray, Kleindienst said, "I don't want to have to shoot any demonstrators on the White

House lawn. I'll have to line both sides of Pennsylvania Avenue with American soldiers shoulder to shoulder."

Sam and Adam, weary of the rhetoric and seriously worried about the possibility of clashes between federal troops and the marchers if the permit didn't come through, took matters into their own hands and met separately with Justice Department officials to secure it. They had another motive as well; they thought this would enable them to exert more control over the tenor of the March. That generated a backlash in the Moratorium and rage in the New Mobe, which charged that the meeting broke the united front of the movement and hurt the negotiating posture. The reactions were so strong that the two agreed not to intervene in the process again and to leave it to the official negotiating team.

Actually, I believe their separate meeting with Justice did move the administration away from a more confrontational stance. There seemed to be a new spirit of cooperation when the talks resumed. Finally, Washington city officials appealed directly to the President and the permit was granted—just in time.

The Moratorium also had to contend with a radical left-wing fringe group called the Weathermen, which had not found even the most extremist of the other groups revolutionary enough, espoused violence, and in Chicago a few days before the Moratorium had embarked on self-proclaimed "Days of Rage" in which they smashed store windows and housefronts, destroyed cars, and careered into police lines provoking shootings, beatings, and arrests. Now they were demanding an immediate meeting with the Moratorium, charging that it had an obligation to defend their court cases in Chicago.

In this case, Sam and I were both hard-liners. We were appalled by their actions in Chicago. Sam, Hawk, Marge, and I met beforehand and decided to bring in some lawyers and activists who we hoped might have credibility with the Weathermen. Coming to any kind of accord seemed virtually impossible, but we figured we would give it a shot. It would definitely not include an agreement to contribute to their legal costs. We could not in good conscience accede to that.

Four Weathermen swaggered in that evening, dressed for trouble in combat boots and military surplus combat jackets. They formed into a wedge, pushing their way roughly through the packed Moratorium offices where hordes of volunteers were busy with last-minute preparations for the March, and into Sam's nondescript quarters.

Our efforts at civility were doomed before they started. They were angry and foul-mouthed. They made clear their disdain for this "fucking middle-class picnic" that we had organized; we were as much the enemy as "those cocksucking war criminals in the Pentagon." Their bottom-line demand was nonnegotiable: The Moratorium must "cough up" substantial funds to pay for their legal fees from their Days of Rage in Chicago or they would not promise that their supporters would not resort to violence and to creating chaos at the March or that our offices might not be "raided and trashed."

Sam held firm that the Moratorium would not even discuss legal fees until after the weekend of the March. If there was any violence, it would make it impossible for us to even consider endorsing their case, much less contributing to their defense. We went at each other for more than an hour, and then they left, shouting epithets.

We took their threats very seriously. We contacted Bill Briggs, a strong opponent of the war and a former football player, and asked him to find the tallest, toughest guys he could to beef up security at our offices throughout the weekend. He did. A dozen huge men arrived at our offices to protect us, but even with their presence, Sam and I thought it wise to move our mailing lists, records, and cash to safer quarters until the weekend was over. We called our good friend and colleague Betty Anne Ottinger and asked if she'd be willing to keep the considerable amount of money we had on hand for all the events in her secluded Washington house.

Betty Anne drove to our headquarters, collected the paper bags stuffed with thousands of dollars, brought them home, and couldn't think of a safe place to hide the money. She ended up sliding it under the mattress in her bedroom. When she and Dick went to bed that night, she confessed to him: "Honey, I have to tell you we're sleeping atop an enormous amount of cash from the Moratorium. I agreed to hide it here over the weekend to protect it from the Weathermen."

Dick was appalled. "Under the mattress?" he said. "That's the most obvious place in the world. Of all places, how could you ever put it under here?" And then he muttered, "No wonder I'm uncomfortable tonight."

On Monday Sam and I went to the Ottingers' to bring back the money. Upstairs in the master bedroom we grabbed one side of the mattress and lifted it so Betty Anne could pull it out. "Oh, my God, it's gone!" she cried. We couldn't believe it. In a panic the three of us sped from room to room throughout the large house, looking in every crevice, yanking out drawers, searching every closet, while Betty Anne kept saying under her breath, "I'll raise the money to replace it. I will. I promise."

No sign of it. We gave up at last. She went off to call Dick with the awful news. We could hear his gusts of laughter right through the receiver. When he was finally able to speak, he told her what he'd done. He'd been so worried about leaving it in so obvious a place that he'd taken it out and put it in a safe. The trouble was, he'd forgotten to tell any of us.

The New Mobe had planned a "March Against Death" at Arlington National Cemetery beginning on Thursday night, to set a peaceful tone for the great March two days later. In the grassy staging area outside the cemetery, we gathered by the thousands to receive candles and placards with the names of the American war dead that we strung around our necks. Patsy came with me. A young staffer recognized me as we got in line and said, "Mr. Mixner, you don't have to wait in line." "Oh, yes, he does," said Patsy. In the great somber stillness I got my candle, lit it, and gave it to Patsy to hold as I slipped the name of William F. Young over my head. Into the night, as far as one could see, stretched an endless line of candles walking against the madness of Vietnam. As we crossed the Memorial Bridge, thousands of federal troops began converging to "protect" the city from the marchers with their candles. Armored vehicles filled with troops and guns rode past us as we walked. We wound our way around the Lincoln Memorial and to the White House. As I passed in front of it I shouted out the name of William F. Young, as if perhaps the President would hear it in the dark night.

Approaching the Capitol, we heard the sound of singing, voices raised in chorus: "Where Have All the Flowers Gone?" At the base of the great white marble building, its floodlit dome aglow, I laid Mr. Young's name in one of the handmade wooden coffins that would be carried back toward the White House, filled with the names of the dead, on Saturday. The procession of candles went on and on. The White House was unnerved. President Nixon went into the office of Bob Haldeman, his chief of staff, and suggested that army helicopters be used to blow them out. Night and day, for almost forty hours, we bore the spirit of our war dead around our shoulders and called out their names to the President even as the government attempted to conduct business as usual.

Saturday was one of those perfect Washington autumn days. We gathered at the base of the Capitol. I carried a small American flag. Hawk hated this gesture and tried angrily to persuade me not to. I refused. It was my symbol, my flag too. Sam had decided on principle that he could not march. To march without him was hard. We had not only always been allies in our politics, we were friends. I couldn't really decipher his point of principle; I could only respect it.

The rally began with speeches by McCarthy, Coretta King, and McGovern. Then with the dignitaries and the Moratorium and New Mobe leaders at the head, the line moved along America's main street, Pennsylvania Avenue, toward the Washington Monument, the coffins with the names of the forty thousand dead borne with it. As the great throng gathered at the monument in petition to their government, it was clear that all the talk about speakers had been irrelevant. Pete Seeger mounted the stage with his guitar, strummed it gently, and in his sweet clear voice began singing our familiar anthem, "All we are saying is give peace a chance." The crowd roared, thrust their hands upward in the "V" for peace sign, and swayed in song.

Half a million Americans had come together to send their message to the heart of their government. The administration did not want to hear it.

CHAPTER SIX
Alone

THE sense of triumph and the exhilarating bonding that comes of shared commitment to a deeply felt cause—nothing takes the place of the human need for intimacy, for love. I saw those around me have the gift of that closeness. Sam was dating and Hawk was in a relationship. This was the year I grew bolder in my hunger to fight my own deep loneliness.

During the summer before the Moratorium I had realized I could no longer deny my homosexuality—the self-imposed celibacy of the last couple of years was taking too great a toll. Increasingly, I found myself having to come to terms with powerful sexual urges. I would do my best to contain them, live in denial, then abruptly seek an outlet when I couldn't stand it any longer. Rather than planning how to meet my needs safely, without any risk of disclosure, I would wait until the frustrations had reached fever pitch and then carelessly seek anonymous sex. I would go to dark parks or walk around gay areas of Washington hoping to meet someone who would give me release. I'd make up a name and background in the hope this would conceal my real identity. Eventually, I found the courage to go out to bars. I learned which ones were straight and which were "mixed" and which were gay, and I sought out dark, out-of-the-way retreats where it seemed less likely I'd encounter anyone familiar. I discovered that as long as I was able to express myself sexually, my anger and tension eased. Even though my human contact was always in a stranger's arms, it was at least some form of intimacy. I needed and wanted that contact.

Shirley MacLaine had also helped me to be more adventurous. She was having an affair with national news reporter Sander Vanocur, and when I was in New York the three of us often had dinner in her apartment and amid a lot of laughter swapped the latest political gossip. Shirley was committed to sexual liberation. She was blunt about her distaste for what she regarded as puritan morality. She did not know I was gay and I longed to tell her. I knew in my heart that she would receive it with love, but I still couldn't bring myself to utter that word—not to Shirley, who increasingly cared about me, or to anyone else.

She also introduced me to her good friends Phyllis and Eb Kronhausen, who were noted advocates of sexual freedom and liberation. They were no more aware of my gayness than she was, but they were eager to open up a whole world of sexual freedom to me. When I was on a trip to California, Shirley had them take me to Sandstone, in the Santa Monica mountains, a swinger retreat where heterosexual nudity and sexuality were expressed openly and with abandon. I kept my clothes on as I explored this sexual playground, walking about in disbelief at what I was seeing. My puritanical upbringing warred with my yearnings—it intimidated me to see conventional boundaries ignored and with such apparent joy, yet I resented not being able to have the same freedom for myself. But most of all I was overwhelmed by the way sex for the revelers at Sandstone was truly a form of connectedness, communication, expression—even a work of art—and never something to be practiced in shame.

I was enriched that day. I learned for the first time that sex could be an occasion of celebration. I began at last to examine my own sexuality with less fear.

But that did not mean the world would accept me for who and what I was. I knew that my political career and my family would be destroyed if my gayness became known. So I went on frequenting obscure little joints and assuming a variety of false identities. A small bar near Thomas Circle became a favorite. It was a classic setting for the time: a narrow entranceway, a dim, windowless room with a long wood bar and shabby booths along the wall, the smell of beer permeating the air. You could sit there quietly nursing a glass and then another one, getting just drunk enough to find someone with whom to have sex but hopefully not so drunk that you could not remember having it. The jukebox played favorite gay melodies like "Over the Rainbow" and "I've Gotta Be Me." Everything about it—the bar, the music, our conduct—reflected the closeted reality of homosexuality in the 1960s.

It was here that I met "Frank." Earlier in the evening I had smoked a joint to garner the courage to go there one more time, afraid as always I might run into someone who knew me. I sat at my usual place at the darkest end of the bar, sipping my Miller's and feeling very down. Then I sensed a presence next to me. At my left was the handsomest man I had ever seen. He had jet-black hair, brilliant green eyes, and a smile that seduced me instantly. He was wearing tight blue jeans and a light blue work shirt, and gave off an air of confidence you almost never encountered in a place like this.

He gave a slight nod when he saw me snatching glances at him. I averted my eyes. I heard his laugh. It was a gentle one. "I don't bite," he said softly.

I looked at him, mute.

"My name is Frank. What's yours?"

A harmless question but one that I rarely answered truthfully. Before I could think I found myself saying "David."

Frank ignored my obvious nervousness and took charge of the conversation. In quick succession he volunteered that he worked for the government, was looking for a relationship, and was tired of the bar scene. My tension eased without my even realizing it and I joined in. We were elated to find that we enjoyed the same poets, couldn't get enough of Janis Joplin, loved long walks in the woods. He confessed to being a candles and wine man who thrived on romance. I already was imagining us walking along an empty beach, hand in hand.

As we talked his muscular thigh was rubbing gently against mine in a clear signal that he wanted to go home together. This wasn't like all those nameless encounters since Kit's death. His spirited confidence made me feel safe. His smile reassured me I could trust him. But I was still afraid, for to go with him would open up all those feelings I had suppressed successfully for the last five years. I sat paralyzed by indecision. Frank took me by my elbow, lifted me from the stool, and said, "Come on. You are coming with me."

I followed him in a daze. I walked through the door into the classic small apartment of a midlevel Washington federal worker, but this one was different. The walls were covered with shelves of books and records. I kept frantically busy examining his bookcases—there were Neruda, Yeats, and Tennyson, and I knew he had told me the truth about his love for my favorite poets. Then I felt his arms wrap around me and once again his laughter filled the room.

"I have to be the luckiest man in the world tonight," he said. I thought that should have been my line. The evening proceeded like a first-rate romance novel. Frank lit candles and incense. He put on Mahler's Fifth. He opened a bottle of excellent wine and filled my glass, then for the longest time just held me close. Again I realized I felt safe. Slowly, gently at first, we made passionate love. Eventually I sat up to leave and he pulled me back into bed. "You're not going," he told me. "You are not walking out on me. I want you to stay." I did.

I woke the next morning to Frank standing next to the bed with a breakfast tray and the morning paper. He put down the tray, sat down at the edge of the bed, took my hand, and said: "David. I know who you are. I have been a fan of yours from afar. Trust me, I am not here to do anything except to be supportive of you. We can pull this off together. I want to see you again."

Never had I been happier or felt freer. Here, at last, was another Kit. There was something about his assurance and his kindness that enabled me to walk through my fears and put them away. But most of all, I was so very ready to find another person to share my life with. With this handsome, intelligent, caring man, at the end of a hard day I no longer had to return home to a bleak room and an empty bed. We became lovers.

The month that followed was joyous. We were together at every opportunity. I broke away from the office to meet for lunch, go to a museum, see a movie, take a long walk along the mall. The nights were celebrations. We made love, and afterward I'd sit up at the end of the bed while he lay back against the pillows and we'd read each other the poems that were special to us. The line we loved most was from Tennyson's "Ulysses": "Come my friends, 'tis not too late to seek a newer world." In so brief a span we had truly created our own safe "newer world."

Frank's apartment was home. I could come back and talk about my day, share the intrigues and problems we were wrestling with at the office. Our affair began around the time of the Moratorium's problems with the New Mobe and it was wonderful to have someone with whom to confess my anxieties. He didn't know Sam, Marge, or Hawk. He had no involvement with what I did. It was safe to examine my concerns about the movement or to talk of my exhilaration after the November March. It was so good to have him in my life.

One Friday morning a month or so after we met, Frank had to go away for the weekend on government business. We made love. From the bed, I watched him pack his bags and place his plane tickets in his suit jacket. We made plans to meet for lunch at the Statler Hilton coffee shop on Monday. He leaned down to kiss me good-bye. When he left I showered, locked up his apartment, and went off to mine.

At noon on Monday I walked down the steps of the Statler Hilton coffee shop looking for Frank. He wasn't there so I took a table and waited for him. A few minutes later two men came over and sat down. I was startled. "Frank's not coming," said one, "and we need to talk."

Frank? Who were they to know about Frank? Frank and *me*? Simultaneously the nightmare of Kit surged over me. I was frantic that he had been in an accident. The men smiled, pushed an envelope toward me, and told me to open it. On the table lay photographs of Frank and me having sex.

As I looked up, stunned, they were holding out badges of identification. To this day, I don't know who they were. I was so terrified by the photographs that I didn't have the presence of mind to examine their IDs carefully. They could have been from a government agency; they could even have been from a private group posing as government officials. I will never know. All I wanted was to die. I was drowning in fright. I had trouble breathing and chills went through me. I could not move. I wished they would pull out a gun and shoot me out of my misery.

The men proceeded with deliberation. Their message was simple. They wanted my cooperation in gathering information on the movement. If I did not comply, and promptly, they would send the photographs to my parents and to the press. I sat facing these two nameless men absolutely speechless. My mind did not even know how to process what I was hearing. It jumped from Frank, to my parents, to being laid out in disgrace for all the world to see. My life was over. I just stared at them.

Finally I heard them say, "David? David? Are you listening to us? We will contact you in three days for your answer."

I said in panic, "I don't understand any of this and I can barely hear you. Don't you understand what you are doing to Frank and me? It will destroy us both. It will kill my parents. Don't you understand?"

I heard one of them snicker. "See you in three days," he said, and with that, they got up and left.

An eternity passed. Finally, I stood and went to pay the cashier. She looked at me with concern. "Are you all right?" she asked. "Do you need help?" I mumbled a reply and headed up the steps and out the door. My first thought was to warn Frank. I ran all the way to his apartment. I opened the door and faced totally empty rooms. There was no art, no bookshelves or records, no Neruda or Yeats. All I saw were bare white walls and rugless parquet floors. It was like walking into my own tomb. I went back down in the elevator, and laboring to sound calm asked the doorman what had happened to Frank. He looked at me as if I were mad and said no one had lived in the place for months.

The apartment that had been so full of love and safety and that was home to my sensitive, handsome lover was a mirage. The relationship that I had grown to trust and value more than anything in life was an illusion.

Then it became clear. "Frank" was an agent and I was his assignment.

I went back home to Eighteenth Street and started belting down scotch. It was the beginning of a two-day binge. Hiding away from my roommates, I took acid, drank hugely, and stayed in bed hoping to die. In reaction to the drugs and alcohol, I vomited severely and shook with chills, and my housemate and dear friend Susan Werbe, thinking I had a bad case of the flu, did her best to nurse me and to get me to eat something. Whenever I sobered up enough to appraise my situation I'd be overwhelmed all over again and reach for the bottle under my bed. All I could see ahead was death or eternal shame. If my family, friends, or the press knew of my homosexuality, my life would be destroyed. I would be banned from the Moratorium and I would never work in politics again. My family would disown me. Suicide was the one recurring option. For two days I wrestled with the urge to take my own life.

Then, as the clock ticked away, I started sobering up. I have no idea where the clarity of mind came from to arrive at my decision. Perhaps it was a gift from God. But I realized that whoever the people were who had broken the law by taking the photographs probably couldn't send them to anyone—especially if they were actually government agents. After all, someone was paying Frank to have sex with another man. The two men didn't know me well enough to tell whether I would blow the whistle on them or not. I would turn the tables on them. I made a pact with myself: I would ignore them until and if anyone received the photographs. If that happened I would kill myself.

On the third day they were waiting for me in their car as I walked down Columbia Road. One of them rolled down the window and asked, "Well?" I looked him in the eyes and said, "Send the photos out. I don't care," and walked on down the street. But for months to come, every time the phone rang and one of my housemates said it was my folks, I thought they had just opened the photographs. Their calls turned into a nightmare.

I never saw or heard of Frank again. I have often wondered where he is today.

In December of 1969 Mary McGrory's apartment once again became the site of a "summit" meeting between the Moratorium and the Nixon administration. This time it was Henry Kissinger's turn to reach out to the antiwar leaders. The protests and demonstrations were having a continuing impact on Nixon's famous "Silent Majority" voters, and Kissinger had told Mary that he would like to meet with these "young, well-meaning activists." Being Mary, she promptly offered her home.

Sam Brown, David Hawk, and I trooped off to Woodley Road to meet with Kissinger in quiet. This time there was to be no food and no haircut. Even Mary did not feel like serving the architect of the bombing of North Vietnam. This time we were angry and cynical instead of full of hope. We knew it was our obligation to meet with anyone anywhere in the effort to end the slaughter in Vietnam but we had no expectation that this meeting was anything but window dressing. Kissinger was anxious to be perceived around the liberal academic dinner tables of Cambridge as a closet dove in the Nixon administration. He was meeting with us to strengthen those credentials.

As soon as he walked into Mary's home, my anger surged. There he was smug in his perfectly fitting suit and trademark horn-rimmed glasses, smiling and shaking our hands. It was hard to take—seeing in person the man I had watched nightly on television defending his policy of massive bombing. I respected him even less than others in the administration because he would bomb during the day and be a dove at night. I thought he was dishonest and unprincipled. I was pretty sure Mary sensed how we felt, but being the gracious hostess, she quickly led us into her living room and offered drinks.

Unlike Ehrlichman, Kissinger sat and listened thoughtfully. He reached out and solicited our views on the war. We explained yet again our vehement opposition to his policies and our determination to fight against this awful war with every fiber of our bodies. Sam said firmly, "There is only one answer to this madness, and that is to bring the troops home now. Not next year but now."

"Sam, you know that is not possible," said Kissinger.

I joined in. "Of course it's possible. All that is lacking is political courage and will. Nixon, of all people, can bring them home. Just do it."

Kissinger gave me a patronizing smile and went right on. "I urge restraint on your part. This administration will not tolerate domestic violence or disruption because of the war. I warn you that there are elements in the White House who would welcome the opportunity to take reprisals against any of you if you provide them the excuse."

His statement flung me back into my chair. I knew firsthand what he meant by reprisals. For me it had already happened. I wondered if he had seen the pictures of "Frank" and me, snickered over them with other White House staff members. I was numb.

Hawk jumped in next: "Sir, your policy of Vietnamization of the war is a total failure. It isn't going to work."

"Yes, it is."

"No it isn't. Let's assume that this is one more failed governmental policy around Vietnam. What next? Will you withdraw our troops then?"

"It won't fail. We need no other options."

"But what if it does?"

"It won't." He would not even entertain any alternatives.

Yes, no, yes, no. We were at a stalemate. I hadn't said another word after the mention of reprisals. Kissinger got up, shook our hands, thanked us for "caring." He smiled at Mary, and told her how much the meeting meant to him as he left.

Several people who were at formal dinner parties with him in Georgetown later that week told us he said we were "lightweights with no real understanding of the intricacies of foreign policy." And during the Christmas holidays two years later, when his policy did indeed collapse, Kissinger was to resort to one of the most massive and devastating aerial bombings ever to take place against another nation.

The tension surrounding the "Frank" incident was beginning to take its toll. I was haggard, pale, and exhausted from the lack of sleep. I would beg out of meetings, go back to the house, and sleep through the afternoons. I couldn't eat, and sometimes my hands would start shaking and I'd have to hide them. I walked slowly, like an old man. I lied, telling everyone it was a heart condition brought on by exhaustion from the pace of the Moratorium and the March, and waited for the call that would tell me the "agents" had sent the photographs to my parents.

Suicide was still on my mind. At last, concerned and discovering that I was one of the few among them who had never traveled out of the country, my coworkers decided I needed to get away and bought me an airline ticket to Europe. In many ways, this trip saved my life.

To actually find myself going to Europe was almost beyond belief. I had always thought only the rich went there. When I was a child I read tales of transatlantic crossings on great ocean liners and in my imagination saw them full of elegant men and women dancing to music under crystal chandeliers. Even the stories of the immigrants who were crowded into the fetid bowels of those same ships hadn't destroyed my charmed fantasy. Now here I was, about to fly to places I had only dreamed about. I was so tired I could barely make it onto the plane. All I knew was that I wanted to be far away from the fear.

But when I actually walked off the plane onto English ground, all that began to change. I saw the fabled red double-decker buses at the airport and a thrill went through me. As I traveled into London for the day and night I was to spend there before I went on to Oxford, I looked wide-eyed at historic sites that I'd only seen on postcards from abroad. I felt a surge of energy. I was excited at last.

My first stop was Oxford because I'd cabled Bill Clinton and he urged me to come visit and stay at the Leckford Street house where he and Strobe Talbott and Frank Aller were roommates. The university was magnificent in its weathered Gothic grandeur, but where Bill lived was a down-at-the-heels working-class area of row houses and small backyard gardens, and it was about as bare and worn as any place I've ever seen. The only gathering place was the kitchen. I never felt warm the entire time I stayed there and I rarely left the side of the old gas heater. Strobe was not to be seen, although I could hear the continual clacking of his typewriter. Later I learned that he was in his room translating Khrushchev's memoirs, which were to become a bestseller when they were published.

I met other Americans studying at Oxford through the guys in the Leckford Street house, and we spent night after night in bull sessions, mostly arguing about the war. I don't recall any dissension about opposing it; our debates centered around the issue of violence and the best tactics for ending the slaughter. Many of them, like Aller and David Hawk back home, were defying the draft and were willing to go to jail if they had to. Some were considering becoming expatriates in Canada or Sweden. Bill was usually with us, and we'd often come home from a late-night session in someone else's house and keep on talking until we couldn't see straight.

We spent nights and days together. He was obsessed with his draft status and whether or not to serve in Vietnam. All his peers and many others he greatly respected were still vehemently opposing the war and acting on their belief. I remember one very cold morning when we were the only ones in the house. We huddled around the heater bundled in heavy sweaters and sipping hot tea. "My visit to the Moratorium offices had a real impact on me," he said.

"I didn't realize that. I guess when you're there on a daily basis, you lose track of what it's like for others to see it."

"That's really why I got involved in the demonstration at the embassy. I felt as though I hadn't made a statement against the war. It was an astonishing day. I wish you could have seen it."

"It got great coverage in the States," I told him. "There's nothing like fighting back."

He agreed. "No wonder you've done this for so long," he said.

"Well, we have to. If not us, who else will speak out? You should be proud. You did a good thing."

"It was my first demonstration. I've always been a little afraid of participating in them before."

I could see that Bill's involvement in the embassy protest was a source of much pride. It gave him the credentials that let him feel a part of the great struggle that was consuming his friends. But he was different from us in one respect. He knew it and we knew it. None of us were planning to return to our hometowns and run for office. He still planned to go back to Arkansas, as he had said at the Vineyard, and the way Arkansas felt about the war hadn't changed. He struggled with his dilemma. It still mattered greatly to him that we not disapprove of his spectator status, even as he was planning a future that would not tolerate the kind of stand we had taken.

I really didn't know what to make of all the conflicting emotions I saw in Bill. Indeed, he generated conflicting emotions in me. I liked him immensely. There were moments when he talked about the failure of our policy in Vietnam with such clarity and knowledge and passion that he swept me away. But how to reconcile this with the man who could in the next moment equivocate about what to do because his ambitiousness took the upper hand?

We took long walks through the lush deer meadows around Oxford and talked again about the conflict between the hometown values we had grown up with and the intrusion of the war into our lives. Once Bill turned to me and asked outright, "What would you think of me if I served in Vietnam?"

He had to be feeling very vulnerable then. I said, "Bill, if you believe this is a just war, then I would admire your courage and your conviction. But—I hate to say this—if you believe that the war is wrong, and you were there because you were afraid of offending some people back home and you killed someone, then I would believe you to be a coward."

He was taken aback.

"What if refusing to serve killed all of your dreams?"

"Better the dreams than people."

I saw tears in his eyes. "It's so unfair!" he burst out. "Old men in Washington are stealing our dreams."

There was no doubt he was right: that if he openly refused to serve, it would mean an end to all he aspired to. The bitter truth, as I knew, was that I could more easily refuse service because being a homosexual had already killed my dreams. So even as we bared our souls to each other about our personal struggles to come to terms with Vietnam, never once did I come close to revealing my deepest fears, or the blackmail, or my shaky mental state.

We cemented our friendship in those Oxford days. He valued friendship. He had a compassionate and loving heart. Unlike those of us who were so immersed in the antiwar movement that we rarely thought of what lay ahead, he had committed himself utterly to a vision of his future beyond the war. Each step he plotted took his political plans into consideration. He was struggling to find a way to live in the turbulence of the day while not sacrificing his tomorrow. I could see his ambivalence clearly; I recognized the times when he was indecisive, even weak, and sometimes it troubled me. But ultimately it didn't matter. His intellect and openness and charm won me. I felt very close to him.

Before I left home Shirley MacLaine had made arrangements for me to meet her European representative, Margaret Gardner, and it was Margaret who made the entire European trip memorable. She treated me to wonderful restaurants and arranged for me to meet with some remarkable people—heady indeed for a young man with such a limited knowledge of the world. From Oxford, I went to London to do a series of interviews with Robert MacNeil of the BBC about the antiwar movement. Not at all surprisingly, his questions were informed and pertinent, and I was very glad to have a forum that would allow the world outside our borders to know what was being done.

Then Margaret took me to meet actress Vanessa Redgrave in a dingy office of the Workers Party and we listened to her as she spoke eloquently against our policy in Vietnam. But what I remember most about the encounter is that she could not look us in the face. Her eyes stayed focused on the floor the entire time and her voice was a monotone. It was eerie.

In Paris, Jules Dassin and Melina Mercouri invited me to dinner in their apartment. I was so nervous my hand trembled as I knocked on the door. She stood there, passionate and beautiful, and flung her arms around me with maximum drama shouting, "My brother, how good to have you in our home!" She took me by the arm and introduced me to friends from Greece, then left them to guide me around the elegant apartment, filled with mementos not only of her acting career but her struggle for freedom in her homeland. She dismissed the photographs from Hollywood with a flip of the hand but paused at each item that had to do with the plight of her country. She would caress it as she told me about it, and all the stories centered around someone who had been beaten, jailed, or killed by the Greek Junta. I was enthralled not by the woman I had met on the screen but by this ardent, articulate defender of human rights. As I left, she rumpled my hair. "What would we ever do without the spirit of the young?" she said, and gave me a big kiss.

In Paris, I put on my blue suit to dine with Ambassador and Mrs. Shriver at the elegant American embassy. Sargent Shriver was one of Nixon's most improbable appointments. He was married to Eunice Kennedy, so was the brother-in-law of the man who had defeated Nixon in his first bid for the presidency; had been the first director of the Peace Corps; and was a committed Democrat who would later be McGovern's running mate against Nixon in 1972. Mrs. Shriver greeted me with warm, generous praise for my work against the war and escorted me into a handsome reception room for drinks. Only then did I realize this was a small dinner party in honor of Mrs. Martin Luther King. I was awestruck in her presence—she had spoken and marched with us at the Moratorium and the March but to be with her at so intimate an evening was different. In fact, she and my hosts were so welcoming and gracious that even the array of silver at my table setting did not daunt me. We ended the evening gathered around the piano singing "We Shall Overcome," and I found myself wondering what Nixon would have thought if he'd been a fly on the wall watching us in his embassy.

As I look back on it now, the entire trip was crucial to my survival. Away from Washington I grew stronger because I felt validated. The Moratorium had been covered extensively by the European press and everywhere I went—London, Paris, Amsterdam, Vienna, and Prague—I was treated with respect by the European left because it knew of my work against the war. And just as important, I had time for reflection. During the long train rides between cities I thought about the life I had been living—always on the edge, balanced precariously between my visibility as an activist and my subterranean sexual activity. For the first time, I started to think of leaving Washington. The thought of moving to a safer place was enticing.

When I came back home in February 1970 the Moratorium was struggling with a growing division between the political and the grassroots activists. Marge Sklencar was pressing for a "Fuck the Military" USO-style concert tour of leading leftist entertainers. Sam and I were committed to the 1970 elections, which we wanted to make a referendum on the war. Hawk was immersed in his draft resistance work and his own case, and couldn't understand why we couldn't do everything, why something like the tour and the politics were incompatible.

Inevitably we began to focus on internal disputes about strategy rather than on substantive issues. At times we stopped speaking to each other. We diligently planned several days of protest in the spring, but the heart had gone out of it.

To add to the dissension, Senator Gaylord Nelson and national environmental activist Denis Hayes had called for a major national protest centered around the environment to be held on April 22. This first "Earth Day" was to be an environmental moratorium, with rallies, vigils, and actions. The debut of the environment as a national issue took the steam out of the Moratorium. Whether we liked it or not, students and activists were feeling powerless to alter the administration's unbending Vietnam policies and sought a new outlet for change. We became yesterday's story. As the bitterness toward Earth Day mounted, I set up what I called a summit of the tree-huggers and the peace lovers in our Eighteenth Street house and Sam Brown and Denis Hayes met. It helped. Tensions between the two groups eased somewhat when they got to know and trust one another. But the writing was on the wall.

We organized one last pair of protests: a three-day "Fast for Peace" in April and a day of demonstrations on April 15, income tax day. Although we worked hard, we knew that they would not come close to the visibility or the passion of October. Perhaps the administration knew it too. They were more relaxed with us. On the first of April I received a call from Kissinger's office asking me to come to the White House at once to meet with him and the President, but to keep the invitation a secret. Naturally I went straight in to see Sam. Of course I had to respond to a request from the President, he told me. Still, before I left I called Patsy and told her where I was going. If she didn't hear from me, I instructed her, she was to call the papers. As I walked over to the White House my thoughts alternated between ego and fear. On the one hand, here was the President of the United States wanting my counsel on how to end the war, and on the other, he was going to tell me personally that my worst fear was going to be realized and I was going to be indicted!

Richard Blumenthal greeted me and took me into the West Wing. There he handed me an envelope that Kissinger wanted me to read before the meeting. As I pulled out the "briefing paper" I could see there were only two words, although they were written on White House letterhead. "April Fool!" The White House and the Moratorium laughed their heads off all day long. Our receptionist kept saying, "David, it's the President on the phone, he needs to see you at the White House!" but she'd break up before she got to the end every time. I joined in. I liked being the focus of the fun.

The time had come for the Moratorium to close. Our April protests were mere shadows of our efforts in the fall. We lacked purpose now, and were losing definition as an organization. In our own way, each of us was involved in personalities and our individual egos. Being the good and honest friend that she always is, Marylouise Oates called shortly after the April protests. "Honey, get out," she said.

"What?" I was startled.

"It's time to get out. I don't like the person you are becoming. You care more about what people think of you than the war. Trust me, it's time. You're spending more time at Washington dinner parties than working."

I knew she was right and I hated hearing it. We had not only lost our edge, we had increasingly become part of the Washington establishment—even the White House staff was comfortable participating in an April Fool's joke. In the evenings we went to dinner parties at the home of Washington hostess Barbara Howar or *The New Republic*'s publisher, Gilbert Harrison. Much of the time in the office, we were simply going through the motions.

It also dawned on me that this might provide the opportunity to escape from the blackmail attempt at last.

"What should I do, Marylouise?" I asked. "Where should I go?"

"Anywhere. Just get out of this city. Go out and organize for a peace candidate, work at the grassroots, find a project. It doesn't make any difference. Go."

It was the spark I needed. I thought hard about what she had said, then went into Sam's office and shut the door. There were just the two of us.

"Sam, I think it's time we fold up shop."

Much to my surprise he said, "I know. I've been thinking the same thing myself. How do you think Marge and David will feel?"

"I don't think Hawk will care. He'll always find a way to work against the war. I think Marge will be angry, but she won't have a choice if the three of us decide to close down."

Sam said, "Let's do it."

We took the idea to Hawk and Marge. Marge was adamantly opposed, but I think even she knew that the time had come. Strangely, there was little nostalgia. Only a little over six months ago we had brought the country to a halt and forced the President of the United States to speak to the nation in order to stem our momentum. Now what was left was a shell, and four people anxious to move on with their lives. It was time for other young people with a fresher vision to take over.

A few weeks after the April 15 demonstrations, we held a press conference to officially announce the closing of the Vietnam Moratorium Committee. I still value an editorial that appeared in *The Washington Evening Star*:

> One of the hallmarks of maturity is the ability to recognize when it is time to quit. It is a maturity that does not necessarily come with the passage of years, as the example of Harold Stassen so vividly illustrates.
>
> Four young people who do know when to shut up shop are the leaders of the Vietnam Moratorium Committee.
>
> The four leaders, Sam Brown, David Hawk, David Mixner and Marge Sklencar, have accomplished much of what they set out to do—more, perhaps, than they now realize. It is to be hoped that the meteoric rise and decline of the Moratorium has not left any of them embittered to the point of giving up on the system they fought so hard to convert to their point of view. America needs them, and others like them, to keep its conscience exercised and alert.

CHAPTER SEVEN

Precipice

THE first years of the seventies were my wilderness years. I had no base. I knew I was embarking on a search for the freedom to be myself, and by the end of the decade I would emerge from the turbulent journey openly gay and happy. But turbulent it was, and when I left Washington I had no idea what I would be doing or where. My only strategy was to keep moving.

I headed to New York first. Dick Ottinger was seeking the Democratic nomination for senator, and the antiwar forces were split between him and moderate Republican Charles Goodell. Dick respected my political skills, and I went to work for his campaign. Having one of the former coordinators of the Moratorium on his side gave him an added boost with the liberal New York Democratic Party.

The war was at the forefront of everyone's mind that spring, for on April 29, on President Nixon's orders, American troops invaded Cambodia, students rose in protest, and in the next two weeks four students were killed by National Guardsmen at Kent State University in Ohio and two by state police at Jackson State in Mississippi. The war had erupted at last on our own streets. Enormous demonstrations broke out on campuses across the country protesting the invasion and in shock at the deaths.

In New York there was one mass demonstration after another—candlelight services, vigils, rallies on Wall Street, marches by students, medical personnel, and religious leaders. At the end of the week, I flew to Washington, where Sam and I joined a small group of ministers, teachers, and activists kneeling in prayer in front of the northwest driveway of the White House in protest of the Cambodian invasion. We were herded into a van, handcuffed, and driven to a police station in Northwest Washington, where we sat in the stifling van for several hours before we were booked. Betty Anne Ottinger had been going from one precinct station to another bailing out old Moratorium staffers. She greeted us when we emerged from the back of the station: "Boys, next time please let me know what jail you're arrested in so I don't have to run all over the city looking for you all!"

Dick won the primary in June and began to prepare for the general election, but I was too restless to stay on. I headed west to Colorado, where Michael Driver was the campaign manager for a Democratic primary race that was a test of the peace movement's strength in the party. Colorado had long been dominated by Republicans and conservative Democrats, but it was beginning to attract activists from around the country who had burned out on protests and were looking for a more tranquil setting. There was reason to hope these new arrivals, united by a populist domestic agenda and a peace platform, could change the old balance.

I saw Colorado as a fresh start. I could choose those issues and individuals I believed in away from the infighting of Washington politics. I was lucky to find myself working with an extraordinary group of young antiwar insurgents, including Pat Schroeder, Gary Hart, and Tim Wirth, in Mike's campaign for Craig Barnes, a young Denver lawyer. Barnes won the primary by a bare thirty votes, and although he lost the general election, we were not discouraged. There would be another chance two years hence, and work to do before then.

Barnes and I and Paul Herzmark, a young Texan, organized a populist attack on the Colorado establishment with strong support from Common Cause's John Gardner. We formed Colorado Project/Common Cause and focused on three populist issues to mobilize grassroots support: legislative reform, insurance reform, and a fight against public utility rate increases. We researched the abuses of the legislature and utility companies and exposed them to the public. We organized hundreds of volunteers at the local level and succeeded in creating a coalition of farmers, labor, students, and environmentalists—a genuinely populist mix—and placed four initiatives on the 1972 ballot aimed at reform.

We were also determined to regain the Denver congressional seat that Barnes hadn't been able to capture, but if we were to do that we needed to offer the voters a clear choice and something truly different. Colorado had never elected a woman to the United States Congress. There was one logical choice—Denver attorney and activist Pat Schroeder. Her husband, State Representative Jim Schroeder, had initially considered the race but decided against it. One night, several of us paid the Schroeders a visit. We sat around the kitchen table in their Denver home and urged Pat to run. She was reluctant at first, but Jim joined in and she was persuaded. She liked the idea of being Colorado's first woman congressperson. We toasted her courage.

In 1972, in a year when Nixon and Agnew were reelected in a landslide, defeating the principled George McGovern, we were able to provide liberals with some of the little good news there was. Pat Schroeder won her race, and went on to become one of the House's most distinguished and outspoken members. We lost on utilities and insurance reform, but won our very important legislative reform package. Our dream of changing Colorado from a conservative Republican state to a young Democratic one was starting to come true.

Still, despite all my activities in Colorado and the terrific people I was working with, I didn't think of it as home and I never did have a permanent home in those years. In fact, my Colorado friends were never quite sure where to find me. I entered into a series of consulting contracts to earn enough money to keep myself alive and they took me to other places around the country. One of these assignments lasted a year, and sent me to Hartford, Connecticut, for the noted urban developer Jim Rouse. In 1972 Rouse started the "Greater Hartford Project" to renew the entire metropolitan area, and he offered me a job organizing citizen support for the innovative programs that the project was recommending to the local governments. I took it, and I learned a great deal about the complex workings of a major metropolitan area and the difficulties of governing a diverse group of citizens.

I also got to learn a great deal about New York City. Although I had often been there for political reasons, this was the first time I was able to explore it on my own. I'd head for the city almost every weekend, and I

found it magical. I walked for hours along the carnival streets of Greenwich Village looking at the eccentrics who peopled them, marveling at
the street life. I couldn't stop staring at gay and lesbian couples openly
holding hands. Through ads in *The Village Voice*, I figured out where to
find other gay men. I still wasn't at the point where I could be honest
about myself in these liaisons, but they were highly pleasurable. Then,
when Sunday rolled around, I boarded the train back to Hartford and
resumed my straight identity. I was still living two lives.

I visited Los Angeles too. Shirley MacLaine introduced me to her
friends in the entertainment industry. A number of them were gay, and
although I was still not out to Shirley, I'd listen as they chatted and
before long I had a road map of where to go in gay Los Angeles. Then
I'd fly back to Denver or Hartford and turn into a different man. Appar-
ently it never occurred to people in any of these places that I should have
a love life. I often wondered what they thought I did at night. When I
came out of the closet later, they all expressed surprise that I was gay.
What did they think I was?

When the Rouse job ended in 1973 I went back to Colorado. I had a
wonderful personal tie there now. Patsy had come there to live. Several
years earlier she had given up nursing in Baltimore to devote full time to
reform politics. She ran insurgent campaigns, became an expert organizer, and helped elect several reform candidates to office. Then in 1972,
when her marriage broke up, she decided to become an "advance person" for the McGovern for President campaign. She wound up working
for the campaign in Texas, where Bill Clinton was directing the statewide McGovern campaign; and after McGovern's huge loss in November she moved to Colorado to take a job running Lieutenant Governor
Mark Hogan's campaign for governor. We were both absolutely elated
to be close at hand after so long.

Colorado was a hotbed of political activism when I returned. The
1974 elections were looming. Gary Hart came back from running the
McGovern presidential campaign and was seeking a Senate seat. Reformers Dick Lamm and Mark Hogan were vying for governor. Tim
Wirth was running for Congress from a Denver suburb and Sam Brown
was seeking to become state treasurer. The entire state was jumping.

But I didn't head into politics when I got back. Instead, I went to
work with Marian Wright Edelman, the remarkable, heroic African-
American woman who founded and heads the Children's Defense Fund.
Trained as a lawyer, and a worker for civil rights since the 1960s, Marian

had established the Fund to protect the rights and answer the needs of poor children, and today it has grown into one of the most powerful advocacy organizations in the country. I had first met her when her husband, Peter, was working for Senator Robert Kennedy, and I often visited them when I was in Hartford and they were in Boston, where Peter's work had taken them then.

I was to open a low overhead office in Denver for the Children's Defense Fund. It was conducting several major surveys on the status of poor children in America in order to create legislation to protect them from abuse and neglect. I found it exciting to be involved in so worthwhile a project at first; but I soon discovered something about myself. I simply wasn't good at this kind of systematic, academically rigorous research. I didn't have the skills, the aptitude, or the patience for it. I hadn't expected this—after all, my political organizing required enormous attention to detail. But I could not shift those skills to this type of work. I knew both instinctively and practically how to work a precinct, but I had no idea how to structure and conduct the kind of survey necessary in academic and legislative circles. With much graciousness, Marian let me off the hook and found others to continue the work of the CDF in the Denver area.

That November, Richard Lamm was elected governor, Gary Hart a senator, Tim Wirth a congressman, and Sam Brown state treasurer. A clean sweep. Four years of intensive organizing changed a solidly Republican state into a bastion of progressive Democratic politics. The results surpassed our dreams.

But while I shared the exhilaration I had no desire to work for any of our victors in Colorado. I wanted to build a life of my own. My future brother-in-law, Michael Annison, asked me to join him in the Rocky Mountain Federation of States, an organization headed by the region's governors whose purpose was to promote their common economic interests. Michael wanted me to serve as liaison between the governors and members of Congress, and to travel to states outside the region to explore innovative programs their governors were attempting.

I traveled for the Federation through much of 1975, meeting key political leaders who could be helpful to its agenda. It was interesting work, and it had the additional advantage of sometimes taking me to cities where I was not known, so that I could have anonymous encounters that would not jeopardize my identity.

That spring I went south for the Federation to meet with some key political leaders. One of them was Jimmy Carter, who invited me to spend several days with him and Mrs. Carter in the governor's mansion in Atlanta. The family was in a second-floor sitting room when I arrived. The governor had just come back from duck hunting and was walking around in his hunting pants, without a shirt. Rosalynn Carter was sitting cross-legged on the floor sewing needlepoint and Miss Lillian, Carter's wonderful, feisty mother, sat in a chair, her presence dominating the room. I felt as if I had just walked into a Norman Rockwell *Saturday Evening Post* cover.

I was curiously uncomfortable throughout the visit. The Carters were gracious hosts who did everything possible to make me feel at home but I had a hard time relating to their rather sanctimonious style. They were so sure of their views that it left very little room for dialogue. When we talked about the possibility of a pardon for those who had fled to Canada in order to avoid serving in Vietnam, Carter spoke with the crisp assurance of an engineer who had a job to do. He seemed just as impervious to the tangled emotions of those who had left a country and families they loved for reasons of principle as he was to the anger of those who had served and wanted no amnesty for those who had not. That may not have been a fair assessment, given that, in fact, he did courageously issue a pardon in the very first month of his presidency. But the Carters' righteousness got to me, it was so unremitting.

I think what bothered me most was how much they reminded me of my neighbors in southern New Jersey: also so sure of that righteousness. By the time I left I realized I had been invited to court me for the upcoming 1976 presidential race, and to tap into my network of contacts. That was perfectly standard political practice, but it too put me off. In both the 1976 and 1980 Democratic presidential primaries I would support other candidates.

Very gradually, I started to make gay and lesbian friends. When I visited Washington, I became friendly with a young and very closeted attorney who arranged several dinner parties for me to meet other closeted political and successful gay men. Now that I was no longer in the very public kind of role I'd had in the Moratorium, I could start being more honest with other gay and lesbian people who seemed "safe." My criterion of safe was simple: They had just as much to lose as I did if their homosexuality was exposed. It was these dinner parties that began to teach me about how to function safely as a gay person in a very straight world.

But learning how to handle myself on the outside did nothing to resolve my internal confusion. It didn't matter that these people I was meeting in Washington were healthy, successful, contributing citizens who seemed to be in reasonable charge of their lives; that the gay and lesbian couples I saw on the streets of Greenwich Village looked happy in their togetherness. I was still a prisoner of the definition of homosexuality that I had found in my high school library. I believed deep within that I was a pervert, even mentally ill. I knew the people I was encountering in my new world were neither perverts nor psychiatric cases, but it didn't help. Angry, hurting, ashamed, and thoroughly mixed up, I finally sought the help of a psychiatrist when I went back to Denver.

For several weeks I spent therapy hours with Dr. Kelly. I talked with him about family issues, my childhood, the pressure of politics, my doubts about my academic skills—everything but my gayness. Then one day as I sat in his office in a high-rise building overlooking the Rockies, he said, "David. You know and I know that you are not telling me the truth. It's time to come to terms with your pain. What is the problem?"

I stared at him. I shifted my gaze to the floor. When the silence became too much, I stuttered, "I think I am a homosexual."

It was the first time in my life I had shared this with a straight person. I started to weep.

"Look out the window, David. Has the traffic stopped? Has the world stopped spinning? Has God created a thunderstorm with this news?" His voice was matter-of-fact. "No, the world continues. It is not earth-stopping news. Let's get to work so this can be a healthy part of your life."

I had truly expected when I spoke up that he would institutionalize me. It was another step, and an enormously important one, in the long, difficult process of coming out.

Shirley MacLaine was the next person with whom I shared my secret. It came out one night when I was having dinner with her and New York writer Pete Hamill and was pushing my food around on the plate, barely able to swallow. "Mixner, what's wrong with you tonight?" Pete asked. "You're not eating and you're not your upbeat self."

I looked at the two of them and said, "I am gay."

The sky did not fall in this time either. I saw no revulsion on their faces, just caring and affection. They were great. By the time she was clearing the table, Shirley was busy running through a list of friends who could arrange a date for me. I blushed and Pete laughed kindly at my discomfort.

Shirley was insistent that I get away from the constraints of Colorado and head to California, where I could explore my sexuality without worrying about friends and family. In fact, she and Pete had some work for me: helping them research a potential movie project about Amelia Earhart they were working on. I could live in her house in Los Angeles while I was there. I discovered I could breathe again. I could hardly believe it. I had told three people the truth and they had given me nothing but support.

Throughout the fall of 1975 and much of 1976, Shirley's Encino home became my base. It was a calming place to be, nestled in the hills of the Santa Monica mountains, surrounded by flowering plants, shade trees, and a view of the San Fernando Valley below. Inside I looked at the reminders of what she had achieved—certificates of her Oscar and Golden Globe nominations hung on the walls—and thought for the first time about making my own mark instead of always operating in group efforts and behind the scenes.

I found part-time work to supplement the film project and keep me going while I sorted through my life, traveling back and forth between Los Angeles, Washington, and San Francisco and coming back to Encino when it was done. I had a consulting contract with the liberal Energy Action Committee, which was attempting to break up the major oil companies, that took me all over the country building grassroots and media support for divestiture legislation in Congress. I also contracted with political fund-raiser Lori Horne to help her efforts in San Francisco—and that was the place where I finally began to come seriously to terms with the burden of keeping my gayness under wraps.

San Francisco had become a place of liberation for American homosexuals. Many thousands of them had flocked to the more accepting atmosphere of the city from their homes in the American heartland. The thriving Castro District at the end of Market Street had become a "Gay Ghetto," teeming with gay- and lesbian-owned businesses, bars, discos, and bookstores. The project with Lori Horne took several months, and I rented an apartment right in the Castro District.

It was an expansive time for me. When I first came to San Francisco, a camera shop owner named Harvey Milk was busy organizing the community into a political force, efforts that would eventually lead to his election to the San Francisco Board of Supervisors. I went to some of these meetings. I listened to lectures on the history of the gay and lesbian community. I met successful, openly gay people. One such person was physician Tom Waddell, a former Olympic athlete who later founded the Gay Games. He and his lover, Charles, took me under their wing and made me welcome in their house on Albion Street. It was an enormous place, whose cavernous interior was a vast hall with a stage at one end and a kitchen and dining room at the other. Night after night it was home to artists, writers, politicians, and professionals of every stripe, who gathered around the table to argue over the future of the gay and lesbian movement. On weekends there were poetry readings, chamber music, folksingers, even small stage productions—all with gay performers.

It was in their home, and in the city itself, that I discovered a positive and thriving gay and lesbian world. For the first time in my life, I realized that I had a history, that other brave and lonely individuals had paved the way for people like myself. As my knowledge of my community grew, so did my anger for all the years of hiding and pain. For almost twenty years, fear had separated me from my own. To realize that there was no logical basis for all that pain was almost unendurable.

I knew it was impossible for me to remain in the closet any longer. I could not justify working for the rights of others without fighting for myself. It was in San Francisco that I first saw gays and lesbians actively resisting the hatred of people like them. It made me ashamed that I was not doing my share. But I recognized that I could not join them unless I first had the courage to tell my family who I was.

In 1976 there were no support groups for families, no articles in newspapers and magazines, no active political players who had come out of the closet. I would tell my family but I decided I would remain closeted professionally. In January I wrote my first letter, to Patsy:

> From what I was told by Dr. Kelly and by the Counseling Center here, you might have two reactions. One is to feel sorry for me. I cannot stress how unnecessary that is. I only feel sorry for my lack of courage in the past, and for wasting so much time because of the pressures of society. For the last year, I have known freedom I didn't know was possible, and for the first time I have started to live.
>
> Second, it is natural and reasonable for you to be concerned about what others say. That's a tough one, which I am still dealing with. Rest assured I have no intention of being a gay martyr or sending out announcements. I have just recovered my personal life and have no intention of surrendering it again. But I will also be living here and elsewhere as a gay person. I intend to keep it as private as possible but I would be kidding you if a lot of

people we know in common didn't eventually know about me. I am sorry you are dragged into something you can't control, but it was a choice of life or death for me. I have chosen to live.

Patsy and her husband Michael were instantly and wholly loving and supportive, but they were very concerned about my telling Mom and Dad. Patsy was afraid they couldn't handle it. I understood what she was saying—I was worried about it too—and we talked about it over and over. But in the end she recognized that I had to for my own well-being. Still, it was many more months before I could muster up the courage to write that letter. The possibility that I might lose them was shattering. Here is some of what I wrote:

Dear Mom and Dad,

This is the most difficult and most important letter of my life. It will be the same for you. I wish there was an easier way to tell you this but I can think of none. Please make an effort to finish this letter and to understand.

I am a homosexual (gay) and have been all my life. I know this is a shock and will cause you great sorrow. I write to tell you for several reasons. One, I love you both more than I love anything in the world. I couldn't stand the thought of lying to you any longer, or that the two people who mean the most to me would never know who I am. Second, for the first time in my life, I have found happiness and a peace with myself and I could not imagine not sharing it with you both. Third, I am being more open about it, and I wanted you to hear from me and not someone or somewhere else.

I am the same son who you have known all your lives. Nothing has changed except that I am now putting incredible faith in your love, and sharing everything with you. . . .

I know this will knock the wind out of your sails. I have dreaded writing this letter all my life. I don't expect you to approve or even to understand right away. I know it is a world unknown to you.

Please don't feel you have to respond either positively or negatively right away. This is why I have chosen to write instead of calling. Take what time you need to think this through. Call and talk to Patsy and Mike. Do what you have to do—feel what you have to feel.

I don't know what else to say. I understand how hard this is for you. I have so much to share with you, to show and to learn from you yet. There is a South American poet called Neruda and one of his poems ends this way—and it is how I will end this letter:

Laugh at the night,
at the day, at the moon,
laugh at the twisted
streets of this island,
laugh at this clumsy
boy who loves you,
but when I open
my eyes and close them,
when my steps return,
deny me bread, air,
light, spring,
but never your laughter,
for I would die.

I will love you always and will always be your son.

David

The days after I sent the letter were the longest wait in my life. I wasn't sure I would even hear from them. Finally, the phone rang. They were both on the line.

Mom was crying hard. "How could you do this?" she asked. "What you are doing is a sin against God. It is the lowest you can sink to. We didn't raise you this way."

With my own voice quavering, I said, "Mom, it has taken me a long time to reach this point. I am proud of who I am. It is not bad."

She was shouting now. "You *can't* be proud! It is dirty and wrong! You need help. Dad and I will pay for whatever help you need."

"I've been to a therapist," I told her. "I am getting help. I do understand how you feel—he said you would need time." All I wanted to do was weep.

"He's no therapist. He must be one of them." It was my father, speaking for the first time and the last.

"Dad, he isn't one of *them*. *I* am one of *them*."

Between sobs Mom said, "Your life is over if you continue this path. No one will want anything to do with you. Your friends will be ashamed. Your political career will be over. You'll be forced to live in shame and disgrace for the rest of your life."

"Mom, I've already told some of my friends."

"Oh, my God!" she cried. "You aren't telling other people, are you?"

"Yes I am. Listen, you need time. It has taken me thirty years to accept this in myself. I don't expect you to do it in thirty seconds."

"Time will never ever make me understand this," my mother answered. "Your daddy and I love you and we always will, but never, never, *never* will we ever accept this—it is *wrong!*"

I went into my bedroom, threw myself on my bed, and broke down uncontrollably. When I called Patsy at last, she had spoken to them and was in tears herself. She had promised to help them through it, but she acknowledged it would be tough. My mother would eventually come to terms with it, although it took a long time. It took my father nineteen years. Not until his doctor finally explained to him that it wasn't a life choice—that his son was born a homosexual—did he understand and accept my gayness. I grieve for all those years we lost.

For many months, I internalized my anger, fear, and hurt. It helped greatly that I had Tom Waddell when it became too much to bear—he and Charles stood by me, and he was a loving force. It had taken me thirty years to come to terms with my homosexuality, he kept reminding me, I should not expect my parents to accept it in thirty seconds or even thirty months. And it also helped to be able to throw myself into the world of gay and lesbian activism that I found in my new community. I volunteered to walk precincts for Harvey Milk's organization, to work on fund-raisers, and to help Tom and Charles organize their weekend evenings. On my own I threw myself into the sexual abandon of the gay male world of San Francisco, from the bathhouses where everyone engaged in open sex to the bars with their back rooms for sexual explorations. I frequented them all. I relished the freedom and the anonymity. Intimacy was still dangerous—I recognized I still had plenty of confusions about my identity—but to be a part of this wonderful wildness was enough.

One of my projects in San Francisco was to assist antiwar activist Tom Hayden in his Democratic primary campaign against United States Senator John Tunney. Hayden lost, but a leader of Tunney's campaign, who had been watching my work, asked me to help Tunney in the November election, and impressed by my organizing skills, then suggested I go to Los Angeles to meet Mayor Tom Bradley. Bradley was the first black American to have been elected mayor of a predominantly white large American city, and while he was widely admired and had a broad base of support for reelection to a second term, he was taking nothing for granted.

We met in Bradley's office in City Hall and it was clear I was being considered for the role of campaign manager. He asked me about my work in the Moratorium and the Energy Action Committee, my political activities in Colorado, and my fund-raising abilities. He had obviously been briefed about me beforehand, and to my very great satisfaction I got the job. I packed my bags and headed south.

Before I left San Francisco, Tom Waddell gave me the name and number of the mayor's openly gay liaison to the gay and lesbian community, Bill Carey. Carey was especially pleased to have me there. Even though I was still in the closet politically, he thought I could be helpful to the community by building access to the mayor's campaign.

Bill hosted a brunch for me to meet a small group of professional and politically involved gay men at Butterfield's restaurant. It was a day that changed my life. A tall, handsome man with jet-black hair and a black mustache walked toward our table and sat down next to me. His name was Peter Scott, and within minutes we realized what had happened. Over the next twelve years, Peter was to become the most important person in my life: best friend, intimate, business partner, companion. That day, all I knew was that instant intense connectedness.

Peter was the informal leader of the group. He had organized it a year or so before as a combination encounter group and an activist organization. Most of the participants were just coming out, and it helped to share their fears and concerns. They had called themselves Orian at first, a name with no special meaning, but when they emerged in short order as the nation's first openly gay and lesbian PAC—political action committee—the group changed its name to MECLA: the Municipal Elections Committee of Los Angeles. They were looking for ways to become involved in the Los Angeles political scene.

In 1976 most candidates resisted that kind of involvement. They returned money they received from openly gay or lesbian groups and individuals. Most gays and lesbians were just as reluctant to contribute to an openly homosexual political cause or organization like MECLA because the law required that contributors' names appear on a campaign disclosure list. The world at large would assume they were homosexual themselves, and that was a dangerous implication. At the very least, they risked losing their jobs. When MECLA hosted small dinner parties in the Hollywood Hills and asked their guests to give money to the PAC, most of the guests wrote checks for ninety-nine dollars—one hundred meant they would have to go on the disclosure list. A hundred-dollar check was considered a significant victory and five hundred a major one. I went to many of these "closed" dinner parties and sometimes spoke at them, although my presence was always unofficial since it was unheard of for the campaign manager for the mayor of Los Angeles to attend events like these.

But I was convinced it was time to legitimize a PAC like MECLA and I set out to do just that. I met in quiet with their leaders and suggested a strategy that in the end would give MECLA real credibility in the political world. The president of the Los Angeles City Council, John Gibson, was notoriously anti-gay. He represented the largely blue-collar harbor area of the city, and for years he had used his position in the council to vent his homophobia. Like Bradley, he too was up for reelection in 1977 and had no serious opposition. The only pro-gay candidate on the ballot running against him came from the fringe Peace and Freedom Party.

We met in the back room of the Carriage Trade restaurant to discuss the problem of Gibson. The mood was gloomy. We knew that if he was reelected, there was no hope of getting a gay and lesbian civil rights bill for the city of Los Angeles. We weren't protected now. I had a weird proposal, so I felt a little silly when I spoke up.

"Listen, guys, I have a suggestion that's going to seem out in left field but hear me out."

"Oh, God," said Peter. "Mixner's going to get us into trouble!"

"Here goes. We can't defeat Gibson because there is no opposition. It's impossible to launch a write-in campaign with the time we have left and our limited funds. But what we might try is to cripple him in the election so he looks less powerful. That would lose him the council presidency, and if he's just an ordinary member he won't be able to block our legislation."

"How in the hell are we going to do that?" someone asked.

"Why don't we take five thousand dollars and give it to the Peace and Freedom candidate?" I said. "That'll be a huge amount of money for him, and Gibson will be totally ignoring a fringe party like that. If we work it right, the Peace and Freedom guy can pull a sneak attack on Gibson and get a large enough vote to embarrass him politically and cost him his power in the council."

Another member looked at me as if I were nuts. "You really mean you want us to give five thousand dollars to the Peace and Freedom Party? How do we explain it to our contributors? Most of them don't even know what it is and those that do think it's some sort of lefty craziness. Are you serious?"

"I'm dead serious. Look, political reputations are made and broken by daring action. This man is hurting us. We have the five thousand. If we succeed we'll have a victory to boast about and if we fail we'll eat shit.

That's the risk. But I can't think of any other way to do damage to that man. Anyone else have any suggestions?"

"Hell, what do we have to lose?" another guy pointed out. "Half the council is scared to death of us. If we pull this off they'll still be scared of us—but not because we're gay, because we can hurt them in a district where there aren't any homosexuals. I say let's give it a try."

By a narrow margin the group voted to give the money to the Peace and Freedom candidate and we sat down to work out a detailed strategy against Gibson. On election day the Peace and Freedom Party won nearly one-third of the vote, in a stunning display of political weakness on Gibson's part that cost him the presidency of the Los Angeles City Council. I was exhilarated by this outcome, which put MECLA on the map in the Los Angeles political scene and made me a part of the emerging gay and lesbian movement in Los Angeles. People in MECLA became friends, and the city itself was beginning to feel like home. Besides, there was Peter. We were still feeling our way into a very complicated relationship, but I knew he was the one I had been waiting for.

An ugly specter of backlash had begun to show itself in Dade County, Florida. By now, there had been enough progress in certain parts of the country, and increasing numbers of gays and lesbians coming out of the closet and starting to organize, for some optimism among homosexuals. But in reaction to this progress, religious fundamentalists, forerunners of the Christian Coalition, surfaced with homophobic messages targeting the homosexual rights laws in a number of cities. Dade County, where Miami is located, had added sexual orientation to its local civil rights ordinance protecting minorities from discrimination; and Anita Bryant, a former Miss America finalist and singer, spearheaded a campaign to place an initiative on the ballot in the spring 1977 election that would delete protection for gays and lesbians from the ordinance.

Bryant's visibility was enormous, so her campaign drew national attention. She played to the worst fears of the unsophisticated voter, charging the ordinance encouraged child molestation and rampant sexuality in the schools. A lot of money poured into Miami in an effort to defeat her hate-filled campaign, but the scaremongering tactics worked. On election day the initiative won by a margin of two to one.

The impact of her victory left us stunned. The vote encouraged demagogues everywhere to build their political careers on our backs. It did not take long for the apostles of hate to win similar initiative victories in cities like St. Paul, Wichita, and Eugene. And, of very great importance in personal terms, Bryant's campaign added fuel to the self-hatred that so many of us still felt for being homosexual. However encouraging we found the emergence of some political clout, however satisfying those of us fortunate enough to belong to a gay and lesbian community felt within its confines, most of us were still wrestling with the difficulties of accepting our identity. Whatever confidence we had achieved was badly shaken.

As Bryant's hate-filled campaign revealed itself I began to fall apart. I was living an incessant juggling act. I had no idea where I belonged. Some of my family and friends knew of my gayness. Most of my political and professional friends did not and I was still afraid to reveal myself to them. At that time, the homosexual community still had respect for the closet, and it was possible to be visible inside the community without revealing your orientation to the heterosexual world. But the tension was unendurable. I felt as though I were hanging alone out in space. There was no place to land.

The pressures grew too great. Throughout the Bradley campaign my mental condition deteriorated. The municipal elections were to be held in April of 1977, and starting in early February I began to feel out of control. The first outward symptom came without warning, when I turned to a coworker in the campaign and blurted out that I had cancer. I had nothing of the sort. The news of my "illness" spread throughout the campaign and I did nothing to dispel it. In fact, I wished it were true and I could die. At night I would go back alone to the Royal Oaks Motel where I was living, shut the door, and break down in tears. In the morning I would get up, shower, put on my blue suit, and drive to the headquarters as if nothing were wrong. For most of the campaign I was able to perform my duties and perform them well. But eventually I reached the end of my emotional tether. I was losing my ability to spin out the lie about the illness any longer. I was afraid and I didn't know where to turn.

By then the leadership circle around the mayor recognized that I was under severe mental stress, not physically ill. When they approached me about it, I'd become indignant, continue the lie, and give them elaborate details of doctors and hospitals where I was being treated. But I was barely able to hold on, and by the election, which Bradley won soundly, I had completely unraveled.

Shirley MacLaine and Peter Scott took charge. Shirley was out of town on location, but she kept in touch on my condition through Peter and had me moved out of the Royal Oaks into her Malibu home by the ocean, which she thought would help soothe me. I lay in bed all day, crying and sleeping, too deeply depressed to eat. In my mind I became hostage to repeated visions of my parents' shame. I replayed the blackmail attempt and saw myself banished from political work forever. Most nights Peter brought me food and stayed with me. On those nights when I was alone, I would secretly take acid, which I foolishly hoped would let me escape from the torment but only made matters worse. I hallucinated horrible images of being hauled into court, tried for disgracing and betraying my family and friends, and being sentenced to live forever in a desert, alone and abandoned. I would end up screaming into the dark, begging God to take me and end the pain.

It was clear that I urgently needed professional help. Shirley called her friends in the medical community for recommendations—she wanted a psychiatrist who was "gay positive" since there were still many practicing psychiatrists who viewed homosexuality as a mental illness. She chose Dr. Klaus Hoppe at the Hacker Clinic in Beverly Hills, and paid for my initial visits so that I could begin treatment immediately. Dr. Hoppe put me on heavy sedatives to ease me back into some degree of control. I slept almost around the clock. Once I was able to function a little better I went to see him daily. Peter came every day. "David, honey, pull it together," he'd encourage me. "Come on. Give it a try. We need you. I need you. The community needs you. You are a gift to us. Don't hide out in that head of yours—come back to us."

I had done everything possible to hide the breakdown from Patsy and Michael and for a while I was able to pull myself together enough to be convincing on the phone. But she grew suspicious. One May morning she asked me, "David, are you okay?"

"Sure, I'm fine," I said, my voice choking.

"Stop it. I need to know. I'm worried. Are you all right? Do you need me to come out there?"

My facade cracked. I began to cry and I couldn't stop. "Patsy, I'm in real trouble," I told her between sobs. "I don't know if I can make it. Can you help me? I'm losing my mind."

She was there with Michael the next morning. They moved me from the Malibu house back into the Royal Oaks Motel so I would be closer to the Hacker Clinic; Patsy didn't like the idea of my having to drive so far in my state of mind. She and Michael had the room next door and she'd hold me at night when I cried uncontrollably and stay with me during the day. Not until she was certain I was going to make it did she go back to Denver, and even then she came back and forth to keep watch over me.

Sedatives at night enabled me to get some rest, and gradually the sessions with Dr. Hoppe began to bring me back to some level of functioning. I was utterly honest with him about my shame and my sense of limbo and my fears of failure and abandonment. By the end of May, thanks to therapy and my loving circle of Peter and Shirley, Patsy and Michael, I was making progress. The sobbing had mostly stopped, I was eating regularly, and Peter was picking me up for dinner or a movie. But I was quite sure my political career was over. News of my breakdown spread. Clearly, people had reason to be concerned. Politics is demanding—you have to be able to think quickly, act intelligently, and respond decisively to a crisis. The state of my mental health did nothing to reassure people that I still had this capacity. I didn't know myself.

Moreover, politics can be cruel. There are plenty of people who can't resist kicking someone when he's down in order to build up their own political clout. Sometimes it works. More often than not it doesn't, either because they're shooting a corpse one more time or because the corpse proves to be a live body who's provoked into regaining power just to prove them wrong. In early June Peter took me to a political dinner, one of my first ventures out in company since the breakdown. I didn't want to go but he insisted. When I entered the ballroom of the Beverly Wilshire, most people were warm and generous and glad to see me back. But as we worked our way through the cocktail reception, I overheard a hushed conversation behind me.

"Yeah, that's David Mixner. He's crazy as a loon, you know."

"Really?"

"Yep, he went over the hill—bonkers, nutcase. I'm surprised to see him here. He shouldn't be here—it makes us all uncomfortable. He's done for politically. Stay away from him."

I turned to look at the person pronouncing me a nutcase and found myself face-to-face with a man to whom I had been extremely helpful in the Bradley campaign. I'd not only cleaned up a huge political mistake he had made, I'd protected him. I was in shock. Unaware I had overheard him, he saw me, gave me a great big bear hug, and said, "David! It's great to see you out. I've been so anxious about you."

I kept my face composed as I answered, "You ungrateful son of a bitch. I will never forget what you just said. I'm recovering and I'll be back and you'll be the first to know."

The guy looked stricken and disappeared into the crowd. Peter started to laugh. "Now that's the Mixner I know," he said. "Welcome back."

What I'd heard hit close to home. I am a stubborn man. I give no one the power to write me off or determine my future. This was just the boost I needed. I was damaged goods but I knew I wasn't dead. It was up to me to make the repairs and get on with my life. The breakdown had slowed Peter's and my evolving relationship and sorting out who we were to each other. The intimacy we felt when we first met went into suspension when he became my devoted caretaker during these months. I wanted to get it back. I wanted to work again. There was a lot to be done.

I had no car and no home and Peter called David Goodstein, who owned the gay magazine *The Advocate*, and asked whether any of his friends could offer me shelter for a month while I got on my feet again. Together they found me a place to stay and a car to use. Peter kept pressing me back into the real world, insisting I go to lunch, to MECLA meetings, and to parties. Patsy phoned two or three times a day. Shirley called from the road.

Coming up from the abyss, I realized I was beginning to discover a self I had never known. I didn't have to hate myself for being a homosexual. I was a person of value. I was ready to not only pronounce myself a gay man but to start living as one.

CHAPTER EIGHT

Good Times A-Coming

IN many ways the nervous breakdown was liberating for me. Until then, despite San Francisco, despite MECLA, I had been able to evade my gayness by refusing to deal with it on an intimate scale, not acknowledging at a human level: "I am one of you." I had avoided the reality of being homosexual by throwing myself into the politics and not the substance. And most importantly, I had avoided dealing with the basic issue of intimacy and my love for Peter.

Peter and I never did stop struggling to define our relationship with each other. Being together was a source of joy and excitement mixed with anger and confusion. Ironically, the same Peter who nursed me back to mental health was himself tormented by his gayness. Not until years later could he bring himself to tell his family he was gay. He too struggled with intimacy, because to love a man too closely meant he truly was a homosexual. In those times, it was not unusual even for open gays and lesbians to work desperately to sustain some of their psychic closet, to hold on to denial and to be filled with their own homophobia.

Peter was no exception, any more than I had been. When we were first together he would often ask me, "When are you going to stop hating yourself for being gay?" I came to a time after my breakdown when I accepted who I was. He never did.

I don't think anyone who ever met Peter Scott doubted that if he had been born into a world that didn't discriminate against homosexuals, he would have had a distinguished, high-level political career. It was certainly what he longed for. He had the skills and brains and smarts. He was well read, personable, poised, focused, and charismatic. He was a political junkie—he thrived on politics. He had always wanted a career in public life and trained as a lawyer, but he decided early on that he would never be able to participate in a major way because he was gay. He had a great deal of anger because of it, and he became a heavy drinker. When he was drunk, his rage often surfaced and he would storm about the injustice of being gay. Many times he drank in order to be intimate with a man.

Peter and I were like two people in a lifeboat frantically holding on to each other in order to survive. We clearly loved each other. We loved what the other had and we wanted it to be part of our lives. I fell in love with his grace, his Marlboro-man good looks, his dependability—and his torment about his gayness. For him, I opened a world that he had given up. Through me, he could at last start fulfilling some of what he had yearned for. He admired my experience and skills as a political strategist. He relished my determination not to be separated from political opportunity because I was gay. He loved my yearning to love unconditionally. He wanted to be with me and to experience it all.

Unfortunately for us both, neither of us was ever able to overcome our fear of intimacy enough to fully commit to our relationship. Through most of our years with each other we spent most of our time together. We vacationed together, we worked together, we politicked together, and we socialized together. But we were too afraid of the intense feelings we had for each other to live together, to articulate our commitment, or to act on our feelings. That struggle bonded us as tightly as two people can be bonded, but in the first years after we met it also filled us with confusion and resentment and anger.

By mid-June of 1977 I was back in pretty good shape and able to consider making a living again. Peter was still practicing law and hating it. I had no idea what I was going to do, since I wasn't sure anyone would offer me political assignments so soon after my breakdown. One night, as we were having dinner, he made a bold proposal: "David, why don't you and I go into business together?"

"Doing what? Being born-again homosexuals?"

"Listen, you have years of experience planning out campaigns, mapping out strategy for candidates, and handling political crises. Why not offer the same services to corporate America?"

"Peter, I can't spend my life lobbying. I'm not that good at it and it's hard for me to advocate things I don't believe in. I don't think I'm that good at public relations either."

"I agree. But you are good at strategy—there's no one better. And you're terrific with people. Let's open a strategic planning firm."

I still thought it was a crazy idea. "I've done some consulting but only on an informal, one-on-one basis," I said. "I don't know the first thing about opening or managing a consulting firm."

"That's where I come in," Peter answered. "I know business, I understand budgets and management from my corporate law practice and the family ranch. We would make a good team. Hell, David, both of us are miserable where we're at right now. You're as poor as a goddam church mouse. I can keep us alive financially until we see if it works."

We talked over the idea for the next couple of weeks. We spent time looking at what would be required from each of us and where we might be able to locate some initial clients; and we outlined a rough budget that would enable us to survive financially. By the end of the month we had filed a legally required DBA (Doing Business As) form and established the strategic planning firm of Mixner/Scott. Although both of us were total novices in the intricacies of starting a new business, we did believe that as a team we had talents to offer to prospective clients. Peter had some money in a trust from his family's West Texas ranch, and we used some of it to open an office, actually an apartment on Cynthia Street in West Hollywood, a gay area of Los Angeles. I was still homeless, so I placed a mattress on the floor between the filing cabinets and lived in the office. Each morning I rolled it up and placed it in a closet so we could begin our business day. For the next two years that was my home as well as our office.

One of our first tasks was to open a business account for the new firm, and we put on our most proper clothes and went off to the local branch of a large California bank to set it up. It was a humiliating experience. We sat down at a desk in the new accounts division, told the banker what we wanted, and gave him our DBA, our lease for the Cynthia Street space, and a page-and-a-half description of the business. We expected it to be routine—we would fill out the necessary papers, the account would be opened, and we'd go back to our office. We couldn't have been more wrong.

The banker looked at us coldly and said, "I know this address on Cynthia Street. It is an apartment house, not an office building."

Peter was not very concerned. "Yes, we know," he answered, "but we opened our office there because the landlord is a personal friend."

Naively I chimed in, "And I'm living there as well."

The banker's voice turned meaner. "This isn't actually a business, is it? We don't sanction gay couples setting up bank accounts as businesses. We can open a personal account for each of you but we won't open up a business account to facilitate such a relationship."

Peter was steaming. I put my hand under the desk and touched his leg in a signal to keep calm. "I'm sorry," I said. "There must be some misunderstanding here. This is a real business. Take a look at the plan."

With a sarcastic edge to his voice, the banker answered, "Excuse me. I have to get approval on this." He left the desk and went off to his superior. They huddled for half an hour, casting disapproving looks at us now and then. Several times the senior man picked up the phone and made calls.

Peter and I sat there stunned. We felt dirty, as if we had done something wrong. Peter was livid. "Let's get the fuck out of here," he said. I was just as angry but I was damned if we'd move. We were going to win this battle.

The banker reappeared at his desk and said, "Listen, guys, this would be so much easier for us if you just opened personal accounts. We promise you good service."

I had had it. More than an hour had passed since we entered the bank. "We are not leaving until we open this business account," I told him. "It is a perfectly legitimate business. We have all the papers." Peter flinched when I went on: "We are gay but that has nothing to do with it. This is a *business*."

"You know, this might be easier if you took this to a more local bank. You don't have to press the issue."

"Yes, we do," said Peter.

The banker pushed our papers across the desk and said, "I'm sorry, we just can't help you."

I pushed them back. "Yes, you can. Now do it."

Peter barked, "I am a lawyer and you go tell your asshole boss that I will sue your asses off and you can explain to corporate headquarters why you cost them so much money in a lawsuit."

"The law is on our side, Mr. Scott. We don't even have to serve you people." That was true enough; it was the reason it had been so important to defeat Gibson. "Yes, you're right about that," said Peter. "But do you really want to pay thousands of dollars in legal fees because you refused to open a small business account? I don't think so."

Once again, the banker left the desk and huddled with his superior. By now every staffer in the bank was looking at us as if we were criminals. I was in shock. Here we were, in a bank in the middle of a gay and lesbian neighborhood, being treated like the plague because we were gay.

We had been there for two hours by this time, and at last, with great reluctance, they agreed to open the account. We left totally drained. Every time I pass that bank today, I remember the incident with irony. It is now extremely gay- and lesbian-friendly and actively seeks these accounts.

The first months of Mixner/Scott were difficult. We made a list of our contacts in both the political and the gay community and approached them systematically to ask for possible business or referrals. We watched for companies seeking bids and submitted detailed proposals. The experience was an eye-opener. We discovered that some of those bidding against us sent plain envelopes to the companies with clippings inside from the gay and lesbian press about our gay rights work. Many midlevel managers told us directly that to hire us would jeopardize their status within their company. Closeted gays working for corporations were especially afraid of us, as if guilt by association would reveal their sexuality should they recommend hiring two openly gay consultants. We had the office, the stationery, the cards, and the business plan, but we didn't have any clients. We couldn't find anyone willing to hire us. Peter's family trust enabled us to survive. Without those funds we would have folded Mixner/Scott within a month or two. As it was, in the course of the first year we gradually built up a clientele, but the beginnings were decidedly stressful.

The stress added to the complexities of our relationship. Our feelings for each other grew stronger, so much so that they sometimes frightened us. Although Peter had made it clear that he was not physically attracted to me—he had always been drawn to young blond men—he felt a strong emotional and intellectual pull that he said left him confused and baffled. I was as afraid of intimacy with another man as ever, and could not express my feelings of love to Peter for fear of another loss or betrayal. When we both were drunk and on drugs, we would find ourselves attempting intimacy, but it always would end in distrust or a rage to the point where we wouldn't even speak to each other. We continued to live in separate quarters and even had other lovers. Yet day by day our lives became more intertwined. We shared business, politics, and social activities. There was little we didn't know about each other.

About two years into our business, Peter and I traveled together to New York for a client. We took a fair amount of drugs and went out drinking. Earlier that evening Peter had been with another man, and he was very drunk by the time we came back to the apartment where we were staying. He blacked out in the living room, so I staggered over, hauled him up, and took him back to our bed—we usually shared a bedroom when we were traveling. Later on he struggled awake and we began to make love. Suddenly he bolted out of the bed, still high from the drugs, and started screaming, "This fucking around is driving me crazy. I can't take it anymore! Get away from me!"

I was scared. I tried fruitlessly to calm him down. He stormed around the apartment knocking over lamps. When I grabbed at them, he swung at me. For twenty minutes we tangled in a raging fistfight. It was the only time in my life that I had ever engaged in violence of any kind. At one point, he flung open the window in the high-rise apartment and screamed, "Just jump! Let's both of us end our misery! It isn't fair. I can't stand the pressure!"

With that he flung his clothes into his suitcase and stormed out of the apartment. We were both scared enough by the intensity of the fight to realize that if we were to go on together, we had to have help. We found a couples counselor, and for the next three years we worked at sorting out who we were to each other. The first year in therapy was rough. For entire sessions we'd sit in Dr. John Lundgren's office and not say a word. We refused to deal honestly with the issues that were tormenting us; much of the time we simply traded charges. But gradually, with the help of the very patient Dr. Lundgren, we began to open up. Lundgren made it very clear that if we were to have any chance of sustaining our friendship and partnership, we had to come to terms with the enormous dependency we felt on each other and be comfortable with it. We also had to stop worrying about how others perceived our relationship. "You are not a traditional couple," he told us, "and given where each of you is in your lives, there is not much chance you'll become one. You have to accept and develop your own model for this relationship if you are to have any chance of surviving together."

We did, although it was a long process. Ultimately we decided that what we had was right for us. We would continue to live apart and with other people in our lives, but we never again doubted our intense love for each other.

•   •   •

The reverberations of Anita Bryant's campaign were continuing to spread, and gays and lesbians throughout California realized it was only a matter of time before her crusade of hate reached us. Many of those in our Los Angeles community were afraid of losing their jobs and their families. No one had greater fears of this than our close friends Roberta Bennett and Diane Abbitt.

Peter and I were devoted to them. They were lesbians who had first met when each was married, and who when they left their marriages and became a couple, had made a commitment between them to raise their children together—Roberta had two daughters, Diane two sons. Both went to law school at night, and were actively engaged in the struggle for civil rights for homosexuals. Roberta was an articulate, no-nonsense type who made up her mind what should be done, got on the phone, and made things happen. Diane was more the visionary and dreamer. She had a gift for articulating her ideals and convincing others they had to join the fight. The Bryant crusade terrified them. If we weren't able to stop it, there was a very real possibility their children would be ripped from their arms by the authorities simply because they were lesbians.

And then the hate surfaced around us. Orange County State Senator John Briggs decided to join the Bryant bandwagon. He announced a statewide drive to place an initiative on the California ballot that would make it illegal for homosexuals to be schoolteachers. Any teacher accused of being a homosexual would be brought before the local school board to face the accusation. If found "guilty," he or she would be dismissed and forbidden to teach again in California.

The proposed measure sent shock waves through California gays. Our own community divided into three camps: one that advocated fighting the initiative vigorously; one that said we wouldn't be able to defeat it at the ballot box, so we should let it pass and fight it in the courts; and one that went into total denial and was ready to hide its head in the sand. Roberta, Diane, Peter, and I were with the fight-back contingent. The first polls indicated that over 75 percent of Californians supported the Briggs initiative, and the prospects of defeating it looked pretty grim.

For the first time, lesbians and gay men in the fight-back camp joined forces on equal terms. For years there had been tensions between them. Lesbians were decidedly unhappy about the lack of support among men for feminist issues, and about what they perceived as the "gay male lifestyle." Gay men had shown very little respect for those issues, and they weren't about to change their lifestyle. In this case, however, both sides knew that we had to work together to defeat Briggs or we would perish together.

In northern California Harvey Milk mobilized a grassroots campaign to oppose the initiative. In the south, the factions continued their in-fighting. We four decided to take action. We called together a group of activists and suggested we create an organization whose sole goal would be to do the political work and fund-raising necessary to prepare for the coming battle. It would operate only until a regular campaign committee could be formed. The group we assembled was delighted to stop talking and start working. It named itself New AGE (New Alliance for Gay Equality), rented office space, was soon overflowing with precinct maps, charts, fund-raising files, and volunteers, and raised enough money to support Peter's and my efforts to prepare the campaign.

Outside Los Angeles a lot of people had still not heard about my homosexuality. While I still didn't feel ready to deal with it on a personal level with my political allies, expressing it as a "political act" was different, so I decided to send a letter to all my political, entertainment, and personal friends around the country. I wrote that I was gay, and asked for their political and personal help in the fight against the Briggs initiative. Some friends sent small checks with warmly supportive notes; among them were Anne Wexler and Richard and Doris Kearns Goodwin. Marylouise Oates, Michael Driver, and Don and Judy Green not only wrote but became vocal advocates of gay and lesbian rights from day one. Others were less forthcoming, and some I never heard from. I found it interesting that only a few mentioned my personal divulgence.

One especially welcome call came from Bill Clinton in Arkansas.

"I received your letter, David. There's nothing ever boring about you, is there?"

"I'm just trying to make sure you all don't forget me out here in California," I said.

"Mixner, all kidding aside, that took a lot of guts, and I want you to know that Hillary and I know that. We will always be your friends and you can count on us."

I was touched, and told him so.

"Well, you take care of yourself," he answered. "I've heard you've been through some rough times. Don't let anyone get to you. You're doing the right thing. We're proud of you. Both of us love you."

Another bright spot for us in New AGE was the reaction of Senator George McGovern. We needed national attention on the initiative if we were to raise money outside California to defeat it. Although he had been soundly beaten by Nixon in the 1972 election, McGovern remained a hero to American liberals for his principled race. His presence in California to fight the Briggs initiative would be a terrific boost to our efforts and our morale. Bob Shrum, a member of McGovern's staff who had a national reputation for his commitment to human rights, set up a meeting with Peter, me, and McGovern at which we asked him to speak at a New AGE fund-raiser open to the press. A United States senator had never attended an openly gay and lesbian fund-raiser before. Moreover, he was facing reelection in his rural home state of South Dakota in 1980, where conservative factions were strong. But Bob made a strong case for the importance of standing up against tyranny, especially when it is unpopular to do so, and with his usual courage McGovern agreed to come.

We rented the ballroom of the Beverly Wilshire Hotel and sent out invitations. We had a packed room that evening, and for many of those who came it was their first gay and lesbian event. The senator, community leaders, and a scattering of local politicians sat on the stage. Linda Hopkins sang some of her wonderful blues songs and McGovern spoke movingly of the battle for human dignity and his willingness to stand by our side. It was a memorable evening, not only because we raised critical funds but because it was a big step toward the community's being accepted by mainstream politicians.

While New AGE was at work, factions throughout California met to plan a statewide response to the initiative, which was now designated Proposition 6 on the ballot. There were many who wanted Peter and me to run the campaign and there were many vehemently opposed to us. Some of those had legitimate concerns about my breakdown and the extent of my recovery. But the majority had something else on their minds: the fact that Peter and I were openly gay. David Goodstein of *The Advocate* led the faction insisting that if the campaign were to have credibility, it had to be managed by "straight consultants."

His was by no means a unique stance. At the time, many acknowledged homosexuals still felt that gay causes had to be led by straights in order to legitimize them in the eyes of the larger society. Our very shaky self-esteem lay at the heart of this attitude. But I wasn't about to take this anymore. I knew my years of political experience and Peter's management skills would be invaluable. I had a no-strings gift to offer my community at last, and no one was going to take it away from me because I was gay.

We reached a compromise at last and the NO on 6 campaign was officially created. Harvey Milk would run the north, Peter and I would manage the south, and Don Bradley, a straight man with valuable skills, would be the statewide campaign consultant. New AGE agreed to fold its operations into the NO on 6 campaign.

But the campaign had an immediate and formidable problem: money. Then an extraordinary individual came to our rescue. The Reverend Troy Perry was a big bear of a man who was a pioneer and hero in the gay and lesbian community. He had been raised among Southern Pentecostals and Baptists, married at eighteen, had two children, and became a pastor for the Church of God in an Illinois community until he was excommunicated for his homosexuality and lost his church, his wife, and his children. But Perry was not a man to accept defeat. In October 1969 he had brought twelve people into his small living room to worship together as open gays and lesbians. That small service led to the founding of the Universal Fellowship of Metropolitan Community Churches—MCC—that today has forty-two thousand members and churches in nineteen countries. It was as founder and head of MCC that the Reverend Perry decided to begin a fast outside the Federal Building in Los Angeles until the community had raised a hundred thousand dollars to defeat the Briggs initiative. Sixteen days later the money was in hand. Without it our operation in the south would have fallen so many weeks behind in organizing that this might well have affected the outcome. Perry was also key in keeping the various factions of the community united, not always an easy task. His unshakable faith that we could win was contagious.

The struggle against Proposition 6 took the lesbian and gay community of California to a new level of sophistication and responsibility. Many of those working against Briggs were novices. We trained them in the basics of politics: taught them how to run a field operation, raise funds, work with the press. They were exultant at learning the skills to fight back. Everyone worked like crazy. Realtor Gayle Wilson was a superb fund-raiser and used her client list to reach out to the straight community. Her business competitor Clyde Cairns organized dinner parties throughout the Hollywood Hills to help her. Neither had ever been involved in a political campaign before but they were naturals. Diane and Roberta worked around the clock uniting the men's and women's communities. Our grassroots effort was headed by Ivy Bottini, a feminist comedian with political experience who worked hard to build a field and precinct operation.

But money continued to be a desperate problem. Then Gayle broke new ground. Large numbers of homosexuals worked in the entertainment industry, and she recognized that Hollywood was becoming increasingly concerned about the anti-gay wave spreading around the country. Memories of the McCarthyism of the 1950s were all too vivid; it had had a shattering effect on the industry and Proposition 6 set up ominous echoes of that terrible time. Gayle planned a women's lunch at the Beverly Hilton Hotel, and knew that if it was to bring in big bucks, she needed celebrities. Everyone in the business knew someone gay or lesbian, and the threat the initiative posed brought out big names ready to speak out against it. Gayle lined up Cher, Donna Summer, and other powerful Hollywood women to attend her lunch. It turned into a standing-room-only event and raised over fifty thousand dollars for our media fund. Moreover, it was a breakthrough. Other celebrities quickly offered their services for fund-raising events. Burt Lancaster, John Travolta, and Lily Tomlin agreed to headline a black-tie dinner where one thousand people contributed over a hundred fifty thousand dollars to fight the initiative. For the first time ever, Hollywood got heavily involved in fighting for the rights of homosexuals.

I drove to Malibu to enlist the support of an old comrade from the antiwar days, Peter Yarrow of Peter, Paul and Mary. Sitting around Peter's kitchen table overlooking the Pacific, I described the ramifications of the Briggs initiative. He hadn't been paying attention to it until then, but he was appalled. He promptly called on the folk music community and asked leading singers for their commitment. Joan Baez, Harry Chapin, and Holly Near joined Peter in a benefit concert at the Santa Monica Civic Auditorium. Despite a bomb threat that emptied the building, they sold out two shows.

Slowly all these efforts helped our cause gain in the polls, and our confidence about winning increased, although there were setbacks from time to time. We were startled one day to learn that with no advance notice the Beverly Hills Chamber of Commerce announced it supported Yes on 6. Although we realized this wouldn't have much of an impact on the campaign, some of our major donors went into a frenzy. I couldn't see why. Gayle straightened me out. "You don't understand, honey," she told me. "We shop there!" Within twenty-four hours hundreds of credit cards were turned in to Beverly Hills stores, hairstylists in one salon refused to cut hair, and celebrities announced that they would not shop in the city of Beverly Hills. That did it. The chamber of commerce went into emergency session and rescinded its endorsement.

The gap in the polls kept on narrowing. Victory seemed more and more likely. Still, there is nothing in politics more dangerous than over-confidence. We decided we needed a campaign bombshell to put us over the top. One day Peter and I had a call from closeted homosexual Don Livingston, a senior executive with the Carter Hawley Hale department stores, who asked us: "Would the endorsement of Ronald Reagan be helpful?" Would it! Previously Don had been a member of Governor Reagan's administrative staff and he thought that through his contacts there was a fair chance of obtaining this endorsement. Because Reagan was beginning to plan his run for the presidency, any effort to reach him had to be conducted in total secrecy, and Don was our liaison in setting up a confidential meeting between a member of the governor's staff and Peter and me.

We met at a Denny's in Hispanic East Los Angeles—about as safe a place as we could conceive, since the likelihood of a Republican showing up there seemed minimal. The staffer too was a closeted homosexual, but he ended up confident that he could trust us not to reveal this and that we would make a good impression on the governor. He agreed to arrange a meeting.

When the time came he warned us that we'd have only a few minutes to make our case. He urged that we stick to libertarian principles. He reminded us that there were those on Reagan's staff opposed to the meeting and it was the governor himself who had made the final determination to see us. The staffer felt that Nancy Reagan, who had many gay friends, would play a part in his decision on the initiative. Rarely have I been more on tenterhooks.

Peter and I were escorted into a bright office with windows overlooking West Los Angeles. Reagan rose from his desk, gave us his famous smile, extended his hand, and said, "How nice of you boys to come over to chat with me about this issue."

He made us feel more at home than most Democrats did. He directed us to chairs and offered us soda. It was hard to believe that this smiling gentle man was the same person who had sent in three thousand bayoneted National Guardsmen to "protect" People's Park in Berkeley.

He opened the discussion. "I understand you boys have a case you want to make to me," he said.

"Governor, you know about this initiative that would allow any school child to file a complaint against any teacher that he thought was homosexual," I began. "This initiative would create anarchy in the classroom. Any child who received a failing grade or was disciplined by a teacher could accuse that teacher of being a homosexual. Teachers will become afraid of giving a low grade or maintaining order in their classrooms."

We could see a surprised look come over Reagan's face. I think he expected to hear a human rights argument. "I never thought about that. It really could happen, couldn't it?"

"Governor, the kids will control the classroom," Peter said. "Teachers will be terrified of their students. It will be chaos."

"You mean, *any* accusation by a student must be heard by the school board?"

I knew we were making progress. "Exactly," I answered. "The law requires a public hearing before the local school board to decide if there are grounds for the charges or not. Each school district's school board meeting will become a circus."

Reagan smiled at us. "This just might be a good day for you boys. Don't think we can allow something like that to happen here in California."

Clearly, our argument was having an impact. He asked a number of questions about the wording of the initiative. He seemed to be well informed, and he spent a lot of time discussing its details. While he officially refused to tell us that he would oppose it, we left the meeting with very little doubt. He stood up, shook our hands, patted us on the back, and said, "Thanks, boys, for coming to see me. You're fine young lads. Your parents must be proud."

When we came out of the office Reagan's staff cornered us and made it very clear that if word leaked about the meeting and if we didn't keep silent about the governor's apparent support, our efforts could be derailed. We were on cloud nine when got back to headquarters but we kept our mouths shut. We held numerous private phone conversations with the Reagan staff on wording and background information. At last, in a mid-September newspaper column, future president Ronald Reagan called for the defeat of Proposition 6, citing the "mischief" it could cause between students and teachers in the classroom. The column became front-page news all over California and the polls showed a strong shift against the initiative.

We set up our election night party at the Beverly Hilton—the room would either be jam-packed or empty. We didn't have long to wait to find out. When the returns started coming in, it was clear that Proposition 6 had been defeated. The margin was enormous: over a million votes. We carried almost every county in the state, including, thanks to Ronald Reagan, ultra-conservative Orange County, Briggs's home base. The ballroom of the Hilton overflowed with weeping, cheering people celebrating the first defeat of Anita Bryant's forces. Homophobia would go on being virulent in the years to come, but we had disposed of at least one of its fanatical manifestations.

•   •   •

The victory transformed the gay and lesbian community in Los Angeles. We had proved we were capable of organizing, fund-raising, and winning, and we felt empowered to continue our drive to protect ourselves. Lesbian and gay professionals and businesspeople who had participated in the campaign formed business guilds and professional organizations and started effective outreach among the city's realty groups, bar associations, and chambers of commerce. Many of our new grassroots activists, trained by Ivy Bottini, joined organizations like NOW and the NAACP and assumed positions of responsibility and leadership. What emerged from this campaign was a jubilant community excited about building a future.

MECLA, in particular, was emerging as a real power in California politics. Politicians, seeing our ability to raise substantial funds and turn out voters, started to court us instead of our pursuing them. The political world was finally opening up to us. But our very success forced the organization to face up to some difficult and important issues and wage some sharp battles. One of them was the long-standing estrangement between lesbians and gays. While the NO on 6 effort had forced the two communities to work together—and effectively so—the tensions between them were real. Gay men, like straight men, were not immune from the sexism prevalent in the sixties and seventies. Our civil rights organizations tended to be dominated by gay white men who neither acknowledged nor shared power with the lesbian community. Not surprisingly, they distrusted us profoundly. Diane and Peter pushed the MECLA board to become co-sexual: half the members men, half women. The men on the board were very reluctant. They were even more hostile to the idea of a man and a woman as co-chairs. But we four mounted a careful campaign to implement these structural changes, soliciting influential acquaintances of the board members to press them to vote for reform; and in a very close vote, the MECLA Board of Directors did just that. MECLA became the first truly co-sexual gay and lesbian organization in the nation.

From then on gender parity became a fact of life for Los Angeles lesbian and gay organizations. It certainly didn't mean that the struggle to come together was over, but we did make progress. NO on 6 had been encouraging. So was another effort just before that campaign. Women wanted to elect a "lesbian-friendly" slate from California to the International Woman's Year Conference in November 1977. This conference was to bring women from all over America—and the world—to Houston to discuss a plan of action for women's progress. The conference was under bitter attack from the radical right, with Phyllis Schlafly and homophobic California Congressperson Robert Dornan leading the charge. Each state established a selection process to elect delegates to Houston. California became a battleground between Schlafly's forces and the feminists. Anyone, man or woman, who appeared at the balloting location and paid a registration fee could vote. Roberta and Diane asked Peter and me to muster gay men to go to the University of Southern California voting site, pay the fee, and vote for the feminist slate. The two of us established a phone tree, asking ten men to find another ten men, and so on, who would be willing to vote for the slate. On the day of the vote, many dozens of gay men stood in the long lines, paid their fee, and voted for our sisters' slate. The show of solidarity laid substantial groundwork for building trust and unity between the two communities.

MECLA's success enabled the community to showcase its new political power. The organization pioneered black-tie fund-raisers in the community. Although the first one it held drew three to four hundred guests, not a single elected official was willing to attend. But that changed. At the organization's peak, the dinners attracted thirteen hundred people, including local, state, and national politicians. They became an important venue for Democratic Party leaders and potential presidential candidates. A parade of Democratic "stars" keynoted the dinners, among them Governor Jerry Brown, Senators Thomas Dodd, John Kerry, and Gary Hart, Congressperson Geraldine Ferraro, and our particular champion, Senator Edward Kennedy. We recognized some necessary realities, and there were intricate negotiations beforehand to ensure the speakers that they would not be politically embarrassed—arranging, for example, that same-sex dancing would not begin until the speaker had left. We did not see this as a problem, and MECLA endorsements and checks were eagerly sought by local, state, and national politicians. We also brought many of Los Angeles's more prominent social figures onto the board and they worked hard to mobilize support in the non-gay community. The organization became an integral part of the political scene and filled us with hope.

As the political power of the community grew, so did the firm of Mixner/Scott. We finally moved out of the Cynthia Street apartment into handsomely furnished offices in the Beverly Boulevard building in West Los Angeles that occupied two floors, including a kitchen and a large conference room, and had a staff of over twenty. The successful NO on 6 campaign built our reputations as effective strategists and our business flourished. My close friend from the Moratorium, Michael Driver, opened the door to the corporate world for us. Mike was moved by our efforts in the NO on 6 campaign and pledged to help us find some corporate business. His largest client was an energy company named TOSCO and he convinced the executive officers to hire us as strategists. TOSCO became our first corporate client and allowed us to demonstrate our abilities to other corporations. As our work became known for its excellence, our homosexuality became less and less of a liability, and in some areas an asset. I did most of the client work and Peter managed the staff, the business, and the firm's investments.

Personally the two of us were on top of the world. For the first time in my life, as an open gay man I was delighting in political victory, financial security, and the honesty that came of being myself. It felt free and wonderful. Our world was filled with "out" gays and lesbians who were celebrating the new openness. For gay men, it was a time of enormous sexual liberation. We rejoiced in the sexuality that had separated us from the larger society. It was a time to throw away shame and to embrace our gayness. Discos were a place to dance on drugs into the early hours of the morning. Designer drugs were commonplace and we had sex with numerous partners.

Amid this exuberant openness, Peter and I bought a house together in Palm Springs. It was a wonderful place, with vaulted ceilings, fireplaces, a sauna, a Jacuzzi, a pool, and lush green lawns. It was both our refuge and a glorious place to party. Closeted politicians came from all over the country to join us and our friends. We filled these weekends with dinner parties, dancing, late-night nude swims, and gossip. On Sundays we recovered from our partying around the pool, reading the Sunday *New York Times* and drinking gallons of coffee, before we finally headed back to Los Angeles and elsewhere and to our work.

Those years in the Palm Springs house were the happiest times in my life. We were carefree. We were finding political and social acceptance. The house became a place for old friends and visiting firemen, lively minds and cheerful spirits, to gather around our dining-room table to laugh and to argue, to share serious concerns and high-spirited pleasure. We stocked the television room with old movies and served the best champagne. Peter cooked all day, making elaborate meals and spectacular homemade desserts. The future seemed infinitely bright.

My success enabled me to reach out to my family. I wanted to prove to them that I could be openly gay and still flourish. I flew Mom and Dad, Patsy and Michael and their girls, Julia and Elizabeth, and my brother Melvin and his wife Donna and their children, Brad and

Monique, out to Palm Springs for a week at our house. I had kept my word to my parents and had yet to talk to Melvin and Donna about my homosexuality, but I knew they knew. It was simply not spoken about between us. Each evening we enjoyed lavish dinners and at the end of the week we posed for a family portrait. I went overboard (and realized it) to prove to my family how complete my life was since I had come out of the closet.

Our success in business enabled Peter and me to become contributors to politicians all around the country. Doors are always open when you're a donor, and we were able to expand our political contacts all over. We not only contributed to candidates, we also held fund-raisers for them in our homes. There were very few elected officials we wanted to reach who did not welcome us. We gave receptions for prominent politicians at Peter's Nichols Canyon house and elegant dinners at the beautiful L'Orangie restaurant, so they could meet the movers and shakers of West Los Angeles. These events were the first evenings in which politically active gays and lesbians integrated socially with the non-gay community at private dinner parties, and they were a rousing success.

In 1980, on a trip to Los Angeles, Bill Clinton took the opportunity to express his friendship for me. He asked that Peter and I host a reception for him with both the straight and the gay and lesbian community at Peter's home. I hadn't realized that Bill even knew about Peter, and I was touched by his awareness and his respect for our relationship. Bill was taking a powerful political risk back home in Arkansas by having two very visible, openly gay men hold a reception that would include a large number of homosexuals. I believe he took that risk out of friendship and to show his support of my coming out. Peter knew how important this event was to me both personally and politically. "David, don't worry," he assured me. "I'm going to take care of this for you. We'll show those Arkansas folks a little bit of gay Hollywood."

That night, torches outside Peter's home lined the way to the front door. Inside were glorious arrays of exotic flowers, bars serving fine wine and champagne, and tables of wonderful food. Lit candles floated in the pool. When Clinton arrived he was overwhelmed. He greeted me with his usual bear hug and hugged Peter as well. He said hello to old friends and welcomed new ones and he charmed every person in the room. At the close of the evening, he thanked Peter for his generosity and told me how much he valued my friendship and advice. I will never forget his courageous gesture. No other politician had risked as much in the name of friendship as he did that night. The memory of that evening made it easy for me to be there for him a dozen years later.

In the 1980 presidential race, other candidates began at last to reach out to the gay and lesbian community. Governor Jerry Brown appointed us to positions in his primary campaign. Ted Kennedy made an appearance at one of its fund-raisers in Los Angeles and insisted that the press be admitted. Even President Carter sent his mother to the Gay and Lesbian Community Services Center black-tie dinner. As always, Miss Lillian provided humor to the evening. When she arrived outside the Beverly Wilshire Hotel, the press crowded around her. One reporter shouted to her, "Miss Lillian, how does it feel to be at a gay and lesbian dinner?" She looked up and said as if surprised, "Oh, my. Is this what this is?" Then she proceeded inside to the ballroom laughing out loud.

The political fund-raising and organizing we were doing started to yield concrete results for communities elsewhere. Elaine Noble of Massachusetts was the first gay or lesbian to be elected to a state legislature, and Harvey Milk was elected to the San Francisco Board of Supervisors. In Los Angeles, we saw Governor Brown rip down the barriers by naming Stephen Lachs the first openly homosexual judge and appointing acknowledged gay lawyer Sheldon Andelson to the California Board of Regents.

Our dreams were boundless. I was out, participating successfully in politics at the national level as an openly gay man. Peter and I, as business partners and best friends, continued to build our lives together, now much more comfortable in our relationship. On my thirty-third birthday Peter gave me a gold Tiffany watch and a note that said, "You have enriched my life beyond my abilities to thank you for it. But I do, and I wish for you the place in the sun you so richly desire and deserve." We were so happy that it was hard to imagine life could hold any greater heights for us. But we were sure it would. The possibilities seemed endless.

Then came AIDS.

CHAPTER NINE

The Nightmare Begins

ONE day early in 1981 Peter Scott brought the first news that would change our lives forever. "I just talked to Joel," he said, "and something is wrong with Ken Harris. He's in UCLA Hospital with some sort of strange ailment. He's very sick. They don't think he is going to make it."

"Ken Harris" was a friend of ours. Joel Weisman was Peter's doctor, and Ken's. I couldn't believe it. "What in the hell is it, Peter?"

Peter described Ken's fever, his chills, and the fact that none of the antibiotics seemed to have any effect at all. "Joel indicated that the doctors at the hospital think it may be 'gay related.'"

I laughed sourly and said, "Of course they do. They blamed us for the last earthquake."

"David, Ken *is* gay, and he is very, very sick. Something's wrong. I don't like the sound of this."

That was our introduction to AIDS: a strange ailment infecting a friend. At first, we were skeptical about the vague claim that gay male sex might be involved in the transmission of this "ailment." There were hardly any cases in Los Angeles; most were in New York and San Francisco. Even the few cases here appeared to be among people who spent large amounts of time in New York City or Fire Island. Then each month, each week, then almost each day, we heard of another person stricken with this unexplained illness. The symptoms were always similar: unbelievably high fevers, chills, abrupt weight loss, a strange form of pneumonia, and sometimes unusual purplish markings appearing on the body.

At first, I kept denying that there was an emerging epidemic hitting the gay male community; if there was the government would be alerting us. But the reports kept coming. Peter and Diane, who had less faith than I in the government's protecting our health, took them seriously right from the beginning. They kept insisting we had to find out more about what was happening to these young gay men. Initially, of course, they really didn't know how to do that. No one did. We were all trying to guess what was going on and the government wasn't telling us anything.

By the end of 1981 the conversations in the living room of Roberta and Diane's San Fernando Valley tract house had shifted from visions of building political power to this unknown disease that was stalking us. One night Peter sat on their wraparound sofa looking very glum. I was on the floor across the room, leaning against a big pillow next to the wall, holding forth on the upcoming 1982 elections. Peter looked up angrily. "Mixner," he said, "none of that election shit matters anymore."

"What do you mean it doesn't matter? Of course it matters. It affects our whole lives."

"Look, Tom Pollack died today. He didn't know he was sick four weeks ago and today he's dead. Another one. I am telling you something awful is happening. In New York it's a fucking nightmare."

"Peter, if this was a crisis the government would be gathering us all together and letting us know. I think it probably has something to do with amyl nitrate or maybe some sort of badly made drug."

Peter snapped back at me, "Hell, this government would let all of us die as long as they don't think it's going to hurt anyone else. The fact of the matter is that we have no idea of what's causing this and your guesses aren't going to help. Neither is the goddam government. Mixner, you have to deal with this because otherwise it is going to bite you in the ass."

Roberta spoke up. "I agree with Peter. They'd kill us all if they could get away with it."

Diane, her legs folded underneath her in her favorite chair, attempted her frequent role of peacemaker. "Listen, guys, you're both right. Something *is* happening and the government should be letting us know. I'm not sure they would actually let us die, but for some reason they're certainly not telling us anything. This is like our political work. We can't count on anyone except ourselves and we'd better get busy figuring out what the hell is going on."

"The activists in San Francisco have had some meetings with their local health department but our county health department hasn't done shit yet," said Roberta.

"Come on, gang," I protested, but beginning to get the point at last. "Don't you think they'd tell us if they had something?"

Diane reminded me of the wishful thinking that said the disease wouldn't really hit us in Los Angeles. "Face it. Our hope that it was going to be mostly confined to San Francisco and New York was obviously false. It's here. You know it. Too many of our brothers are starting to get sick. We've got to *do* something."

I went home shaken. Now I look back in amazement at those early years of the epidemic. When I read books like Randy Shilts's *And the Band Played on* and learn of the number of meetings and briefings that had taken place in various health departments and at the Centers for Disease Control by mid-1982, I am stunned at the way we were left to our own devices. Most of what we heard came second- and thirdhand from friends around the country. It was largely anecdotal, "information" passed on by a friend of a friend who had talked to some unnamed health official or doctor. It was clear simply from the volume of rumors and reports that something major was happening to the health of gay men, and that alone should have put me into an action mode. But I was naive for an astonishingly long time, still wanting to believe that if something this serious was occurring, we would surely hear from our government.

As a person heavily involved in the leadership of the Los Angeles gay and lesbian community, never once was I asked to attend any briefing by a governmental agency or official to alert us to this growing epidemic or to give us any advice. Now and then the media ran an article on a new "gay cancer." We knew cancer was not a contagious disease. There was nothing in those occasional reports to sound warning bells about our vulnerability to this plague. What information there was, as I learned so much later, was confined to a small circle of researchers, health care workers, and medical personnel. Nothing reached the community at large.

Part of the problem was a reluctance on the part of some public health officials to create panic among the general public about a new disease

among gay men that might create a backlash against an already belea-
guered community. In fact, the community itself, whose memories of
what the radical right had tried to do to it were still fresh, had its own
reluctance about facing reality. It knew just how many public officials
had failed to speak up against those attacks. It knew of too many politicians who had instigated such attacks, or tried to build their careers by
using gays and lesbians as their favorite whipping posts. We were averse
ourselves to believing that a disease attributed only to gay men could
actually be hitting us.

Those who were infected in those early years usually seemed to die
very quickly. We didn't know then that you could be infected for months
or even years before you got sick. When a friend had a fever or came
down with diarrhea, we thought it was probably the flu, not the beginning of a deadly illness. By the time full-blown AIDS finally surfaced,
the victim went fast. We did come to realize that very few were surviving
once the illness surfaced. One day a strong vital man would be at your
dinner party and the next month he would be dead.

There is nothing more frightening than evil that lurks in the dark
when you have no idea what it is. Is it real or just a nightmare? There
was no test then to tell if you would get the disease, whatever it was, but
we did realize it seemed to be traveling in "circles of friends." Once one
person became ill, the odds were high that others of his friends would
get sick too. Slowly, we started filling in some of the missing pieces. We
began to recognize that it could be transmitted sexually. By the beginning of 1982 we started seeing articles about it in the gay press. The
Centers for Disease Control had just given it a name: GRID, for Gay-
Related Immune Deficiency. We searched among ourselves for explana-
tions, but the only common ground we found among our friends was
their gayness. Rich or poor, black, white, or Asian—this was an equal
opportunity assassin.

Diane was right that night in her living room. No one was going to
help us but ourselves. We could not expect anything from the government. It was the community that would have to educate itself, provide
care, push for research, fight public backlash, and sound the warning.

A community meeting got us going. In 1982 activists Matt Redman
and Nancy Sawaya Cole set up a hot line to manage the rampant rumors
and to provide as best they could what limited accurate information
there was. Increasingly the hot line became the source of referrals to
doctors, dentists, and lawyers who were willing to work with people with
AIDS, the name finally given it that July. Then in early 1983 Joel Weisman and Diane Abbitt established AIDS Project-Los Angeles: APLA.

They mustered enough funds to open a small office and hired a tiny staff. In addition to the hot line, APLA created a "buddy system" in which an individual teamed up with an AIDS victim, providing assistance with daily needs and emotional support and companionship. APLA became the city's major AIDS service group, and today has a budget approaching twenty million dollars.

As the disease and word of it spread, the straight community panicked. Often, the news of a son or brother's fatal illness was the first knowledge many families had that he was a homosexual. Some parents were loving and supportive. Many refused ever to see him again, and often APLA "buddies" became family to those rejected by their parents and stayed with them until their death. Undertakers turned away the bodies of victims, churches and ministers balked at conducting their funerals. Many doctors and dentists refused to treat people with AIDS for fear of catching it. The practices of doctors who were themselves homosexual swelled. Where they had been used to treating garden-variety complaints like the flu, they quickly became specialists in this new disease. Young men in committed relationships could find themselves in a legal nightmare, denied access to their loved ones as they lay dying, or facing hostile lawyers hired by families challenging the AIDS victim's will and their legal rights as long-time companions.

Then another nightmare arose. There was growing evidence that AIDS was being transmitted to hemophiliacs and others through blood transfusions. The issue of screening donors was an incendiary one. Many community leaders saw banning gay males from giving blood as a form of blacklisting, an invasion of their civil rights. Blood banks dragged their feet because of the possibility of liability cases. Even hemophiliac groups tended to be resistant to the possibility that the clotting factor that had been a lifesaver to so many with the disorder could itself be infected with this mysterious virus. While within its confines the CDC had identified groups at high risk for AIDS, not only gays but Haitians and intravenous drug users, all these conflicting pressures put off the problem of establishing donor guidelines to control a possibly infected blood supply to some indeterminate time in the future.

By 1983 AIDS was coming closer and closer to Peter and me. In mid-January, Peter's roommate and our close friend Dan Indelli came to our new offices looking pale and grim-faced—very different from the exuberant man whose infectious cheer raised everyone's spirits, who shared my passion for African art and loved opera just as fervently as Peter. Today, though, his smile was nowhere to be found. He was pale and drawn, which I chalked up to the flu he'd been struggling with the last couple of weeks.

"I have something not very good to tell you two," he said. "I have it."

I had been leaning back in my chair, my feet on my desk. I sat bolt upright. "What? You're not serious, are you? Oh, God!"

Dan began to sob. I went around the desk and held him in my arms. Peter sat stunned, unable to move. When he was able to speak, he reached for Dan's hands. "Dan, we'll be here for you," he said. "Always, all the time. Whatever you need, just let us know. You are not alone."

We comforted him as best we could until he left, and then faced each other. "David, he's going to die," Peter said.

"I know. I know. I feel sick with sadness."

"I feel helpless." Peter's voice was almost inaudible. We knew so many in the community who had died of AIDS. Five of our very closest friends had already been diagnosed, and all of them were dead. Dan was the sixth.

We were grieving and we were afraid. That was the moment when Peter and I became certain that we were infected ourselves. There was still no way to test whether the virus was present. We had to live with the fear. It was made worse by a growing sense of isolation. We never knew whom we could count on. In the straight community devoted friends like Shirley MacLaine and Jane Nathanson, an art collector and warm supporter, threw themselves into our cause, but others whom we thought were friends and allies disappeared overnight. Our phone calls would go unreturned; dinner invitations stopped; if we encountered them at receptions they would quickly turn away. In those last years before the advent of the epidemic, Peter and I had taken great pride in having opened up so many doors to the greater Los Angeles community, in breaking down the separation between gays and straights. Now many of these doors slammed shut. AIDS was re-creating the discrimination we had worked so hard to end.

One clear October Los Angeles night as the Santa Ana winds were blowing, we went to a dinner party at the home of a West Los Angeles political power broker. Ten of us were engaged in a lively and animated conversation about politics. AIDS was never mentioned. That seemed strange to us, probably because in our personal world it was omnipresent. Then our host, who was a political ally of ours, called the guests in to dinner. It was served buffet style, and as we approached the table Peter and I noticed the paper plates. The hostess saw us exchange a look. She knew that we knew what was going on. "I want everyone to relax this evening," she announced to the room, deliberately sprightly. "Let's all be casual—that's why I'm using paper plates."

I was enraged. Peter was amused. He pictured her picking up the plates with gloved hands when the guests left and throwing them into the trash. He was not amused later, when we heard she had called around town afterward and urged her friends to use paper plates "to protect their families" if Peter and I were coming to dinner.

At first, we had attempted to continue politics as usual. Despite the repeated shocks when we heard of yet another man stricken, by maintaining some sense of normalcy, we were often able to play down the reality of the approaching storm. One of the key players in our community at that time was West Hollywood lawyer and property owner Sheldon Andelson. A small, intense man with thinning hair and designer glasses, he had been one of the founders of the Gay and Lesbian Community Center in Los Angeles. To many in the community he was the symbol of success. It respected his financial and political influence. His Bel Air mansion was the site of political fund-raisers, straight weddings, and great festive parties.

Peter and I were good friends of Sheldon and business colleagues as well. After our miserable experience with the bank branch, Peter did not abandon his idea of a "gay bank" that would service the needs of the gay and lesbian community. We certainly didn't have the assets to start a venture like that, but Sheldon had both the economic means and the contacts in the financial community that could make the idea a reality. We worked together to refine the concept so it would be economically feasible. Many successful gays were still very much in the closet, and we worried whether they would place their funds in a bank that had a clear gay and lesbian identity. Sheldon resolved this by proposing that the bank's board of directors be half gay and half straight, helped us create a list of potential directors, and worked with us on the location and the design of the bank. In due course the Bank of Los Angeles was established in the center of West Hollywood. Sheldon was chairman and Peter went on the board. Peter and I invested in the initial stock offering. It was exciting to be involved in a venture that could create real economic power for the community.

We also worked closely with Sheldon in creating political power. He was on the MECLA board and wanted to be known as a "major donor" in political fund-raising circles. I opened my numerous political contacts to him, and we were the ones who introduced him to Governor Jerry

Brown. In 1983 Brown named him to the Board of Regents of the University of California, a very prestigious post and a very controversial appointment. If confirmed, that position would make Sheldon one of the highest-ranking gays in the country and the radical right was determined to stop his confirmation. We prepared volumes of briefing books for his testimony before the California State Senate and lined up key state senators who would act as "floor managers" for his confirmation battle. The carefully planned effort worked, although it took several tries before the Senate finally voted to confirm him.

Sheldon had made some of his fortune from his partial ownership of the city's most popular gay male bathhouse, the 8709 Club, where a great deal of sexual activity occurred every night. Without the revenues from the bathhouse, his ability to pump large amounts of money into his political ventures would be limited. But the season of AIDS was upon us. Bathhouses were now being recognized as a source of spread. Sheldon's property was turning into a personal albatross and a source of embarrassment to the community. It had nearly become an issue in his confirmation hearings but a legal rearranging of his ownership enabled him to sidestep it.

In San Francisco that May, the gay community had been bitterly split by an attempt to shut down the bathhouses. How fine was the line between protecting individual rights—a valid, indeed urgent concern for homosexuals—and trying to control a dangerous epidemic? Would closing these places where casual sex took place actually save lives and slow the spread of the disease, or would the people who frequented the bathhouses seek other, less controllable locations for sex? Like the issue of blood banks, there were no simple answers, and the debate in our community was often bitter and angry.

MECLA, under the able leadership of Larry Sprenger, became the first Los Angeles community organization to urge the "voluntary" closure of the bathhouses. I strongly supported its position, though not until I had spent some difficult hours wrestling over the problem of infringing on civil liberties. But there was so much we did not know about AIDS that it would be irresponsible to keep them open. Even if the patrons of these bathhouses went elsewhere, we had sounded a very serious warning about casual unsafe sex.

Behind the scenes, Sheldon fought MECLA very hard. He had been on its board for a number of years and he was outraged that it took a position that threatened his economic base. Then we learned that a local newscaster who had discovered Sheldon's involvement with the bathhouse was going public with the news: Here was a member of the prestigious California Board of Regents responsible for a bathhouse that was contributing to the spread of AIDS. Sheldon appeared in our office in tears, asking for help. We told him he had no recourse; he had to divest himself totally and quickly of any interest in the 8709 Club. Even in the face of devastating publicity he was resistant; only when he finally grasped the fact that we couldn't stop the story any longer did he finally agree to close the place down.

Marylouise Oates acted as an intermediary and asked her journalistic colleague to meet with me. I told him we had been attempting to close the bathhouse for some time and the threat of this story would finally do the job. If Sheldon agreed to shut it down, would he be willing to stop the story?

No, he wouldn't—not under any circumstances. But he would change its thrust, presenting it in a more positive light and not making it the lead, if, and only if, Sheldon told him himself that he was a participant in the bathhouse and was going to close it. Even at this juncture Sheldon implored me to stand in for him. But he had no choice, so he, I, and the reporter finally sat down together. It was painful to watch him. He had given so much to the community, yet in its time of terrible crisis he could not acknowledge the dark truth of what was happening or accept responsibility for his own actions. But he did admit his participation in the bathhouse and say he was closing it immediately. The reporter was satisfied, and the evening news ran an item about the closure, barely mentioning Sheldon. His service on the Board of Regents was not affected, and he continued to do an outstanding job.

How could this devoted, committed, and extraordinarily gifted advocate on behalf of the community behave so strangely? Certainly money played a part, but denial even a greater one. Sheldon himself had AIDS. He could not deal with it—not within himself and not in the community. He refused to acknowledge his illness publicly, and even when he was bedridden or in the hospital, he would have calls to his office patched into his room, pretending he was at work there. He maintained the fiction to the day the disease killed him.

1983 was the year when every gay man had to confront his own sexuality. We all knew by then that the only way to completely avoid the possibility of contracting AIDS was to abstain from sex altogether. Abstinence. Such a straightforward word, such a glib evasion of an overwhelming human drive. I was an intensely sexual being. It was so fundamental to my feeling alive that to deny it would be like not eating, not breathing. I had won my way to an open sexuality through the nightmare of breakdown. I could not give it up. I loved having sex with friends in the spirit of Plato's *Symposium*. I still had my share of casual encounters with lovers I met at parties or in bars.

The alternative to abstinence, of course, was to practice safe sex. There was still conflicting information about exactly what "safe" was, which meant every gay man had to determine this on his own. I took my own definition of it from what I could learn from medical experts, insisted on condoms, and checked my mouth for any sores or bleeding gums that could serve as a conduit for the virus before engaging in oral sex. But what motivated me to these practices was not really my own safety. I believed it was too late for me. I assumed I already had the virus, but because there was as yet no effective way to test for it, I didn't want to convey it to anyone else.

All around me friends were getting sick and dying. Every day brought another name, another casualty. I felt I was in a never-never land of the doomed. Some mornings I would wake up and think it was time to start planning my own death and by afternoon I would be in total denial that the plague even existed. I'd find myself in a rage about the limits I had to place on my own sexuality and the next minute be furious at those practicing unsafe sex. Teetering without end on the seesaw between fear and denial, in those initial years of the plague I was too often paralyzed to be able to come to terms with it.

I also had to come to terms with a new factor in Peter's and my lives. In 1983 Peter met a young New York banker, David Quarles, who came to Los Angeles and moved into his house. David was a handsome, enormously charming man with engaging southern manners—he was Georgia-born—and everyone liked him at once. I found this a miserably difficult and painful reality. Thanks to our therapy, Peter and I had established a stable, warm relationship in which we were at ease, with just the level of closeness that would not be threatening to either of us. Now there was David. First I was angry, then withdrawn and depressed. I knew from the past how devastatingly that mood could escalate, so I sought psychiatric help for ways to come to terms with David's arrival. Given how stubborn Peter could be, I realized that if I fought over David's presence our friendship would be over. I could not let that happen, so with my therapist's help I accepted this admittedly appealing addition into our lives and masked the pain I felt. Indeed, David Quarles became my good friend too, and we all moved on together in both our business and our personal lives. Instead of Peter and I going to our house in Palm Springs, Peter, David, and I went to Palm Springs. In town I worked for both their interests, opening doors to my political world, resolving disputes between them, and finding them remunerative work.

But throughout 1984 Peter became increasingly restless and depressed. He was pessimistic about the prospects of a cure for AIDS and he was absolutely convinced he had it. He lost interest in our consulting business, and spent weeks away from the firm sitting in the sun in Palm Springs preparing for what he believed was the inevitable. I would go off to the desert on the weekend, then come back alone and try to run the firm in his absence. By this time, I knew the business side well, so I worked long hours supervising our staff, handling clients, and keeping Mixner/Scott going. I sent him his share of the revenues, never questioned or confronted him about his behavior, and juggled my feelings as best as I could. I was terrified at the possibility of losing him from my life. Anything was endurable as long as it did not jeopardize the fragile arrangement we had created.

But in fact I was on the edge of another precipice of my own making. I had used drugs and alcohol "recreationally" for years, but since the early 1980s they had become a way to avoid some of the conflicted feelings about my relationship with Peter, about AIDS, about the frightening, uncertain future. By now there was nothing recreational about my intake. My weekend trips to our home in Palm Springs became three- or four-day alcohol and drug binges. I would take acid to escape and Quaaludes to come down from my high. I started to miss work, not turn up at events where I was expected, forget important political meetings.

In January of 1984 a good friend named Larry Weghorst came to my apartment and became the first person to confront me about my addictions. He sat down on the sofa, looked directly at me, and said, "David, you have a problem. You are a drug addict and an alcoholic."

I knew Larry himself was a recovering addict. I laughed aloud. "Larry, I'm a child of the sixties," I told him. "I know how to handle my drugs. But thanks for caring—it's good of you."

Larry would not be distracted. "Listen carefully," he went on. "You are missing work and social engagements. More and more, people are seeing you loaded. I think you have a problem."

I didn't feel like laughing anymore. He was hitting close to home. But I wasn't giving up. "I don't have a problem. I know how to handle my drugs. Just because you can't doesn't mean I can't."

Larry got up from the sofa and walked into my tiny kitchen. He called out, "Come in here, Mixner."

He was holding open the door of the refrigerator and pointed into the freezer. "Take a look. What do you see in there?"

In front of his finger were several lids of grass, a dozen hits of acid, Quaaludes, and speed. I fell silent. "Mixner, most people have lettuce and tomatoes in their icebox," he said. "You have it filled with drugs. Something is wrong here. If you don't have a problem, you should be able to stop anytime. Right?"

"Sure. No problem."

"Why don't you try to stop for thirty days and see what happens?"

"Okay. No big deal. I'll stop for thirty days."

Within three days, I was experiencing withdrawal. I knew I was an addict. With the help of my two loyal Larrys, Larry Weghorst and MECLA chair Larry Sprenger, I enrolled in a well-regarded recovery program. The first two months were hell. I could barely function. But it forced me to reexamine every aspect of my personal and business life, and I was able to recognize that oblivion was not an answer. My drug binges made me forget my life and I wanted to remember that I had lived it.

By the end of 1984 Peter had ceased to participate in the firm in any way. My newfound sobriety made it impossible for me to hide my anger. I found myself increasingly supporting Peter and David financially as they lived in our Palm Springs house. They kept saying they were looking for "investments" in real estate in the desert, so that the money I made in the firm could grow and we would all become richer. But the investments never materialized and I soon realized they didn't exist. It was only my hard work that was financing them. I became furious. I demanded that they come into the city to talk about our situation.

They were both in a rage. I didn't really blame them. They had a good thing going. By the time they arrived, I had already checked with a lawyer about what was required to dissolve the firm if that were the outcome of our meeting. I sat there with Peter and David and we glared at each other. It took a lot of time before we finally opened up. Peter said, with evident difficulty, that he didn't want to spend whatever life he had left working at Mixner/Scott. Clearly he was convinced he had the AIDS virus. David argued for continuing to look for "investments." All I wanted, as I listened to them, was to be out of it all. It took some blunt talk and some difficult and painful soul-searching to move to a resolution, but we finally came to terms. We would end our involvement in

Mixner/Scott, and each of us would go our own way. Soon after the meeting, we arranged to turn over the firm to two of our most outstanding employees, Ron Hampton and Larry Irvin, who received all of the clients, the Palm Springs house, and the firm's indebtedness.

Peter decided to devote himself to battling AIDS. He became chair of AIDS Project-Los Angeles and went on to organize APLA's first million-dollar event, the Commitment to Life dinner that brought in Elizabeth Taylor, Betty Ford, Burt Reynolds, Linda Evans, and dozens of other stars. David Quarles went to work in the cable industry. And I thought long and hard about what I wanted to do.

I was literally unable to throw my entire life into the AIDS battle—I still couldn't face it. To acknowledge the presence of AIDS in our lives would be to admit that Peter and I could die. I think I was less afraid for myself than of the prospect of life without Peter. Most of my friends had moved past denial by then, but I still couldn't handle the truth about what was happening to us. I decided to focus on territory that was familiar to me.

I turned to the peace movement.

CHAPTER TEN

Losses

By the middle of the 1980s, the proliferation of nuclear weapons and the brinksmanship of the great powers had seeded a spreading movement. The purpose of "Nuclear Freeze" was to freeze the production of these weapons at current levels and to begin the process of dismantling them. There was wide concern that the lethal course the world was on was moving it to the verge of a nuclear holocaust.

Massive nuclear disarmament marches took place all over the country. It was a genuine grassroots movement, demanding that we as a nation take the lead in halting the proliferation. Whenever I joined the marches, I would think about the four youngsters who mattered more to me than anyone in the world—my nieces and nephew, Julia and Elizabeth, Monique and Brad—and wonder what world would be there for them when their generation came to leadership. Every time I saw them, I would feel that if I didn't do more to stop the madness I would have failed them.

So that became my focus. My experience with the Vietnam Moratorium made me believe that even now, one individual, starting from scratch, could move millions into action. My vision was to tap into the enormous existing Nuclear Freeze movement and mobilize the participants into forcing our leaders into serious nuclear arms negotiations.

As it was to prove, the self-confidence I had gained from the Moratorium experience and my own ego led me into a huge, well-meaning disaster.

In late 1984 I sat down and wrote a "call to action" to halt the nuclear arms race. The document included a four-step plan that would eventually mobilize citizens around the world. The centerpiece of the plan was to bring together five thousand marchers who would take a year out of their lives and walk across America for nuclear disarmament. The walk would leave Los Angeles in March of 1986 and arrive in Washington in November. The marchers would live in a tent city, travel through deserts and mountains, and hold major rallies in each city they came through on their way to the East Coast. I called the document "Because We Have No Choice . . ." and it read in part:

> *The time has come for another way.*
>
> *PRO Peace is an organization formed to build a massive international citizens movement to immediately create the climate necessary to impel leaders to reach an agreement on nuclear disarmament. PRO Peace is not made up of special interests, only of the one overwhelming interest of sustaining life on earth. It is not confined to one group, one state, or ultimately to one nation. It will not be confined to one action, to one request, or to one constitutional resolution. PRO Peace will be a well-organized, professional, well-financed, forceful organization with a powerful strategy for success.*
>
> *PRO Peace believes deeply in and is committed to non-violence in the spirit of Dr. Martin Luther King, Jr., and Mahatma Gandhi. We believe it is absolutely impossible to achieve our goals by adding to the world's anger, chaos or division. But we also, in that same spirit, passionately reserve our right to peaceful civil disobedience in the service of others, as a sign of our seriousness, our decision, and our profound commitment to make nuclear disarmament happen.*
>
> *We, the citizens, do not bear the awful responsibility of leadership. But we have chosen, in the wake of international governmental inertia, to become leaders. To begin to communicate directly with each other, wherever we are; to force action for as long as it takes.*
>
> *PRO Peace believes this will happen, but only by touching in a*

*humanistic way that core in each of us that wants to survive. What it
will take is courage, commitment, and action.*

From the very beginning, I made a classic organizer's mistake: the
assumption that I could repeat the Moratorium experience and impose a
new organization on an existing mass movement without any clear indication from the people that they desired such an effort. Nevertheless, the
reaction to "Because We Have No Choice . . ." was instant and overwhelming. Every time I spoke to people about the concept, they immediately wanted to participate. By January of 1985 the first seams of the
PRO Peace structure (the name was a partial acronym for People Reaching Out for Peace) began to appear. Peace activists Cass Ben-Levi and
Tim Carpenter joined the staff and Hollywood executive Kathleen Unger agreed to head the finance committee. Together we got to work to
implement the vision.

PRO Peace began to plan what we called the Great Peace March
Across America. Our offices were in the same building that had first
housed Mixner/Scott. Donations began to arrive in significant numbers,
and we had some major contributors. Hollywood celebrities, among
them Barbra Streisand, Richard Dreyfuss, Madonna, Paul Newman,
Sally Field, Jodie Foster, Judd Nelson, and Rosanna Arquette made the
Great Peace March a priority in their giving and their support. It was an
exciting time. Advance teams planned the trek; logistical experts mapped
out the tasks of feeding, bathing, and equipping five thousand marchers
for 255 days. Artists prepared murals for the campsite and recruitment
teams sought out potential marchers. The press gave the preparations
massive coverage, and I found I was drawing increasing attention. In
mid-April, CBS news correspondent Bruce Morton gave the organization—and me—a wonderful boost on national radio:

> *Sixteen years ago, when I was covering protests against the Vietnam
> war, I met a young organizer of those protests named David Mixner.
> David went on from there to do a lot of other things . . . but he is
> back now organizing again with a goal more ambitious than ending
> the Vietnam War. He wants to end the nuclear arms race.*
>
> *David Mixner had, all those years ago, a genius for organizing
> . . . Still later, he went to California and discovered he also had a
> knack for making money. . . . But he has stopped that now, sold the
> various enterprises back to their employees, taken the proceeds, and
> organized a group called PRO Peace, which will try to mobilize people*

on both sides of the Iron Curtain for nuclear disarmament. Its first project is a march across the United States by five thousand people, starting in California on March 1, 1986, ending 255 days later, November—election time—in Washington. After that, he says, there will be other phases of the campaign, including civil disobedience. Idealism? Mixner is an idealist, but he is also a skilled political professional, and the PRO Peace press releases say over and over that the march and everything else will be professional—smart advance people and schedulers and so on.

Can it matter? The idea that one man can make a difference—or thousands—seems almost dated now in a decade of massed government and missiles. But David Mixner thinks he has to try and there seems nothing wrong with that.

Morton's piece captured the tone of the whole thing. My ego wanted complete control of the operation and staff. The press and the peace establishment gave it to me, but the grassroots did not feel invested. They supported the idea and loved the excitement of a new venture, but it did not originate from them. They were participating in someone else's vision, not their own.

I recognized none of this. Until early autumn, nothing went wrong. The press was very supportive, the money arrived at our doors daily, and a young, committed, professional staff worked day and night. My job was to take this momentum and direct it into a well-financed, successful operation. All the early returns suggested we were likely to succeed.

The first attack in the planning stage was aimed at me and it was a personal one. An East Coast congressperson visited our office in Los Angeles. He was outspokenly antinuclear, and as we did with most visiting politicians (and there were many of them), we took him on a tour of the operations and then he spoke to the staff. Afterward, he asked if he could talk with me alone. We went into my office and closed the door. I could see he was very uncomfortable. We skirted around a variety of subjects until I decided to be blunt.

"Congressman, clearly you have something on your mind. Please feel free to tell me what it is."

David, several key individuals, both in and out of Congress, have been meeting about PRO Peace and we have a major concern."

"What's that?"

"Well—it's about you."

"What about me?" I knew I wasn't going to like the answer.

"Well, it's about your lifestyle."

"What lifestyle?" I was damned if I was going to make it easy for him.

He took a deep breath. "David, you are to be commended for the success of PRO Peace and it is a remarkable asset to the antinuclear movement. But given the visibility that you have achieved, we think it is unfair for you to burden the movement with your open gayness. Not that we think there is anything wrong with you being gay—certainly not—but you are mixing the two. Your presence as such an openly gay man distracts from the antinuclear movement. We would like you to become—well—like an honorary chair—and allow someone else to be the spokesperson."

I was incensed, not least because the congressperson had the reputation of coming to Hollywood and partying very hard. As I saw it, my personal morals were in better shape than his.

"Congressman. That is not going to happen. Thank you for your honesty and your willingness to be direct. I look forward to working with you. Now, I have to go back to work." And with that, I ended the meeting and escorted him to the door. It took everything I had not to give him a big wet good-bye kiss.

His visit was like bad karma. Problems began sprouting everywhere. It was becoming apparent that my vision was overly ambitious. Unlike the Moratorium, where many of us had a decade of involvement with the civil rights and antiwar movements and were well-seasoned veterans, many of the staff of PRO Peace were participating in this kind of organization for the first time in their lives. The enthusiasm of the fresh staffers was contagious and I failed to listen to the warnings of the few experienced staff members. If we just kept hammering at the vision, our determination and enthusiasm would make it happen.

Then there was that problem of my ego. I wanted control and I wanted to be liked. I wanted everyone to accept me. It was critical for me to have the approval of my staff and everyone else involved in this great effort. As a result, I made some wrong decisions and some bad ones. For example, we had asked each participating marcher to raise three thousand dollars in pledges to help us meet the enormous budget of this effort. When some of the staff objected to an "economic criterion" for being a marcher, I yielded. I don't think the phrase "politically correct" had been coined back then, but that was certainly how I wanted to be perceived. In fact, I knew better than to give up that much income, and I made a serious mistake. It was to cause critical cash flow problems. Those marchers who arrived to make the trek raised an average of only a little over five hundred dollars each. This generated only half a million dollars in funds instead of the three million we had originally budgeted.

I spent most of my time frantically trying to raise money to cover the shortfall. I sincerely believed that once the marchers arrived at the campsite, the public would be moved by their courage, dedication, and commitment to their sacrifice of a year of their lives in pursuit of a vital and noble end. Surely at that moment we would obtain the needed funds. It was very wishful thinking on my part. Planned-for corporate sponsors and proposed fund-raising concerts never materialized. Word of our money troubles spread, and that made other prospective donors nervous about contributing.

Anytime serious problems develop in an organization, internal dissension spreads. Staff meetings were turbulent. Even when we reached a consensus, it was likely to evaporate once the meeting was over. Serious, bitter, and destructive factions developed within the organization and everyone started choosing sides.

Although I had often faced a divided movement during our antiwar activities, here I had so personalized the effort that there was no backup for my decisions. There was no way out of people personalizing their own judgments in terms of how they viewed *me*. If they were in accord with the basic vision of the march, I was on a pedestal. If they viewed the project as a mess, I was the evil character who had misled them into it.

I had no experience with being the source of an organization's pervasive dissension and it was now too late to build an infrastructure to pull us out of this spiraling disaster. Every single person in PRO Peace had his or her own differing priority for the meager funds available. Every single person had strong feelings about how to salvage the Great Peace March. In the early days, when PRO Peace was capturing the imagination of the nation, I readily accepted the glory. I now knew we were heading into a major political and economic failure, and the blame was mine. It was my vision. I was in charge. I had all the information. I had made the decisions—for better or worse.

The marchers were scheduled to arrive at White Oaks Park in the San Fernando Valley in late January 1986. All winter long the weather in Los Angeles had been picture perfect, not a drop of rain. As we pitched our North Face tents at White Oaks, the skies opened. We were soaked. We slept in mud and we walked in mud. The spirits of those thousand marchers would not be dampened, however, and they sang as they worked preparing for the trek. The third day at the campsite, I fell as I stepped out of a PortaPotti and badly injured the muscles in my foot. For the first days of the march, I was on crutches. A doctor donated his time to care for my foot every night as Kathleen Unger and I frantically worked the phones seeking funds to keep the march alive. The march staff was frazzled and acted out their exhaustion in a number of ways—some helpful and some not.

At last the weather cleared. We pulled up camp and moved to Griffith Park for our final week of preparation. I felt a little more hopeful. The press was beginning to cover the assembled tent city and the visuals began to generate more funds. There were arguments among our legal staff because we had no permits, but I knew that the local governments would not stop the march. We had no money for security but the marchers arranged a security system themselves. Perhaps—just perhaps—a modified Great Peace March might work after all.

But underneath I knew that for the first time in my life I was facing failure in a political venture. I was absolutely terrified. I wasn't sure how to handle it. At night I lay in bed reading accounts of other public figures and how they had handled failure—Dr. King when he was jailed in Albany, Georgia, and McGovern after his massive defeat in the 1972 elections. In the morning I prayed for guidance and the strength to do the right thing, not flee in fear. All day long I put one foot in front of the other, desperately attempting to turn the march around. Every time I found myself tempted to protect myself and my reputation, I caught myself. I had only one responsibility, and that was to the marchers. I wanted to cry, but bit it back because I would become completely unraveled if I let go. I put on a show of confidence. No one could see inside.

On March 1 we moved to downtown Los Angeles to march to a major rally at Los Angeles City Hall. We paid rock stars Mister, Mister and Melissa Manchester (who were extremely supportive throughout PRO Peace and even wrote us a song) to perform at the departure ceremonies. One of Los Angeles's leading weekly newspapers, *The LA Weekly*, ran a front-page editorial calling people to attend the departure to show support for the marchers. Radio stations were covering it live.

I expected fifteen to twenty thousand people at the rally but when we arrived at City Hall there were no more than five. At that moment, I knew that the Great Peace March was not going to happen. We had failed to stir the imagination of the people and they were letting us know it. They were not moved. It was over.

For the next several days, Kathleen Unger and I worked out of motel rooms along the route trying to raise enough money to keep the march moving across the desert. But the money ran out and my credibility was wholly gone. In a late-night meeting, the staff finally convinced me that PRO Peace was over and that I had to tell the marchers. I found a phone, called my sister, my family, and Peter to let them know I would be facing the marchers the next day to declare PRO Peace dead, and lay sleepless the rest of the night in my motel room while the light of a neon sign flashed on and off outside my window.

I went back to Los Angeles the next morning, met Kathleen at the PRO Peace office, and started the drive in her car to Barstow, where the marchers were camped. I sat next to her in silence, wondering what I would say to them and where I would get the courage.

As we drove into the campsite, marchers came clustering around the car. I felt an overwhelming sense of shame. In a trance, I walked to the gathering area where the marchers and the press had congregated. I took up a bullhorn and announced that we had run out of money to escort them safely across the country. I had failed them. PRO Peace was over. It was up to them to meet and decide what they wanted to do. I handed the bullhorn to one of their leaders and walked back slowly to the car. Some of them trailed after me, yelling in anger. I just kept moving forward, climbed into the car, and Kathleen drove me back to the office. By the time I arrived, the staff had emptied it out. I looked over the space, the gaping file cabinet drawers, the papers scattered all over the floor, the colorful charts ripped off the wall, and realized this was all that was left of a shattered dream.

The marchers refused to be discouraged. The real story of the Great Peace March was their unshakable determination to make it across the country. They took responsibility for succeeding at their venture, raised some minimal funds, and with extraordinary courage took off. With great difficulty, they made it, marching into Washington, D.C., in November. It was a remarkable accomplishment. One marcher wore a ribbon with my name written on it, so that in a very small way I would be present as they entered the capital. I still have it.

I focused my life on cleaning up the mess caused by the collapse of PRO Peace. I was deeply ashamed, but I was determined to conduct myself with dignity. The debt was massive. Tens of thousands of dollars of employment taxes were owed. I was hit by a barrage of lawsuits. I forced my way through each day. My friends rallied around—Peter, Diane, and Roberta—and Patsy and Michael. I had run up huge amounts on my personal credit cards to help finance the march, so I had no choice but to declare personal bankruptcy as well as bankruptcy for PRO Peace. I had another quick lesson in reality the day of my bankruptcy hearing. In their anger, some of the PRO Peace staff came to the courtroom to witness my public humiliation.

For the next six years, every spare cent I made went to paying off the thousands and thousands of dollars in taxes and debts that I was legally and morally required to pay. Some friends suggested that I should do a fund-raiser, but I thought it inappropriate. The failure was my responsibility.

My family gave me strength. At the end of the encampment in Griffith Park, my mother, father, and Patsy and Melvin and their families had come to participate in the departure ceremonies. I can still see my mother sitting in a lawn chair as the marchers gathered on a hillside, singing with Holly Near in the twilight. She never seemed happier. She and Dad were so proud of PRO Peace. When it died in a glare of national publicity, their only concern was my well-being. Mom called every day and wrote me warm notes of encouragement. My taciturn dad, in one of his rare phone calls, said, "Son, the only failure would have been not to have attempted it. You believed in it. It was not for greed, it was for peace. You have nothing for which you should be ashamed."

I loved them for their love.

What was urgent now was to find work. Over the years, as I immersed myself in various political ventures, I had lived off the scanty wages of an organizer and slept on many couches around the country. The success of Mixner/Scott had changed that for a while, and I had been able to be a full-time volunteer in my activism. Now, my life in a shambles, I sat alone in my apartment with no idea where to turn. I had lost belief in myself. Torie Osborn was my savior. She was a bright, energetic redhead, a lesbian who had long worked in the women's movement, and at PRO Peace she had raised money and handled media. She had been a loyal supporter throughout the ordeal, and she was not about to let me sit alone now and wallow in my self-pity. Torie made it her personal project to help me regain confidence. She turned up almost every day to take me to lunch and talk to me about moving on to other things. Her vigor and her insistence were effective. She started to make me believe in myself again.

Peter urged me to get involved in the fight against AIDS. He would say, "David, you've attempted to save the world. Now how about giving us that extraordinary gift of organizing so that we can save ourselves?" I knew he was right. There were twenty-one thousand documented cases in the country by then, and I knew over fifty who had died. My deep belief in God and in serving others required that I join the battle. My time for denial was over.

As usual, Roberta and Diane had an agenda for me. Right-wing extremist Lyndon LaRouche had placed a measure on the November 1986 California ballot that would make it mandatory to quarantine people who had AIDS. The measure, called Proposition 64, was drawing a fair amount of public support, which gained momentum when Rock Hudson revealed that he had AIDS in 1985 and set off a national hysteria. Diane was co-chairing the campaign committee against the proposition and wanted me to be the statewide campaign manager. The committee was a Who's Who of the movement, but some of its members were concerned about my recent experiences around PRO Peace. Diane, Roberta, Larry Sprenger, and Peter were adamant that I could run a campaign in my sleep. They knew I would bust my ass to prove myself. In June the campaign committee agreed to hire me on the condition that I keep a low profile and report directly to Diane. Torie Osborn became the southern California manager. Dan Bross, who was later to be the executive director of the AIDS Action Council, worked the field operation. Ivy Bottini took on the grassroots organizing once again. Unlike NO on 6, this battle proved easy. We won with over 70 percent of the vote statewide; in San Francisco it was 86 percent.

But the Proposition 64 work could not compensate for the tragedy that arose in early June. Peter began to suspect he had AIDS. He called one day in tears to say a rash had appeared on his face and inside his mouth. I tried to reassure him, but by the end of the month we knew it was true. He had been having night sweats and skin disorders, and he was tired all the time. By now an antibody test for the AIDS virus was available, and with Peter's illness David Quarles and I faced the fact that we could no longer put off being tested. In the midst of our grief, we went and had it done. David tested positive. I was absolutely joyless when I found out that I was negative. All I could feel was guilt; my anguish for them overwhelmed me. I didn't want to tell Peter my results but he pressed me, and he greeted the news with a great hug. I forced back tears.

Peter continued to decline throughout July. I would go over to his house and sit by his bed while we watched old movies. Then the night sweats increased, so every morning I would go over to change the drenched sheets; David was in no condition to help. One day in early August I went over to Diane and Roberta's office to talk about how we could get Peter Compound S, a drug developed by the National Cancer Institute that was still in clinical trials by Burroughs Wellcome, the drug company the NCI had licensed it to. All reports indicated it was the most promising drug therapy so far, but not available for general use. I walked into Diane's office and found her sitting behind her desk with tears streaming down her face.

"David Quarles just called. We have to get to Sherman Oaks Hospital

Family Album

ristmas 1950 I am smiling but Melvin is
ng serious. [Author's collection]

1967 At Patsy's house in Baltimore, addressing
envelopes for a political mailing.
[Patsy Annison collection]

1971 Mom and her trio: Patsy is between me and Melvin. [Author's collection]

1982 Assembled for a grou portrait at the Palm Spring house: Mom and Dad in front, me, Patsy, and Melvin standing behin [Author's collection]

1994 With the loves of my life—my nieces Elizabeth and Julia Annison. [Berliner Studios]

1968 Sam Brown at the National Action Corps office. [Author's collection]

1969 The "Easy Riders" take off on a Moratorium organizing trip: From the left, Rick Stearns, me, and Dan MacIntosh. [Author's collection]

1969 At a McGovern Commission hearing in New Orleans with Patti Knox and Eli Segal. [Author's collection]

Los Angeles

1978 The fight against the Briggs Initiative: Me, Peter, and campaign worker Sallie Fiske. [Author's collection]

1979 With Shirley MacLaine at Peter Scott's house in Los Angeles. [© Barry Levine]

1982 Peter Scott and me at work at Mixner/Scott in West Hollywood. [Marsha T. Gorman]

1982 My friends gave me a birthday party when I turned thirty-six; from the left, Peter Scott, Roberta Bennett, Diane Abbitt, and me. I was in one of my thinner phases for the moment. [Author's collection]

1985 Announcing the PRO Peace March at the Los Angeles Press Club. [PRO Peace Collection]

1985 Showing Cesar Chavez the campsite for the march. He had been a hero of mine ever since I had worked for his cause as a student. [Author's collection]

1991 In Sacramento, protesting Governor Pete Wilson's veto of gay rights legislation. [Alex Koleszar]

July 1992 On the floor of the Democratic National Convention at Madison Square Garden. [Dr. Scott Hitt]

My credentials are hanging around my neck. [Author's collection]

July 1993 I am being arrested in front of the White House for protesting "Don't Ask, Don't Tell." [Peter A. Harris/*The Washington Times*]

January 1993 At the Gay and Lesbian Victory Fund Salute to me in Washington. [Author's collection]

A Clinton Album

1970 The Oxford years. Rick Stearns and Bill Clinton on a visit to Stonehenge. [Author's collection]

1980 At a party at Peter's house in Los Angeles. Very few politicians were willing to attend a gay-sponsored event in those years. [© Barry Levine]

1987 Governor Clinton at Patsy's house in Denver. [Patsy Annison collection]

1992 At a gay and lesbian
fund-raiser for Clinton in
Los Angeles in February.
Roberta Achtenberg is shak
ing hands with the Governo
[© Barry Levine]

December 1993 With Vice
President Gore and White
House aide Marsha Scott.
[White House photograph]

December 1993 The Oval
Office. A meeting with the
President after the arrest and
fallout following the "Don't
Ask, Don't Tell" protest.
[White House photograph]

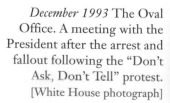

right away. They've admitted Peter with *Pneumocystis carinii*—AIDS pneumonia."

The mention of Sherman Oaks sent chills up my spine. It was known as one of the best AIDS care centers in the country, but for us it was the place where we sent our friends to die.

"How bad is it?"

"They don't know if he'll make it through the weekend."

We sped to the hospital. I took the elevator up to the third floor, terrified at what I might find. The nurses' station directed me to Peter's room. On his door was the brightly colored tag that indicated an AIDS patient was inside. I felt sick to my stomach. Peter weakly turned his head to me as I walked in and began to cry. Holding him in my arms, we wept together.

It was touch and go for two days. He was afraid of being alone at night and David, Diane, Roberta, and I took turns sleeping in his room. I knew he was rallying when he complained of my snoring and asked if I could take the day shift.

On August 16 I turned forty years old. My friends wanted to throw me a party but I couldn't imagine one without Peter. Instead we decorated his hospital room, invited four other friends and the medical staff, and held the party there. After I blew out the candles, we brought cake and ice cream to the other patients and their families and friends on the AIDS ward. Peter motioned for me to come over to his bed. "I am going to get better," he whispered to me. "That's your fortieth birthday present."

He did. I could have had no better gift. At the end of August I brought him home. Daily throughout the fall, I picked him up in the morning, drove him back to the hospital, and sat with him during his IV treatments. All around us the news was getting grimmer. My wonderful San Francisco friend, Tom Waddell, developed AIDS. Jerry Smith of the Washington Redskins died of it. David Quarles's T-cell count dropped to 280. Michael Newton of the Los Angeles Music Center and Sheldon Andelson's half brother Roger Horwitz died of AIDS. Mark Coleman, another close friend, told me he was HIV-positive. Every day brought more bad news.

The one hope on the horizon was Compound S. The drug trials were indicating it actually prolonged the lives of AIDS patients. Peter was frantic to obtain it and so were we. Even if you were participating in a drug trial, you never knew if you were receiving it or were in a control group getting sugar cubes in order to test the effectiveness of the treatment. We weren't interested in getting Peter into the trial; we wanted to

be sure he got the real thing. We went to our devoted friend Jane Nathanson and her husband Marc because we knew they were friends of
Congressperson Henry Waxman, who headed the Health Care Subcommittee in the House. Appropriately, Waxman refused to intervene. What
he did instead had a much broader impact. Working with Senator Edward Kennedy, he pressured the FDA to cut short the Phase Two trials
of the drug, given the excellent results in Phase One, and to release
Compound S, now renamed AZT, for public sale by the fall. In addition,
Waxman and Kennedy put through legislation that ensured AZT would
be obtainable by everyone with AIDS by making funds available to them
for what was a very expensive drug.

We were jubilant. AZT, we hoped, would keep Peter alive until the
next treatment breakthrough. He had a bad reaction to his first dose in
October, but within a week was tolerating it better and taking it daily.
There was a brief moment of panic at the end of the month when the
drug company ran out of AZT but we soon found new supplies. Then
just before Thanksgiving Peter had a massive heart attack. He bounced
back quickly, but all around us the news grew worse. By now, the death
of several friends in a single week was not uncommon.

By mid-December Peter was in a severe depression. I struggled daily
with rage and fear. Peter was dying, my friends were dying, and I was
powerless to stop it. All my life I had felt that I could change the course
of events if I dedicated myself to the task at hand. I could no longer
believe this. Each morning I asked God in my morning prayers for the
strength to get through another day. I prayed for my rage to be removed
so that bitterness would not take control of my soul. I was determined
that AIDS not steal my capacity to love and forgive. I took long walks
along the beach and in the hills seeking moments of peace from the
plague. Every day I talked to Patsy to keep myself centered and to receive her love. She was my rock.

On December 15 there was another blow. I found a message on my
answering machine from Michael Annison: "David, your mother has had
a heart attack. She is in bad shape and you need to get home as soon as
possible."

I caught the first plane to Denver, where my parents had been living
since Dad's retirement so they could be around Patsy and Michael's
children as they were growing up. Patsy greeted me at Rose Hospital
and said it didn't look as if Mom would make it. The room was filled
with equipment keeping her alive. She was asleep. I kissed her gently on
the forehead. She opened her eyes and squeezed my hand. Gasping for
breath, she said, "I'm so sorry, honey. I know you have been through so

much this year." I kissed her again, held tight to her hand, and said, "Mom, I love you so much. You have given me so much. Please don't go. I'm not ready." She smiled at me.

Late that night Patsy and I sent Melvin, Michael, and Dad home to get some sleep, and we dozed in the waiting room. Toward morning the nurses came in and woke us to say we had better get to Mom's bedside. We found the room full of medical personnel trying to save her life. Patsy and I stood at the end of the bed, resting our hands on her legs as she struggled to stay alive. I went to the elevator for Dad, Melvin, and Michael, and when we came back to the room Mom was dead. Patsy and Michael's pastor arrived and we formed a circle around the bed, took Mom's hands, and recited the Lord's Prayer. Then I knew she was gone.

I loved her very much. Her death devastated me. I had talked to her every day and every day she gave me the strength to continue. I would have to find my own strength now.

CHAPTER ELEVEN

Into the Night . . .

For the remainder of the decade three commitments drove my life: taking care of Peter, working as an activist against AIDS, and paying off my responsibilities from PRO Peace. To deal with those responsibilities—and to fund my everyday expenses—I built a small consulting practice based on old Mixner/Scott corporate clients and worked out of my apartment. Almost all my free time went to caring for Peter and fighting to find something that would prolong his life. And to implement the battle against AIDS, I called on long-time skills and practices.

By December 1986 there were AIDS organizations in every major city. Some groups were dedicated to the care and treatment of people with the disease. Others engaged in a wide range of political actions to increase federal funding, speed up the release of other promising drugs by the FDA, and fight discrimination against people with HIV. Most of these groups were gay and lesbian. Communities everywhere knew they had to take care of their own. People like Jane and Marc Nathanson and Marylouise Oates were the exception to most of my liberal straight friends. Most didn't want to hear about AIDS. There was a clear implication that it was our own behavior that had created the epidemic, and they gave more lip service to the "rights" of AIDS victims than help.

In Los Angeles at least a dozen significant organizations and groups were fighting hard against the disease and caring for our sick and dying. In December a group of fund-raisers and activists in the battle against AIDS in our community decided to meet in my apartment to plan more effective ways to pool our resources and efforts to combat AIDS, both in government and politics. We sat late into the night figuring out what we could do collectively that would contribute significantly to the efforts around the country to find a cure.

We decided that we didn't want to form yet another organization, so we named ourselves the Book Study Group and told anyone who asked that we got together to discuss what we had been reading. We had no formal structure. Each of us had a particular sphere of influence we could tap into to reach a variety of communities. Thus, Roberta and Diane could liaise with the lesbian and women's movement, Jean O'Leary with the legal community, Duke Comegys with the Gay and Lesbian Community Center, Rob Eichberg with his Advocate Experience network, Larry Sprenger with local elected officials, Sheldon Andelson with Jewish leaders. I had a network of national political contacts. Coordinating these varied accesses, we were able to tap into a broad range of constituencies, and as we utilized our fund-raising skills, the group proved to be very effective. We began to meet with major public officials like United States Senators Alan Cranston and John Kerry, presidential candidate Jesse Jackson, House Majority Leader Richard Gephardt, and presidential candidate Gary Hart. AIDS was a national disaster. It required the help of a national leadership.

Our most important achievement was creating a California alternative to the slow and bureaucratic FDA. The group met with California Attorney General John Van de Kamp in May of 1987 and made a passionate plea for his help in creating the first state-run equivalent of the FDA. Van de Kamp later described the meeting to *The Los Angeles Times.* "It was," he said, "a cry of frustration . . . one of the gloomiest evenings I've spent in a long time." He left the meeting committed to creating a state operation that would enable California to conduct its own research and drug trials. He had his staff look into ways to structure the entity without entangling it in federal regulations that could bring the courts to overturn it. Then he proposed a bill to the legislature, AB 1952, that would allow independent research and drug trials for pharmaceutical companies headquartered in California. Our group mobilized support for the bill by calling our friends in the legislature, briefing the press, seeking editorial board support from the newspapers, and obtaining endorsements from a wide variety of state leaders.

The FDA was extremely unhappy with the legislation. Publicly it kept a low profile, but it made calls throughout the California research, scientific, and political community to try to stop what it clearly viewed as an intrusion into its turf. Despite this, the attorney general shepherded AB 1952 through the legislature and then in a private meeting convinced Republican Governor George Deukmejian to sign it. It was an extraordinary victory. In the last few years the Salk Institute has been utilizing this law for its research on AIDS. Moreover, the law's passage helped serve as a wake-up call to the FDA itself, and spurred it to further internal reforms. In gratitude for his effective labors on behalf of people with HIV and AIDS, the Book Study Group worked hard and raised significant funds for Van de Kamp's losing race for governor.

By 1987 the anger in the AIDS community toward President Reagan and his White House staff was at the boiling point. If they had treated this epidemic as they did other public health crises, thousands of lives could have been saved. They ignored their own health officials who pleaded for a coordinated response to the epidemic. If they had reacted to AIDS the way they had to toxic shock syndrome, the nation would have been better prepared to take effective action dealing with the surging number of cases. But it was gay men dying, so they played politics, acceded to rightist pressures to stifle AIDS education, left researchers uncoordinated and underfunded, and kept the homosexual community vulnerable and miserably uninformed. Not only had they failed to warn us, mobilize the nation, and assume a leadership role in the search for a cure, they were openly hostile and homophobic. Indeed, the only leadership there had been came from the gay community. I do not think it is an exaggeration to say that the policies and actions of the Reagan administration were directly responsible for the deaths of thousands upon thousands of young men from AIDS.

In June 1987, at the Third International AIDS Conference in Washington, D.C., Ronald Reagan gave his very first speech on the subject. It was six years since the epidemic had begun. Thirty-six thousand Americans had been diagnosed with AIDS. The death toll stood at almost twenty-one thousand. Even the President and his senior staff recognized he could be silent no longer. At a fund-raising dinner of AmFAR—the American Foundation for AIDS Research—which had been launched by the country's most famous AIDS victim, Rock Hudson, the summer when he went public with his diagnosis, and was spearheaded by the indomitable Dr. Mathilde Krim, Reagan stood up in a huge tent set up for the purpose and launched his speech to the standing-room-only black-tie audience with a not very funny anecdote. He focused most of his words on testing for AIDS. He said little about research, little about education, nothing about ensuring the civil rights of those tested. He mentioned the victims of transfusions, hemophiliacs, the partners of IV drug users, but never said a word about homosexuals. The speech was pure politics.

While many of us in the gay community understood the political necessity of the invitation to the President, we had argued for several weeks beforehand about the appropriateness of protesting it as he spoke. AmFAR leaders pleaded with us not to disrupt the ceremonies. Finally, we agreed to Peter's suggestion simply to stand up in silence. A man behind me angrily shouted for me to sit down. We could hear the chanting of demonstrators outside.

Activist Duke Comegys, a member of our Book Study Group, had urged that we be arrested in front of the White House as a protest against the President's policies. The protest had mushroomed by the time of the conference, and was being organized by the National Mobilization Against AIDS. On June 1, the day after the speech, a hundred national community leaders gathered in the basement of the New York Avenue Presbyterian Church. Of our group, only Roberta Bennett and I had been arrested before. The Human Rights Campaign Fund— HRCF—the homosexual community's national political action and legislative advocacy organization, had arranged for the Quakers to train us in nonviolence and how to respond if provoked by the police. Their instructions were practical and levelheaded, but the tension was palpable. Some broke down at the possibility of arrest.

Dressed in sedate business attire, we all marched out of the church at noon in procession to Lafayette Park. Awaiting us were hundreds of cheering supporters who had left the AIDS conference to show their support. Dan Bradley, who was now dying of AIDS, weakly ascended the makeshift podium. Dan had formerly run the Legal Services Corporation, which provided legal assistance to the poor, and he was known throughout Washington as a man of great integrity. His presence brought a moving dignity to the assemblage. Dan spoke about the "crime of silence," not only the President's but all those liberals who were failing to speak up in fear of offending some unknown political constituency. He spoke of his bitter disappointment in onetime progressive allies who were letting him die without a fight. We wept in accord as we listened. Then Dan stepped down and led us across the street to the gates of the White House. Sixty-four of us stepped across the barricades and sat down on Pennsylvania Avenue. The police arrived and before our eyes pulled on brilliant yellow rubber gloves that reached to their elbows to protect themselves from us. The gloves became an instant symbol. Across the street supporters started chanting, "Your gloves don't match your shoes!"

There were two buses standing there, one for men and one for women. Those of us who had been arrested previously let the newcomers go first so that they wouldn't have to sweat out their fear any longer. When a police officer finally got to me, he said softly as he put on the handcuffs, "I'm really sorry. I have a brother who has AIDS." He led me to the "men only" bus, and I couldn't help myself as I climbed in and saw thirty of my brothers, all handcuffed like me. "Oh, my," I said. "Thirty men in handcuffs—it's a queen's dream come true!" It broke the ice. As the buses pulled away, the hundreds lining the street called out to us, "Thank you! Thank you! Thank you!" It sent chills up our spines.

In jail, the lesbians were placed in one big holding cell and the gay men in another next to it. We sang, told jokes, and laughed together. Roberta and I kept knocking on the walls pretending we were doing code for a "breakout." I did a Susan Hayworth imitation and flung myself against the bars shouting, "I want to live!" The guards seemed sympathetic to us all as we waited to be booked and then let out. Newspaper reporters and TV cameras had recorded the protest, the arrests, the gloved police. AIDS was becoming a national story at last.

In the fall we all came back to the capital for the second March on Washington. On Sunday night, October 10, the Human Rights Campaign Fund held a large fund-raising dinner. Sixteen hundred gays and lesbians had come together from all over the country to honor our two openly gay congresspersons, Barney Frank and Gerry Studds. It struck me how very few straight politicians were in the ballroom. Most elected officials would normally kill to be in a room with a crowd like this, each of whom had paid $250 for their tickets. Even those who had received large checks from HRCF to push for our concerns were somehow unable to join us. Breaking bread together was something different from taking our money. Despite the success of local organizations like MECLA to pull in candidates when elections were looming, despite the courage of a few national figures who had spoken out on the community's behalf—and despite all the attention AIDS was now getting—one basic reality hadn't changed. This community would still have to fight for its own survival. We could not rely on others.

After the dinner several of us from California went over to the Lincoln Memorial. Bathed in moonlight, it was like a temple. I looked toward the Washington Monument and thought of Dr. King and the 1963 civil rights march. Twenty-five years later, here I was with my brothers and sisters, this time marching for *our* freedom. I moved to the south wall of the Memorial and reread the words of the Gettysburg Address chiseled into the marble: ". . . that we here highly resolve that these dead shall not have died in vain . . ."

Now, a century and a quarter later, that was our resolve as well. It was up to us. I was ready for sunrise and the march.

It was enormous in size and powerfully moving. The organizers estimated half a million people had come from around the nation in protest against the nation's policies in the epidemic. There were twenty-five thousand from Los Angeles alone. In front of the Capitol the vast crowd listened to the speakers and joined hands, swaying back and forth, as Holly Near sang "We Are Gentle, Angry People" . . . Then we left and went to view the AIDS Quilt. It was the first time I had seen this astounding memorial to all those who had died of AIDS. As we joined the thousands moving slowly along the length of the quilt, we wept uncontrollably. Friends and families had each created three-by-six-foot segments on which they stitched the name of the one they had loved and lost, and then the segments had been sewn together to form the great sweep of quilt. We walked along reading the names, looking at the poignant mementos embedded in the segments—a pair of blue jeans, a baseball cap, a teddy bear, a page of sheet music—and we swallowed back our sobs. It was unbearably sad—the most overwhelming, gut-wrenching experience of my life.

I came home from the march to find Peter holding his own. He and David and I decided to fly to Kauai for Thanksgiving. We rented a house right on the beach on the north shore of the island. David and Peter were both feeling great so it was a celebratory time. Three other friends joined us and we spent a joyful week hiking, lying on the beach, and playing. Each morning Peter got up and practiced his golf shots in the sand. Thanksgiving dinner was a grand spread of traditional foods. Each of us made our favorite dish from childhood and I baked my mother's pecan pie. As I write this nearly ten years later and remember that glorious dinner, I am struck by the knowledge that of us six, Larry Sprenger and I are the only ones still alive.

Thanksgiving was only a respite. The dying went on around us: within months Sheldon Andelson, Dan Bradley, others. And then, through the spring of 1988, Peter began to decline. Simultaneously David became seriously ill and for the first time had to be hospitalized. By summer they were in poor shape. We who were their friends did what hundreds like us were doing across the country: We set up a primary care group to take care of them. Each week we talked on the phone and set up our assignments. We decided who would feed them; who would take them to the hospital for transfusions; who would make sure they had a ride to their doctors' appointments, handle the finances, be the liaison with the health care nurses, make sure the house was cleaned, cope with the legal and insurance problems and paperwork. Our lives were about taking care of them. Every day I picked up Peter and took him into the San Fernando Valley for his IV treatments, and we'd sit together and talk as they pumped him full of antibiotics.

In August he had to be taken off AZT since he could no longer tolerate the drug. By the end of the month, he was back in the hospital, running fevers of 104 degrees. David was hospitalized at the same time. We rushed from one room to the other administering care and love to both of them. There was no time even to think about what was happening. I would get up at 4:30 A.M. to tackle my consulting work so I could be in the hospital by 8:30 for my shift. As I drove down the streets of West Hollywood on my way, I passed hand-lettered signs reading "Estate Sale" in front of the houses of all the young men who had died of AIDS. I took care of Peter until late in the day, when Roberta, Diane, or our friends Tom Moore, Jane Nathanson, and Steve Lachs arrived to relieve me. Then I'd speed home, answer my business calls, tend to personal affairs, and head back to the hospital to spend another hour or two. Other friends would bring food and relieve us when we became too exhausted to function.

Peter and David both came home in September. David was much better, but Peter had lost so much weight and was so weak that he was largely bedridden. Once in a while he felt strong enough to sit up and every now and then we took him out, but those times became rarer. October 19 would be his fiftieth birthday. It was clear that this would be his last. A group of us decided to hold a small dinner party at his home to mark the milestone. David and I were determined to do it up right; no matter what, this was going to be a celebration for Peter, not a wake. We took ourselves to a local videotaping studio, put on wigs, long stunning boas, and elaborate outfits and sang "You Have a Friend." That evening, as the guests arrived in black tie as requested, we gathered them around the television set, inserted the videotape of our drag performance, and sent Peter and everyone else into gales of laughter. From that moment on, the evening was about fun, love, and celebration.

The first Tuesday in November was election day: George Bush vs. Michael Dukakis. We had to cast our votes against the Reagan years. Peter refused to vote by absentee ballot. He was determined to go to the polling place and vote in person. I carried him down the steps and placed him in the car. "I know this is a lot of trouble, David," Peter said, "but if it's the last act of my life, I want to vote against the people who I believe killed me." We pulled up in front of the house that served as his local polling place. An election official came out to help me get him out of the car. Peter pushed us away. "I'm going to walk into that place on my own," he told us. He struggled up the drive and into the house, frail and stumbling, entered the voting booth, and made his choices. We had to carry him back to the car.

Soon Christmas was upon us. Peter had improved enough to be up and about. Our friend Michael Roberts, chef of Trumps restaurant, volunteered to prepare Christmas dinner for us all. Roberta, Diane, David, and I worked hard to make sure this would be a loving holiday. We put up decorations, bought special gifts, and invited our closest friends to Christmas dinner. Peter and David gave me a Tiffany clock that was inscribed on the back, "With eternal love . . ."

But we knew time was running out. That spring Peter wanted to see Hawaii one more time. Larry Sprenger and I went with him, but the trip was so hard for him that we weren't sure he would make it home alive. By the end of April, the death vigil began. Peter was bedridden. His favorite operas played by his bedside. His feet were sore and I massaged them several times a day. Sometimes it tickled. He would giggle in delight and ask for more, and I'd agree only if he would tell me how much he loved me. But little routines like this didn't last long. As May arrived, Peter slowly began to slip in and out of consciousness. We spent hours talking to him and holding his hand, but he no longer registered what was happening around him.

By the second week of May, he was in a coma. Roberta, Diane, and I visited his doctor and told him of Peter's wish to have all medications stopped when he slipped into a coma. Diane wanted to ask Peter if it was time. None of us thought he would be able to understand her, but she lay down next to him and asked for his permission to stop the medications. As if a bolt of lightning had hit him, he opened his eyes and said in a clear voice, "No, I am not ready." Stunned, we watched as he got out of bed and started walking around the room. For three days, he was

vigorous, lively, and happy. Friends came by to visit. We realized what
had happened. He needed the extra time to say good-bye.

On Friday, Peter and I spent three hours alone. He patted his bed and
asked me to lie down next to him. He took my hand and held it, and for
half an hour we lay next to each other in silent peacefulness. Then, with
difficulty and careful not to pull out any tubes, he turned on his side and
faced me. He was smiling.

"David, you know how much I love you, don't you?"

"Yes, I do. I never have doubted that."

"Well, I have never loved anyone more than I love you. We never
really talked about it, but you must know the depth of my love for you."

I struggled to hold back tears. "Oh, Peter," I said, "we were two
stubborn old fools who just couldn't say it. We knew how unique our
friendship was."

"No, David. It wasn't just a friendship. It was one of the most special
things in my life. Please know that. I will always be grateful to you."

I realized this was our farewell. "Peter, I have always loved you," I
said, my voice quavering. "Thank you for everything."

He smiled again, closed his eyes, and fell into a restful sleep. I lay
there with him for another hour, now and then massaging his feet.
When I finally got up to leave the room, he jolted awake.

"David?"

"Yes?"

"When I'm gone, don't ever date an actor!"

I laughed and gave him a wink.

"David," he called out again.

"Yes, Peter?"

"I love you."

I went back to his side and kissed him. I ran my hand through his hair
and said, "I know. See you later, baby."

At 5:30 the next morning, May 13, my phone rang. It was Peter's
nurse. "David, Peter is failing quickly. I don't think he has much longer.
You'd better get over here immediately."

I was there in minutes. He lay in a coma, his breathing labored. The
nurse and I telephoned his special friends. We gathered around the bed,
and I began to massage his feet. He heaved one great deep breath and
then let go.

I wept. I had never in my life felt more alone.

We held a memorial service for Peter at St. Augustine-by-the-Sea
Episcopal Church a week later. We who loved him were there. Patsy and
Michael flew in with Elizabeth and Julia. Melvin and Donna sent flow-

ers. But with the few usual exceptions—Bob Shrum and Marylouise Oates, Marc and Jane Nathanson—very few of my straight friends even acknowledged his death. Hardly any of the dozens of elected officials we had assisted over the years even sent a note. Even in death, we didn't count.

It was a beautiful and moving memorial. Members of the Los Angeles Philharmonic called and asked to be allowed to play before the service began. Two singers from the Los Angeles Opera Company had read in Peter's obituary of his love for opera and volunteered to sing. The church was filled with music as we wept at our loss. Broadway director Tom Moore, a close friend of Peter's, gave a reading. Then openly gay Los Angeles judge Steve Lachs mounted the pulpit and gave an extraordinary eulogy. He had been devoted to Peter and he captured perfectly that independent spirit, the leadership that was so magnetic, and the human qualities that aroused so much devotion in his friends.

Then the church fell silent, and the bells began to toll as if to announce the death of a fallen leader. An opera singer sang "The Lord's Prayer." We left the sanctuary slowly to the tolling of the bells.

In the middle of the service, David Quarles had been taken ill and had to be assisted from the church. He felt strong enough to come to the reception at the Nathansons' afterward, but the next day we had to take him to the hospital. There wasn't much time to mourn Peter because almost immediately our life centered around taking care of David. For the next six months the same devoted group who had helped Peter became David's primary caretakers. He died over the Thanksgiving weekend.

I had to leave Los Angeles. The losses and the memories overwhelmed me. I was filled with anger at Peter's death. I had no more to give to anyone. I was a burnt-out case. If I were to survive, I had to renew my faith, my commitment to life, and my will to fight. I closed my apartment, had a farewell gathering with my friends, and drove around the city to say good-bye to all the places that had meaning for Peter and me. I did not know if I would ever return.

When I made this decision, I had called my long-time friend from the McCarthy campaign, Anne Wexler, and asked for her help in finding work somewhere remote enough to be away from the daily horror of AIDS but not too far from a metropolitan area. Anne ran a consulting firm. Within two days she called back with a possibility in Connecticut. It sounded perfect.

About two months before Peter died, I had met a young, talented actor named Bradley Laughlin. The gentlest of men, he became amid all this tragedy a source of deep strength and unconditional caring. He had no history with any of my dead friends. He was not a reminder of the dreadful past and the awful present. I told him about Connecticut. He made a decision to leave acting, and applied and was accepted at Yale Divinity School. The day I flew out of Los Angeles, Bradley came with me.

We rented a house on Long Island Sound, in East Haven, and for a year and a half I did nothing but heal myself—physically, emotionally, and spiritually. I rarely went out or saw other people. I took long walks along the beach and through the Connecticut forests. During the day, I earned a living of sorts by consulting with the insurance industry. At night, I read, listened to music, and shared long conversations with Bradley, trying to understand a world in which there was so much cruelty and evil, and hungering for the faith I had lost. I devoured books about the Holocaust in World War II, seeking for answers in the struggles of survivors. Out of the ashes and their devastated lives these extraordinary people built a new nation. Of all that I thought about and talked about and read about in those months, it was the stories of courage that I found in these books that helped me to heal.

In August of 1990 I reached the conclusion that I was in fighting shape again. It was time to rejoin the battle. I decided to return to Los Angeles.

Part Two

Commanding Respect

". . . from now on
let your pureness and your strength, your solemn story
be known by children and by men, by women and by old men,
let it reach all men without hope, let it go down to the mines
   corroded by sulphuric air,
let it mount the inhuman stairways of the slave,
let all the stars, let all the flowers of Castile
   and of the world
write your name and your bitter struggle
and your victory strong and earthen as a red oak.
Because you have revived with your sacrifice
lost faith, absent heart, trust in the earth,
and through your abundance, through your nobility, through
   your dead,
as if through a valley of harsh bloody rocks,
flows an immense river with doves of steel and of hope."

                        —*Pablo Neruda*
        "Arrival in Madrid of the International Brigade"

CHAPTER TWELVE

A Reason to Hope

O F all the cruelties inflicted on gays and lesbians for their sexuality, the cruelest may be the loss of their dreams. Children are born hopeful. The fables of childhood promise happy endings. Their schoolbooks tell them stories of victory over adversity, of heroes who fought for the right and won. Fables are just that: fables; and the simplified versions of complex events and heroes who had more than their share of human frailties do indeed reshape historical fact. But how much does that matter when set against the importance of hope and the belief in heroes that allow the young not only to dream but to believe in the possibility of achieving what they dream?

For tens of thousands of young gays and lesbians their dreams of glory have involved serving their country. They envisioned themselves in the military, running for office, serving in Congress or perhaps as an ambassador to a faraway land—maybe even, in the ultimate dream, as president. You could be born in a hut or a log cabin, grow up poor, wrest your way to an education, and make it—you had only to look at those history books and believe the American dream: Anything is possible.

But if you were born a homosexual, those dreams of service weren't likely to endure very long. As I traveled around the country the last several years, I have encountered thousands of our best and brightest who turned away from public service because of the closed doors that awaited them. I knew those closed doors from my own closeted past and my experiences when I came out of the closet. I knew it from child-hood—you can never erase the early memories of epithets like "fag," "queer," and "pervert" tossed around so casually even among family and friends. The message of disapproval, of revulsion, was terrifying. I was too young to be paying close attention to it, but I vaguely remember hearing adults in my neighborhood talk about the witch-hunts orches-trated by Senator Joe McCarthy, and all those "homosexuals in the State Department." I remember reading articles in the newspapers about homosexuals being forced to resign from the armed forces, and of prom-inent local citizens being arrested for homosexual sex and shamed by the entire community. Young gays and lesbians knew from a very early age that they were not welcome in government service of virtually any kind.

Then, slowly but surely, the pioneers of our political movement started knocking on those doors, and as noted earlier, in the 1970s and early 1980s there were some breakthroughs—to elective office, to the court, to local government. The first time that I was granted respect as a political individual who happened to be gay was during the 1984 presi-dential campaign. My old Colorado friend Gary Hart called to ask for my support for his presidential bid. Once I would have supported him unquestioningly, but I was not the same person I had been before I had come out publicly in 1978. I was a lot more militant about the issue of gay and lesbian rights since MECLA and the successful campaign to defeat the Briggs initiative. Even more important, my old desire to be the "best little boy in the world," to be granted the approval and to live out the expectations of others—all that was rapidly diminishing. I wanted to be openly gay and proud. If others disapproved, too damn bad.

So I said to Hart, "Gary, we have to talk."

"Don't tell me that you're going to support Mondale."

"No. But before I can support you I have to know that you're going to be there for us on AIDS and gay and lesbian issues."

"Dave, you know who I am," Hart answered. "We've known each other for a long time. You know that I'm with you on this. If it requires me to demonstrate it, then let's get on with it. I want your support."

Gary agreed to meet with Los Angeles gay and lesbian leaders in the Mixner/Scott offices and asked me to be one of the numerous honorary co-chairs of his national campaign. He came with his bright, capable young California campaign manager, John Emerson. We were proud to have them there and proud of the handsome offices. The staff had arranged lunch around our massive oak conference table for the eighteen participants. Looking very western in his cowboy boots and engagingly Jimmy Stewart-like in style, a youthful, energetic, and confident Gary Hart took his place at the head of the table.

Around it sat the leaders of the gay and lesbian community in Los Angeles: Roberta Bennett, Diane Abbitt, activist Jordon Mo, Sheldon Andelson, David Quarles, and others. One by one we went around the table and told him our personal stories of discrimination, of fighting for custody of our children, of our fear for our jobs. We spoke remarkably little about AIDS. It had happened, it was striking some of our friends, there were evidences of fresh discrimination, we were often afraid, Diane had issued her call to arms—but it had yet to become the all-consuming issue in our lives.

Gary was relaxed and at his best. He listened intently and asked numerous questions. He told us how moved he was by our courage and our stories. As the meeting ended, he made remarkable commitments for a front-runner candidate at that time. He agreed to have a fund-raiser in the gay and lesbian community. He understood our desire to have him mention the words "gay" and "lesbian" in one of his speeches. Until then, hardly any candidates would mention us by name. They would always speak in terms of civil rights or human rights. That way they could never be quoted as having actually said those three dangerous words. To listen to these evasions for the sake of political safety was humiliating. It continued to keep our community in the political closet. When I look back I am amazed at how modest our desires were, how little we asked. To have Hart honor those requests of ours was a major victory. We agreed to support his presidential race and we went to work. We kept our efforts in California low-key so as not to attract undue attention from the press.

That spring Hart gave the keynote address at the MECLA dinner at the Hollywood Palladium on Sunset Boulevard. As we approached the Palladium, the famous Hollywood klieg lights searched the night skies. It was a big night for the community. More than a thousand of us sat at candlelit tables in the huge hall as Hart rose to give his speech. He talked about his usual campaign themes and building a better tomorrow. Then he spoke briefly of our struggle, stated his commitment to work with the community, and used the words "gay" and "lesbian." The entire room came to its feet and cheered. It was, for the time, a genuine act of courage.

The community's fund-raiser for Hart came soon after. It was held at Sheldon Andelson's hillside Bel Air home, on the terrace overlooking the entire Los Angeles basin. It was one of those wonderful clear summer evenings in southern California. A light Santa Ana wind had pushed the smog out into the Pacific, and the sun was setting as Hart arrived, a busload of reporters trailing his motorcade. He worked the large crowd of gays and lesbians comfortably, patted people on the back, and made his way to the edge of the terrace.

We used the wide ledge of the terrace for our speaker's platform. Sheldon welcomed everyone to this historic evening. As I stepped up to introduce Gary, I realized that just behind me was a drop of thirty feet. I introduced Hart as a long-time friend committed to our community and praised his courage in coming. Then he jumped up on the ledge to speak, and all I could think of was my God! What if he falls? Hart gave a graceful speech and spoke of how honored he was to be there with the gay and lesbian community. As it turned out, the event was to prove costly to him, but not because of us. With the press crowded into one end of the patio, he smiled, turned, and took in the sight of the glorious California twilight. He swept his hand toward the magnificent view and said, "My wife Lee sends her best. She wishes she could be here. I have the better deal. She's campaigning in the toxic waste sites of New Jersey and I get to witness this stunningly beautiful Los Angeles evening."

My smile froze on my face. It was a whopper of a political blunder and the press came to life. New Jersey was holding its primary election the same day as California and their voters would not be thrilled at the candidate's put-down of their state. Many political observers came to believe that remark cost Hart the New Jersey primary and perhaps the nomination that year. It completely overshadowed his appearance at a gay and lesbian fund-raiser.

Hart understood the political advantage in California of his outreach to the community. He wanted our money and our votes. Still, I did not doubt his commitment to our struggle for freedom. He kept his word to us. Working with our ally John Emerson and the political organizations of congresspersons Henry Waxman and Howard Berman, we were able to secure over a dozen gay and lesbian California delegates to the San Francisco convention.

That June convention was a very special one for us. Roberta Bennett, Diane Abbitt, and I were all delegates, and we felt a sense of responsibility not only to our community but to a greater good. We already had experienced four years of Ronald Reagan. We were appalled at the dismantling of social programs for the poor, for women, and for children. We had seen the government retreat from the protection of the civil rights of women and blacks. We had experienced firsthand the administration's active hostility toward people with AIDS. We had watched in horror as the President entered into political alliances with people like the Reverend Jerry Falwell, who demonized homosexuals. We had seen the eighties turn into years of greed, ostentation, and voracious corporate takeovers. This convention was an opportunity for us not only to give a voice to our own community but to show others its commitment to equity and decency.

One morning soon after we arrived, Roberta and I sat in the lobby of the St. Francis Hotel, the convention headquarters, watching the circus of delegates, elected officials, and media stars heading for meetings and seeking out stories. Roberta turned to me with a big smile on her face.

"Do you see the people looking at our badges?" she asked.

"What?"

"Watch carefully, David. They're looking at our badges." She held up hers. Our community had created the badges. They said "Gay and Lesbian Delegate."

She was right. And she was beaming.

"David, who would have thought when we sat in our living room only five years ago that we would be openly gay and lesbian delegates to a national political convention?"

"Pretty amazing," I answered. It was.

"Yep. And if we're going to wear these badges, we better be the best damn delegates possible. We represent a whole lot more than just a good time at the convention."

"Doesn't it all seem a little unreal to you?" I asked. "Being here? Being open? I don't know. I never thought I'd be able to be a delegate and be openly gay. It's all so strange. I almost don't believe it."

Roberta felt the same way. "It's like we've been given parts in a Broadway play and we're just playing the role. It *is* strange. Except here we really are, and we better make the best of it."

The Moscone Convention Center took our breath away that first night when the convention opened. In front was the massive podium, looming over the entire hall. Television network booths ringed the ceiling level, and we could see the headphoned anchors through the glass. Each state's standards jutted up from the floor, road maps for delegates to their seats. Bright red "Hart for President" signs vied with the blue ones of "Mondale for President." Delegates in gaudy dress and crazy hats sported gigantic buttons for the cause or candidate of the moment. Roberta, Diane, and I looked at each other and laughed at the joy of being part of it all.

Waxman waved us to the front of the California delegation. He took us by the arms. "I know this is the first convention where gays and lesbians have had significant representation," he said. "I feel like we're all part of history. I've saved three seats for you in the first row." He paused a moment, then went on, "You have waited too long and worked too hard not to sit up front where the whole nation can see your progress."

We were enormously moved. Bursting with pride, we took our places in the front-row seats. We knew Hart did not have the votes to win but we raised glorious hell on the floor when he was nominated for president. There were no major floor fights or speeches about gay or lesbian rights and we did not expect any. But it was a triumphant convention nonetheless. The highlight was the nomination of Congressperson Geraldine Ferraro to be Mondale's running mate for vice president, the first woman in history to be on the ticket of a major party. As Ferraro spoke to the assembled delegates, the three of us hugged. She stood before us all and moved us with her eloquence. We were witnesses to an enormous breakthrough. Someday, we prayed, there would be one for us.

Mondale lost to Reagan in the greatest Republican landslide in history, and today those victories in the 1984 election seem minor. But to us they represented a significant step forward. Gary Hart was to be the first of a generation of politicians who had openly gay and lesbian friends. Although the issue and his awareness of it were new to him, he recognized that it affected the lives of people he cared about. Mondale's campaign made no serious outreach to the gay and lesbian community. The leadership did not treat us seriously. Democratic Party officials in California who understood the importance of the community's vote there pressed for him to acknowledge us, and he finally agreed to make an appearance before MECLA in Los Angeles. He came to a breakfast in a packed hotel ballroom, gave his standard campaign speech, and never mentioned the words "gay" and "lesbian." He was of another generation. For those like him, we were still to be feared. Hart, responding to our pleas, enabled us to feel pride that we indeed could be seated with the rest of the nation. He gave us permission to dream even greater dreams. He empowered us to work toward still greater heights.

•   •   •

By 1988, four years later, the community was consumed by AIDS and we were frantically seeking assistance in the battle. The presidential race that year could actually save our lives. It was the year that Peter was dying. Michael Dukakis was the Democratic nominee. The mean and brutal inaction of Reagan's administration had doomed thousands. At all costs we had to make a change.

One day I had a call from Los Angeles entertainment attorney David Wexler asking me to a small dinner in his Hollywood Hills home. David was openly gay and had been a generous contributor both to MECLA and to candidates favorable to gay and lesbian rights. There were just four of us there that night: David, millionaire Randy Klose, Duke Comegys, and myself. David had called us together to urge that we coordinate an effort that would raise a million dollars from the community for the Dukakis general election campaign. We were unquestionably committed to the broad social and economic agenda that would end the eight cruel years of Reaganism, but almost our entire focus was on AIDS, on saving the lives of our friends. If we could contribute at a serious level to the election of a Democrat to the presidency, we would have a president more responsive to the desperate urgency of fighting AIDS. That kind of money would make us a serious player in presidential politics. It would give us a place at the table.

David finished. We laughed uncomfortably. Raise a *million* dollars from our community? For a political campaign? But David hadn't gone off his rocker. Randy began writing down a list of potential thousand-dollar contributors and he got to a hundred people without much trouble. Cheers all around. We knew at that moment we could raise the money.

The group asked me to hold a meeting with the Dukakis campaign to make arrangements to coordinate our fund-raising drive. The next day, filled with excitement, I called a leading fund-raiser with the Dukakis campaign. With great pride, I told him we believed the gay and lesbian community could raise over a million dollars for the presidential race. The fund-raiser asked whether the source of the money would be identified. "Of course it will!" I said. He told me he had to make a couple of calls, but he would be back to me within the week.

Two days later, the phone rang. He spent the first five minutes of the call making small talk. Finally he said, "We can't accept the money."

I felt as if the breath had been knocked out of me. *"What?"* I asked.

"We can't accept the money. It's too risky."

"Are you telling me that you are turning down a million dollars because it is being raised by gays and lesbians?"

"Yes."

"You're kidding."

"No. I am sorry. There is nothing I can do. I have to go."

We were all livid and we immediately ceased our efforts. That was the end of my involvement in the Dukakis campaign. I didn't even go to the convention.

Gradually the message became clear. Although national organizations like the Human Rights Campaign Fund and local ones like MECLA were having an impact as advocates and PACs, we had to do more to develop our own political power base. It was clearly no longer enough simply to educate candidates and to make contributions to those who responded to our concerns. We had to develop our voting strength. We had to be tougher and more effective in our political giving. We could no longer rely on the kindness of others to represent us on our issues in legislative or political matters. We had to start looking at running openly gay or lesbian candidates for office. Every time we started feeling comfortable about our emergence into the political process, we were dramatically reminded that we were not considered a serious political or civil rights movement.

Only by creating our own political and financial base and accepting responsibility for our own future would we be able to function as peers of the power brokers. Death had taken its toll of the Book Study Group and left a serious void in our community. While I was in Connecticut healing from Peter's death, Randy Klose, Dr. Scott Hitt, Diane Abbitt, and Roberta Bennett re-created the Book Study Group model into an organization named ANGLE, an acronym for Access Now for Gay and Lesbian Equality. The purpose was the same but they approached the political process with a new sophistication and determination. Initially the group focused on raising funds for local candidates, and then branched out to raise tens of thousands of dollars for national candidates.

When I came back from Connecticut in August 1990, I joined AN-GLE. That year one of the members, Bob Burke, ran for the Democratic nomination for a State Assembly seat in the Los Angeles area. This was to be a historic race for the community and an opportunity to elect the first open gay or lesbian to the Assembly. ANGLE and other community organizations committed themselves fully to this race and expected that many of the straight candidates we had supported over the years would now return that support to our candidate. We were stunned when most of them and their political organizations supported other candidates who were straight. Even the powerful Berman/Waxman organization, which had stood behind our selection as delegates to the 1984 convention, ignored years of our faithful support as a community to its agenda and placed a straight candidate on their endorsement mailer to the voters in that district.

We knew what we had to do. It was time to develop a way of identifying voters who were gay and lesbian. We hired a direct mail house and spent more than one hundred thousand dollars to create a methodology that eventually enabled us to pinpoint registered gay and lesbian voters in California. With the assistance of the direct mail house, we developed a "political slate"—a voter guide that is mailed to targeted voters—so that we were able to communicate directly with our own voters. After much work and some slipups, we created a voter list that today approaches several hundred thousand identifiably gay and lesbian registered voters in the state.

Simultaneously ANGLE expanded its funding base. We needed to improve our ability to raise money for candidates, as well as to pay for the list development. The members contributed their personal lists of potential donors and created a base of thousands. We published a newsletter to keep supporters informed of our work and to pass along the latest political news of interest to the community. Because we were so successful in fund-raising, candidates from out of state began asking us to raise money for their own congressional races. ANGLE's reputation grew. It was being seen as a group with real influence at the national level. Before long, it became a "must stop" for candidates around the country who were seeking a variety of nonlocal offices.

By now, of course, my old friend Bill Clinton was beginning to close in on his lifelong dream of being President of the United States. By this time he had served as governor of Arkansas longer than any other person in the state's history: four terms, beginning in 1978, with one two-year interlude after he was defeated for reelection in 1980. He had flirted with the idea of running for president in 1988 but quickly decided against it. Instead, at the 1988 Democratic Convention, he gave a keynote address so endless that it became the brunt of late-night talk-show hosts' jokes. I had had almost no contact with him over the last few years. I had been taking care of Peter and healing myself, and he was busy preparing for his presidential run; but I was of course fully aware of those efforts. For much of 1991 I watched with a mixture of fascination and—being human—envy as he emerged as a serious contender for the presidency. I wondered if I would hear from him. If so, how would he treat me now that he had so much at stake politically? We had been friends. Did that matter anymore? Would he keep his distance because of my gayness? We had been building a significant political power base in the gay and lesbian community over the last few years; would he decide this was worth embracing?

And, of course, I could not help thinking of what I perceived as his charmed life. He was being judged on his skills and experience, not his sexual orientation. I thought about all those doors closed to me and those like me, and I swallowed back the sour taste as best I could.

In early September of 1991 Bill Clinton gave me a call at home for the first time in over two years. It was not unlike the call I had received seven years earlier from Gary Hart. We exchanged pleasantries for a few minutes and then the conversation got down to business.

"You know that I am running and I need and want your support. Mickey and I are anxious to get you involved as soon as possible."

Mickey Kantor was a gifted, intense lawyer with a major Los Angeles law firm. He and his wife Heidi were long-time friends of the Clintons. They were supporters of gay and lesbian rights, and Mickey was also a friend of mine.

"Bill," I said, "I think the world of you. I know Hillary and your convictions on gay and lesbian rights because I have experienced your support and kindness in my own life. But you have no public record to speak of and I can't ask friends in the community to support you without their knowing where you stand. Right now, Bill, I would say that a vast majority will go with Tsongas, who has a long and distinguished record."

Former Senator Paul Tsongas of Massachusetts, who was also seeking the nomination, had been the first person in the history of the Senate to sponsor a gay and lesbian civil rights bill. He had built a loyal and dedicated following in our community.

"I would have one too if I lived in Massachusetts," Clinton snapped back. "What do I need to do? I want your support and the community's. California could be a rugged primary and I need your early support."

"You need to take tough stands on issues of concern to us so we know both that you are knowledgeable and that you care."

"Such as?"

The two of us got down to specifics. "Well, such as gays and lesbians in the military," I said. "We're forbidden right now from serving our country."

"I've already taken a position on that," Bill told me. "I believe everyone should have the right to serve. That's done. What else?"

"We need to know that you will fight like hell to find a cure for AIDS. We need a Manhattan Project kind of effort to find a cure. We need to streamline the FDA. We urgently need money for care and treatment and protection from discrimination. Jesus, Bill, I could go on and on."

"Look, David, can you prepare a briefing paper for me on every one of these issues? Get it to Mickey, and he'll review it and get it to me. If there are problems I'll let you know. Let's just get this moving."

As we signed off, Clinton said he would be delighted to sit down with ANGLE on his next trip to California and promised that Mickey would call to arrange a time and place.

I had a call from Mickey Kantor very soon thereafter inviting me to what was to be the first Clinton campaign event in California, a gathering at the home of Geoffrey Cowan and Aileen Adams. We also set a mid-October date for the ANGLE-Clinton meeting.

Geoff Cowan and Aileen Adams hold a special place in my heart. Today he is the head of the Voice of America and she is in the Justice Department; back in the late 1970s they were among the first on the West Los Angeles political scene to include gay and lesbian couples at both political and social events at their home. It was a gathering place for filmmakers, artists, writers, and politicians—the best and brightest of our generation there—and to be excluded would have seriously hampered a person's ability to network effectively in politics. Along with liberal power brokers Stanley and Betty Sheinbaum, Geoff and Aileen opened their home and their hearts to Peter and me. They were among the few straight people who attended Peter's memorial service. They practiced their politics and beliefs every day.

I asked ANGLE colleague Scott Hitt to come to the Cowan house with me. I had come to cherish the friendship that had developed between us over the last few years. Scott is a physician in his thirties with enormous energy, and he thrives on politics and is passionate on the subject of AIDS. I had first met him when he assisted Dr. Joel Weisman in treating Peter. They shared a medical practice, Pacific Oaks, and have treated literally thousands of people with AIDS. I have always been astonished by Scott's ability to sustain his remarkable humaneness and caring despite the unremitting tragedy he endures in his practice. Nor was his commitment restricted to his patients. He could juggle multiple projects with great skill and devoted endless hours to fighting the disease politically. Scott would be the perfect choice to "work" the Clinton staff at the event on the AIDS issue.

As we drove along the lush Mandeville Canyon Road toward the Cowan house, I missed Peter. We had made this same drive many times to events at Geoff and Aileen's but I had not been to their home since he died—it had been too painful to accept their invitations until now.

Inside, it was like a reunion from the sixties. The house was filled with friends from the Moratorium, the Fred Harris campaign, PRO Peace, and numerous liberal political campaigns. Over the years, Clinton had stayed in touch with us all. There was excitement in the air because for almost everyone there Bill Clinton, their good friend, was actually going to run for president. The room was crowded. As I reunited with old friends, I saw Scott engaged in deep conversation with Hillary. He told me later that he was astonished by the extent of her knowledge about the health care system and about AIDS, and that her questions were informed and to the point, going to the heart of these issues. She knew about the FDA, drug trials, and care problems. Scott was a Hillary convert from then on, and could not stop revisiting their conversation.

Bill gave an effective talk that evening, and grew increasingly relaxed as he realized he was among friends. All I could think of was how much I wanted to be among these friends too. I found myself praying that Bill and Hillary would do well at the forthcoming ANGLE meeting so that I could be comfortable in supporting his candidacy. I had a history with just about everyone in the room and I could not imagine working without them on this effort.

As I had told Clinton when he called, 90 percent of the national gay and lesbian community was supporting Paul Tsongas. The Boston community was reaching out across the country to line up endorsements for him. The staff of a prominent national gay and lesbian organization, while officially neutral, was working hard for Tsongas. Los Angeles was one of the few places where there was even an interest in meeting with Clinton.

Tsongas also requested a meeting with ANGLE, and he came to Scott Hitt and Alex Koleszar's house to meet with us on September 21. Although my connections with Clinton were well known throughout the community by this time, most of the ANGLE participants were either undecided or were leaning toward Tsongas because of his pioneering civil rights record on our behalf. The former senator misread my leaning toward Clinton as the feeling of the entire group. It was a serious miscalculation.

By now ANGLE had the routine for visiting elected officials down pat. Scott and Alex's hilltop home served as our unofficial meeting place. It was spacious, light, and a comfortable setting for free and open conversation. Tsongas arrived that hot day with a huge entourage. Traveling with him were almost as many staff members as there were participants in the meeting. He was formal and somewhat aloof, and he gave what was not one of his better performances. He had his staff pass out his program for "Renewing America," a printed booklet with his complete plan for the nation. Seated with us in a circle of folding chairs, Tsongas proudly held up the booklet and announced that his position on gay and lesbian rights was printed right there inside it. Anyone who read the program could find it.

We turned to the page he specified. He had indeed set down a strong commitment to our issues, including AIDS, the military issue, and the civil rights legislation. He spoke of his powerful record on gay and lesbian rights, but his delivery lacked passion. There was no question that even for a senator from liberal Massachusetts the record was remarkable. Knowing we planned to interview other candidates, he urged us to use his tough stances to leverage other candidates into comparable positions. Then, with the formal meeting over, he left quickly, not staying for lunch.

One of his top staffers later confided in me that Tsongas was resentful that he had to explain his distinguished record to this small group of donors. I don't think he felt that there was anyone else running, including Clinton, who would take as strong a position as he had. But even if that was true, aloofness, perhaps even arrogance, was not the way to persuade us. While Tsongas was familiar to the East Coast gay and lesbian community, this was his first exposure to many of us in the room. He did not make a significant impact on the group. It felt he lacked the charisma to win and was put off by his remoteness. I was delighted, since I had been concerned that he would nail down ANGLE's support before Clinton had a chance to make his pitch. As it proved, Tsongas's failure to win converts in that meeting set the stage for Clinton's visit in October.

Two days later, the next potential candidate came to see us: Congressperson Richard Gephardt. He had met with the group once before and had promised to look into becoming a co-sponsor of the gay and lesbian civil rights legislation. He wanted to be sure that there was nothing in it he found objectionable, but he promised he would be back to us soon. We never heard from him. This time we focused on the subject of gays and lesbians in the military, and asked him to use his influence as House Majority Leader to arrange for public hearings that would educate the public about the intense discrimination they were subjected to. We stressed that he did not have to take a position himself; we simply wanted fair and open hearings.

Gephardt responded very positively to the suggestion and promised that his staff would be back to us in the near future. It was the same story as before. In fact, we never heard from him or his staff about it until after the right wing seized control of the issue in the early months of the Clinton presidency.

ANGLE's meeting with Clinton was set for October 14, but in the two weeks preceding it, all hell broke loose in the Los Angeles community. For more than a decade, California gays and lesbians had been pressing for a civil rights bill that would protect our jobs and our homes. When Pete Wilson ran for governor, he promised us he would sign such legislation and many in our community supported his bid for election. All through September, our advocates worked day and night to shepherd the bill through the legislature, and saw it passed and placed on Governor Wilson's desk. We assumed he would keep his word and sign it.

We were aware that the Christian Coalition and others in the radical right, whose strength had been increasing in California, had initiated a phone and mail campaign urging Wilson to veto it, but the governor's office repeatedly assured our advocates that he would not bend to the pressure. He did. His political advisers and his own ambitions for eventual national office won out. He needed the right wing of the Republican Party more than he needed us. On September 29 he vetoed the bill.

That night, in a rage, five hundred of us gathered at the main intersection of West Hollywood, the heart of the Los Angeles area gay and lesbian community, and stopped traffic. As the police arrived, we moved our demonstration and acts of civil disobedience elsewhere, and then kept shifting around the city so that the police were kept off guard. I remember lying down and blocking traffic on Sunset Boulevard and having an African-American man honk his horn and shout at me to "move my fat white ass" out of his way. I raised myself up and said, "Brother, I went south to help you fight for your freedom. Give me fifteen minutes to fight for mine." I could see the surprise on his face. Then he grinned and said, "Take your time, brother. Take your time."

Every night for two weeks the Los Angeles community met in streets of the city to vent our fury at the betrayal. Act Up/Los Angeles orchestrated the demonstrations. Act Up is an organization that uses militant and often disruptive tactics to force the government and its decision-makers to move forward on finding a cure for AIDS. It was not as strong in Los Angeles as in New York and San Francisco and some in our community were offended by its tactics, but I found it uniquely effective in these demonstrations. (In fact, although elected officials would never admit it, the organization was also effective in forcing reluctant politicians to come to terms with AIDS.) Under its direction, the crowds grew nightly, until anywhere from five to ten thousand people were participating. United in their sense of betrayal, every conceivable element in the community demonstrated as one, from wealthy donors to the hardened street activists of Act Up. In a final protest on the weekend before ANGLE was to meet with Clinton, thousands of us marched in Sacramento to protest the veto. This was the climate that was waiting for Clinton when he arrived.

When I drove up Doheny Drive to Scott and Alex's house on October 14, I was wiped out from two weeks of unceasing demonstrations. I was also nervous and scared. I was in a strange situation. To have a personal friend be a serious contender for the presidency of the United States was still hard to grasp. I didn't quite know the rules. And if Clinton and the ANGLE participants failed to connect, I knew I wouldn't be able to support his bid. It would be awkward and painful for me personally, but I hadn't the slightest doubt that my vision and my dreams were with my friends from the gay and lesbian movement.

As I saw it and hoped, the friendship between Bill, Hillary, and me could serve as a dramatic building block for ushering the Clintons into the White House and the gay and lesbian community into a society of freedom. If we were able to convey to Bill and Hillary the story of our struggle and our pain, a true alliance could develop. After watching Bill Clinton over the years, I knew that with his intelligence, charisma, and will, he could win. This meeting could be crucial to the community's taking a huge step toward its inclusion in the fabric of American life.

Bill, Hillary, and Mickey Kantor arrived around noon. They mixed easily with the twenty or so people there and Bill showed them the famous Clinton charm by smiling, touching, and listening intently. Then he and I walked out to the pool and I briefed him once again on the issues the group would raise. He looked reflectively out at the ocean and said, "It's sort of strange, isn't it, David? Here are two friends, standing in this beautiful setting, one running for president and the other a freedom fighter. We both need each other. Did you ever think years ago that we would end up here?"

"No, I didn't. In fact, I wouldn't have predicted most of my life. You know, this is a day I really miss Peter. He would have loved this meeting."

Clinton seemed caught off guard by the intimacy of my mentioning Peter, but he looked at me gently and said, "We will make Peter proud today."

"Bill, so many of us in that room inside have lost so many of our friends. Please be there for us."

"I wouldn't be here if I didn't care," he told me. "You won't be disappointed."

The group sat in a semicircle in the living room facing Bill and Hillary seated in front of the fireplace. Each of us shared our personal stories and what we had experienced as gays and lesbians over the years. Roberta and Diane spoke of their fear in the early years of their relationship of the courts taking away their children. Scott spoke of the enormous numbers of people he was treating with HIV and AIDS. Alex spoke of suicide among the young. Executives Bill Melamed and Leslie Belzberg shared what it was like to be gay and lesbian in the entertainment industry. Former banker Ed Gould talked of his career as a banking executive and his HIV status. Activist John Duran outlined the issues around the massive demonstrations of the past two weeks. David Wexler shared the problems that he was facing as chairman of AIDS Project-Los Angeles and how it was barely able to meet the rising caseload. Richard Colbert talked of the battles he faced as a gay Republican. Businesswoman Chris Hershey discussed her lover and their child. I noted that if he was elected and should want me to serve, by law there were a number of positions I couldn't be appointed to. As we spoke of the discrimination we faced, about the death of hundreds of friends and of the systematic exclusion we faced in virtually every aspect of our lives, we could see by the tears that glistened in his eyes how moved he was. We were reaching him.

Hillary spoke first. My relationship with her over the years had been mostly through Bill, but I had come to know and admire her for her strong convictions, her sense of self, and her impressive intellect. She was calm, pleasant, and articulate in her speech, and there wasn't a person in the room who wasn't impressed with her intelligence, her grasp of health care issues, and her understanding of the epidemic. Then it was Bill's turn. He told us how touched he was by our sharing. He assured us that he and Hillary would be our allies in the struggle for freedom. Without prompting, he volunteered his determination to issue an executive order banning discrimination against gays and lesbians in the military. He said that if he were governor of California he would have signed the legislation that Wilson had vetoed. Finally, he talked with passion about his commitment to find a cure for AIDS and to end the horrible "cycle of death" that we had been experiencing for the last decade.

There was a lot of dialogue between Clinton and the group when he was done and I could see that he was connecting with them. The one issue where differences surfaced was the national gay and lesbian civil rights legislation. He was concerned about the content, and wanted to be certain that it protected religious liberty and would not have provisions imposing quotas.

Then Diane Abbitt spoke up: "Governor Clinton, for the last two weeks we have been marching in the streets because of the blatant betrayal by a man who made similar promises to this community in private. How do we know that we can trust you? What makes you different from all the rest?"

He answered her forthrightly. "You don't know if you can trust me. You'll have to watch my actions but you won't be disappointed. I won't be in the closet on this issue. I promise you that."

With that, we all sat down to lunch. I was very proud of my friends from Arkansas. Not only had the Clintons taken the right stands; they had shown an enormous compassion for us. They seemed to have felt our pain. My friends in this room had seen what I admired in them. Now it would not just be me alone talking about them in the community. ANGLE moved from leaning toward Tsongas to leaning toward Clinton.

The next day we woke up to an unanticipated headline in *The Los Angeles Times*: "Clinton Opposes Thomas, Backs Gay Rights Bill." "Thomas" was Clarence Thomas, George Bush's nominee for the Supreme Court. The article said:

> On the gay rights question, Clinton said in an interview that he told a group of gay activists at a private luncheon that he considered the controversial state legislation prohibiting occupational discrimination against homosexuals "an appropriate thing to do."

Mickey Kantor said to me later that Clinton had left our meeting and made a special point of telling Ron Brownstein of the *Times* that he would have signed the gay rights legislation. That gesture did more to solidify ANGLE's support than anything else that had happened. He had gone on record publicly with what he had said to us in private.

•   •   •

Despite this very positive meeting, ANGLE wanted to hold off any official endorsement or involvement for several months. It was still feeling the shock of Wilson's veto and felt caution was indicated. But the omens continued to feel good. In December Hollywood power broker Dawn Steel and her husband held a fund-raiser for Clinton. By then he had built up considerable support in the entertainment community through Mickey Kantor and the Cowans. A number of us from ANGLE decided to buy tickets and listen to what he would say in a mixed group of straights and gays. Once again he was excellent and forthright, and repeated unprompted his statements about the California civil rights bill and the military. Our group was impressed, and now started planning how to support this new and relatively unknown champion of our freedom.

As for me, I was feeling hope after years of darkness and despair. My friend of many years was willing to build an alliance with us. As he traveled the road to the White House, we would travel with him, hoping that his election would open the doors of freedom to us. Maybe this really was someone who would battle with us to save the lives of our friends. I felt that Clinton had the capacity to build an alliance with the traditional Democratic coalition and middle-class America. He would be able to articulate our common vision without spurring fear among the American people. With him, we could not only win back the White House but also our dreams, our hopes, and our lives.

CHAPTER THIRTEEN

On the Campaign Trail

AT the beginning of January, campaign chair Mickey Kantor asked me to serve on the National Executive Committee of the Clinton for President campaign. This, Mickey indicated, would become the "kitchen cabinet" for Clinton. These committees are not the governing body for the campaign; their purpose is to showcase for the public the kinds of people and advisers who will surround the candidate. An invitation to join such an "elite" group was also a way to reward key supporters and fund-raisers by giving them a prominent position and title. Once an initial formation meeting is held, the members rarely meet again as a group. Individuals on the Executive Committee become advisers to the candidate based on their particular area of expertise, their network of contacts, or their ability to raise funds. My invitation to join the committee was the first gesture to our community to become partners in the campaign.

Both Clinton and Kantor made it clear that they wanted me not only to mobilize the gay and lesbian community but to use my years of political experience to outreach to other key communities outside ours. In fact, this last never happened. My outreach was almost entirely confined to the homosexual world. It wasn't because I wanted this to be the case. I received requests only for the network of contacts I had in the homosexual community. From the moment I came out of the closet, those who wanted my support ignored all my years of experience in the wider political world, and I could not break through that barrier.

Eventually, I came to understand this as a political fact of life—my life. Although I have constantly resisted being segregated from the mainstream of American politics, the reality is that if integration moves beyond their rhetoric, even progressive politicians become very uncomfortable with it. I appreciated Bill and Mickey's asking me to broaden my base, but I was cynical about their ever following through in ways that might put teeth into it. As it proved, I was right to be cynical. Nevertheless, I was extremely proud to be the first openly gay man to occupy so prominent a position in a national campaign. It was not a token appointment.

Knowing that my responsibilities would involve extensive travel around the country to mobilize the gay and lesbian community behind Clinton, and that my office would be flooded with phone calls, paperwork, and faxes, I began searching for someone to assist me. At the same time, a gifted young man named Jeremy Bernard approached me about working for the campaign. Jeremy was raised on Texas politics by his parents, who are active in the liberal wing of the Democratic Party there, and is one of those rare young people who has innate political instincts. He had been interested in politics all his life, but he originally pursued an acting career because he felt there was no room for a gay man in the political process. I hired him on the spot.

He came to work in January of 1992. He was exactly what I needed to handle the onslaught. His only weakness was his shaky self-esteem around his gayness. He was new to gay activism and had to struggle with the personal issues that arose from it. Since his arrival, he has come out to his family and friends, become very involved in the struggle for freedom for gays and lesbians, and turned into a major political operative in his own right. Jeremy could be a "poster child" for what coming out does for a gay or lesbian. He has blossomed into a strong, sophisticated, and powerful young man. He not only proved indispensable to our efforts, he has become like a brother to me.

I wanted to have as much in place as possible before the first meeting of the Executive Committee. San Francisco had to be the first stop because of its large and politically powerful gay and lesbian community. By now, it had elected a number of its own to key governing positions in the city, and Jeremy and I hoped to persuade some of them to support Clinton. Our first meeting was with openly lesbian Supervisor Carol Migden, who was leaning toward Tsongas and was skeptical of anyone becoming president who came from a state like Arkansas. All day long we visited with leaders of the San Francisco community and encountered a Tsongas wall. Feeling rejected and weary, we held my last meeting of the day with Supervisor Roberta Achtenberg and her friend Paul Morabito.

I had met Roberta when she was opposing Proposition 6, but had not really interacted with her since then. She was emerging as a major political power in the Bay Area. She had dedicated her entire life to championing the cause of the powerless. Before she was elected supervisor, she had been the directing attorney for the Lesbian Rights Project, a public interest law firm that fought for civil rights for lesbians. She had also been dean at the New College of California School of Law, and her involvement in a variety of political causes and her advocacy for civil rights had earned her the respect of a broad spectrum of San Franciscans.

We met Roberta and Paul in the redwood-paneled bar of the Clift Hotel. Never a strong supporter of Tsongas, she was leaning toward New York Governor Mario Cuomo. I told her about Clinton's commitments on gay and lesbian rights, and his very effective presentation at the ANGLE meeting.

She was not impressed. "I'm a Cuomo supporter and I hope he is going to enter the race, David."

"He isn't going to and you know it. He might play with you for a while but in the end he won't run."

"Well, so what if he doesn't?" Roberta asked. "Why should I get ahead of the community? They're strongly supporting Tsongas here. I would take a lot of heat, especially for supporting someone from Arkansas, for God's sake! San Franciscans don't have a great image of politicians from the South."

"Look, we have to get rid of Bush," I said. "Tsongas can't do it. I don't think he can even get the nomination. Clinton has the ability to touch working-class issues without surrendering his commitments to the poor. No other candidate, with the possible exception of Cuomo, can do that—and Cuomo is not going to run. I really believe that Clinton may be the only one who can end the nightmare Reagan-Bush years."

Roberta gave a little at last. "If I'm going to take heat for supporting this man," she said now, "it is absolutely essential that the community sees that he respects me, knows me, and values my advice. They have to see that I have been given a serious role in the campaign. When he comes to town, I want to be by his side. When he has meetings with the 'big guys,' I want to be in them. When he wins, I want to be in the administration."

Roberta was talking my language now. "Roberta," I told her, "I have no doubt that all of that can be arranged. I will call Mickey Kantor tomorrow. But you can't go halfway with this if they agree. Your support must be enthusiastic and unconditional."

She was a touch offended by that. "I never go halfway with any-thing—period!"

Meeting with Roberta was like a breath of fresh air. She knew how to ask for power, and she knew how to move the community forward when that power was granted.

This was the break I was looking for in northern California. Roberta had a following not only in San Francisco but around the country. I called Mickey Kantor at once and he was elated. We discussed creating a role for Achtenberg and having the Clintons contact her directly about participation in the campaign. We also decided that it would be an im-portant symbol to have Supervisor Achtenberg ride in the car with Clin-ton on his next visit to San Francisco.

When I phoned to report my talks with Kantor, Roberta agreed to endorse Clinton on his next visit to San Francisco. It was the first signifi-cant community support for his campaign other than ANGLE's in Los Angeles.

Attending the National Executive Committee meeting was another "coming out" for me. Many of my old political allies and friends would be there, and this would be my first major involvement with them since I had come out of the closet over fifteen years ago. My old friend from the Moratorium days, Mike Driver, told me that when they were talking my name would come up now and then as this long-ago old friend in Cali-fornia lost in some fringe effort for gay and lesbian civil rights. They had a vague impression that I had made a lot of money in business but was really not taken too seriously in politics.

In truth, none of them had any idea of my life over the years since I'd left Washington. Nor did I think they could ever understand it. Not those fifteen years on the tumultuous road toward self-acknowledgment, of love and terrible loss, of plague and death—all those deaths. The last time I had worked with them I was in the closet. Even the man they remembered had never really existed. The man who was to walk into that meeting room that morning was a stranger, and they didn't know it.

I was torn with conflict. There was a side of me that desperately wanted to belong to the group again and to be accepted by them as a peer. I wanted them to like me. I wanted their respect. I wanted them to give their approval of the journey that had brought me to this room. I yearned to resume where we had left off. But the other side of me knew I could never again be a member of the team. I was still a political animal—I could not *not* be one; it was bred in the bone. But I had seen what naked political greed and infighting could do—too many brave young men lay dead because of it. Even as I came back into the arena, this time truly believing change was possible and the fight worth it, I had to swallow my bitterness. I wanted the respect of those in the room for the hopes and aspirations of the millions in the community that I represented. I wanted to enter that room in Washington with dignity and authority.

Before I left for my red-eye flight the night before, I carefully packed the new suit, shirt, and tie I had bought for the occasion. As the plane became airborne, I realized that I had on my sneakers and had forgotten my cowboy boots. The meeting was scheduled for early in the morning. There was no way I would find a shoe store open at that hour and I didn't know any friends who had size thirteen feet. When I landed I went to a friend's house to shower and shave, and then I put on my new suit and tied my sneakers. In the taxi to the meeting, I was suddenly overcome with fear. I prayed. I asked God to remove my ego and allow me to be of service to my community.

Entering the meeting room was like attending a class reunion. It was filled with old friends from the past. There were Eli Segal, Anne Wexler, Mike Driver, and Tony Podesta, my old allies from the days of McCarthy and the Moratorium. Just like 1968, there was tall, lean, pale Harold Ickes with his heavy five o'clock shadow huddling in the corner with short, intense, no-nonsense Susan Thomases plotting their strategy for the meeting that was about to happen. The two of them had coordinated the New York McCarthy campaign in 1968 and they were now the coordinators for Clinton's New York campaign. They had always seemed joined at the hip back then. Some things hadn't changed.

The place itself was the standard-issue Washington legal conference room, though a very large one. At one end we visited with one another and held whispered conversations. At the other end tables had been arranged into a square that made it look as if we were assembled for some grand summit. When I took my chair I felt victorious. Not since I came out of the closet had there been a place at a table like this for me.

Campaign officials James Carville, Mickey Kantor, Eli Segal, and others took turns bringing us up-to-date on the progress of the campaign. They reviewed the latest polling information, ran through the lists of endorsements, and told us the timetable for the campaign. They gave us the proposed strategy for the campaign, including their expectations for the various primary states and the fact that they planned to highlight the economy as an issue. Carville presented his set performance piece, "It's the economy, stupid!" that he was to repeat so often in the coming months. He was amusing and articulate but his good-old-southern-boy persona distracted from his message. I thought he wasn't trying to convince us as much as entertain us. By making us laugh, he was hoping to minimize the number of questions and move the agenda forward. As I saw it, he felt he already had the answers and had no interest in our opinions. This was a man who hid his arrogance in his humor—and not that well. Now and then people would question one or another aspect of the various reports, but generally there was silent agreement with what was being presented.

Fund-raising was another important item on the agenda. Rahm Emanuel took the chair at the head of the table for this one. Rahm had come to the campaign from the organization of Chicago Mayor Richard Daley (the son of 1968 Mayor Daley of convention fame—or infamy), and was considered an uncompromising political pro. He had the personality of a battle-ready soldier, and came across as tough and superbly organized. Rahm made a brilliant presentation to the group and then proceeded around the table demanding to know what each of us felt we could raise for the campaign.

After his presentation, each member of the Executive Committee was asked to give a report from his and her area of expertise. When it came my time to speak, I was able to tell with pride of the progress I had made in my community: the endorsement of Supervisor Achtenberg, the AN-GLE endorsement and commitment to fund-raising, the huge computerized lists of names that we would make available to Clinton, and the growing number of endorsements from key grassroots activists. Almost no other community could report this level of accomplishment at that point.

By and large, the group around the table was genuinely excited by the involvement of the gay and lesbian community. Former Carter White House adviser Anne Wexler spoke about the importance of the gay and lesbian votes in key primary states like New York and California. She reminded the group of the problems that Dukakis had had with the community in the 1988 election, and how important it was to build good relations with it early in the campaign.

Nonetheless, I could see that some individuals, mostly from southern states, were nervous about this involvement. They worried about the possibility of backlash from southern fundamentalists but clearly felt they would be viewed as homophobic if they spoke up about it. They picked their words carefully and avoided looking at me. The thrust was that the gay and lesbian community might not be able to deliver enough votes in the large industrial states to justify taking the risk of backlash in the South. I genuinely did not believe the campaign was taking a risk, but I knew it was important to allay their fear. During the coffee breaks I sought out those who had expressed concerns and tried to reassure them. They pointed out that the community had never been a major player in a presidential election. I told them this one was going to be different, and why. They wanted to be sure I wasn't biting off more than I could deliver. That one made me seethe inside, since no other participants were having *their* credentials or abilities questioned. But I knew my job was to make allies of the skeptics. I repeated all the reasons why this vote mattered and why we could deliver it, and felt by the end that I had eased their qualms—at least somewhat.

The group really bonded as a team. At the end of the meeting everyone traded cards and promised to stay in touch. Again I realized how exhilarated I was to be in this company, to be participating at a level of real power. But I was also struck yet one more time by the differences between them and me. In the course of the day everyone caught up on children, families, home life. Never once did anyone ask me anything about mine. When I mentioned someone I was dating or said I was taking a trip with a friend, there was an awkward silence. So, much to their relief, I dropped any further personal talk. I was "different"—not one of them. No matter how open and accepting politically they might be about my sexuality, they could not be at ease with gay relationships. We had come a long way in some respects, but we had a long way to go in that one.

As the day ended, a group was going out for dinner and invited me to join them. I begged off. I had about as much of heterosexual America as I could handle for the day. I needed to be with my own. I went and joined friends at a gay restaurant and relaxed in my own world.

We never met again. Almost everyone who was there became a major player or adviser in the campaign but we ceased to function as an organized group. We had been successfully brought together, and as a result were able to call on one another when we needed to. The meeting had accomplished its purpose.

In California the community started integrating into the campaign. The national campaign asked ANGLE members Scott Hitt, Bob Sertner, and me to be on the Western States Finance Committee. Rahm Emanuel had broken down the country into different regional finance committees. He gave each region the amount he expected them to raise. Membership on such committees was easy. Anyone who was willing to pledge to raise tens of thousands of dollars could join. Membership put you into an elite circle and usually guaranteed better access to the candidate. The three of us were invited to a meeting in Occidental Petroleum executive Jerry Stern's office in Westwood to help plan a major western states fund-raising dinner for Clinton to be held the week after the New Hampshire primary. At this initial meeting, the enthusiasm was high. Clinton had been on the cover of several national publications and his numbers in the polls were rising rapidly. We all thought we had a winner on our hands. Stern and fund-raiser Mary Leslie briefed the group on the plans. Mickey Kantor called us from Little Rock with a progress report and asked all in the room for assistance with the fund-raiser. To be listed as a co-chair, one had to pledge to raise a minimum of fifty thousand dollars for the dinner. Clinton had agreed to do a private reception for each person who did so.

Scott Hitt and I were sitting next to each other. Scott turned to me and said, "Let's pledge fifty from ANGLE and do the reception with the community."

"Scott, that's a lot of money for us to raise in one month's time."

"Well, if they list us on the dinner invitation as 'ANGLE—Access Now for Gay and Lesbian Equality'—that would be something spectacular for everyone to see."

As we huddled over on the side of the room, I kept on worrying. "If we fail to raise it, then no one will ever take us seriously again. Besides, we'd have to obtain everyone in ANGLE's approval first."

But he had my number. "I thought you liked living on the edge," he shot back. "Getting chicken in your old age? We can agree, based on the others approving. Anyway, we have an ANGLE meeting in just two days."

The edge comment got to me. "Okay. I'm willing. Let's go for it."

As Stern and Leslie went around the room there were a lot of ten-thousand-dollar pledges but only two for fifty thousand. When they came to us, we said that ANGLE, if its members approved, would agree to be a co-chair of the event and raise the fifty thousand dollars. There were surprised looks all around the table. Jerry Stern said "terrific." With that, we set up the first test for the community in the campaign.

ANGLE met two days later and took on the challenge. Ed Gould would organize key contributors to community-based organizations, David Wexler would hit major AIDS contributors, Bob Sertner and Skip Paul would work their contacts in the entertainment industry, Scott would call his medical community peers, Diane, Roberta, and I would call traditional gay and lesbian contributors, and the others would hit family and friends. We knew that this was our big chance to prove our abilities to the campaign and increase our influence.

The next day disaster struck. Gennifer Flowers, a young woman in Arkansas, claimed that she had a long-term affair with Clinton and the story broke on the front pages around the country. Simultaneously, questions arose around Clinton's draft status during the Vietnam War and whether he had used influence to avoid serving.

My heart went out to him. As a gay man who had seen his personal life discussed from one side of the country to the other, I knew what it was like to have one's private life placed under public scrutiny. I had no idea whether the Flowers charges were true, and I couldn't see what bearing they had on the kind of president he would make. I felt very strongly that this was a matter between Hillary and him, and not the voters. In 1987 I had seen my good friend Gary Hart, a man extremely qualified to be president, lose his chances to lead the nation because of his own personal behavior. I was afraid history was about to repeat itself. The thought of wasting such a remarkable gift for a reason like this made me angry.

But if I was angry about the Flowers mess, I was livid at the issue of the draft. My generation had urged others to avoid the draft as a way of protesting a horrible, unjust war. I remembered this patriotic young man from Arkansas struggling in pain to come to terms with his love of his country and a war that should never have been fought. Thousands upon thousands of us had decided not to serve, to go to jail, or to leave the country. He was a part of all that was good in the sixties, and now he was being roasted for having had the courage of his convictions. Ironically, his involvement in the antiwar movement had been minimal, but it was taking a heavy hit now.

Equally disturbing, though, was the way that Bill and the campaign were responding to the charges. Instead of presenting the draft issue as a matter of conscience and moral courage, the campaign baldly tried to explain it away as a "misunderstanding." I didn't get it. I thought Clinton should have taken pride in his stand against the war. To be defensive implied he had done something wrong. The whole episode left me unsettled. I was astounded that this issue could surface two decades after it had happened, and I was greatly troubled by the spectacle of Clinton rationalizing his concern about the war as he did.

Politically, the two problems presented me with some tough choices. I had invested enormous credibility in the campaign and now all that was at risk. I urged ANGLE to meet again to make certain they were still comfortable with our financial commitment. Even if we were, we had to assess whether we would still be able to raise the money we had pledged. The group decided to hold to its pledge. If we succeeded under these circumstances, we would truly gain points. A number of people on the finance committee had already bailed out or lowered their pledges. We figured that even if Clinton lost the nomination, we would be sending a message to other candidates about our loyalty and ability to be good allies even in times of trouble. We went to work.

February proved to be a difficult month for the Clinton campaign. The impact of the scandal and the draft issue had some political observers deciding he was ruled out of the race. We were finding it hard to raise funds for a candidate who might not be around very long. We also found ourselves facing the first problem to arise between the gay and lesbian community and the campaign.

That this should develop wasn't really surprising. We had been on a honeymoon and reality was creeping back into our alliance. Up to this point, there had been enthusiasm on both sides. The campaign was delighted to have a new funding base, and being correct on this civil rights issue made them feel good. But many people in the campaign had no experience with gays and lesbians, and even less with the issue of our rights. Complicating our side of the partnership was the fact that most of the community had never participated as open homosexuals in a presidential race and didn't know how far it was appropriate to push the campaign on our issues. Given all the ingredients in this stew, it was just a matter of time before a misunderstanding arose between us.

Early in the year, the Human Rights Campaign Fund had sent all presidential candidates a questionnaire asking their positions on a number of gay and lesbian and AIDS issues. Senator Tom Harkin, former Senator Tsongas, Senator John Kerry, and Clinton all returned the questionnaire. But one question asked if the candidate would sign the national gay and lesbian civil rights legislation if Congress passed it. No one from the Clinton campaign called to ask my advice in filling out the questionnaire, and I woke up on February 11 to headlines in the San Francisco papers that said, "Clinton Dissents on Gay Bill." HRCF, while officially neutral on the race, was full of Tsongas supporters and they jumped on Clinton's answer: that he couldn't sign the legislation as it was currently written. A day later a headline in the *San Francisco Sentinel* screamed "Clinton Says No to Gay Rights."

My phones were ringing off the wall. Furious gays and lesbians were shocked by Clinton's answer. ANGLE members called to express deep reservations about the group's endorsement and warned that if something wasn't done to straighten out this fiasco, they'd find it impossible to raise the money. I was stunned by the blunder. I knew exactly how this had come about. I knew where Clinton stood, and the concerns he had expressed when he met with ANGLE back in October. If they hadn't been so stupid and had coordinated with us, none of this need have happened.

I swallowed my rage, called the campaign, and was put in touch with the person who had answered the questionnaire for Clinton. He was condescending and arrogant. He knew what he was doing. They'd worked for civil rights for years. Of course they knew how to answer a questionnaire. My problem was that I really didn't understand the complexities of the issue and the "political problem" it presented to the campaign.

I told him that my whole life had been about the "complexities of the issue" and that Clinton believed in this legislation, but I realized this conversation wasn't going to accomplish anything worth a damn. It was a crucial moment for the alliance. If this blunder wasn't corrected, the Clinton organization would have a serious credibility problem with the community.

I placed a call to campaign chair Mickey Kantor in New Hampshire. He returned the call within two hours.

"Mickey, we have a problem," I began.

"What is it, David? I have to be in a meeting with Bill."

I gave him a concise report on the questionnaire and the impact of Clinton's answer.

"Damn! Didn't you see it before it went out?"

"No."

"They can't send that stuff out without showing it to you—that's crazy," he said. "Let me visit with the boss and I'll get right back to you."

"Mickey, we have to move quickly," I warned him. "The Tsongas people have the questionnaire. There's a HRCF board meeting this weekend. If we don't have a response by then, we're dead meat!"

Kantor was back to me in short order. Clinton "was livid at the response and wanted it corrected immediately." We agreed that he would send a letter to HRCF co-chair Randy Klose to be distributed at its board meeting. He asked me to draft the letter and fax it immediately. The campaign made some revisions and dispatched it to Randy in time for the meeting:

> Dear Mr. Klose:
>
> I am writing to clarify some misconceptions about my position on the subject of civil rights for gays and lesbians which have arisen from the answer to your recent questionnaire.
>
> I am a strong supporter of civil rights for gays and lesbians, as I am for all Americans. As President, I will sign the federal gay civil rights bill as long as the final version addresses my concerns on two matters, which I believe will help facilitate the passage of the bill.
>
> In my answer to your questionnaire, I mentioned that the current version of the legislation will need to undergo further clarification on the issues of enforcement of non-numerical affirmative action and the hiring of secular employees by religious organizations. These issues raise important questions about the right to privacy and freedom of religion, and should be addressed. My concerns are shared, I believe, by many legislators in Washington who support the legislation but think that the current version of the bill will need technical changes prior to passage. In pointing out my views about these areas, I was trying to give a thoughtful and responsible answer to your question about the legislation. This does not, however, reflect on my fundamental commitment to sign the legislation when it is passed by the United States Congress.
>
> I think that if my position on the civil rights bill is read in the context of my commitment to the rights of gays and lesbians— my call for a repeal of the ban on gays and lesbians serving in the military, and my pledge to issue an executive order if elected prohibiting discrimination against gays and lesbians in federal

hiring and contracting—it will be clear that I am fundamentally committed to the protection of the rights of gays and lesbians.

Sincerely,
Bill Clinton

The letter was released publicly, soothed a lot of uneasy supporters, and was enough for ANGLE members to continue bringing in the checks. But the Tsongas supporters, sensing blood from the Flowers scandal, the draft issue, and the HRCF questionnaire, moved quickly into the gay community around the country. On February 18, Tsongas carried New Hampshire with 33 percent of the vote to Clinton's 25 percent. Earlier we had thought Clinton had a chance to defeat Tsongas in his own backyard, but all the mess slowed down his momentum.

Still, although Tsongas's strong showing in New Hampshire spurred his community supporters to work harder on his behalf, the checks kept coming in to ANGLE. The Los Angeles community began to know Clinton better and they liked what they were hearing from him. In addition, ANGLE members were now invested in the campaign and determined to keep our word and meet our goal.

By February 28, the day of the dinner, we had collected over seventy-five thousand dollars. Gathered in a conference room at the Beverly Wilshire for our reception, we had a call from Jerry Stern. As always, Clinton was running late. The forty-five minutes allotted to it would have to be cut down. I assured Jerry that we would be pleased to have Clinton simply say a few words and have his picture taken with the donors.

More than sixty of them were there. We were feeling very proud indeed. We had exceeded our financial commitment to the campaign, and accomplished it while the campaign was in the midst of a crisis and others were having a hard time fund-raising. Clinton arrived exhausted, looking much more tired than on his last trip. The crises had clearly taken a toll. But when he began to speak, all that vanished. He was passionate and eloquent. I had introduced him, and he talked of our friendship and how much it meant to him. Then he addressed the issues of concern to the gay and lesbian community. He said he was "tired of the politics of division and denial . . . tired of seeing the American people put each other down because of their differences." I listened, feeling proud to have brought my friend to this community. He said what we needed and wanted to hear.

Then he shared a startling insight into his personal life. There was a quaver in his voice as he talked about his life without his father, about his mother having to leave him behind because she had to work, about his loneliness as a child, about his brother's addiction. The room was very quiet. We realized he was reaching out to us by reaching deep inside himself. He had made the link between his feelings of isolation from his neighbors with our feelings of isolation from society. He won the hearts of those in the room. I had never heard him so self-revealing in a speech. "I will be there," he concluded. "I want you to play a role in the life of this country. . . . I want you to have the opportunity to just be people, and live up to your fullest potential. This is my commitment. I could do no less and still hold my head up."

With that appearance Bill Clinton nailed down the Los Angeles community.

As we filed into the ballroom, ANGLE's success was clear. More than one hundred of the over six hundred people who attended the dinner were members. Attorney Warren Christopher introduced Clinton, Mickey Kantor spoke, and Maxine Waters, a congressperson from Los Angeles, endorsed him. He gave a very effective speech, and then, when he was about to leave the room, hesitated, turned around, and came back to me. He gave me a big bear hug and, as the crowd cheered, whispered into my ear, "I love you. I will never forget your friendship and loyalty."

As the primary campaign season continued, Clinton regained his lost momentum. One by one he picked off his opponents; Kerry fell in Georgia and Tsongas was derailed in Illinois and Michigan. It looked as if everything was on "go"—no more obstacles awaiting us on the road to the convention in New York in July. We should have known better. This was politics.

The voters had something else in mind. After the collapse of the Tsongas and Kerry candidacies, former California Governor Jerry Brown, who up to then had been viewed as a minor player in the Democratic presidential primaries, suddenly became the focal point of the anti-Clinton vote. Still viewing him as a fringe candidate, Clinton's staff ignored Brown's surge in the Connecticut primary on March 24. Brown had beaten Clinton by just twenty-seven hundred votes, but his upset victory made him a credible candidate and sent the Democratic race into yet another frenzy. Again Clinton was put on the defensive. He faced a crucial showdown with Brown in the New York State primary.

Brown's sudden emergence as a populist candidate was a tough one for me. I had been a long-time supporter and had worked on his California races and his two previous tries for the presidential nomination. As governor of California from 1974 to 1982, he had one of the best records anywhere on gay and lesbian rights. His appointments and policies were outstanding. This was one of those times in politics where I had to juggle divided personal loyalties with the reality of practical leadership. Clearly Brown wasn't going to be the nominee, and the only result of a Brown victory in New York would have been to badly divide the Democratic Party. I had one overwhelming priority: to end the nightmare years of Reagan/Bush and to increase the survival odds for my friends. So despite Brown's record and some significant support for him in the community, I stayed strong for Clinton.

For weeks I had been attempting to schedule Hillary Clinton for a tour of AIDS Project-Los Angeles, the city's chief service group for AIDS patients. We finally set a date for March 26, and I met her as she finished speaking at an elementary school about ending violence in the school system and achieving excellence in her life. Children were Hillary's passion. She had been serving as national chair of Marian Wright Edelman's Children's Defense Fund, and when she speaks of the plight of children in America she becomes animated and passionate. I listened as she spoke from the heart in the auditorium full of children and teachers. Then, as we entered the van to drive to APLA, she whipped out my briefing paper and fired off dozens of questions. They were informed, sharp, and to the point. She wanted to know as much as possible before we got there and she stayed away from any personal conversation. With AIDS, my usual practice with decision-makers was to try to convey the reality of the plague through personal experiences I had had with it; but I knew Hillary had had friends who died of the disease so she was fully aware of its awfulness. I realized she wanted to focus on policy and the work of APLA, but I suggested she also share her own experiences of sickness and loss. She grimaced. "I understand why it's important to do that, but I hate it. My relationship with Dan and the others was so personal."

There was pain in her voice when she mentioned Dan Bradley, who had been a very close friend. Hillary had been chair of the board of directors of the Legal Services Corporation when Dan was heading its daily operations. Dan had come out of the closet while at Legal Services, and even five years after his death she was clearly still grieving for him.

I could understand her reserve. Still, I told her, "Hillary, I know it is an invasion of your privacy but it is important."

"I know. I know."

"You should also know that at this visit there are going to be a num-

ber of people who will approach you and share the fact that they are
HIV-positive. They will be very sensitive to how you react. So many
people they meet recoil and refuse to hug or touch them. It would be
absolutely great if you gave anyone who approaches you a hug."

"David. I am not a hugger."

Her comment caught me by surprise. I realized for the first time how
difficult certain aspects of campaigning had to be for Hillary. In the past,
I had only seen the more personal side of her when she was warm and
embracing with her friends. Bill was a born hugger and toucher. He was
like this with his friends and with the people he met on the campaign
trail. In one-on-one situations, he rarely tried to connect through his
ideas or his very considerable knowledge. Instinctively, he relied on his
extraordinary personal skills. Hillary reserved her displays of affection
for her family and a small circle of intimates. When it came to public
situations, she much preferred to utilize her knowledge and intellectual
mastery to achieve her purpose.

Now I could see her wrestling with my request. It was clearly difficult
for her. "Well, I guess I can handle a handshake," she said at last.

We were greeted by APLA chair David Wexler and Lenny Bloom, the
executive director. They gave her a tour of the large, warehouselike
facility, and she peppered them with questions on health care, governmental response, and the needs of the project. At the end she met with
APLA clients—and she did indeed shake hands. In 1987, just before the
Third International Conference on AIDS, President Reagan had acceded to pressure and formed a presidential commission on AIDS, but
its recommendations had largely been ignored. Hillary pledged to "dust
off" the proposals and make AIDS a priority in a Clinton White House.
Karen Ocamb, an openly lesbian reporter, was in the van with us as we
headed toward Hillary's next stop and interviewed her on AIDS and gay
and lesbian issues. She talked about Dan Bradley with Karen, and in the
next issue of the gay and lesbian newspaper *Update*, Karen recorded Hillary's thoughts on him:

> "I visited him for the last time shortly before he died in Miami,
> where he was living at the time. . . . He got dressed up and came
> down and had breakfast with me in my hotel. That's the kind of guy he
> was. He never complained about anything and just went on with his
> life. He was indignant over some great injustice that he was attempting
> to undo. It didn't even have to do with AIDS—it had to do with some
> problem in the Dade County school system that he ranted and raved
> about for thirty minutes. . . .

"He was a great friend, and he was a very effective advocate for whatever he believed in. I didn't know that would be the last time I'd ever see him. He knew he was very sick but he never talked about it. . . . I wish he was here today. I wish that he had not died. He taught me a lot."

It was a personal side of Hillary that I had rarely seen. If elected, I realized, Bill and Hillary would be the first occupants of the White House who had close openly gay and lesbian friends.

That night Jeremy and I flew to Oregon for an HRCF dinner. I found an urgent message waiting for me as soon as we landed—Clinton's New York campaign coordinators Harold Ickes and Susan Thomases needed me there to help with the April 7 primary. Brown was running stronger than expected and had significant support in the sizable New York gay and lesbian community. He had been attacking Clinton's lack of a record on AIDS issues in Arkansas. That was true enough—Arkansas had so small a caseload that Clinton had practically no record on AIDS. In addition, Brown was fanning the Northeast's usual suspicion of southerners when it came to civil rights issues.

Ickes bellowed into the phone in his usual style: "Mixner, we need your ass here to turn around our problems in the gay community. The race is closer than we want and we're getting clobbered among gays."

"What's been done so far?"

"Marty Rouse is working hard on it," Ickes said. "Give him a call."

Marty Rouse was an openly gay aide to Manhattan Borough President Ruth Messinger. "Harold, if I come all the way back there, can we arrange a meeting between Clinton and some of the activists?"

"Just get here. We'll work it out."

While I gave my dinner speech Jeremy was on the phone canceling all my appointments and making arrangements for us to get to New York. We were there two days later. It was one week to the primary. The Clinton headquarters at the Sheraton Towne House was loud with the usual campaign madness. The corridors were filled with people having hush-hush meetings while volunteers ran back and forth past them on ostensibly urgent business. Sections of the floor were classified off-limits except to senior campaign staff. We walked through this invisible barrier into the select offices, received our credentials, got on all the "access lists," and figured out the lay of the land.

We had meetings with Mickey Kantor and David Wilhelm, who was

sharing campaign management duties with him, and with Ickes and Susan Thomases. The polling results looked bad. The race was very tight
and the report that Clinton was hurting badly in the gay and lesbian
community was accurate. Tsongas was starting to make a comeback and
Brown was getting very favorable coverage in the community's press. I
said, "Let me find out what's going on. I'll come back to you with a
strategy for the community that we can handle in the one week we have
left."

The first job was to meet with strong Clinton supporters in the community. I saw the very able Marty Rouse, who was the gay and lesbian
coordinator for the New York campaign. I followed up with meetings
with respected civil rights attorney Tom Stoddard, environmental adviser Bob Hattoy, and activist Ann Northrop. They were all very frustrated and all had the same report. They had been trying to set up a
meeting between Clinton and AIDS activists for several weeks, and had
consistently hit a dead end with the campaign staff. The problem, they
kept being told, wasn't substance; it was "scheduling." That was absolute
evidence of a runaround. Campaign schedules are extremely flexible
when they need to be. If there are people it's important for the candidate
to meet, the time will be found for him to meet them.

This was not the first time I had to deal with homophobia, perceived
or actual, in a campaign. It was always hard to tell whether the concern
was based on the political judgment of a backlash from straight voters, or
if I was dealing with personal prejudice and intolerance. The motive
really didn't make any difference. The only way to deal with it was to
face it head-on.

I went back to Ickes and Thomases, the two most powerful and sympathetic people in the New York campaign, and said we had to set up
that meeting between Clinton and AIDS activists, and quickly. They
understood its importance immediately. Mickey Kantor agreed, but he
wanted to be sure the meeting was a productive one, not the kind where
hard-core activists ended up screaming at the candidate. Clinton had
already had several confrontations with Act Up on the streets of New
York, and the staff was growing weary of those encounters. I could understand that. I assured Mickey this meeting would stay under control.

I was able to set up the meeting for Saturday evening, April 4, in
Clinton's suite at the Sheraton Towne House. Rouse and Northrop had
already gotten together with David Barr of the Gay Men's Health Crisis—GMHC was the largest and most powerful AIDS organization in
New York—and prepared a list of invitees. The list covered a broad
spectrum of the AIDS community. Barr stressed to me that this was an

AIDS meeting and not a gay and lesbian meeting. This was a compromise I could live with if that was what it would take to turn around the community's vote. I realized that for many gays and lesbians, AIDS was more momentous than some civil rights issues. I knew that such a meeting would have a major impact on the community—and not only in New York.

The next urgency was to prepare in-depth briefings for Clinton that gave him essential background data and also focused on such controversial issues as needle exchange, condom use, and sex education in the schools. We made sure he had the latest figures on AIDS, was informed about the diversity of the AIDS community, and understood the correct rhetoric. While we were working on the briefings I constantly reassured the staff and protected the time slot from all those who tried to grab it away. In between the staff meetings, I made appearances and speeches for Clinton throughout the community. One of the problems of a hot and heavy campaign is that you don't have time to reflect either on your commitment or on the candidate. It usually takes a huge scandal or violation of trust to trigger individuals into reevaluating their choice. In New York that crazed week, despite what the scheduling difficulties probably signified, I felt no need to think about any of this. I knew that the problems we faced were not unique to this campaign. I was enthusiastic about Clinton and welcomed the opportunity to campaign for him in New York.

As the time for the meeting neared, we all became nervous. The staff worried about political fallout and we worried because we understood the long-term impact for our community. Saturday evening arrived at last. The several dozen participants came from every conceivable background and every culture, but most of them were leaning toward Brown or Tsongas. Ruth Messinger greeted them in Clinton's personal suite, together with Bob Hattoy and Ann Northrop. Congressperson Barney Frank of Massachusetts waited with me down the hall, in the room of Bruce Lindsey, who was an adviser to Clinton and a long-time personal friend from Arkansas. We were there to brief Clinton before he entered the meeting.

Clinton walked into Lindsey's room clearly worn out from nonstop campaigning. That was worrying. He dropped down into one of those horribly uncomfortable hotel chairs, with Barney and I sitting on the bed facing him. Lindsey stood in the doorway. Barney did most of the substantive briefing and I added the political background. Clinton's knowledge of the issues was already impressive and he had obviously read our briefing papers. As Barney and I went down the list of concrete proposals that the activists would be raising, Clinton would occasionally look toward Lindsey to be sure he was on the right track. You could see the trust he put in Lindsey and their closeness.

By the time Clinton rose wearily from his chair and headed for his suite where everyone was waiting for him, the meeting was already an hour and a half behind schedule. The place was filled. Those who couldn't find a seat in the circle of chairs sat on the bar, the floor, anywhere there was a space. There were gay men, lesbians, people of color, mothers with AIDS, mothers whose children had AIDS. They were old and young, rich and poor—and they were Clinton's kind of crowd.

The minute he entered the suite, his tiredness vanished. They energized him. As he introduced himself around the room he tried to have a personal moment with each person there—asking a question or simply giving a warm handshake or a hug. A chair had been held for him in the circle, and I sat directly opposite. You could sense the excitement in the room, but you could also sense the urgency. There wasn't a person there who didn't have a message for Bill Clinton that evening.

David Barr of the GMHC started off the meeting by presenting Clinton with a condom. He blushed a little, coolly accepted it, and then quickly tossed it over to me. Mine wasn't just a blush—I turned scarlet.

I knew that Clinton was exhausted and I was afraid that if someone in the meeting pushed him too hard, he would lose his temper. While I'd never seen it in action, his "purple rages" in the campaign were legendary. Whoever was closest to him when he exploded bore the brunt. I was also concerned that his fatigue might prevent him from answering questions sharply and clearly. But I needn't have worried. The questions were to the point and well presented. The participants pressed him to agree to endorse the concept of a Manhattan Project for an AIDS cure, to give a major AIDS policy speech before the end of the campaign, to have an HIV-positive person speak at the convention in prime time, and to reform the drug trial approval process. Clinton not only agreed to these requests, he often went further. Even in his tiredness he was articulate and compassionate, and the people in the room sensed his caring. Several times senior staffers tried to bring the meeting to a close and Clinton waved them off. Finally, Mickey Kantor passed me a note saying we had to get the candidate to bed and would I please end it. I looked at Clinton and said that it was time to disband and for everyone to get to work. He gave a resigned smile, but before he left he took the time to thank each participant personally for coming.

Word of the meeting and his promises quickly spread through the

New York community and across the country. Clinton won New York with 41 percent of the vote and Tsongas was second with 29 percent. Brown placed a distant third. Bill Clinton's path to the nomination seemed almost certain.

I headed back home feeling good about my work but I was burnt out and exhausted. If I was to be any use to the ongoing campaign, I had to take a break. So I went off to Europe for two weeks with Larry Weghorst, the friend who had made me confront my addictions and pushed me to recovery. London was our first stop. Through friends of Larry's we got great seats to the memorial concert for Freddie Mercury, who had died of AIDS. I am a huge rock music fan. When I'm at a rock concert I can let loose in the music and forget about everything else in the world. I could listen to Bob Dylan, Bruce Springsteen, and Janis Joplin forever. We sat and watched Elton John, David Bowie, Guns N' Roses, George Michael, Liza Minnelli, and dozens of others belt out songs from the group Queen. At one point, David Bowie knelt on stage and starting reciting the Lord's Prayer for Mercury. I joined him and prayed for Peter.

We went on from London to Amsterdam and Paris. During the day I walked all over the streets exploring, ate in sidewalk cafés, drank tons of coffee, and people-watched. I read several books, caught up on some badly needed rest, and had some equally badly needed casual sex. Larry and I ate some first-rate meals and talked about everything but the campaign. I put it out of my mind for fourteen glorious days and then we headed for home.

Just as Larry and I were boarding our plane at the Paris airport, the jury in the Rodney King case returned its verdict and rioting broke out in South-Central Los Angeles. Our plane left Paris late and we had to run to make our connection in New York, so we hadn't the faintest idea of what was happening at home. As we were flying over the Midwest, the captain announced that we would have to land in Las Vegas because people were shooting at the planes landing in LAX. A flight attendant told us what was happening. In the seats next to us were an Italian news crew, who had boarded in New York and were on their way to cover the riots. While we sat on the ground at the end of a runway in Las Vegas, I spent the time briefing them about Los Angeles, and they asked for my card in case they had any more questions.

Five hours later our plane was released to fly into Los Angeles. We landed at midnight. We could smell the smoke and see the burning fires, but no one had given us any updates on the situation. I found a phone and called Jeremy to ask where my ride was. He was dumbfounded. There was nothing he could do; a tight curfew had been placed on the entire city. Still not really grasping the extent of the disaster, Larry and I went down to retrieve our luggage and to hail a cab. There were no cabs, no police, no airline personnel, and hundreds of passengers were waiting at the curb trying to figure out what to do.

I caught a ride to the Hertz Rent A Car building and found long lines and an almost empty lot. Then an attendant behind the counter recognized me because of my Clinton work and pulled me out of the line. In the back office, he saw that I got one of the last cars. "That's for the work you do for us in the community," he said. "Please, Mr. Mixner, be careful out there. It's wicked."

The car was a station wagon. When I drove back to pick up Larry and our luggage, he had found other friends from West Hollywood who were desperately looking for a way to get home. We loaded the rear of the station wagon with our bags, packed ourselves into the seats, and turned on the radio. The rioting had spread from South-Central Los Angeles into all areas of the city. We were very scared.

We decided that we'd stop for nothing, drive through red lights and stop signs. If we had to, we would drive on the sidewalks to avoid being trapped by cars backed up on the streets. The fires were all around us as we drove down Century Boulevard, and we quickly maneuvered ourselves onto the San Diego Freeway to avoid the rioting in Inglewood just a block away. For the first time in my life, the freeway was totally deserted. The highway lights were off, nothing but empty dark road ahead. Off to the side we passed burning buildings and the blinking red lights of emergency vehicles in the smoke. But I got everyone home safely and finally reached my house in West Hollywood. Buildings were on fire a couple of blocks away. I walked inside, barricaded the doors and windows, and then wondered whether I was overreacting. Later I found out that everyone did the same thing.

The next day I sat on my roof and witnessed the anger of years of repression explode in my hometown. I abhorred the violence as I always had, but I understood the pain that had led to this havoc. If I had a child who was hungry, went to a hopelessly poor school, was likely to drop from a gang bullet every time he went out of the house—if all my child faced was an abyss for as long as he lived—I too would be tempted to riot. At night, a rigorous curfew kept us isolated and an eerie quiet fell over the city. When I couldn't sleep, I read Gandhi and Thoreau. I searched for answers but there were none.

On Saturday the Italian news crew called to ask whether I would serve as a commentator for their broadcast. We drove around the city filming the devastation. National Guard troops stood on every corner. Then, as the day went on, we witnessed an astonishing sight. Black, white, Asian, people of every race were appearing on the streets holding shovels and brooms to clean up the debris. Against the massive destruction looming around us those small brooms looked so futile at first. But they came to symbolize the future. The citizens of Los Angeles weren't going to be defeated by the violence. We were all on the same course. We could only be as free as our neighbors.

When the riots were over, I went back to work on the campaign. When Jeremy and I were in New York for Clinton, we had a meeting with Rahm Emanuel. From that very first day at the National Executive Committee meeting, Rahm had recognized the fund-raising potential for Clinton in the gay and lesbian community. The two of us worked closely to develop fund-raising contacts in different cities around the country. In New York we came up with the idea of a "million-dollar" fund-raising evening in the gay and lesbian community. Clinton would be at a location in Los Angeles, and his speech would be broadcast by satellite to dozens of other cities holding simultaneous fund-raisers. Hillary would anchor the New York dinner. Our goal was to raise a million dollars in a single night for the campaign.

Jeremy and I briefed ANGLE on the concept and it was greeted with enthusiasm. Scott Hitt, Diane Abbitt, Roberta Bennett, and I called around the country to explore the possibilities. A week or so later, Rahm called back to say the costs would be prohibitive and the technology too difficult. I had doubts about his analysis and I suspected that the campaign's inner circle wanted to avoid so public a gay and lesbian event. I did some quick calling around and I was right on both counts. But I had to be realistic. We were making great progress in this campaign and this was not the place or the issue on which to do battle with the staff. It was important that from time to time we be seen to yield to some of their concerns and to save the battles for when there could be no compromise.

Rahm proposed that, instead, ANGLE host a major event for Clinton on May 18 in Los Angeles. We agreed, with the stipulation that it be opened to the press. The Los Angeles community went all out. A pre-speech reception would be held for the major donors and a massive rally would follow where Clinton would give a major policy address on gay and lesbian rights and AIDS. Hollywood producer Art Arellanas agreed to produce the rally and had some of the best sound, light, and staging technicians in Los Angeles donate their services. Everyone was pushing ticket sales so that the room would be full and we would meet our goal of one hundred thousand dollars. For the first two weeks of May, no one talked to anybody in the Los Angeles community without selling them tickets.

The advance team arrived and started making the changes required for a presidential candidate's visit—moving the press stands, checking the exits, and testing the sound and lighting. They were amused at the specific instructions they had received from national headquarters to not deny access to the press. Head advance man John Tooley was laughing when he told me how many times he had been warned about the press issue. "David," he said, "I think they got the message!"

On May 18 I went to the Van Nuys airport to meet Clinton and escort him to the Hollywood Palace Theater for his speech. Earlier, I had faxed a draft of a proposed speech to the plane. As usual, Clinton was running an hour and a half late. Inside the campaign we joked about buying watches that ran on "Clinton time." We had to cancel his appearance at the private reception. Mickey Kantor spoke to the major donors and briefed them on the campaign, and then they went downstairs to join the hundreds packed into the main room waiting patiently for Clinton's arrival.

While this was going on I sat in the Van Nuys airport and was a nervous wreck. I kept calling Scott Hitt on the advance staff phones to check on the crowd size at the Palace and to update him on the latest arrival time. Scott assured me that several hundred people were packed into the main room and it looked impressive. This evening was important. My head kept circling around all the things that could go wrong: Would Clinton give a tough speech? Would he move the community? Would the crowd be big enough?

The advance staff watched me pacing back and forth on the tarmac and laughed at my nervousness. I couldn't help wondering what advice Clinton was getting on the plane. Was the staff toning down his speech? And when I wasn't worrying about Clinton, I'd switch back to the Palace and dwell on how the community was going to respond. I began to feel whiplashed.

The plane landed at last and the motorcade pulled up to the ramp. The advance team placed me in Clinton's car and the Highway Patrol motorcycle cops pulled in front to lead the procession to the Palace. It was at that moment that I realized that the world that Bill Clinton and I had known together had vanished. No more intimate talks, casual walks along a beach, confidences exchanged. My friend was running for President of the United States.

Bill came down the ramp and entered the car. He looked over at me, grinned, and said, "You're scared to death, aren't you?" I wasn't sure how to relate to him now. I laughed nervously and acknowledged my fear. He gave me a pat on the leg and said, "Don't worry. Not one person in that room is going to be disappointed. I know what this means to you and I am not going to let any of you down." The motorcade proceeded out of the airport and onto the freeway. All traffic was stopped and people waved from the sidewalks. I couldn't help myself. As Bill worked on his speech, I waved at the crowds.

Every once in a while he would look up and ask a question, then start writing again. Finally, he stopped and looked over at me. "You know," he said, "I just got off a plane where no one wants me to give this speech and I am going into a room where no one believes I will give it." I knew then that the speech was going to be a special one. The long motorcade pulled in front of the Palace. Just before we got out, I received one more reassuring pat, a thumbs-up sign, and a "Let's go get them, David." We headed down the side of the building and through the stage door.

The ANGLE gang was there to greet us. We all posed for pictures and Clinton started going over his speech one more time. A giant screen came down over the stage and a film was shown on Clinton. Then Diane, Roberta, Scott, Bob Sertner, Roberta Achtenberg, and I walked out on the stage to cheers. There were the usual preliminaries of introducing dignitaries, an appeal for more checks, and a plea for the crowd to understand the historic significance of the evening.

Diane and Scott gave me a generous introduction and I proceeded to the microphone. I had to take a deep breath:

> *My brothers and sisters. We have all come a long way to this place. No one handed us this event. No one has done us a favor. We have earned this evening inch by inch, step by step, moment by moment, and it is ours. . . . The last twelve years, especially for this community, have been a long, hard, and difficult road. . . . We have buried thousands of our dead. We have cared for tens of thousands of our sick. . . . We have done it with anger. We have done it because we had to. But don't forget, most of all, we have done it as a community together, with dignity, nobility, and we have every reason to be very, very proud tonight. . . . I didn't think I could allow myself to dream any-*

more. . . . I am allowing myself to dream again. I am allowing myself to believe again. And it is because of this man.

This man comes here tonight to share his vision of how we belong in his America. It is this man who will be our Harry Truman and sign that executive order. It is this man who will be our John Kennedy and include us in the vision of a greater America. It is this man who will be our Lyndon Johnson and fight like hell and effectively work to get a cure for AIDS out of the Congress of the United States. . . . My brothers and sisters, the next President of the United States, my friend Bill Clinton.

Bill came out from the side of the stage and the crowd roared its approval. He stepped to the podium and began his extraordinary speech to our community and to the country:

You know that I have said many times that a campaign for president has two purposes. One is for the country to get to know the candidate, and the other is for the candidate to get to know the country. If the candidate does not grow and deepen in understanding and compassion and feeling, then the race itself is already half lost.

There are people in this room today to whom I owe a great debt of gratitude, for you have helped me to get to know my country better than I did when I began. . . .

Tonight, I want to talk to you about how we can be one people again . . . without regard to race or gender or sexual orientation or age or region or income, how we can become one again.

This country has often been divided, especially at election time. The pollsters and the political consultants tell people all the time how to cut the electorate up in just "this little slice and that little slice" so that we cannot be one again. Yet it is against all our natures, against our basic values, against the statements of all our basic laws, and still we do it, over and over again. . . .

And the great passion of my life has been education and telling people we don't have a person to waste. The great heartbreak is seeing people wasted. . . . And those of you here tonight, you represent a community of our nation's gifted people whom we have been willing to squander. We can't afford to waste the capacities, the contributions, the hearts, the souls, the minds of the gay and lesbian Americans. . . . For every day that we discriminate, that we hate, that we refuse to avail ourselves of the potential of any group of Americans, we are all less than we ought to be. . . .

Regarding the military, Clinton said:

> *. . . [a study] said that there was no basis in national security for discriminating based on sexual orientation of Americans who wish to serve in the military. I said I would act on that study. It seemed to me elementary that if a person, man or woman, wanted to serve their country, they ought to be able to do it. . . .*
>
> *. . . The Secretary of Defense himself, obviously personally very uncomfortable at not changing the rules, said it was a "quaint little rule." Well, my fellow Americans, we have too much to do to endure "quaint little rules" . . .*
>
> *I want people like David Mixner and Roberta Achtenberg, Dr. Scott Hitt, some of you in this audience, to be a part of a Clinton administration, not because of or in spite of your sexual orientation, but because America needs you. And if I become the President of the United States, I owe it to my country to find the best and most gifted and most knowledgeable people in the United States of America to solve the problems and embrace the challenges of this time. . . .*

Bill outlined his commitment to battle AIDS, including the pledges that he had made in the New York hotel room to the AIDS activists. Then, movingly, he thanked the community:

> *And now, before I leave, I want to say something which is not part of a political program. I just want to thank the gay and lesbian community for your courage and your commitment and your service in face of the terror of AIDS. When no one was offering a helping hand, and when it was dark and lonely, you did not withdraw, but instead you reached out to others. And this whole nation has benefited already in ways most people cannot even imagine from the courage and commitment and sense of community which you practice. . . .*
>
> *The nation owes you thanks for that. I want to give you my thanks and respect for that struggle today. . . .*

From the stage, as I looked at the crowd of my friends, I saw tears streaming down their faces. For the first time a potential president had acknowledged their pain, their journey and struggle. Then Clinton, his own eyes moist, moved toward an emotional close.

> *Finally, let me say again, this is not an election, or it should not be, about race or gender or being gay or straight or religion or age or region or income. What kills the country is not the problems it faces. . . . What kills the country is to proceed day in and day out with no vision, with no sense that tomorrow can be better than today, with no sense of shared community.*
>
> *What I came here today to tell you in simple terms is: I have a vision and you are part of it.*

His voice cracking, Clinton finished:

> *If I could, if I could wave my arm for those of you that are HIV-positive and make it go away tomorrow, I would do it—so help me God, I would. If I gave up my race for the White House and everything else, I would do that . . .*

The crowd roared its approval and surged forward to touch his hand. Those of us on the stage hugged, almost unbelieving at the power of what we had heard. Those in the audience who were skeptical became true believers. As I wiped tears from my eyes, Clinton gave me a great big bear hug and disappeared into the night. He was off to his next engagement.

The effect of the speech flashed across the nation. Alex Koleszar had the wisdom to have the speech videotaped, and we found ourselves overwhelmed with requests for copies. Alex organized the duplicating and sent them out as fast as he could. All around the country people arranged parties in their living rooms so they could watch it with their friends. People who received the tapes made their own copies and sent them on to others. Then Alex did a three-minute version to be played in gay and lesbian video bars until election day in November. He made a list of every single one of these bars in the major industrial states and got help calling them to tell them to play the tape over and over until victory. Alex reached one bar owner in Dayton, Ohio, and said, "We are asking bars to play a three-minute clip of the Clinton Palace speech on gay and lesbian rights. Can we send you a copy, and would you be willing to play it to your patrons?"

"Nope," said the bar owner. "We don't need the three-minute tape."

Alex gently tried to persuade him to change his mind. The man laughed. "Nope. We don't need the three-minute tape. We've already been playing over and over the thirty-minute version. Keep up the good work!"

The Washington Post carried the Clinton speech on its front page on May 20. The headline read, "Clinton Finds New Voice of Emotion" and the article said:

> *The moment [Palace event] was historic in its own right: the largest fund-raiser ever held openly by the gay community for a candidate for President. It raised an estimated $100,000. But for Clinton, the beneficiary of the event here Monday night, it could mark a turning point in his campaign, a point where it seemed that his political and emotional sides converged to give his voice a deeper sense of conviction.*

The next month Clinton won the California primary and became the surefire nominee at the Democratic convention in New York in July. With the help of California campaign chair Bill Wardlaw and campaign manager John Emerson, ANGLE members Scott Hitt, Diane Abbitt, Roberta Bennett, Chris Hershey, and I became Clinton delegates to what promised to be a momentous convention for our community.

On Gay Pride Day at the end of June, not long before we were to leave, a major earthquake struck southern California. We took to calling it the "Queer Quake." In some ways it was an omen of what was to come.

CHAPTER FOURTEEN

"Happy Days Are Here Again"

THAT July the convention hullabaloo took over midtown New York. Media vans lined the curbs. You couldn't walk a block without bumping into sidewalk interviews, vendors hawking buttons, delegates from Iowa munching big pretzels covered with mustard, store windows promising sale prices to those with delegate badges. Red, white, and blue banners hung from the lampposts. Everywhere you turned there were pictures of the Clintons for sale—on posters, plates, and coffee mugs. Shuttle buses ran between the delegate hotels and Madison Square Garden, and the delegates waved banners and posters out the windows. Even blasé New Yorkers caught the spirit. They made us all feel very welcome.

The official opening was on Monday, July 12, and Jeremy and I came in the Friday before. The campaign wanted us close to the central action so they gave us a suite in Clinton's hotel, the Intercontinental. I had asked two personal friends to come with us to help with what was going to be a barrage of work. Jeff Gibson, a successful young San Francisco lawyer with great political judgment, and Mark Coleman, a passionate fan of the Dallas Cowboys, were devoted friends. At one time we had all lived in Los Angeles, and they were my sane refuge in my often crazy life. I'd call them when I needed a respite and we'd go out to dinner, laugh, and gossip, never mentioning politics once.

We found ourselves swamped in meetings, interviews, caucuses, and a whirlwind of receptions. Most of the serious work and most of the real battles are always fought beforehand, during the campaign for the nomination, so there was little of major importance to be decided at the convention. The wording in the party platform about AIDS and gay and lesbian rights was acceptable to us and had been cleared weeks before. Clinton had kept the promise he had made to the New York AIDS activists, and there were to be two HIV-positive speakers at the convention. The Human Rights Campaign Fund had done a great job preparing for maximum visibility for the gay and lesbian community, and had organized signs, hospitality suites, and buttons proclaiming the wearer's sexuality. Our job in the suite was to insure inclusion and visibility and to make sure there were no unpleasant surprises.

On my first day in New York, I met with convention honchos Harold Ickes, Sky Johnson, and Kevin Thurm to confirm all this, and to check that our major donors, leaders, and delegates were assured access to the convention proceedings, the special finance committee receptions, and the media, and were given the necessary credentials. They had already assigned personnel to liaise with us at the convention to prevent any problems from developing that would create difficulties for all of us. The name of the game now was to avoid screwups and have the whole thing run smoothly.

The national media found a major story in this first-ever significant presence of the gay and lesbian community at a national political convention. They were intrigued by the great amount of money the community had raised for the Clinton effort and the sizable number of gay and lesbian delegates, and they were stunned by our high visibility at the convention. I was asked for interviews almost daily; as the BBC was taking down their cameras in our suite NBC would arrive to set up theirs. As a delegate I had to attend the meeting of the California delegation every morning, make the round of the receptions sponsored by every national gay and lesbian group, and participate in the daily caucus of gay and lesbian delegates; and I also had to go to the meetings called by the Clinton staff so I could make certain everything was on target.

We had raised a lot of money for Clinton out of my office in Los Angeles and many of our large donors were coming to the convention to enjoy our moment of triumph. Although I had pinned all this down with

Ickes, Johnson, and Thurm the first day, I didn't want any inadvertent foul-ups. It was essential that they be given VIP status and that we get them on the floor of the convention at least once. If they felt excluded, there was no way we could ask them for large donations for the fall campaign. Jeremy took over the job of handling them and their needs. He went downstairs every day and charmed the credentials committee out of dozens of floor passes and invitations to VIP receptions and to the exclusive "Sky Boxes" at Madison Square Garden. He was so good at all this that the campaign dubbed him "credentials king." By the end of the convention many straight donors and even Clinton staff were calling him asking if he had any extras. I was reminded of a political boss handing out patronage to those who had been loyal to the organization.

There were more than one hundred openly gay and lesbian delegates to the convention and thirty-five were from California. At the beginning of the week there was clearly some distrust and concern about our visibility. The first day or two, speakers tended to mention almost all the constituencies present except us. This was not a minor matter. Acknowledgment of the community went to the heart not only of our self-esteem but our political power. Moreover, we had earned that right by delivering for Clinton. I hammered home that point in several meetings with key campaign staff. Ickes and Thurm put out the word that we were to be fully accepted and included in this convention. Suddenly, all over the convention floor signs sprouted reading "Lesbian and Gay Rights NOW." Speakers like Paul Tsongas, Mario Cuomo, Tom Harkin, Jerry Brown, and Jesse Jackson spoke of our struggle in their speeches. Round one accomplished.

On Monday, Scott Hitt, Chris Hershey, Diane Abbitt, and I entered Madison Square Garden together for the opening. It was a big day. History was about to be made. We stood in the crowd waiting to clear security proud of our gay and lesbian delegate badges with the pink triangle. Many of our fellow delegates asked about them, and when we explained they'd smile with approval. As the delegates from the fifty states streamed inside the enormous hall, a team of volunteers from gay and lesbian organizations handed us signs that said, "Gay and Lesbian Rights . . . Now!" We found our seats in the California delegation. Bill Wardlaw, the chairperson of the California Clinton campaign, and John Emerson, the campaign manager, seated me on the aisle right behind Wardlaw so I would be readily available when needed. Bill was evidence of the progress we had made in the campaign. A tall Irishman with prematurely gray hair, he is a major political power broker in California. I knew him as a devoted family man, Catholic, and a close friend of

Roger Cardinal Mahoney in Los Angeles, so I had laid my own stereo-typical presumptions on Bill and didn't expect him to be supportive of our efforts in the campaign. So much for stereotypes. I learned an important lesson. He was unquestionably one of the most open-minded and fairest individuals I dealt with in the entire campaign, and he was adamant that we receive our share of delegates, be accorded total respect, and have complete access. We became friends as the campaign progressed, and each of us increased our respect for the other's viewpoints.

It was an emotional week. A number of times, as I sat with the California delegation, straight delegates from all around the country stopped by my seat on the aisle and shared with me word of their lesbian or gay child or sibling and how proud they were to see them represented at the convention. I will always remember what one of them said to me.

"Mr. Mixner, may I interrupt you for a second?"

"Sure," I said, and stood up to greet him.

"My son died of AIDS about two years ago." He swallowed. "He would have loved so much being here. I had to come in his place."

A sob escaped, and I put my arms around him. "I'm sorry," he said as he broke away and wiped his tears. "I didn't mean to do that, sir."

"Please, please don't be sorry. There isn't one of us here who isn't carrying the banner for someone not with us. By our work we give your son's life additional definition and purpose and dignity."

He smiled at me, I thanked him for his courage, and he disappeared into the crowd. I sat down and all I could think of was Peter. I wanted Peter here with me. He would have loved this convention. He would have been so proud of me. I held back the tears and settled down to work.

The real moment for us, of course, was to come when Clinton kept his promise and there was an AIDS speech before the whole convention. In the weeks before, any number of people jockeyed for the role. My office alone received dozens of calls, résumés, and even some political threats on behalf of potential candidates. It was clear from the day that Clinton made his promise to our community that Elizabeth Glaser, a close friend of the Clintons and of Mickey Kantor, was a leading contender. Elizabeth was an extraordinary woman who had contracted AIDS through a transfusion and unknowingly passed the virus on to her two children. The wife of successful actor Paul Michael Glaser, she could easily have retreated into a very comfortable private world and spent the time that she had in the safety of her family. But there was no way that Elizabeth Glaser was not going to confront this disease. She was a founder of the Pediatric AIDS Foundation and became a national spokesperson in the battle against AIDS. Tireless in her efforts on Capitol Hill and with the White House, her effective politicking enabled the AIDS community to make great strides. While there was tension and even anger directed toward the gay community by some straights who had contracted AIDS through transfusions, Elizabeth would have no part of it. She believed strongly that we were all in this together. We were not going to be separated in the battle.

Most in the AIDS community held Elizabeth in very high regard, but the gay and lesbian community also felt it was important that a gay man be included in the presentation at the convention. In a memo I wrote to Clinton aide George Stephanopoulos and Ickes in early June, I warned that no matter whom we selected, others who weren't chosen would be upset, but that it was important that the person not be a newcomer. He had to have credentials born of fighting the disease for several years.

San Francisco newspaper reporter and renowned writer Randy Shilts called and asked to be considered as the speaker. This was the first time many of us realized that Randy was HIV-positive. Randy's remarkable 1987 book on the evolution of the epidemic, *And the Band Played on*, had become a classic; no one knew more about the subject than he did. He was seriously considered up to the final decision.

During the campaign Clinton's friend and his environmental adviser, Bob Hattoy, had found out that he was HIV-positive. The news sent a shock wave throughout the campaign and had a deep impact on Clinton. When I saw him in California during the primary, one of the first things he said to me was, "Have you heard about Bob?" and asked me to do whatever I could to be of help to him. There was no question that once Bob shared his health status with Clinton, he too would be seriously considered as the speaker.

Thus the choice of speaker turned into a problem. Ickes called to say he was going to ask Hattoy to introduce Glaser and hoped this would satisfy everyone. Bob didn't find this acceptable. He made an announcement that he had been asked to be one of two speakers on AIDS. Weary officials from the convention office called to ask me whether I could possibly get him to accept the introducer role, but I told them it was too late—the lesbian and gay press all over the country had picked up his announcement by then. Finally, it was agreed we would go with two speeches on AIDS.

For the community, Tuesday night was the highlight of the week. The presentation of the platform would come first, and one of the presenters was our friend Roberta Achtenberg. She was one of the first open lesbians ever to address a national party convention and as she came to the podium, our delegates cheered wildly. I thought Diane would break my hand, she was squeezing it so tightly.

Finally Congressperson Pat Schroeder came to the microphone and began the introductions for the two AIDS speeches. The hall was in the usual hubbub that passes for normal even when speeches are going on. But as Bob Hattoy mounted the podium, a stillness fell over the entire place. One by one, the delegates stood up, until all five thousand were on their feet in respect. The hush was palpable. When he paused, and said as he looked out over the crowd, "This is difficult," he won the hearts of a nation.

"I am a gay man with AIDS. If there is any honor in having this disease, it is the honor of being part of the gay and lesbian community in America. We have watched our friends and lovers die but we have not given up. Gay men and lesbians created community health clinics, provided educational materials, opened food kitchens, and held the hands of the dying in hospices. The gay and lesbian community is a family in the best sense of the word."

Elizabeth Glaser was equally eloquent in her powerful and moving speech as a woman with AIDS. By this time, any of those who had not wept when Bob spoke were in tears. "I am here," she told us, "because my son and I may not survive four more years of leaders who say they care—but do nothing."

I thought of Jim Foster, who first spoke about gay rights to the 1972 convention at two o'clock in the morning with no one listening. Jim had died of AIDS but he was very much with us that evening. People were listening at last.

When I got back to the hotel that night there was a message that Bill and Hillary wanted to see me. The hotel had provided them with a small conference room where they could greet close friends each night. When I walked in, they were with some friends from Arkansas. Bill saw me and came right over. He couldn't contain his excitement. "Weren't Bob and Elizabeth incredible tonight? Talk about a home run! Those two moved the nation."

"Bill," I said, "please know that we will never forget this evening and it would have never happened without you. There is no way I can thank you enough or describe what it meant to us."

"There is going to be a lot more where that came from," he promised.

Then others joined us. Hillary and I exchanged hugs and I told her about the man who was representing his dead son, and how much I missed Peter tonight. My voice cracked, and gently she put her hand on my arm in support. A little later Bob Hattoy and Elizabeth Glaser arrived and everyone applauded their entrance. They were the true heroes of the evening.

On Wednesday night the convention nominated William Jefferson Clinton to be the Democratic Party's candidate for President of the United States. After the balloting, he came to the hall and everyone cheered, paraded, and shouted their enthusiasm for the promise of a whole new way for the nation. It had felt strange to be casting my vote for Bill. Surely I was too young to actually know someone who was running for president—and someone my own age at that.

The last night of the convention was Clinton's acceptance speech. We were concerned about whether he would acknowledge the gay and lesbian community. If he didn't spell out any constituencies at all, that would be fine; but if he gave the usual political litany, group after group after group, and failed to mention us, that would be a disaster. I emphasized how important this was to Ickes and Kantor and Segal. Eli asked me to write out some comments that he could pass on to Clinton's speechwriters.

On Thursday night, as I sat with the California delegation waiting for Clinton, New York delegate Ann Northrop came rushing up and thrust a rough draft of the speech hot off the wire services into my hand. I got a sick feeling in the pit of my stomach. The usual litany was there, but gays and lesbians were not in it.

This was not how I wanted this convention to end. I reassured Ann this was only the rough draft but that I'd check on it, and got hold of Bill Wardlaw and John Emerson. Both realized the impact this would have in California and placed calls to the operations trailer behind the podium. Meanwhile I met in the aisle with some gay and lesbian delegates from different states and we organized a strategy. Each of them went back to their delegations and had the chairs call the operations trailer to insist that our community be included. We tried to do all this quietly. We didn't want to attract the attention of the press.

The group worked the convention and reported back to me as unobtrusively as it could, but one of the network news teams noticed all the activity and started moving a camera crew over to my seat. I told the reporter we were just planning our floor demonstration for Clinton after the speech—the last thing we needed on his big night was to have controversy over this splashed across the nation's television screens. John Emerson went off to the trailer with Ruth Messinger and reported back that they had reached Clinton in his car on the way to the convention and that the speech would be amended.

I believed them but that didn't relieve my anxiety—I wasn't going to relax until I heard Bill speak the words from the podium. With our ears poised for the slightest nuance and our eyes riveted on the close-up of his face on the two huge video screens fixed to either side of the podium, we listened as he began the list of constituencies. I held my breath. As he reached the end of the list, there was a slight pause—and then the word "gay." The convention roared its approval. My tension vanished in a flash, and for the first time that night I let myself share in the celebratory spirit filling the entire hall. When Clinton was done our team formed a jubilant conga line and wound our way around the floor to the music of Fleetwood Mac's "Don't Stop Thinking About Tomorrow." We had crossed the finish line. We had won our race.

Back in California we got going at once on the campaign for the general election. John Emerson asked me to be part of the general staff meetings to be sure we mobilized the gay community. Three community activists—Richard Ryan, Susan Grant, and Tony Leonhardt—also went onto the statewide staff. It was the first time in all my years of politics that we didn't have to plead for inclusion in a general presidential campaign.

By the end of the convention there weren't very many gays and lesbians we had failed to convert to Clinton, and they quickly came on board after the Republican convention in Houston in August that renominated George Bush. Pat Buchanan gave a keynote speech so charged with hate that he genuinely frightened much of the nation. Filled with sexual innuendo and the zealotry of the religious right, it proclaimed that there was "a religious war going on in this country for the soul of America." Later that week Pat Robertson of the Christian Coalition echoed Buchanan's message, charging that Clinton's agenda was out to "destroy the traditional family." Their harsh words brought the extreme right delegates to their feet in cheers, and moved every moderate who heard them closer to Clinton. Throughout that week our phones never stopped ringing with people from our community eager to work for and contribute to the

Clinton/Gore ticket. Unsolicited checks poured into the office to be forwarded as "gay and lesbian" money for the campaign. No more anonymity at last—they wanted to be identified.

And everywhere I traveled I was told, "All my life I've wanted to participate in politics and I never thought I would be allowed to because I'm gay." I talked with people in their sixties who had had to opt out, and I watched our young community members participate without that fear. I envied them their sense of autonomy. But young, old, or in-between, all had the enthusiasm of the freshly liberated.

I had two major assignments from the national campaign: to generate press that would mobilize us to turn out at the polls in November, and to travel around the country raising money for the ticket.

Historically, about 35 percent of the gay and lesbian community were Republican. That had its roots in the fact that until now neither major party had ever taken a strong stand on civil rights for homosexuals. But given the two recent conventions, we had the opportunity to deliver a sizable bloc vote to Clinton and Gore. The first job was to make sure they were registered and then to get them to the polls. San Francisco Supervisor Carol Migden would estimate that over 25 percent of the newly registered voters in California were gay and lesbian.

Our computerized donor base was invaluable in our fund-raising, and we got key individuals in different cities to spearhead the push there. We worked closely with the national campaign finance committee to add important gay and lesbian donors to the committee and on local steering committees. By late September, we had passed the three-million-dollar mark nationally and over one million in California. All this was money whose source was specifically identified as gay and lesbian. There were numerous large contributions that did not go through our operation and were counted in the overall total. By election day we had raised at least three and a half million dollars and it is likely that the actual figure was much higher. For obvious reasons, our ability to raise funds for Clinton increased our access to the campaign.

I recognized the importance of my press assignment but it was much less congenial than the fund-raising responsibilities. Even back when I had a very visible role in the Moratorium, I had never been comfortable in the role of spokesperson, probably because of a lifetime spent fearing exposure. I certainly relished media praise for my efforts—in fact, I worried when my appetite for it got too great—but I much preferred to work behind the scenes. In 1992, however, the participation of the community was a new and newsworthy element in a national election, so in each new city I found myself in interview after interview. The pattern was always the same: visits to the local gay and lesbian press, interviews with the local network news affiliates, the area papers, and radio talk shows. Talk shows were always the most unpredictable; you never knew who would call in. Sometimes they'd just scream "Fucking faggot!" into the phone and hang up. Sometimes they'd expound on my sinfulness for being gay or slam at Clinton for "pandering to the queers." No matter how skillful I got at fielding these calls, they always left me unsettled. Hate is scary. But the job had to be done; media coverage was important. And all in all, most of the attention was positive. It escalated throughout the campaign and right into inauguration week.

My high visibility had some bizarre side effects. The radical right attacked me personally and constantly. Fringe ministers called me the "Satan behind Clinton" or the "head faggot in the Clinton campaign." Leading members of the religious right talked seriously about my having used my friendship with Clinton to mobilize the gay and lesbian community to "infiltrate and take over" the Democratic Party. I could always tell when I had been attacked over the airwaves because without fail, I would start to receive death threats. They'd usually come late at night. I would pick up the phone, hear "We're going to blow your fucking brains out, faggot!" and then the sound of the receiver slamming down.

Some were more threatening than others. Once a caller said he was outside my house with a gun and described my home to me. I resisted doing anything about these calls because I felt that by acknowledging them I was giving the haters power. But Jeremy kept pressing me so I finally saw Bruce Boland, an openly gay Los Angeles County deputy sheriff, and asked his advice. He insisted that I install a new security system right away, briefed the nearest sheriff's station, and gave me direct phone numbers to call.

The day the sophisticated system was installed, I was in a foul mood. I did feel relieved at the added protection. The alarms and panic buttons meant I could do something to defend myself. On the other hand, I loathed this intrusion into my privacy. For days, I glared at the system control panel every time I passed it.

The increased press exposure also brought some very colorful characters to my door. One day the bell rang and I went downstairs to answer it. At the door was a good-looking man dressed in a conservative business suit. He was holding a neat stack of papers about a foot high.

"Yes, may I help you?" I asked.

"Are you Mr. Mixner?"

"Yes, I am. What can I do for you?"

"I have in my hands a detailed economic proposal for Mr. Clinton and I need to give it to him personally. If you read it, you will see that it is serious but I can't leave it here alone with you. I must give it to Mr. Clinton directly."

I asked whether this was his own plan or whether it came from a university or a group of economists.

"I received this plan from Mars. They sent it through my tooth and I have typed it all down."

He looked so sedate, so conventional. I kept a straight face and said, "There is no way I can arrange for you to hand this economic proposal to Clinton directly, but I will be delighted to send your proposal to the campaign staff if you'd like me to."

He turned angry at that, and I excused myself and closed the door. But throughout the rest of the campaign our office kept getting his irate calls insisting that he had orders from Mars to carry out his mission. For reasons I do not understand, the passion of politics brings a lot of unstable people out of the woodwork. They can be very frightening. They stalk highly visible leaders, send threatening letters, make menacing phone calls, and are very persistent. No one in the business takes them lightly.

The campaign also had its glamorous moments. More than in any campaign since McGovern's 1972 bid for the presidency, the Hollywood entertainment community came forward to participate in Clinton's bid. On September 16, the Hollywood Women's Political Caucus (HWPC) held a fund-raiser for the campaign at Green Acres, a magnificent Beverly Hills estate then owned by entertainment executive Ted Fields. HWPC had lined up a spectacular array of performers, including Barbra Streisand, Tammy Wynette, Dionne Warwick, Mike Nichols, and Elaine May. There were onstage appearances by Glenn Close, Warren Beatty, Geena Davis, Mary Steenburgen, Christine Lahti, Christian Slater, Dustin Hoffman, Danny DeVito, Rhea Perlman, Richard Dreyfuss, and Louis Gossett, Jr. The place was sold out, and there were as many celebrity guests in the audience to greet the candidate as there were performers.

We sold thousand-dollar tickets to the fund-raiser, Patsy flew out for the occasion, and HWPC gave us a front-row table. I wanted to visit with my old friend Shirley MacLaine, whom I had not seen in a long while. As Shirley became a very visible spokesperson for the New Age Movement, we grew further apart. I admired her search for answers, but we had less and less in common. But I was very fond of her and would always be grateful for her great generosity to me, and I wound my way through the crush to her table. Shirley gave me a wonderfully warm greeting and looked as radiant as always. Indeed, I thought that her explorations had made her happier and more at peace. But she startled me now. "It doesn't look good for him," she said.

"Do you mean Clinton and the election?"

"My people say that the atmosphere is just not right. The karma is all wrong. He isn't going to make it. I have consulted a number of people. They know what they're talking about."

Knowing that Shirley had always been more right than wrong, I suddenly found myself nervous about the election.

When Clinton arrived he walked over to our table, gave Patsy and me big hugs, and thanked us for all of our efforts. The evening ended with the gaggle of entertainers, led by Streisand, singing "God Bless America." I joined in and loved it. I realized how terrific it was to feel patriotic again. A lot of us were feeling that way.

By early October, Bush was in trouble, his polling figures bad. There is nothing unusual about a political party resorting to hard-nosed tactics in the last weeks of a tight political race, but the Republicans had a special reputation for the "big smear" in such circumstances. Everyone remembered the 1988 Willie Horton ads that had done such damage to Dukakis, no different in kind from those of the old southern racists in the 1960s. In 1992 the Bush campaign seized on the issue of Clinton's draft status during the Vietnam War and his alleged involvement in the antiwar movement, and it went to town in the final weeks.

Since the August convention, the Republicans had been attempting to paint Clinton as a militant antiwar activist who had ties to Moscow and had been a leader in the demonstrations against the Vietnam War. They distorted the facts so that it appeared he had been unpatriotic, a Communist sympathizer, and a hippie radical in the sixties. This was McCarthyism revisited, and like Joe McCarthy's charges, they hadn't the remotest basis in fact. We had been through some of this back in the primary season, but it was much more vitriolic now. Clinton never was a leader in the antiwar movement, he had visited Moscow as a tourist like many other Americans, and I knew from my own experience just how painful the struggle had been between his moral objections to the war, his deep love for his country, and his ambitions.

In a desperate attempt to keep the issue alive until the end of the campaign, the Republicans seized on Clinton's presence at our 1969 Martha's Vineyard retreat. Most of us had been in politics a long time so we weren't surprised to see a smear campaign erupt now. But to take a simple retreat that was more like *The Big Chill* than a serious political get-together and turn it into a "secret meeting to plot against the government" did startle us. It was grotesque. This was conspiracy theory run amok. But Bush's campaign fed information to sympathetic talk-show hosts, who perpetuated the "big lie" and thereby allowed Bush to distance himself from such dishonesty.

Newspapers around the country picked it up. *The New York Times* wrote in a front-page article:

> In a series of television appearances and press releases this week, Bush campaign officials have spotlighted Clinton's anti-Vietnam days, in effect broadening their earlier attack on his attempts to avoid being drafted and on his visit to Moscow while a Rhodes Scholar at Oxford. Clinton "played fast and loose with his 1969 visit to Martha's Vineyard to meet with anti-war activists," said an official Bush-Quayle campaign press release earlier this week.

The Times had called me when it was preparing its piece, and it quoted my answer to the charges in the same article:

> Said Mixner, who is now a strong Clinton backer: "He was in Washington for a few weeks in the summer of '69. . . . He was not a major or minor figure in the movement. . . . He was the conservative. In many ways, he was mistrusted by many of the organizers, because he was struggling with whether to serve in the armed forces."

In fact, most of the media did do some further probing and many placed the retreat in its proper perspective. But the genius of a smear campaign is that once the big lie is disseminated, it takes on a life of its own. It becomes almost impossible to persuade the public of the truth. The "Martha's Vineyard Conspiracy" brouhaha lasted only a week or so, but the perception of the big lie still festers.

On October 27 I went to the national Clinton campaign headquarters in Little Rock for the first time. I was excited. I thought the campaign had been brilliantly run. There had been the standard-issue problems and internal bickering common to every group enterprise, but overall it was an astonishing performance. If in the following week Clinton was elected to the presidency, as seemed likely, it would be because he had brought together an extraordinary team of individuals to assure that victory. He had overcome the kind of Gennifer Flowers incident that had destroyed Gary Hart four years earlier. He had managed to convince the public of his patriotism in the face of the Republican attempt to portray him as a radical and a subversive. All this was testimony to the competence of his staff. I had met the key players throughout the campaign but now they were all together in Little Rock, their agenda to plan for the transition following victory. Campaigns may have been old hat to me, but it was brand-new to know at first hand the president-elect and his closest advisers. I could hardly wait.

Little Rock seemed such an unlikely setting for such a historic moment. I was shocked at the small-town atmosphere of what was, after all, the capital city of Arkansas. I thought: This is what it would have been like for me if I had returned home to southern New Jersey to run for office and spent most of my life living in Trenton. At least there I would have been two hours from New York and a short ride from Philadelphia. I understood once again why gays and lesbians left their small towns to seek the anonymity and freedom of the big cities. There was no question that I could not safely walk arm in arm with my friends in downtown Little Rock. The gay bars were in a remote industrial part of the city, hidden from the public eye.

The Clinton campaign was big business for Little Rock. Walking from the Hotel Excelsior to the headquarters, I saw the streets full of stores selling Clinton-Gore souvenirs and restaurants advertising their support of the ticket. The city was making the most of its favorite son. The headquarters was in a drab, block-long building that looked like a warehouse. I walked inside and found myself in the middle of hundreds of energetic young political activists. It was like a college campus. At last the yuppies had found a political home.

The top brass of the campaign was there: George Stephanopoulos, David Wilhelm, Mickey Kantor, James Carville, Susan Thomases, Harold Ickes, Eli Segal. The only one missing some of the time I was there was Bruce Lindsey, who was traveling with Clinton. What I also found at the headquarters was a sky-high level of tension and intrigue. It wasn't because of the election, imminent though that was. It was because everyone there was already jockeying for power once the election was over. It seemed clear that Clinton was likely to win, so *real* power was now at stake—the presidency of the United States. As I walked down the corridors on the first day, I recognized all the signs of infighting: closed doors, huddled groups in the hallways, people not acknowledging each other as they passed, strained faces and whispered conversations that stopped the moment someone else came near.

The focus of a lot of the intrigue seemed to be my good friend Mickey Kantor. In early fall Clinton had asked Mickey to prepare for the transition that would be required if he won in November. Most of the staff was delighted that he would be off on the sidelines handling something that was not yet real to them—a Clinton victory. But Kantor understood that if Clinton won, his would be a position of real power. Controlling the transition process between two administrations gives the person in charge access to the president-elect and major input to all presidential appointments. He sets the tone for the incoming administration, helps the president-elect determine his immediate staff, and puts that person directly in line to become the all-powerful White House chief of staff.

Kantor had quietly been building a tightly controlled, detailed plan to insure an orderly transition. Then, as election day neared and victory seemed probable, the other key players realized that a great deal of power lay with him and they wanted their share of it. Utilizing leaks to the press, direct conversations with Clinton, appeals to Hillary, and some subtle undercutting of Kantor, many of the brass sought a place for themselves in the transition process. But first they had to free it from the tight control that Mickey had imposed, and that meant they had to diminish his power. When I arrived in Little Rock they were in the process of trying to do just that.

I am a fan of Mickey Kantor. Throughout the campaign he had consistently been open and honest with me. When I placed urgent calls about problems like the HRCF questionnaire, he always recognized the need to move fast and got them solved. Although we had minor differences, he understood the gay and lesbian community and its importance. He had always been a civil rights and civil liberties advocate in Los Angeles. He practiced his practical politics with a heart. Hardened politico though he was, he had never lost his passion to give voice to the powerless. I was delighted that he was in charge of the transition process because I knew that the community would be treated fairly and with integrity. The attempts to undermine his authority in the transition were disturbing.

I went to see Mickey. His door was always closed throughout most of my visit, entry to it guarded by a faithful staffer. He let me in. Mickey struck me as very tired, but he greeted me warmly and as a friend.

"Mickey, how about the transition? How as a community should we plan on plugging into the process?"

He laughed. "David, Clinton isn't even elected yet," he said.

"Come on, Mickey, you and I know that's likely to happen. I need direction."

He sighed. "Right now it's like a thousand bees going after one flower. Everyone smells power and I can't promise you how it's going to work after the election. But I will promise you this. I will always be available to you and I will do my best to insure that the gay community is treated fairly."

That was both welcome and unsurprising, but I needed more. "I know that and I appreciate it, but I'm very concerned. Once the election takes place, all hell will break loose and I want to be able to answer with credibility what our community should do."

"Look, David, I'll set you up with Jerry Stern. He's my top guy on transition and has pulled together lots of teams. Let's work with him to get your people on some of them now, and then stay in touch throughout the process."

That was good news. I thanked him.

"Well, get ready for a roller-coaster ride. It's going to be interesting."

In every office I went into, each person spent time speculating on the appointments and his role. When I visited Eli Segal, he asked me anxiously what I had heard from the others. Stephanopoulos was one of the very few who seemed confident of his role after election day. James Carville was continuing his "performance art," acting as if it were all beneath him while actively participating in the intrigue. Ickes was still holding his whispered conferences, and David Wilhelm gave the impression that he knew exactly how everything was going to unfold.

Given everyone's priority of post-election power, it was hard to get any one of them to focus on what they perceived as a secondary matter—the transition plans for gays and lesbians. The attitude in every top-level office was, "Don't worry, Dave, we'll take care of you." I had no idea what this meant, if anything at all. The air of self-confidence and self-congratulations made it difficult to get specifics, and so did the ongoing battle for control. It was unclear who would have the power to make decisions after the election.

I had several goals in this visit: to push for the promised AIDS speech in the last week of the campaign, to prioritize the agenda for the gay and lesbian community after the election, to make my own desires clear to the transition team, and to insure the community's full participation in the transition process.

One of the few focused people I met was Hillary Clinton's friend and staffer Susan Thomases. She worked hard to see that Clinton fulfilled his promise to give that major AIDS policy speech. We had only a few days to go, and I was convinced it wasn't going to happen. But Susan finally received a commitment from Clinton that he would give the speech in New Jersey, and she was frantically working out the logistics. If it hadn't been for her, there would have been no speech. But Clinton did give it. It contained very little that was new, but it meant a lot to us. He had now fulfilled every one of his pledges and promises to the community during the campaign.

In my meetings with Eli Segal, Mickey Kantor, and Jerry Stern, I made it clear that I would not be seeking any position in the administration. I had come to this decision after some serious reflection. First and most important, I believed that my visibility in advocating Clinton to the community required that this advocacy not be perceived as a way to personal political advantage. This election had inspired so many people in the community that I would have felt uncomfortable using their efforts for my own gain. I also knew that I would have a greater influence in pushing for appointments and setting the agenda over the next couple of months if I wasn't using up all my chits for myself. Then there was the fact that I have led an adventurous life. I am a recovering drug addict. The initial nominees from our community would have to be able to survive an in-depth FBI investigation required by the Senate for every major presidential appointment. Appointees would have to have a spotless background report. They would also have to deal with the realities of a national press that views an individual's personal life as fair game.

And finally, now that I had a chance to realize my childhood dream of perhaps working in the White House, I discovered it had lost its appeal. I am in many ways a free spirit. I could not imagine working seven days a week, eighteen hours a day, in the confinement of a small office, unable to speak out if there was serious disagreement. What had not changed in me was my passion to fight against injustice. I had to have that freedom, unhampered by loyalty to another person's agenda. It was far more important than any possible appointment.

My visits with Mickey Kantor and Jerry Stern and the temporary transition team were focused on placing key gays and lesbians on the developing task forces that were preparing for different aspects of the transition. I urged them to have a detailed plan for our issues and cautioned them on the number of enemies the community had in the political process. I found an unwillingness to focus on either the military issue or gay and lesbian civil rights legislation on these visits. Every time I tried to bring them up, I was greeted by understanding smiles and reassurances that when these issues surfaced the community would be fully consulted. Most, perhaps even all the staff, had never experienced the nastiness of an anti-gay and lesbian campaign. Although I believed it naive, the staff really did not expect a battle and at this time certainly did not want to hear about one from me. The issue of gay and lesbian rights had not hurt them in the campaign and they had seen Republican attempts to exploit it at their convention backfire. They were confident that they understood how to proceed.

Common sense told me that no more could be accomplished in Little Rock. Their minds were on their own agendas after the election. I decided to head home. My friends in the campaign urged me to stay or at least to come back for election night. There were elaborate plans for a celebration and all my old comrades from the 1960s were flying down for a reunion centered around Bill's election. But somehow, after this visit, I didn't feel that I belonged in Little Rock. I was going to spend that night with my community in Los Angeles. They would understand what election night really meant to us.

I woke up on the morning of November 3 and immediately had an anxiety attack. I had placed such great hope in the hands of one man. The voters would either accept him or reject him that day. It scared me to reflect on how much depended on the outcome. I don't believe God ever created a longer day than election day. In my youth, you literally had to wait up and hear the returns with the rest of the country. Now you received the news of the first exit polls by late morning or early afternoon in California. Of course, as soon as you got them you started dialing all your friends and your family and the major donors and sharing the good news or the bad with them. If it was a sweep, it could all be over long before the West Coast polls closed. If it was close, you'd have the network projections by nine or ten Pacific time at the latest.

Jeremy and I started receiving the first exit polls about 11 A.M. and it looked very, very good for Clinton and Gore. The second spate of polls came in around 1:30 and the trend was holding. By 3:30, just before some of the East Coast voting sites closed, I knew that we had elected Bill Clinton President of the United States. I was speechless.

Scott Hitt, Alex Koleszar, and I decided to hold an election night party at their home to raise money for the National Gay and Lesbian Victory Fund, an organization dedicated to electing openly gay and lesbian candidates to office. What better way to celebrate the election of Clinton and Gore than to contribute to building political power for the community?

People arrived early. Television sets had been set out in every room and out in the pool area. NBC's *Today Weekend Show* had sent a camera crew to follow me around on election night. The party was a must stop for local elected officials, who arrived after their obligatory election night appearance at the Biltmore Hotel in downtown Los Angeles. The house was filled with hope. We had invested our heart and soul in this election—our ticket to our freedom. At last, the long, isolated nightmare years of Reagan and Bush were over. Maybe our friends would no longer have to die from AIDS. Our lives were at stake this night. Our dreams were at stake. We deeply believed this would be a turning point in our history.

When the networks started predicting the election of the Clinton/ Gore ticket, the house exploded in celebration. I stood on the steps by the pool and faced all those who had dedicated their lives over the last year to electing this man. I thanked them. I spoke of the new world that awaited us—an administration that finally included us. I spoke about the hope that we would be able to grow old with our friends.

Then we all crowded into the living room to watch Clinton and Gore speak to the crowds in Little Rock. Diane Abbitt slid next to me. "Do you wish you were in Little Rock with them tonight?" she asked. I looked at her and said, "Nah. I'm right where I want to be—with my family."

As I drove home through the streets of West Hollywood, hundreds of gays and lesbians were dancing in the streets as if it were New Year's Eve in Times Square. I didn't know quite how I was feeling. I experienced an extraordinary sense of accomplishment but I was also exhausted and frightened. I was not sure what was ahead. I knew deep down that this election meant I would have to draw on new and uncharted territories within myself. I realized that my having played a part in this victory was creating a slippery place for my ego. I knelt down by my bed and prayed.

CHAPTER FIFTEEN

The Roar of the Crowd

I WOKE up the next morning not sure what the next step should be. Making the transition from a campaigning mode to governing was new territory for everyone. As pioneers, we in the community had to look warily over every hill. I knew that the ugly face of homophobia would surface when we attempted to make the campaign promises a reality. All my life, I had seen the hatred that arises against homosexuals whenever we become visible. This election increased our power but it did not protect us from attack. In fact, I expected the attacks to escalate as we proceeded along the road to full inclusion. The more successful we become, the more hostile a climate we will face. Eventually, if we do not bend in our pursuit, the hostility will change to uneasy acceptance. Only then will we have the luxury of contributing our talents to this nation unhindered.

In the climate of celebration that followed the election, it was hard to keep focused on realities like these. In Little Rock, my impressions of the young president-elect's staff was that they too had been struggling to shift from a campaign mode to organizing a government. But they didn't recognize they were struggling. They seemed confident to a fault. They believed that there was nothing they couldn't handle. They had made it clear they didn't feel the need to seek out advice from anyone.

Immediately after the election Clinton himself focused on the transition. He broadened Mickey Kantor's plan dramatically, and asked former National Urban League President Vernon Jordan and former South Carolina Governor Richard Riley to head his transition team. The two of them established task forces for each cabinet department, the major agencies, and issues of significant concern to the administration. If these task forces fulfilled their mandate, by inauguration day the new administration would be ready to take over the government from twelve years of Republican rule.

The real power in setting the tone of the new administration and overseeing the transition still lay in the hands of the top campaign brass. It was quickly clear that George Stephanopoulos would be a key adviser to the President and that David Wilhelm would head the Democratic National Committee. Ickes and Thomases had direct access to the president-elect and Hillary Clinton but were not seeking positions. They, along with Carville, seemed to be content to be major behind-the-scenes players. Mickey Kantor, who had now been shunted aside in the transition, was soon to become the American Trade Ambassador. It had been so long since the Democrats had held power that it was a whole new world, not only to the Clinton team but to Democrats all over the country—and to constituencies like ours. The baby boom generation was jubilant at finally having elected one of our own, but no one quite knew how to proceed.

Many of the people we had worked side by side with on the campaign were now busy positioning themselves in the new administration. California campaign manager John Emerson found himself assisting Riley and Jordan. Clinton friend and adviser Cindy Liebo was creating a new team for the Justice Department. Issues adviser Sandy Berger was thrust into the foreign policy transition efforts. New York organizer Kevin Thurm started working on the Department of Health and Human Services.

Others who had been key campaign workers discovered they were out in the cold. Positions of responsibility went not to them but to more prominent Democrats, such as former San Antonio Mayor Henry Cisneros, former Democratic National Committee chair Ron Brown, and Texas Senator Lloyd Bentsen. They found themselves working on the plans for the inauguration. Meanwhile they circulated their résumés, hoping that someone they knew from the campaign would be given a major appointment that might lead to a job for them.

One thing was obvious. The name of the game was appointments. It soon became clear that the best way to discover what was really going on was to assist someone in obtaining an appointment. If the effort worked, the appreciative appointee might provide access and information. But keeping track was no easy thing. The centers of power kept changing with each new appointment. You could have authority one day and the next day find yourself superseded by a new face. Navigating in this whirlwind was often bewildering.

This transition was a first-time experience for those in the community because both parties had thought us a political liability up to now and systematically excluded us from the process. Thanks to the president-elect's campaign promises, however, our expectations were very high. We had been a valuable ally in the election. We knew that our contribution to his victory was a critical one. Exit polls by CNN and others indicated that we delivered a significant percentage of the vote to him. We had earned our way to the table and deserved to be treated as full partners. However, I don't think that is how the new staff of the president-elect viewed us.

Right after the election, all the major gay and lesbian organizations held meetings to plan our involvement in the new administration. That first weekend I went to several such sessions in Washington focused around the issues of appointments, legislation, AIDS, and the military. Most of the participants were new to this process but we were learning quickly and responding professionally. The community was willing to be a team player with the president-elect's transition team, but we wanted to be sure its members had the information they needed to make appropriate decisions. Since we had had no input from the White House transition team, we started preparing for the change of government on our own.

In one of the meetings I went to there were more than seventy participants, representing a diverse spectrum of AIDS groups, who had come together in Alexandria, Virginia, to outline an attack on AIDS for the administration, beginning with a plan of action for the first hundred days. They asked me for my assessment of the political realities of the transition. All I could offer were reassurances that this was a priority for Clinton. I promised I would do everything possible to see that their recommendations got to the right decision-makers in the administration.

Within three weeks the group had put together a detailed planning document for those hundred days. Several of us worked hard to place the document before the key players in the transition, but these were constantly changing. I took the plan, plus reminders of the campaign promises, to the health care transition task force, the emerging soon-to-be White House staff, and other leaders in the transition. I also sent a copy to the president-elect, asking him to please review it.

There were so many task forces that as I entered and left each office, I had a sinking feeling that the report was viewed as yet one more proposal dumped on the huge stack already there. Initially there didn't seem to be any procedure to separate out the important ones or see that they received serious attention. You found yourself educating the new members of the changing task forces on work that others had already completed. We were fortunate to have Tim Westmoreland appointed to the health care task force. He had worked for years for Congressperson Henry Waxman on the House Health Care Subcommittee, and he was one of the most knowledgeable people in the country on AIDS issues. His presence on the task force made it more likely that there would be quick and decisive action on AIDS.

That same weekend that the AIDS group was meeting in Virginia, the Human Rights Campaign Fund called a meeting in Washington of its board members and key supporters. HRCF handles a great share of the community's advocacy work on Capitol Hill and was gearing up for a new legislative agenda. Its major donors had raised significant funds for Clinton.

Roberta Achtenberg and I outlined the political realities of a transition for them. Senator Kennedy's staff member and AIDS expert, Michael Iskowitz, mapped out an advocacy plan for legislative action on AIDS. Then the meeting touched on the military issue. Based on Clinton's promises in the campaign, the staff had indicated that they were planning to proceed with an executive order. We were waiting to hear from the transition effort to begin our planning for this. Although a few of those present indicated some worry about congressional opposition, there was overwhelming agreement that we had ample time to plot strategy with the new administration. After all, the assurances could not have been more explicit.

The real discussion in the meeting centered around the gay and lesbian civil rights legislation and appointments. We knew that there was hesitancy among some of the Clinton staff around this. We remembered the campaign foul-up with the HRCF questionnaire. On election day Colorado had passed an anti-homosexual amendment modifying its civil rights law. This certainly highlighted the need for national legislation, but it was also going to make elected officials more nervous about supporting it. This clearly had to be a high priority, and HRCF started laying the groundwork for moving on it.

When I spoke to the group, I urged people to think long and hard before applying for appointments with this new administration. I was clear about my own public decision not to seek an appointment, which made it easier for me to speak frankly. We had to put not only our best and brightest before the administration and Congress, but our "cleanest." Anyone in the room who had anything in his or her background—such as drugs, sex, and rock and roll—that might cause problems in confirmation should not seek a job. I spelled out the rough sledding that every one of our appointees would have in the Congress, from Senator Helms to the press. The scrutiny would be unremitting. We owed it to our community to be honest with ourselves before we acted. Most potential nominees understood the message and many quietly withdrew themselves from consideration. A few blindly insisted on pursuing their dreams of an appointment despite obvious problems with drug use, financial concerns, or public misconduct. We had too much at stake to let them proceed, and we quietly alerted the various transition task forces of the potential problems.

I found the entire appointment process a nightmare. Overnight my small office was swamped with résumés, faxes, and phone calls. There were times in the months following the election when no one could get through because the lines were filled with job seekers. The requests weren't confined to gays and lesbians; dozens of prominent straight people, old friends, and acquaintances called to ask for my help in their efforts. Several times I was asleep in my Washington hotel room when the phone rang to tell me a governor or former senator was in the lobby wanting to talk about his eagerness to be part of the new administration. Because of my visibility in raising funds in the campaign, former members of Congress, governors, and mayors sought my help with their electoral hopes. I recognized this as further signs of how this election had made the community a player. I made calls and wrote letters for those who had been long-time friends of the community or whose appointment would open up access for it to the new centers of power. The transition team had a special code to identify key supporters of the President and guarantee that our recommendations received attention.

William Waybourn, the talented organizer and executive director of the National Gay and Lesbian Victory Fund, had had the foresight to organize a coalition of all the major national community groups, and

"Coalition '93" became the vehicle that professionally screened gay and lesbian applicants, trained them in applying, and helped them with access to the various teams. This effort had the additional benefit of introducing large numbers of community leaders to members of the new administration. Before applicants' names were submitted to the administration's transition team, five working groups within the coalition screened them thoroughly and then sent them to the coalition's oversight body. The very thorough procedure meant that only highly qualified applicants actually competed for appointments. We were not going to let slipshod vetting waste our new opportunities. Only after the recommendations were finalized did Bob Hattoy, Roberta Achtenberg, and I lobby for them with our friends in the new administration, such as Emerson, Ickes, Segal, and Wilhelm.

Riley's and Jordan's offices received more than one hundred thousand résumés for the four thousand jobs available and the competition was fierce. There was dissension within the transition team as to whether gays and lesbians should be considered part of the "diversity plan," a plan created to ensure that all elements of American society had the opportunity to participate in the new administration. Clinton was very concerned that his new team reflect the presence of the African-Americans, Hispanics, and women who had been crucial to his victory. In general, other minorities had no problem with our being included in the plan; ironically, it was white straight males within the team, who were themselves seeking jobs, who objected to any further inclusions.

Because of her wide experience, early support of Clinton, and hard work in the campaign, Roberta Achtenberg was both the best shot and the leading choice of our community for a major and visible position within the administration. She had taken full advantage of her position in the California campaign and established direct ties to the Clintons. She did not trade on that, however, and wisely chose to use the new community task force to apply pressure to the transition team for the most prestigious appointment possible. Roberta was very single-minded about it. She worked hard to mobilize people on her behalf. She was on me two or three times a week urging me to make more calls and to contact Clinton directly on her behalf.

One morning in early December I met with her for breakfast. She was feeling conflicted. Friends were besieging her for help with their own job prospects, and she was wondering whether it was appropriate to push for others while her appointment was very much undecided.

"All this emphasis on my appointment is making me feel so damn guilty," she said.

"Look, Roberta," I told her, "the political reality of this moment is that we will not get hundreds of appointments—more like several dozen. We don't have many of our own ready to ascend to the level that you are seeking. We can't afford to miss this opportunity. As hard as it is, you have to keep pushing for yourself."

"I know that but the others don't understand, and they make me feel like a greedy power grabber."

"A transition is new to most of these people. They have no realistic idea of what can and can't be done. You know what you have to do. It may not be comfortable, but it's the price of leadership."

She wondered whether it was all worth it.

"Damn right it is. We've been excluded since George Washington. We have to start building power and now is our chance."

We walked over to the transition offices to meet with Bob Hattoy, who was working on the environmental task force and seeking a position within the White House. The three of us found an empty office with a desk and a few chairs. It was so bleak that no one on the transition team had claimed it. We closed the door. There had been some tension between Bob and me for some reason and we worked hard to clear it up. We talked about how we ought to proceed and the kinds of problems each of us was encountering. Bob broke us up when someone stuck his head into the office and asked who we were. "Just the three Clinton queers meeting to overthrow the government," he announced. The head vanished in a hurry.

We were concerned about two major issues. There was a visible lack of appointments of open gays and lesbians to the transition team. Out of several hundred who had been appointed to the task forces for various agencies and cabinet-level departments thus far, only three or four were from our community. We had to make a concerted effort to change that.

We were also very worried about the possible appointment of Georgia Senator Sam Nunn to the administration as Secretary of Defense. The press was full of reports he was interested in the job and that the president-elect was giving it serious consideration. As far as we were concerned, Nunn was the George Wallace of our civil rights movement. He had historically been anti-gay and lesbian. He had come out against homosexuals as schoolteachers and in 1988 had announced his support for Senator John Glenn of Ohio for president, citing Glenn's reluctance to support our rights. A staff member had accused Nunn of firing him because of his sexual orientation. Nunn was bad news.

There wasn't much we could do about the Nunn problem for the moment other than worry about it, but because the community had created an united front with the formation of Coalition '93 under the leadership of Andrew Barrer, we were able to deal effectively with the appointments issue. With a series of high-level calls we increased the number of lesbians and gays on the transition task forces to more than a dozen. That was a first for the community, and the source of a lot of pride.

But there was still nothing for Roberta. By the beginning of January she was beside herself. There had been several false rumors about a pending announcement, and I finally called Clinton himself. He assured me that a major position was coming up for her. "I hold her in high regard," he told me, "and I will not forget her loyalty. Don't worry."

At last she was offered the appointment of Assistant Secretary for Fair Housing in the Department of Housing and Urban Development. This was indeed an important position; among its responsibilities was preventing discrimination in any federal housing. But Roberta was very upset. She didn't think it would be perceived as substantial enough and was thinking of turning it down.

"Listen," I told her, "this is a major appointment. The highest ever offered to a gay or lesbian in the history of the United States. We have to start somewhere."

"I know, David, but is it the right one? Am I accepting something too soon?"

"Roberta, I believe that if you turn this one down you won't be offered another one. This is it. This is the time for you to decide if you want to do this."

The pressures of the last weeks clearly had taken a toll. I put my arm around her. "I know it's a bitch," I said. "Public life is a bitch. Take this position and get yourself some rest. Your confirmation hearings are going to make this process look like a picnic. We need you, Roberta. Take care of yourself. You're a pioneer, and that means you will be fighting some tough battles for us."

She knew that. She knew the radical right would be going after her. I agreed. "There is not one single aspect of your life they won't touch. They will attempt to destroy you. But remember," I added, "there are millions of us standing behind you."

I saw her change before my eyes. She stood up, extended her hand, pulled me out of my chair, and said, "I'm ready. Let's go make history."

Roberta's Senate confirmation hearings were even more nightmarish than we anticipated. Notorious homophobe Jesse Helms of North Carolina led the bitter, nasty fight against her. He focused almost entirely on her sexual orientation. He found not a hint of misconduct in any of her professional or business affairs. He not only attacked her for being a "radical, militant lesbian" but launched a campaign against her longtime lover, Judge Mary Morgan of San Francisco, and their child. It was a disgrace to call them a family, he charged. He was on a mission. If he succeeded in stopping Roberta, the administration would be hesitant to send further homosexual appointments up to the Hill.

As Senator Kennedy said to me in a phone call, "I don't ever remember such a vigorous personal attack on the Senate floor. It is ugly." But Roberta conducted herself with dignity and refused to bend under the onslaught. Her testimony to the Senate committee was powerful and articulate, her grasp of housing issues impressive. She won confirmation despite the virulence of her opponents.

Her victory helped our other appointees. Their hearings went far more easily. More than forty received key positions throughout the new administration, spread through almost every department and agency that historically had been closed to us and in the White House itself. Every single one of them could have been introduced by the sentence: "For the first time in history, the administration appointed . . ."

So yes, there were victories. But when it came to issues of policy, such as our civil rights and our right to serve in the military, the story was otherwise. The newly elected administration made no attempt to convene a meeting of people who had worked on these issues all their lives. They didn't think it important to bring that experience into the deliberations the inner circles were holding about these rights. We would hear reports that they recognized they had to meet their obligations to the community, but no one ever briefed us on these reports or provided details on their meetings. Whatever we heard was secondhand, filtering through the political grapevine, and we spent a great deal of time tracking down rumors.

It was the first time, though not the last, that I saw the "plantation mentality" of some of the new staff. We didn't need to be in on what was being discussed. We were supposed to be grateful to them for whatever we were given—which was, after all, more than we'd ever had before. They knew what was best for us. We ought to wait quietly while they determined how fast we should be given our rights. It was obvious that they didn't want to be publicly perceived as beholden to us as a constituency.

For the first time, I found myself angry. Exactly who *were* these people who were excluding us from deciding our own future? It was hard to get a handle on this opposition, because each time we were passed the name of someone said to be urging caution, the person would always vehemently deny it and point the finger at someone else. No one had the courage to confront me directly with his reservations. Evasion and patronizing were the name of the game.

I kept hoping that sheer persistence would open the door to us because I knew we had a lot to offer. We understood the political dynamics of the issues. There were certainly some on the staff who recognized this but they were often too busy with their own agendas. I used them to gather information and to keep track of who was advocating what within the administration. Time, however, wasn't on my side.

With one simple press conference held on November 16, during the second week after the election, the issue of gays in the military took on a life of its own. A Navy ensign named Keith Meinhold had told his superior officers he was gay, and was faced with dismissal because of it. He decided to fight the ousting, and in a recent decision the Ninth Circuit Court of Appeals had declared the dismissal unconstitutional. The case had drawn wide publicity, and at the president-elect's very first news conference, a reporter asked him whether he still intended to issue an executive order allowing homosexuals to serve openly in the armed forces. Clinton, aware that there really hadn't been any political backlash in the campaign when he advocated lifting the ban, promptly answered that he did.

My guess is that he had had no briefing on this issue. Certainly no one consulted community leaders about its complexities or the timing. We knew firsthand the volatility of Americans' feelings about homosexuality. We certainly knew this was not a subject to be debated without serious planning and a careful strategy worked out beforehand.

The young Clinton staff, who clearly had almost no experience in handling this issue, was not prepared for the firestorm of opposition that hit right after the press conference. It had not only not briefed the president-elect or called on us, no one in the transition had thought to brief the Joint Chiefs of Staff. Unforewarned and unhampered, they felt free to oppose the Clinton statement with vigor. They did. They lobbied to undercut his commitment. Sam Nunn led the charge in Congress. The newly elected White House was unprepared to fight.

As soon as I heard Clinton's pronouncement, I called his adviser, George Stephanopoulos. He was very relaxed about the whole thing. He urged the community to stay calm, to keep a low profile, and to trust them to manage the matter. "We don't want the community in the forefront of this issue," he warned me. "It will make our ability to handle it more difficult. We're on top of it, but we need you to give us some room to maneuver." Then he asked me to write a memo outlining my thoughts on how to proceed.

I found his reaction frustrating and upsetting. He didn't seem to have the first notion of the anti-gay chords this was likely to tap, much less how to deal with them, and the staff was certainly rebuffing our expertise. Nevertheless, it was only two weeks into the transition and I didn't want to be viewed as politically difficult or on an ego trip so soon into the process. It seemed important to be seen as a team player. I was nervous and unhappy but I decided to heed his request. George had always been honest with me and I trusted his instincts. Within a week I faxed him a memo.

I have a call in to Congressman Frank. I am reassuring all the key people in the community and asking them to hold tight. *Remember, this order is supposed to ban discrimination anywhere in federal employment and with federal contractors.* Here, as you requested, are some of my thoughts:

—Lower the debate, if possible. I think that once we start announcing other major actions and appointments that the coverage and the debate will hopefully not be as newsworthy.

—Be sure if you meet with opponents of the executive order to meet with some leadership from the other side. My preference is not to meet with either side. If a meeting was held with the "pro" side, I would suggest meeting with honored, decorated service people who are gay and lesbian and had to leave the military (e.g. Tracy Thorne, Joseph Steffan, Margarethe Cammermeyer).

—Please keep in mind that the March on Washington for Civil Rights for Gays and Lesbians is going to be on April 25, 1993. At this time it is going to be [a march] on Congress for [passage of] a Civil Rights Bill and we want to be sure that the executive order is not caught in this event. . . .

—The order should be signed ASAP. The longer this issue festers the harder it will be to hold the "center" on both sides. We will start losing people to the fringe. The moment it is signed it will start becoming yesterday's news and we can get on with the business of governing.

—Remember that President-Elect Clinton is Commander in Chief and that we cannot leave the image that military leaders can badger the President-Elect into abandoning his positions because of their threats to resign. A tough line by the President-Elect now will show strong leadership and demonstrate his decisiveness and courage on an important issue.

—We should be spinning that these arguments are not new and that they are strikingly similar to the ones used to oppose Truman's 1948 Executive Order.

—We should be sure not to lose control of the issues: Gays already serve in the military by the thousands and this order allows them to serve their nation with dignity and pride. One shouldn't have to lie and live in fear in order to serve one's country. . . .

Clinton's timing was obviously unfortunate, but now that he had announced his intention of signing an executive order, we couldn't put the issue back into the closet. It was a reality, so we had to deal with it quickly. The longer the debate, the more time our opponents would have to organize. I was hoping that they would use as a role model President Truman's courageous executive order in 1948 that integrated the armed forces.

I never received a response to the memo. Every time I inquired, I was told politely, "Don't worry" and "Please keep everyone calm." Community leaders kept being told everything was "on track." No one in the inner circle wanted to be stuck with "the gay issue" so soon into the transition, so no one developed an early or a coherent strategy. It was as if they hoped the whole thing would go away. As a result, opponents of lifting the ban not only had a field day in the press, they determined the tone of the debate.

By early December radio talk-show hosts had grabbed on to the issue with a vengeance and had become a forum for bigots to vent their hate. The extreme right had mobilized its forces to hammer at Congress, and the Christian Coalition hammered their Bibles as they preached their hate. The opposition was unrelenting and it swelled throughout the month. Nothing we could do, no strategy we proposed, got us anywhere. No one wanted to listen.

Unfortunately, by this time the highly regarded head of the Joint Chiefs of Staff, Colin Powell, had added his prestigious voice to the opposition. It became hard to paint our opponents as bigots when so distinguished an African-American as General Powell gave their viewpoints credibility. Allied with Senator Sam Nunn, the pair became a formidable force. (The irony of Powell's stand, given what Truman's executive order had opened up for him, was not lost on me. He insisted that this was a different situation, but when I compared the statements of the segregationists who opposed Truman in 1948 and those of Nunn opposing us in 1992, they were shockingly similar.)

Even more surprising to me was Clinton's failure to assume the leadership role of commander in chief and make it clear to General Powell that he expected his orders and policies not only to be followed but to be implemented with enthusiasm.

Any hopes that the national gay and lesbian leadership had of shifting the debate were doomed from the start. We were faced with powerful opponents and a virtual vacuum of leadership on our side. For better or worse, Clinton's first battle was going to be on the issue of homosexuals in the military.

Inauguration time was coming. Washington was buried in preparations. The reviewing stands were going up, the platforms for the swearing-in. The vendors were out with their flags and buttons and souvenirs. The Republicans were on their way out after twelve long years, and the Democrats were planning a gigantic party.

In early December I sent Jeremy Bernard to Washington to work full-time with the finance and VIP committees of the Presidential Inauguration Committee. He worked with Democratic fund-raiser Bob Farmer raising money for the inauguration, and he handled our VIPs. As usual, it took no time for Jeremy to have everyone on the committees liking him, which meant we could count on our major donors being able to buy good tickets for all the events.

On my visit to Little Rock the last week of the campaign, I had been informed that Rahm Emanuel would be in charge of the inauguration. I made my one and only request for an appointment for myself, and asked Rahm if I could be one of the few honorary co-chairs of the Inauguration Committee. I thought this very important. It wasn't a matter of vanity. It would be a message not only to all of us but to the rest of the world about our presence in the new administration. I never got an answer to the request.

I also pushed for the participation of the Gay and Lesbian Bands of America, the Lesbian and Gay Choruses, and the AIDS Quilt in the events of inaugural week. There was the usual resistance; when I visited the Inaugural Committee headquarters, I'd find myself shunted from the finance office to the events office to the parade office to the special interests office without getting any answers. I didn't enjoy it, to put it mildly, but I was still hopeful of prevailing. Eventually, the bands were asked to play on a street next to the parade route and the Quilt was in the parade itself.

In early November William Waybourn of the National Gay and Lesbian Victory Fund asked whether they could hold a "small reception" in my honor during inauguration week to raise funds for the organization. "Small" was reassuring, although the idea of being "honored" made me rather uncomfortable, so I said yes. Then what I'd assumed would be a private gathering for a hundred people or so in somebody's home quickly turned into a great big occasion, to be held in the International Ballroom of the Hilton Hotel, with guest performances, speeches, and hundreds of guests.

Because this was to be the first time in history that gays and lesbians were to be so visible in an inauguration, the press seized on all the events the community was planning as fresh copy. Given the friendship between the president-elect and me and my visible role in the campaign, there was a lot of speculation about whether he would attend the Hilton party. Everyone assumed he would have to acknowledge our community's role sometime during the week, and the Victory Fund evening seemed the likeliest place. I heard from a number of mutual friends as he traveled around the country that he said he was excited to be coming. "You bet," he told Tom Henderson in Texas. "I wouldn't miss it. It's going to be quite an event."

But we never officially heard from him one way or the other. I have to say that got me angry. I saw it as a lack of courtesy and thoughtfulness. We had been friends for a very long time, and I was proud of the extensive work I had done on his behalf. Part of it was certainly my bruised ego. This was to be a moment of triumph and his ignoring it made me feel as if he were diminishing my contribution. Besides, I didn't think I really deserved the tribute and the slight played right into those feelings. Swinging back and forth between ego, modesty, and self-doubt, I ended up trying my best to block the whole thing out.

Inauguration week arrived and we all flew to Washington. There was a great shortage of rooms and I shared my suite at the Four Seasons with five friends. The city was swept up in euphoria, anticipating all the festivities—the fireworks, the receptions, the concerts, the balls, the parade, and the swearing-in ceremony itself. My days were packed with family and friends, with interviews, with events. But none of this was enough to distract me from the military issue. My deepest hope was that after the swearing-in ceremonies, the President would enter the Capitol and as his first act in his new role sign a number of executive orders, including the one allowing gays and lesbians to openly serve their country. This had some historical precedent; earlier presidents had dealt quickly with controversial issues in their first days of office. My hope was also based on my strong political instinct that this would be the safest and best time to do it. I felt that by timing it thus and including it with other orders, such as one overturning the ban on fetal tissue research, the events of the inauguration would overshadow its impact in the next day's press.

Openly gay Massachusetts Congressperson Gerry Studds and I talked to officials of the incoming administration about this. Studds had taken it on as a personal crusade. He hated the idea that he could serve his country in Congress while others like him were being denied the right to serve their country in its military. He had started to insert himself into the process in late December when he realized that no one was exerting any leadership on the issue, but neither of us got any indication of what was or wasn't being planned. Then came Tuesday evening, the night of what was now called "Salute to David Mixner." Patsy and I were in my hotel room at the Four Seasons and she was helping me tie my black tie—after several fumbling tries I realized I was too nervous to do it myself—and keep me calm. Jeremy came in from the other room and said Gerry Studds was on the line. Patsy sat on one bed and I sat on the other. I lifted the phone.

"You getting ready for your big night, David?"

"Gerry, I'm scared to death. You're used to this. I'm not."

He laughed. "You never get used to it. I have good news and bad news. Which do you want first?"

"I always want the bad news first."

"I just talked to the White House. The President is not going to sign the executive order in the next couple of days."

The knots in my stomach grew tighter. "Jesus, Gerry, you better have good news now."

"Don't worry. It's all taken care of—I have their word. All parties— the Congress, the military, and the President—have reached agreement. There will be a six-month study which will be used as a cooling-off period. At the end of the six months the President has promised that he will sign the order."

I was still uneasy. "Gerry, are you convinced that he will do it in six months?"

"Yeah, David, I am. In fact, if you want, why don't you announce it tonight at your event?"

"You *are* sure?"

"I'm sure. See you tonight. You deserve this evening."

I hung up the phone and turned to Patsy. "I think we just had a big victory," I told her, repeated Gerry's conversation, and called in my friends from the other room. The phone rang again and this time it was George Stephanopoulos. Even more enthusiastically than Studds, George repeated what Gerry had told me. "The President needs this six-month period of reflection," he said. "He needs it to bring everyone aboard to make this work."

"George, is he going to sign it after six months?"

"There is no way that this six-month period should be viewed as a lessening of the president-elect's commitment. David, he is going to sign that executive order. This I promise you. We need your support for the President's strategy. Do we have it?"

I had to make a quick decision and hoped I was making the right one. Under my breath, I said a quick prayer: "Please God, guide me," and then I said to George, "You have my full support. I trust your word. I will support his strategy and defend it."

I hung up the phone. Patsy gave me a big hug and said, "You're doing the right thing, honey."

I hoped so. It may have been wishful thinking but I wanted to believe them. After all, I had received assurances that the President of the United States would keep his word to us. I had received a firm commitment as to when the order would be signed. I also felt good about working as a team player with the President, giving him the room he needed to position himself to end all those years of fear. I started getting ready to be honored.

I walked into the ballroom and saw a great stage with the seal of the President of the United States behind it, and above it Clinton's quote: "I have a vision and you are part of it." I was taken backstage to wait for my speech. I looked out from behind the curtain at the room filled with nearly two thousand people and I could see my history in it. There were friends and family, political allies, and lesbians and gays from all over the country. Mickey Kantor came backstage and gave me a hug, and we looked at each other with tears streaming down our faces. This week was the culmination of a very long journey for both of us.

Patsy and Melvin and their families kept me company backstage. Jeremy kept me sane. Scott Hitt and Lynn Greer worked with William Waybourn to keep the program moving. Art Arellanas, who had produced the whole effort, had his stage manager ready to move each of us on and off as quickly as possible. I thought I was going to be sick.

Peter Yarrow, my old friend from antiwar days, and his partner Mary Travers kicked off the evening with a moving rendition of "Don't Ever

Take Away My Freedom." Waiting backstage I heard two thousand voices singing those words and I almost lost it. Throughout the evening there were video tributes from friends over three decades of organizing. Rhythm and blues singer Patti Austin sang a passionate song about AIDS. Then, in a remarkably powerful speech, our long-time champion, Senator Ted Kennedy, reminded us all of our struggle:

> And I am honored to join in this tribute to a person who did so much to bring us to this moment. David Mixner has won a high place in the annals of a movement to free a whole segment of our people from oppression. He has touched history, and in the process contributed to changing the lives of millions.
>
> In a large part, because of him, we are about to inaugurate a president committed to justice for gay and lesbian Americans. David Mixner helped teach his friends Bill and Hillary Clinton about that cause. He helped mobilize his community so that, last fall, one in every seven votes cast for Bill Clinton—more than the margin of victory—was cast by a gay or lesbian voter. . . .
>
> As a community, gay men and lesbians have been pilgrims on freedom's road. You have stood together—with your talent, your voices, and your strength. With courage, you confronted a terrible epidemic and you warned us about it. At the threshold of liberty came tragedy. But you would not be deterred by a new fear and intolerance. You have gone forward. The irresistible force of your faith has met a seemingly immovable object and the immovable object has moved. . . .
>
> That has been David Mixner's journey—from civil rights, to the antiwar movement, to the liberation of his own community. Tomorrow marks a great victory for him, for all of us . . . because at last, these mighty walls of oppression and resistance are finally coming down.

The ballroom roared in approval. Kennedy promised to be the principal co-sponsor of the gay and lesbian civil rights legislation. Once again, he proved himself to be an unshakable ally.

Scott Hitt and Lynn Greer introduced a video clip in which I talked about AIDS and Peter Scott. As I watched Peter on the clip I could barely control my emotions. We all began to weep. Then the clip ended and the stage manager took me by the arm and said, "It's your turn!"

I found myself on stage facing all those beaming faces, all those dear and loyal friends. I had no idea of what I was going to say. I began to speak:

No one person brought us here. No one organization made this happen. It was all of us as a family—as a tribe of people united by the determination that no more should die and that we have a right to be free. . . .

Bill Clinton had a vision and we are part of it. But we too have a vision. We too are dreaming again. . . .

We have a vision that we can go into our place of employment with our significant other and introduce them as the man or woman that we love.

We have a vision that we will be able to stand up in our classrooms and say that "I am gay and proud."

We have a vision that people can serve their country openly and with honor.

We have a vision that our gay and lesbian youth will no longer kill themselves but will look up and know that they too can be a congressperson, a senator, and, yes, even the President of the United States.

But all of these visions come down to just one vision. No matter what our differences, no matter what our color, no matter what our religion—we are united as gays and lesbians, proud and strong, and we will never, ever be turned around!

With that, I very proudly introduced Patsy and Michael and Julia (Elizabeth was home ill), Melvin and Donna and Brad and Monique. They came up onstage and the crowd cheered them. Too many in that room had faced the wrath of their families when they had told them they were gay or lesbian. To see my family on the stage and supporting me moved many to tears. I felt very blessed.

Democratic National Chairman David Wilhelm came onstage to express his support and to end the program. It had been a glorious evening and a deeply moving one. Still, I was glad that it was over. I was eager for inauguration day.

The sun was shining the next morning and I knew that in every way January 20 was going to be a beautiful day. My long-time friend, Bill Clinton, was going to take the oath of office as President of the United States. We had seats close up, right in front of the Capitol, and as I waited for the ceremonies to begin, I remembered when I was fourteen and watched on television at my Grandma Mixner's house John Kennedy standing in the very same place and summoning us to service. Maya Angelou read her powerful poem and we got chills when she included us in it. Then Bill Clinton, with Hillary holding the Bible, took the oath of office. As he finished, we could not stop cheering—cheering for his victory, cheering in hope, and cheering for ourselves.

We walked down to the bleachers across from the White House for the inaugural parade and found that our seats were directly across the street from the new President. As he entered the pavilion that had been erected to review the parade, he saw me in the stands, pointed, and waved a greeting. I felt proud. When the AIDS Quilt appeared before him, my friends and I stood and held each other tightly. All of us thought of our friends who had died. Somehow Clinton's viewing the Quilt on this ceremonial day gave their deaths a new dignity.

That night as I was putting on my tuxedo to attend the National Ball, I came face-to-face with reality—gay reality. The reality of being gay in a straight world. In so many ways, large and small, this impinges on our lives all the time. I suppose that in the eye of eternity, being able to dance with one's date, or not being able to, is hardly a world-shaking dilemma. But dancing is a joyful thing to do. I love to dance. For weeks I had been debating with myself whether I should dance with my date at the ball. My date for the week was a handsome, personable man named David Davis, who had jet-black hair and vivid eyes. I was very proud to have him with me. If I were going to the California Ball at the Kennedy Center, where most of my friends had been invited, there would have been no problem. The progressive Californians were quite used to same-sex dancing and there would be a large number of lesbian and gay couples there. But I had been invited to the National Ball, in an elegant Washington building. This ball was going to be full of major donors, cabinet appointees, and establishment figures from around the country. There would be very few of our people there, and those who were going had decided not to dance together until later that night, when they moved on to the HRCF Inauguration Ball. I knew many or most of the guests at the National Ball would never have seen same-sex couples dancing. I was not anxious to create a stir or end up in some sensationalized story in the next day's news coverage.

As I wrestled with this question I had grown increasingly angry— angry at myself for all the back-and-forth and angry at my own fear. Angry that on one of the most memorable evenings of my life, once again I had to deal with my homosexuality. I had always dreamed of one day dancing with another man at an event like this. Now it was here, and a source of turmoil, not delight. I was afraid that two males dancing cheek to cheek at an inaugural ball would turn into great copy for the newspapers—that an act so simple would be sensationalized and exploited. All those years of a self-hatred I thought I was done with came writhing to the surface and I had to confront it. David was patient and wonderful about the whole thing. He said simply, "Whatever you want to do that night, I will be there for you."

We went off to the ball in a limousine with Tony Leonhardt and Craig Dougherty. In the majestic setting I felt festive. I looked at the women in their elegant gowns and the men tailored in black and white and I decided to dance. When I told this to some of my straight friends there, they urged me not to. It would draw attention away from the occasion we were celebrating and create an uproar. Even a few of my gay and lesbian friends begged us not to dance. Finally, I couldn't stand it any longer. I turned to David and said, "Let's get this over with." He smiled back, said, "I'm willing," and told our friends gleefully, "I am going to dance at a presidential inaugural ball!" I saw the panic in their eyes and several of them headed for the other side of the room. There was no way they were going to be associated with this daring.

David and I glided to the floor and started dancing. We could feel each other's fear and sense the stares. A little space cleared around us, a distance established, and I felt very vulnerable. Then a much older couple danced near us and smiled. "We always like to dance next to the best dancers," they said. I loved them for it and suddenly felt free and alive. Later that night, we went on to the HRCF ball in the packed National Press Club ballroom, where couples were celebrating in hope and joy. We danced into the early morning without fear of judgment. I felt safe among my own.

As I lay in bed at last, I wondered what the next years would be like. There was no way I could visualize what lay ahead. I made a commitment to myself not to become a prisoner of the power and glory of the White House and to serve my community. We had done our celebrating. The hard work lay ahead.

PART THREE

Let Freedom Ring

"The ceremony of innocence is drowned."
—*William Butler Yeats*
"The Second Coming"

CHAPTER SIXTEEN

Betrayals

THE relationship between the lesbian and gay community and the Clinton administration changed dramatically once the President took the oath of office. Although those of us who were behind the scenes during the transition on a daily basis had grown increasingly concerned, the vast majority of the community was pleased and excited at the prospects ahead. It wasn't until after the inauguration that the concern started to seep into the community at large. The Clinton team's need for our money and our votes had kept in line those within the campaign who were less than sympathetic to our cause. After they took our money and our votes and secured their jobs within the administration, the hostile staff members decided the time had come to put us in our proper place.

The administration was divided within itself about us. Some staff members knew of our struggle for freedom and of our battle against AIDS, and viewed us as a serious civil rights movement. They were seasoned veterans of politics, the antiwar effort, the black civil rights movement, and, interestingly, they tended to have long-term loyalty to the President. Just as energetic in their beliefs were those who judged us on an entirely political basis. If there were gains to be made by supporting us, they would speak out. If there was the possibility of any political fallout, they were the first to advocate pulling back. These fair-weather friends did not view us as a civil rights movement nor did they have any concept of what we had endured. Those who held their fingers to the wind had no experience of any great moral struggle. They made their careers within the Beltway, their life decisions according to the polls, and their careers off this presidency. The schizoid character of this White House caused mistakes, misinformation, and chaos.

As in the transition, our opponents continued to be invisible and hard to identify. Finger-pointing remained the tactic to explain our exclusion from serious decision-making; someone else was always responsible. It was more important to be seen as politically correct than to deal with the substance of the problem. Once their newfound power was confirmed by their titled jobs, that plantation mentality that I saw surface in the transition became even more pronounced. They knew what was good for us. We did not need to be involved; in fact, they resented our insistence on participating in the decisions that would affect the rest of our lives. They had brought us out of the fields of bondage. We were there to serve them. They could not understand why we were not grateful. They did not view us as peers. Even more important, they did not seek out the years of experience that we had gained in battle. They had no interest in learning from our mistakes and our triumphs. When they encountered the forceful hostility of those who were opposed to giving us our freedom, some of the second tier and the younger White House staffers wanted to flee. I often wondered what they would have done in Birmingham or Selma.

Without a doubt, our strongest allies in the new White House were the President and Hillary Clinton. Two years later, when the community needed the President's support to oppose the anti-homosexual initiatives on the 1994 ballots in Idaho and Oregon, he responded to our appeal and spoke out against them. But after the inauguration, my access to the President became more limited. While I didn't have a problem reaching any of his top staff, I was not given the key mailing and phone codes that would have given me direct access to the President. From the swearing-in on, I was dependent on Stephanopoulos, who had been appointed Assistant to the President and Director of Communications, for that to happen.

George was always cooperative when I called but it was very frustrating to have to go through him to talk to a friend. Clearly, becoming

President had dramatically separated Clinton from many of his old friends who were not on staff. Maybe that always happened to presidents—I had no way of knowing—but I did know that he was likely to receive briefings on gay and lesbian matters from the more political types on the staff who would have been happy to see the entire subject disappear. Often he would hear only one side of the debate and would make his decision based on that. This was the climate I faced with the advent of the new administration. There was to be no honeymoon—just the hard realities of our marriage.

None of us had role models. This administration was the first in history to seriously consider the issue of gay rights. It was a new issue for many of its people. There were no former presidents they could consult. They could resort to comparisons of the emergence of the labor or the black civil rights movement but those comparisons were of limited usefulness. Many in the community were novices too. We never had such access before now. Many of our leaders had very little experience in mounting a campaign at a national level to win an important battle, or to holding their own when meeting with national decision-makers. Nor, as we quickly found out, was there time to learn on the job.

The policy about gays and lesbians in the military exploded within days of the inauguration. The President had chosen Wisconsin Congressperson Les Aspin to be his Secretary of Defense. We were exultant. Not only did we not have to contend with Sam Nunn, we had in this cabinet post the chair of the House Armed Forces Committee, who had been a supporter of gays and lesbians in the military. We expected strong backing from the new Defense chief.

So on January 25 we could hardly believe what we were reading when we picked up *The New York Times* and found a front-page article by Eric Schmitt that contained the outlines of a confidential memo from Secretary Aspin to the President warning there was substantial opposition within the Joint Chiefs of Staff and that Congress would never accept an outright repeal of the ban. The article went on to say:

> *The five-page memorandum, a draft copy of which was provided to* The New York Times *by someone not in the military who is critical of Mr. Aspin, includes a detailed strategy to consult with senior officers and senators in the next six months to work out a new policy that lawmakers will not reject. Even if Mr. Clinton ordered the ban lifted, Congress could pass a law reversing him.*

The leaked memo was featured on all the newscasts that night and was instantly seized by the right as evidence that even the President's own Secretary of Defense was acknowledging that the proposed policy had to be modified. Television evangelists like Pat Robertson used Aspin's own words to reinforce their opposition to lifting the ban and urged their listeners to write their representatives to override the President.

The same *New York Times* article referred to General Powell's opposition to lifting the ban:

> *The Joint Chiefs of Staff, headed by Gen. Colin L. Powell, contend that repealing the ban would wreck morale and discipline, undermine recruiting, force devoutly religious service members to resign, and increase the risk of AIDS among heterosexual troops.*

Powell's opposition was not new. It had begun after the press conference and he continued through January to be a vocal critic of lifting the ban. His eminence gave legitimacy to the attacks of right-wing extremists. In a speech in January at the United States Naval Academy, he spoke of how as a black man he could oppose civil rights for gays and lesbians in the military. The February 8 issue of *The Legal Times* reported:

> *Although the analogy is obvious to gay activists, who note that arguments used to exclude blacks and gays are virtually identical, those arguments don't wash with most members of the military, including Gen. Colin Powell, chairman of the Joint Chiefs of Staff. Last month, Powell argued that there was a distinction, telling a U.S. Naval Academy audience that skin color is a "benign" characteristic, like being Hispanic or Asian, while homosexuality "goes to one of the most fundamental aspects of human behavior."*

That was too much for many veteran civil rights leaders. Roger Wilkins, a respected professor of history and a veteran civil rights leader, responded in the same article:

> *Powell's argument does not hold water. Lots of white people don't think that being black is benign even in 1993. The fact is that I was alive in 1948 [the year that President Truman officially ended racial discrimination in the armed forces], and then nobody thought it was a benign characteristic.*

But voices of reason such as Wilkins's were not enough to overcome the high-visibility positions of powerful figures like Nunn and Powell. They were quickly joined by prominent senators—Dan Coats of Indiana, Ernest Hollings of South Carolina, and John Glenn of Ohio—who used Powell's opposition and Secretary Aspin's doubts to call for hearings by the Senate Armed Services Committee on the proposed lifting of the ban. This issue thus became the first crisis for the infant administration and a test of the President's leadership.

Initially, the White House urged lesbian and gay organizations to keep a low profile and let them handle it. It was certainly better politically to have the prestige of the presidency leading the battle on our behalf, and many of the groups complied. Until the leaked Aspin memorandum, many of us, myself included, really thought that the administration had meant what it said.

The memorandum was a wake-up call. Business as usual was not going to suffice. But we had already lost two valuable months organizing a counterattack; it ought to have gotten under way back in November. Even knowing that "if onlys" are a fruitless exercise, I still cannot help regretting that we allowed those in the White House to dictate our initial strategy. Instinct and experience had long made it clear that we could not expect others, not even the White House, to deliver our freedom to us.

I was in an awkward situation. I was the one with access to key staff people within the administration. But I was not a board member of either the HRCF or the NGLTF—the two major national organizations that had strong advocacy components to their mission. Both had entrenched staffs and strong boards of directors that required them to map out their plans internally; and they were very sensitive to the possibility of undue influence on the direction of their organizations from outsiders—including me. I was only one of many who offered assistance when the military issue blew up, but quick decision-making is not a characteristic of established institutions. Within a two-week period community institutions like these were not only being asked to have an immediate plan of action in place, but to be on top of an issue that they had left to the White House to manage. They did not have the flexibility or the resources to do this in so short a time.

They were asked for this plan of action because the political section of the White House finally realized that the extreme right was outgunning them. Organizations like Concerned Women of America and the Traditional Values Coalition generated thousands of letters directed to senators and congresspersons. Capitol Hill was beginning to ask the White

House what it was doing to counter the opposition to the President's announced policy. Behind the scenes the White House political operatives now began to say the gay and lesbian community wasn't doing enough at the grassroots level, and demanded ammunition to help them build favorable public support. The irony left a sour taste in my mouth.

It was not clear who from the White House requested that a meeting be held in late January to deal with the crisis. The site was the Georgetown home of Bob Shrum and Marylouise Oates. I couldn't be there, but among those present were entertainment mogul Barry Diller, EMILY's List Ellen Malcolm, David Geffen's political aide, Bob Burkett, Tim McFeeley and Hillary Rosen of HRCF, the Victory Fund's William Waybourn, and Washington power broker Tim Boggs. It was a combination of first-rate fund-raisers, contributors, and community organization heads, both straight and gay. White House adviser Paul Begula arrived late and kept insisting that his presence was "not official." He was anxious that his participation be kept quiet.

There was an urgent item on the agenda. Senator Jesse Helms was threatening to immediately attach an amendment to the Family Leave Act that would undercut the President and prohibit gays and lesbians from serving in the military. We spent much of this initial meeting devising means to counter him. The idea was to call on members of Congress like Ted Kennedy and Barbara Boxer and others for a "floor strategy" that would either collect enough votes to defeat Helms's amendment or limit it to the six-month study period Clinton had proposed.

The other essential task was to decide how to respond to the critical need for grassroots support. That was going to be an uphill battle. The extreme right already had organizations and coalitions in place; Nunn and Powell had been allowed to set the tone of the debate; and the failure of the White House to bring us in early had given our opponents a huge advantage. The most skilled political talent in the world cannot generate an instant grassroots organization, endorsements, and coalition partners. That takes time, and time was what we didn't have. Even basic organizing is not an instantaneous process. The deadline for the President to present the executive order was July 15. Those present decided that the sphere of influence had to be expanded. Another meeting was called for, with a broader range of participants. It was essential to find out what kinds of resources were available if we were to create a coalition that was able to deliver effective and productive backing for the President's policy.

Meanwhile, the community itself was growing angry over what it perceived as the lack of a strong, articulate opposition to the swelling attacks of the right. Many didn't know their national organizations had been asked to lie low, and blamed them for not countering the barrage of hatred effectively. By the beginning of February I was fielding endless calls from contributors demanding that something be done and done quickly. ANGLE urged me to attend the second meeting in Washington on February 3 and strongly express their concern.

Bill Rubinstein of the ACLU—the American Civil Liberties Union—asked me to fly into Washington the night before, to have dinner with him and legal scholar and rights leader Tom Stoddard to discuss the "crisis of leadership." Bill has devoted his life to fighting for civil rights, and for years Tom, who has AIDS, was the executive director of the Lambda Legal Defense Fund. He is widely respected for his skills and the breadth of his knowledge.

We sat over pasta in a Georgetown restaurant and talked about the next day's meeting. Bill expected it would produce a "campaign," and he felt strongly that Tom should be its manager. It was good news to learn that someone of Tom's stature and reputation was willing to take on the task, but we had to face the sensitive situation that was developing with the established organizations.

"You guys know there is going to be hostility to any new coalition effort. It will be viewed as attempting to create a new organization or as usurping the power of the other ones," I said. "We've got to reassure the participants that this coalition is solely for this issue alone. If we don't, there's going to be nothing but chaos and turf-fighting. Even more important, we'll be dead meat."

"If we don't mount a credible opposition to this firestorm of hatred, we'll be dead meat anyhow," Tom observed.

"Look, I know that. But we have got to insure that any campaign against the ban has the support of everyone in the room. We can't diminish the odds of our success because we failed to appreciate the concerns of the established organizations."

Tom sounded impatient. "David, I am not new on the scene. I have long, historical relationships with a lot of people who will be in the room. I am confident I can assure them of my ability to bring a coalition together. The important thing is that the coalition be structured so that we have the power to get the job done."

We laid out what was needed to build an effective coalition, such as soliciting non-gay support, gathering religious and political leaders' endorsements, implementing a fund-raising drive to bring in hundreds of thousands of dollars, and creating an excellent press operation. The July

15 deadline made all this an organizational nightmare. By the time office space was found, staff hired, mailings created, and a presence created in the national media, it would be the middle of March at best. That would leave us only four months to the deadline to make an impact. Four months was no time at all in politics. The clock continued to work against us.

We wrapped up the discussion by outlining all the possible arguments and concerns that could surface in the next day's meeting and collected our notes, by now stained with red sauce. But before we left the restaurant, I had a few more points to raise.

"What do you want from me in this effort?" I asked.

"We need your readiness to spend a lot of time on the road raising money and also to back us to the hilt in the lesbian and gay press."

I ran through what would be required of me over the next couple of months. All my work for the community in this effort had been on a volunteer basis. I was still doing corporate consulting in order to pay the bills and finance my work in the community. I had only so much time, and my clients had a right to a substantial part of it. I was also concerned about the high visibility of a "campaign" such as this, and whether they would disapprove of my involvement and cancel their accounts. But it took me very little time to agree. "You've got all of that. This is my priority. I just have to figure out how to make a living while I'm doing it. Give me a week or two to straighten things out at my office."

I had one final question, for Tom. "As a friend," I said, "I am concerned about your health. Your involvement in this effort is going to bring you great stress. You'll be attacked by the radical right, you'll be attacked by our own community, and you're going to be under the daily pressure of organizing a coalition in very few weeks. Can your health stand it?"

He laughed. "Fighting this battle will probably keep me alive," he told us.

I felt the tension the moment I entered the high-ceilinged living room of Bob Shrum and Marylouise Oates's hundred-year-old Georgetown house. Never before in an atmosphere of crisis had our national organizations attempted to organize a coalition that would have a life of its own. The reactions we had anticipated the night before were in full play. The leaders of every organization present saw themselves with a dual responsibility: to end the opposition to the ban while simultaneously protecting their turf.

A coalition like this was new territory for us. We had all joined our names on letterheads in the past. We had held joint press conferences. We had endorsed one another's projects and programs. But this was the first time in the history of our community that all the national organizations were attempting to create a single campaign, with a director and staff, to engage in battle. Many people in the room were going to have to let go of their fears and suspicions if we were to achieve this goal. It wasn't going to be easy.

Interestingly, some of the unease centered around Tom. His stature was such that it fed the fear that what we were really attempting was a new national organization—there could have been no better choice to guarantee its chances of survival. But even when there were differences, the tone was respectful. I found this a hopeful sign that we had a chance of emerging from the room with a sound agenda for action.

There was no disagreement that a "coalition effort" was called for. The real job was to persuade the participants that it would be a single-purpose entity and that when the effort was over, the existing national organizations would be stronger. We deliberately named it the Campaign for Military Service (CMS), to make it clear this was a "campaign" and not an organization. Everyone pledged to support the new coalition and approved Tom Stoddard to lead it. I don't think any of us knew quite what to expect—or even whom to trust—but we tried to put that aside for a greater good.

When the meeting had finished, I headed to the Department of Defense for a luncheon meeting with Morton Halperin, who had been nominated by the President to be Assistant Secretary of Defense for Democracy and Human Rights. Tom Stoddard had suggested the meeting; Halperin was an old friend. I had met him once before and I certainly knew of his background. He had been on the National Security Council when Nixon was president, but left when he found out that Henry Kissinger had had his phones bugged in an attempt to identify the source of leaks to the press. He had been working for the Washington ACLU when Clinton appointed him to the Defense Department position.

I wasn't sure why Tom wanted this meeting—perhaps no more than that it was a good idea for us to know each other better. But it would obviously be useful to have information about the status of the military issue inside the Pentagon, and I hoped the meeting might produce this. I would find it valuable in my organizing efforts.

This was to be my first visit to the Pentagon since the 1967 march, and the first time I had been inside the building. I was escorted to

Halperin's office, which was decorated with the Defense Department seals and an array of flags. His greeting was cordial.

"Well, we have quite a problem here, don't we?" he asked.

"We certainly do. I have to tell you that I find it strange being here. This is where I demonstrated against the Vietnam War, and I am a pacifist."

Mort laughed. He too had been in the forefront of progressive politics. "You get used to it. Most of the people here are good folks just trying to do their job."

"I know and believe that, Mort, but can you keep them out of my rights?"

"Let's have lunch and see where we are," he answered.

The department's dining room was full of military brass. I had a feeling that the liberal side of Mort was secretly delighted to be bringing an openly gay politician to lunch here. Several military officials recognized me; I could tell by the startled looks on their faces. A couple of them set down their forks to stare. I relished the fact that I could walk openly and proudly into this room as a gay man. That was the high point of our meeting; as it proved, I didn't learn much of substance, although we did promise to do our best to keep communicating with each other.

CMS needed money and needed it quickly; the days were ticking away. Within a week I had reorganized my office and called all my clients. Jeremy would be the pivotal person in Los Angeles while I was on the road. On some days I had as many as twelve different events, one after another—meetings, speeches, and interviews. On a single day in Texas I went to Dallas, Houston, San Antonio, and Austin, and gave my last fund-raising pitch at midnight in an Austin living room packed with gays and lesbians eager to help the cause. Everywhere I went veterans came up to me to share their stories. There were many times when fundraisers became therapy sessions for those who had never been able to talk openly before.

I crossed paths with some modern-day heroes and heroines on these road trips. The military was still actively dismissing able personnel because of their sexual orientation. These honorable men and women had seen their lives dragged through the mud in the effort to discredit their service and destroy their credibility. Many of them volunteered their time to CMS to let the public know their stories. Randy Shilt's book *Conduct Unbecoming* documents the forced interrogations, witch-hunts, calls to families, friends asked to turn in other friends, and shattered careers.

My encounters with active-duty military personnel who were fighting back were a highlight of my work for CMS. They were no longer willing to lie and dishonor themselves by remaining in the closet. I met people like Colonel Margarethe Cammermeyer, who came out of the closet to her superiors; and Joseph Steffan, who felt obligated by the honor code of Annapolis to reveal his homosexuality; and Ensign Keith Meinhold, whose case had provoked the question at the press conference; and Lieutenant Tracy Thorne, a fighter pilot who gave up his lifelong dream to tell the truth about his homosexuality. Observing their dignity and courage, I knew we could not compromise the honor they brought to us—indeed to the entire country they had chosen to serve.

When I was on a trip for CMS to Washington in February, I made my first actual visit to the Clinton White House. I had an appointment with John Emerson, who was Deputy Director of Presidential Personnel. There were still many jobs that had not yet been filled, and the meeting had been set up to talk about pending appointments of open gays and lesbians. As I walked up the steps of the ornate Old Executive Office Building, I realized I was about to enter a building full of friends, acquaintances, and allies. This was our White House now. It was a strange feeling. I handed the guard my driver's license and waited until John's assistant appeared on the other side of the metal detector and took me to his office.

Our meeting was routine and when we finished, John asked me if I wanted to visit the West Wing. Did I! We headed down the expansive halls of the EOB toward the West Wing entrance and all along the way familiar faces stopped to greet me. What struck me most as I passed the open doorways was how young most of the people in them were. They were also very casually dressed—maybe too much so, I thought, remembering all those admonitions of my mother about "proper" dress. Then I recalled her outrage over the length of The Beatles' hair. I suddenly felt very old.

John escorted me into the West Wing. The President was not in town and many of the staff were traveling with him. Every once in a while, a political ally would pop out of an office at the sight of me and give me a high five. I was even allowed to enter the empty Oval Office. I'd been part of making it possible for Bill Clinton to sit behind that desk and it made me feel proud.

Back in the EOB John dropped me off to visit my close friend from the California campaign, Marsha Scott. She was a long-time friend of both the President and Hillary Clinton and she now headed up the White House Correspondence operation. She shut her office door, we grinned in pleasure at our reunion, and then we sat down to trade political gossip that eventually evolved into gossip about our mutual friends. When we ran out of nuggets and it was time for me to go, I asked Marsha if I needed an escort around the building. She looked at the security pass hanging around my neck and laughed. "Honey, with that pass you can walk all around the place," she said. "Why don't you get a feel of the EOB and say hi to all of our friends?"

I decided on the spot to go visit my old McCarthy/Martha's Vineyard compatriot Eli Segal. We had shared so much over the years. When I launched my calamitous PRO Peace venture, he and his wife, Phyllis, had hosted a fund-raiser in their Boston home. When I came out of the closet and told them I was gay, they had been wonderfully loving and supportive. Eli had worked hard during the campaign to insure that the hierarchy took the community's issues seriously, and I felt very warmly toward him.

He was now Assistant to the President and Director of the Office of National Service. He had a corner office, majestic enough to be daunting, with a ceiling that must have been twenty feet high and crystal light fixtures hanging from it. It intimidated me. Its grandness made it hard to relate to Eli as the old friend he was.

But it wasn't only the office. To my surprise, seeing him behind his desk brought forth a realization of what I had lost. If I had chosen it, surely I too could be sitting in an office like this one, doing work that might change lives for the better as Eli's was. For the first time, I felt a twinge of regret at my decision not to serve in the administration. I had a different obligation and I recognized this: I *had* to fight for our freedom and to battle AIDS. But knowing there was also a wider world to which I could have contributed, I had sometimes found myself feeling bitter at being perceived solely as a "gay activist." It wasn't always easy to acknowledge that this was, after all, how I had chosen to define myself. No one gets through life without making trade-offs. I had chosen my work in the community as mine.

I am proud of being a gay activist. But I did have those moments when I wished I were free of the need to fight for my own freedom, and moments when I thought of what might have been. This was—briefly— one of them. Those moments of nostalgia usually don't last very long, and I greeted Eli and sat down to small talk. But the truth was, our lives had grown apart. We had different priorities now, and different roads to travel. The gap was too great. It was time to move on.

•   •   •

A few days later the White House called to say that the President was going to be in Los Angeles that weekend, and asked me to join a few others in greeting him at the airport. We gathered in a small 1950s-style terminal—lots of glass and brick—at the far end of the LAX complex. There were fifty of us, including David Geffen, Alan and Marilyn Bergman, producer Sean Daniels, Ruth Hunter, and other Hollywood types. I think even the most sophisticated among us were awed as we watched Air Force One land and taxi to our building. Clinton bounded down the steps into our holding area.

He greeted each of us personally; I got one of those famous hugs and he held me by my shoulders, looked directly into my eyes, and said, "We are going to do this and I won't be intimidated by any voice in opposition. Just give me some room to maneuver and we will be just fine."

With that he moved on to give the same intimate attention to the next person: the cordial embrace, the touch on the arm as he spoke to them, the warm smile. Bill Clinton had not lost his touch. He could still make you feel like the most important person in the world when he was with you. But as I watched him this time, I suddenly ceased feeling special. For whatever reason, I found myself remembering all those intensely connecting moments in the past—the night of his great speech at the Palace, the small ANGLE meeting at Scott and Alex's home. I don't think that first meeting at the Vineyard came to mind, but this was the day when I first began to wonder how much of those warm feelings were genuine or how much plain old-fashioned political manipulation.

After he drove off, we were all invited to tour Air Force One. It was like being let into a candy store—I was really going to see the inside of the world's most famous plane. I was as excited as a kid. A military attaché guided us through the fuselage and we saw the massive communications systems for the President's use, his bedroom, the full kitchen, a huge conference room with a table in the center and big leather chairs surrounding it, the seat belts set in them the only concession to the fact that this was, after all, an airplane we were in. We saw where the media sat. We gawked at every detail. I didn't want to leave.

Just as I was walking through the door, a military attaché took my arm and whispered, "Mr. Mixner, thank you. Please keep fighting for us."

Just as quickly he averted his glance and resumed his duty.

•   •   •

I juggled my corporate consulting with my work for CMS and got to know on a personal basis more airports around the country than I care to think of. Each time I changed planes, I'd grab a phone, call Jeremy, get the messages and the status of my client work, and then frantically dial my clients and deal with their problems before it was time to catch the next plane.

Early March brought me back to the East Coast for organizing and fund-raising, and to visit the White House about problems with permits for this year's Gay and Lesbian March on Washington on April 26. Back in February, four of the young organizers had asked me for help.

"The Park Police won't give us a permit because they've just re-planted the grass on the Mall," a young woman who called herself Scout told me. "They want us to have two separate departure points, one per-haps at RFK Stadium and maybe the other at the Pentagon. This is serious. We need your help in getting the White House involved."

I was appalled. "I can't believe the stupidity of wanting to place sev-eral hundred thousand demonstrators who are furious at the Joint Chiefs right outside their door at the Pentagon," I said. "Do they really expect us to be able to control the situation?"

"Exactly. And we won't take responsibility for controlling it either. We've got to reach the police and convince them that grass can be re-planted. Hattoy's also warning the White House how crazy it is but you've got to help too."

Bob was now Associate Director of Presidential Personnel in the White House, but I suspected she was right to want both of us on the case. I was weary of yet another crisis to take into the White House. But I had to do it. By now I had prepared a memo for key staff people suggesting how the administration should respond to the march. I pro-posed examining the way President Kennedy had handled the 1963 Civil Rights March and replicating it. This meant Clinton would not make an appearance at the march, but I did stress that it was very important that he stay in town and not appear to be fleeing the marchers. Again follow-ing Kennedy's example, I thought that on the morning of the march, the President should invite community leaders to the White House for breakfast to hear the marchers' petition for justice personally. We had an excellent model for handling this situation. I saw no need to reinvent the wheel.

I went to see key Clinton people in the Department of the Interior. Clinton appointee Stephanie Solien, who was Director of Congressional Affairs at the time, was working on the issue of permits. I pointed out the potential for disaster if the marchers gathered at the Pentagon and the need for permits. Stephanie recognized the problems and asked for suggestions. My first idea was that for public safety, and to avoid a massive confrontation at the Pentagon, we ask the Washington, D.C., police chief to make an appeal to the Park Police for the permits. That ought to make it politically impossible for them to continue refusing. Stephanie promised to explore this and to look for alternatives as well.

Later that night I went to a fund-raising reception for the Democratic Party being held on Capitol Hill. A very young White House staffer came up to me. He had seen in someone's appointment book that I was going to the White House and he asked what I would be doing there.

"I am trying to have the White House focus on the March on Washington while we have time to make plans for it quietly. It's essential that the President have some sort of meeting with community leaders and not leave town."

The staffer looked very assured. "You have got to be reasonable," he lectured me. "We're taking a battering on this issue. Wisdom and patience are required from you people."

"You people" indeed. I kept my voice calm. "Look, we have a good model in President Kennedy's actions in the 1963 march. It will be more difficult for anyone to slam us if we let it be known that we are following the precedent he set."

The staffer, who had not even been born in 1963, and who clearly needed a history lesson, was oblivious. "President Kennedy didn't have it as rough as we do on this issue. People are really angry at us for supporting your people. Kennedy had it easy compared to what we're going through."

Again. "Get a history book—you need it. By the 1963 march, Kennedy had to deal with firebombings, assassinations, freedom rides, the Birmingham demonstrations, and massive arrests. We're the victims in this struggle, not you. We'll organize the whole thing for you if that's what it takes to get you to stop pretending you're the ones being slammed."

With that, a witness to the exchange stepped in, wanting to avoid an incident at a private party. He took me by the arm and said, "David, someone over here wants to meet with you."

I went off, dumbfounded at the staffer's arrogance and ignorance. I wondered how many more young turks like him there were back at the White House. The exchange left me feeling uneasy.

Over the next several days, I visited a number of Washington officials and staffers at the White House. John Emerson suggested I see Rahm Emanuel, now the Political Director; he ought to be able to resolve the permit question quickly. I was running out of time because I had to give a series of speeches and fund-raisers in the Boston area over the weekend and be back early on Monday for a White House reception, my first, set up for major donors. I changed my Washington–to–Los Angeles plane ticket and made an appointment to meet with Rahm later that Monday.

I arrived in Boston to news that a fierce blizzard was traveling along the East Coast. On Friday evening I went to a fund-raiser for the Fenway Community Center. The next day I had a meeting at Harvard University with leading AIDS researchers Max Essex, Ric Marlink, and others. In each city where I traveled, I made an effort to tour AIDS facilities, meet with researchers and AIDS activists, and get a feel for the problems that needed to be resolved, so that I could take what I learned back to Washington and lobby the administration hard for changes and action. The snow began falling during the Harvard meeting. By evening, the rest of my weekend had been canceled and I was trapped in my hotel by the famous Blizzard of 1993.

The airports were closed and there was no way I was going to make a Saturday evening dinner in Washington hosted by the Vice President and Mrs. Gore. I was disappointed. I had been looking forward to this invitation; I was an admirer of both, although we had never really had the opportunity to get to know each other beyond casual encounters. Back in the Vietnam War years, I had worked hard raising money for his father, who was an antiwar Democrat from Tennessee.

I couldn't get out of Boston on Saturday but no matter what, I was not going to miss my first Clinton reception in the White House. Sunday, as the blizzard eased, I boarded an Amtrak train and headed for Washington. Sixteen hours later, in a ride punctuated by numerous storm delays, I arrived in Washington. It was 4:30 A.M. I had enough time to get to my hotel, shower and change, and make it to the reception at eight.

I plowed through deep snow to the East Wing gate of the White House, cleared through security, and made my way up the small circular drive to the entrance. I had my invitation, yet it still felt strange to see my name on the guest list. I walked through the East Wing, examining rooms along the way and poking my head inside the White House movie theater. I was surprised by the freedom I had to roam. Then I went up the great staircase to the first floor and the East Ballroom. I had so many memories of this room from television vignettes—President Kennedy's press conferences, Pablo Casals playing his cello at an evening recital,

Kennedy's casket lying on the same draped platform where Lincoln had lain, and more. I was moved to be here.

When the President entered, he was mobbed by dozens of contributors and old friends. I shook his hand but the press of the crowd made me feel very removed. He spoke about achieving social and economic justice and the opportunity that we all had to change and make history. I did not linger. It was just another reception after all. As I came down the stairs, a strikingly tall, blond military attaché stopped me and asked me to step into a side room. He was very nervous and kept looking at the door to check whether anyone could see us. I knew why he wanted to speak with me. I had become used to it.

He said, "Please don't tell anyone that I'm talking to you. I could lose my career and everything I've worked for all my life. But I have to tell you that I am gay. I would be too ashamed to have you leave the White House without me telling you this. It's something I just have to do. Please keep it between us."

I shook his hand. I said, "Hopefully in the very near future, because of this president, you and I will be able to meet openly as free people. Stay strong. It shouldn't be too much longer."

Before we left the room, he snapped to attention and saluted me. I thanked him. He was the one who deserved the salute.

I came back to the White House at three o'clock for my appointment with Rahm Emanuel. I had mixed feelings about this meeting. We had known each other from the first days of the campaign, where his intelligence and political astuteness were obvious and impressive. We had had a terrific partnership raising money for the President, and a less productive relationship through the inauguration process. It was further downhill now. In his West Wing office today, I found a different Rahm: very aggressive, restless, and arrogant.

He was full of himself. I thought the aggressiveness that had served him well in a campaign operation was unseemly in a governing situation. Watching him impatiently handle phone calls and pace back and forth was like watching a caged tiger wanting to be let loose to spring on you. He had lost something in the transition to the White House. He was no longer pleasant. He struck me as riveted by his own power.

He made me feel as though I were intruding on the important business of state. In my ten or fifteen minutes in his office he fielded several calls and constant interruptions by the staff. Each time he returned his attention to me, it was as though he were dealing with a house servant. I was certainly not a peer, and he clearly hated being bothered about the problems of the march.

I went through them briskly. First, I strongly urged him to read the memo containing the recommendations for the President. He said he would but he dismissed any discussion of the contents. He made it very clear that *he* would decide what would be recommended to the President. I was to deal with him directly—no one else. Then I brought up the serious problem of the permits and the nightmare scenario of the Pentagon location.

"Can't you get some of your rich boys to pay for the grass on the Mall?" he asked.

That was a nice one. "Rahm, I don't think we should have to put out that kind of money simply to exercise our right to petition our government. We have to raise millions as it is for AIDS and to fight these damned initiatives. We can only raise so much."

"Geffen can do it. So can several others. They'll want to please the President."

"Maybe so, but I don't have a relationship with Geffen or some of the others."

"I do. Well, maybe we can make it some type of 'bond' that will satisfy the Park Police about the grass and get those guys their money back. We'll have to keep it confidential."

"Rahm, if it means avoiding chaos at the march, there may be a few calls I can make to help out— *if* this is the only way we can handle it. But please give some thought to the police chief idea."

"Let me check into it. I'll give you a call."

I was glad to be out of there.

I had no idea how continuously this administration would test me. Another indication that all was not well in paradise came about a week later. I had shuffled down my driveway in my pajamas in the early morning sun to pick up my morning *Los Angeles Times*. There on the front page was a photograph of the President, accompanied by Armed Forces Committee Chairman Sam Nunn, aboard the USS *Roosevelt* looking at several sailors crowded into tight sleeping quarters. I couldn't believe my eyes. How the hell had the President's advance team allowed a setup like this by Senator Nunn and the military? The story reported the "cool reception" the President had received from the military personnel on the ship. The photographers were waiting when he was escorted belowdecks to inspect the sleeping quarters of the sailors. I couldn't help wondering how many sailors on that ship were gay and lesbian and had been sleeping in those very quarters without a problem.

I knew from our friendship during the days of the Vietnam War just how much Clinton was in awe of the military and its leaders. When we had talked in Oxford, he had once said that if it hadn't been for Vietnam, he actually might have been willing to serve in the military.

"I love the power and the order that the military provides a man," he told me in one of our late-night talks.

"Not me, Bill. I can't imagine killing another person for anything."

"Sometimes it's necessary to preserve a greater good."

"Yeah, maybe so. It's the old 'would you have fought in World War II?' argument. I just feel someone has to say no to the killing. I guess that's me. And I hate the blind obedience to authority that comes with the military. It scares me."

He wasn't buying it. "David, I know what it's like to live without structure and an authority figure in my life. It's important for individuals and it's important for a country."

I knew that Bill was referring to the time in his life when he had had to be the "father" in his family. He had responsibility thrust on him at a very early age. When we first knew him in the sixties, unlike most of us he was still very respectful toward those in authority. Maybe it filled a vacuum. Who could tell?

What I did know was that what I saw in the paper spelled trouble—big trouble. I knew that he had never made peace with himself over his draft status in the Vietnam War, and I had witnessed his desperate desire to win the respect of those he believed to be strong and in charge. I thought it very unlikely that he would be able to resist seeking the military's approval for his presidency.

On Tuesday, March 23, President Clinton held his first formal press conference in the East Room of the White House. Andrea Mitchell of NBC News and Mark Miller of *Newsweek* asked him several questions about the pending executive order. They focused on whether he would support restrictions on homosexuals in the military in both promotion and deployment. The President's answer stunned us all. ". . . if you can discriminate against people in terms of whether they get into the service or not based on not what they are but what they say they are, then I would think you could make appropriate distinctions on duty assignments once they're in." A follow-up question asked if that meant that he was "prepared to support restrictions on the deployment of homosexual members of the service." ". . . I wouldn't rule that out, depending on what the grounds and arguments were," he replied.

The President of the United States had publicly refused to rule out the option of segregating lesbian and gay troops in promotion, deployment, or even housing. To be allowed to serve in the military and to be segregated from other troops, to have separate living quarters, and possibly to be denied promotion was a throwback to the old days when black troops were similarly segregated. They too were not allowed to room or eat with their peers. They had separate barracks. They were in separate units. This disgrace ended only when Harry Truman issued his executive order. We were not about to allow ourselves to repeat history.

The irate calls poured into my office all that day, and those who couldn't get through on the telephone sent angry faxes demanding to know what was going on. I truly believed that the President didn't understand the ramifications of what he had said. I urged everyone to stay calm and reassured them that the statement would be clarified to our satisfaction at the next morning's White House press briefing. I pulled that out of the blue—I had no idea whether it was true or not. I placed calls to Stephanopoulos to be sure I was reading the situation correctly. This was the first time I didn't receive a call back from him. Toward the end of the day, I tried to call the President directly. This was the first time I had tried to reach him on short notice. I did not have his direct line and I don't believe he ever received the message.

The truth was, I was terrified that the President really did mean what he had said. When none of my calls to the White House were returned, I became nervous and angry. That night I couldn't sleep at all. I got up at five in the morning and waited anxiously for word of the early morning press briefing. As I was waiting, Rahm Emanuel's secretary called and said that Rahm needed to talk to me. Could I be available at 1:30 P.M. Pacific time? I was greatly relieved. They *were* returning my phone calls. That was a good sign.

The first indication of the morning briefing came when Dana Wolf of ABC's *Nightline* called. She wanted to know my response to the President's willingness to consider "segregation" of homosexuals in the armed forces.

I said, "Dana, I'm waiting for the results of the morning briefing. I am hoping that yesterday's statements will be clarified."

"Well, I can help with that. The briefing's already been held and they are standing by their statements."

At the White House, George Stephanopoulos and press spokesperson Dee Dee Myers had held firm; the President would indeed consider restrictions on homosexuals as an option. They did not back down from the previous day's statement at all.

I was stunned. I wanted to hang up on Wolf and hide. I think she understood my shock, and she proceeded gently. "What do you think of all of this, David?"

I told her of my pain, anger, and sense of outrage.

"Are you willing to go on *Nightline* and say what you just said to me?"

"Dana, I'm expecting a call from the White House at 1:30 P.M. our time. I am still hoping they will give me something to explain this. If they don't and you still want me, I'll go on your show."

It was possible, she said, that they might have someone else by then, but she would get back to me either way.

I hung up the phone and asked Jeremy and Tony Leonhardt to handle the calls. I had to take a walk and think. If I went on *Nightline* and shared my true feelings about the President's statement, it would change my relationship with the Clinton White House forever. I weighed which would serve my community better: to keep my access to the White House or use my position to articulate the outrageous substance of the President's comments. Was I going to be an insider who defended policies I did not believe in, or an outsider who followed my conscience and my convictions?

I came home, went upstairs to my bedroom, and called Patsy. We had talked several times over the last twenty-four hours. She too had had a close personal friendship with Clinton. "Patsy, this is the important one," I said. "If I go on *Nightline*, we both know what the reaction will be in the White House. On the other hand, there's my obligation to the community. I'm the one who went all over the country urging them to vote for him. If I don't speak out now, how can I ever again be taken seriously as a man of principle?"

Patsy, as always, had it right. "If you don't tell the emperor that he has no clothes, who will? The problem with so many of these guys is that no one is willing to tell the truth because they're afraid of being locked out. You have no choice. You must go on the show and you must speak the truth. If we allow statements like this one to go unchecked and they pay no political price, they'll do it to any of us. This is beyond the community. This is about the administration's willingness to listen to dissent. This is a civil rights issue."

She was right about that, but I still worried about the cost. "Will I be hurting the community more by giving up my access?"

"Sounds like the old days. Remember when White House staffers would tell us that they were talking quietly inside about the war while remaining silent on the outside? We've spent our lives fighting for civil rights. You can't remain silent when it comes to your own community. Go for it!"

I told her I was going to wait for Rahm's call and wanted to talk to Jeremy too. "Bless you, Patsy," I said. "I love you."

I hung up the phone and went into the office, which was next to my bedroom. Jeremy was working at his desk.

"Let the machine answer the phone," I told him. "You and I have to talk. Depending on what Rahm says, I am thinking of accepting the offer to appear on *Nightline*. I want you to understand what the consequences will be. My business may well be hurt—clients not wanting to associate with someone the White House is angry at. We could be short of money very quickly. We could face some very tough sledding. I want and need your support but you need to know this. It will affect your life too."

Jeremy didn't even hesitate. "You have no choice. You have my support totally." In an echo of Patsy, he went on: "If you don't speak up now, what will it take for you to speak up?"

"Well, let's wait for Rahm to call. See what they have to say. If we're lucky, maybe he'll give us something—or maybe Dana will have found someone else to carry the ball."

We sat there in a strange silence except for the endless ringing of the phone. Now and then I checked with friends in the movement for their advice. It was divided down the middle. Half said I had to speak out, and half thought I was crazy to risk my access to the White House. They felt strongly about it, telling me it would be "irresponsible" and that I would be "hurting the community." I sweated out my decision.

The phone rang at 1:30 sharp and this time I answered it. It was Rahm's office. Would I hold for him?

He came on the line and without any pleasantries said, "What kind of luck have you had in raising the money for the bond?"

I was taken aback. "What are you taking about?"

"The bond," he said impatiently. "You agreed to help raise money to pay for a bond for the grass at the March on Washington. I am calling for a progress report."

I couldn't believe it. Was he living in a vacuum? And to call and ask me to raise more money to protect this administration's ass? I was livid.

"I don't give a flying fuck about the grass," I said. "As far as I'm concerned, they can march without a permit and trample the hell out of the grass and you can deal with that. I can't believe you are calling me to raise more money, given the situation."

"What the hell is your problem? You agreed to help. Why are you so upset?"

"Rahm, I thought you were calling to explain the President's segregation statement. I have been trying to reach someone in the White House for two days now. I thought this was the return call. Believe me, I didn't want to hear a request for more money."

He was furious. "We don't have to explain or justify our actions to you," he said. "Who do you think you are? If the President of the United States never does another thing for you people you should get on your knees and be thankful. He's already done more for you all than anyone. How dare you question his actions!"

"I am trying to avoid chaos breaking out and I'm getting a lecture as if you're the master and I'm the slave. Look, he is *wrong*. Segregation is wrong. You are wrong. *Nightline* has called and asked me to go on tonight's show. I don't want to do it but you have to give me something."

"You've already had too much. I wouldn't go on that show if I were you if you ever want to see the inside of the White House again. You have got to learn to be a team player and stop being so damn self-righteous."

I had had it. Let him hear it from the gut. "Rahm, how would you feel if the President of the United States said that he would consider creating separate units, separate housing, and deny promotions for all people of the Jewish faith? I don't think you would be a team player, would you? Nor do I think you would quietly accept it. Neither will I."

"We don't have anything more to talk about," he said. "You are unreasonable. I will not talk to you anymore." He hung up on me.

I knew what I had to do. Rahm had taken care of that. I turned to Tony and Jeremy. They were watching me. They had listened to my side of the conversation and they were stunned. "Would you please get Dana Wolf on the phone?" I asked Jeremy. "I have a job to do."

Dana still wanted me on the show. They would be sending a car to take me to their Los Angeles studios by 7:30 that evening. I went out and got a haircut and then I asked the guys in the office to give me some quiet time. I knelt by my bed and prayed to my God to give me the strength to do the right thing.

Jeremy knocked on the door to tell me Bob Hattoy was on the phone from the White House and that it was urgent. Bob wanted to know what happened in the call from Emanuel. He'd been in a meeting and Rahm had come in and said to him, "What's wrong with Mixner? He's off the wall. He's crazy. Can you do anything with him?" Rahm had told him some of our conversation. I filled in more. I spelled out why I was going on *Nightline:* There had to be an effort to put an end to this segregation talk. Bob understood perfectly. He wanted me to know that if it was needed, he was ready to speak out too. (In fact, later that week he gave several courageous interviews for which he would pay a heavy political price.) His call meant a great deal.

The ABC News car came and took Jeremy and me to their studios. Never having appeared on *Nightline* before, I wasn't sure what to expect. I thought we would be taping in a large studio with monitors everywhere so that Ted Koppel and his guests could interact on the show. I was led to makeup and then to someone's office where I assumed I was to wait. Not so. They set up a camera right there and told me to look straight over it into a wall of bookshelves. There was no monitor for me to see Koppel or the other guest, Indiana Senator Dan Coats, a Republican. I felt as though I were talking to a bookcase.

Coats, who was a vehement opponent of lifting the ban, was present in ABC's Washington studio. Dana told me the White House had turned down the request to have someone on the show. Koppel's familiar voice came through my earpiece, welcomed me, and gave me a quick briefing. The program would open with a taped background piece and then he would ask us questions. He stressed that with commercials, we would have only a little over twenty minutes for dialogue, and he urged the senator and me to be brief and to the point. He wished us both well and then I heard the familiar *Nightline* theme music introduce the show. I nearly froze in my seat.

They started with the taped clips, and included in them was a segment of a speech I had given at the New York HRCF dinner promising that the President would keep his word and lift the ban against homosexuals in the military. Then they ran a clip of the President's press conference and wrapped up the opening with reactions to it.

Coats praised the President for a step in the right direction and called for him to continue the ban. I took a hard line, hammering that segregation in any form was immoral and insupportable. I said in response to a question from Koppel that I had doubts about the President's continued commitment. He asked me, "I know you had a conversation with a White House official earlier today. . . . You were asked not to come on our program tonight, is that right?" I had no intention of going into my conversation with Rahm on national television, so I simply said, "That's right," and went back to my point one more time: "There is one thing that is very unacceptable to talk about as a legitimate alternative and that is the segregation of the military once again. It is morally wrong. It is repugnant. It is something we cannot accept."

The program flew by. Finally, Koppel asked me to do a wrap-up. "It is an issue of great principle," I said. "One should stand strongly for one's principles and articulate them clearly. We don't compromise on basic freedom and civil rights. We fight for them."

That was it. I headed home. I found my answering machine full of messages thanking me for going on the air and articulating what needed to be said. They were wonderful people, those callers, but you couldn't do more than a basic job in thirty-second sound bites. I sat down and wrote a four-page speech that I wanted to deliver somewhere soon.

The firestorm continued. Patsy faxed me a shocking clip from *The Rocky Mountain News:*

> *The White House said Thursday it did not try to prevent a top gay adviser from going on television to complain about President Clinton's comments on possibly segregating homosexuals from others in the military. "Untrue," said White House spokeswoman Dee Dee Myers when asked about the accusation made by David Mixner Wednesday night on ABC's* Nightline.

Either Rahm had failed to share his threat that I would never see the inside of the White House again or they had decided it was politically expedient to lie. Certainly no one there had taken a minute to pick up the phone and ask me if there was any truth to it. Instead, they branded me a liar.

The community spoke out. Tracy Thorne called the President's statement "a full retreat." Tom Stoddard of CMS said that unless it was corrected, the March on Washington could turn into an anti-Clinton march. Bob Hattoy said that he could not accept such a compromise and told *The New York Times* that he "almost started crying when he heard Mr. Clinton's remarks." At a New York meeting of contributors to the Democratic Party, fund-raiser and activist Fred Hochberg told Democratic National Committee Chairman David Wilhelm that funds would be pulled from the DNC if the statements by the President became a reality. Tim McFeeley, the executive director of the Human Rights Campaign Fund, said to *The Washington Blade*, "At this point we don't know what the President stands for."

What I had forewarned Jeremy about also started to hit. Within a month, my consulting business dropped more than 40 percent. Under-

standably, clients did not want someone at odds with the President of the
United States on their payroll. The White House staff let it be known
on the political grapevine in Washington that I was persona non grata.
Old straight allies from the past stopped calling and no longer invited
me to dinner. Most of them could not understand why I had to criticize
a president who had done so much for us, but very few took the time to
call and probe further. They just kept their distance. A particularly sad
moment came when I read a profile of me that Daniel Golden of *The
Boston Globe* wrote for their Sunday magazine. It was a fair and insightful
piece but one quote hurt.

> *Despite his success, Mixner felt out of place in the antiwar move-
> ment as he had in Woodstown. Both the McCarthy campaign and the
> Moratorium were dominated by upper-middle-class Ivy League stu-
> dents more self-assured than the working-class Mixner. While he
> slaved behind the scenes, they grabbed the spotlight.*
>
> *"People didn't think of David Mixner as likely to be a great
> leader," says Pulitzer Prize-winning historian Taylor Branch, whom
> Mixner recruited for the McCarthy campaign. "He was 'good old
> David.' Maybe that bugged him."*

It hurt that Taylor was so quick to judge me without making any
effort to understand my journey. To have written such superb books on
the civil rights movement, yet not to perceive that ours too was a civil
rights movement, a battle for freedom too—that was surprising. But he
was not the only one among old friends who chose to take the President's side. I did not think their motives were selfless.

I was committed to giving the speech I had written after *Nightline*. I
called my dear friend, Reverend Troy Perry, and asked him for a platform from which to speak. I was going to be in Texas that weekend and
he offered the MCC Cathedral on Saturday. As soon as I saw him, I felt
safe and in God's hands.

Tracy Thorne and Keith Meinhold had flown to Dallas and had come
to the cathedral to show their support. Any fear I had about making this
speech disappeared when I saw their courage in standing by my side.
The sanctuary was full as the church's powerful organ swelled into "The
Battle Hymn of the Republic."

I rose. I knew that many who were there were waiting to hear what I would say about my old friend the President. I could hear the cameras from the news networks turn on. Now it was my turn.

> *Brothers and Sisters,*
>
> *It is rare that I have the opportunity to speak so urgently among people for whom I have so much love. It is difficult to speak truth and know that it might bring pain between old friends. But today I must . . . because for us truth is the sword. . . .*
>
> *History will not present us with a more historical movement than now. Each one of us will be judged by future generations by our actions in the next several months and years. If, as a family, we rise to the challenge, we truly have the opportunity to change years of oppression into a future filled with hope.*

I continued by outlining the path that had brought us to this moment. I spoke of our work in the campaign and our discovery of our own abilities and power. Then I talked about the opposition the President had encountered in his effort to lift the ban. I spoke about those opponents:

> *In this process of keeping his promise to us, [the President] encountered what we experience every day of our lives—outright bigotry and homophobia. The voices of the past have risen to deny us our moment of freedom. Military leaders are fighting to keep ancient apartheid laws on the books and to resist ending fifty years of repression and persecution. They frighten our neighbors with the big lie. They paint pictures that contain only dark colors. They resort to the same bigoted arguments that have been used for centuries to deny every emerging minority their freedom and equal rights.*

And much to the dismay of many of my Washington insider friends, I decided to remove the air of respectability from Senator Nunn.

> *They sought the cover of legitimacy in Armed Forces Chairperson Sam Nunn. Let me be clear about Senator Nunn. Let us educate those people, including some in the administration, that this is not an enlightened man. Listen to me carefully. Sam Nunn is our George Wallace. He is an old-fashioned bigot who will abuse his power to deny us our freedom.*
>
> *. . . This man does not deserve the respectability that he has been accorded by so many. He has chosen hate over love . . . fear over*

enlightenment . . . and division over unity. We will not quake in his presence. We will not fear him. We will not ever give him the power to determine our future.

Then I said, "This brings us back to our President." There was utter silence. This was not only painful for me but for them also. My voice quavered but I spoke out. I implored:

> *. . . Mr. President, do not give dignity to false compromises. . . . What kind of freedom is it when you ask us to remain silent about who we are? . . . Separate assignments and separate units are no more than old-fashioned segregation. . . . Bigotry that wears a uniform is nothing more than a uniform with a hood. Segregation is morally repugnant to us and we will never, ever accept segregation as a sign of progress.*
>
> *Mr. President, you can make our road to freedom easier. You can speak to this nation of unity, of our unused talents and skills and of our suffering. You can educate senators. You can provide the moral high ground that Senator Nunn is stealing from us. You can provide decisive leadership, courage, and most of all our freedom. But make no mistake—with or without you we will be free . . . we will prevail!*

The crowd cheered as I spoke of what each of them was feeling inside. They wanted to hear that they were not alone. I did not doubt that day that I had done the right thing.

CHAPTER SEVENTEEN
Hard Times

THERE was no ambiguity about my changed status with the White House. My calls were not returned and "anonymous" quotes appeared in the papers about my no longer being welcome at the White House. There was no ambiguity either about the rest of my life. Economically, I was struggling to make ends meet. Personally, most of my straight friends—many of whom had seemed so pleased to hear from me when they perceived I had influence in the White House—had vanished. And even in my own community, there was a small group who gloated over my lost access.

But there was no time to be self-indulgent. Too much was going on. Fred Hochberg and Andrew Barrer, who were the finance co-chairs at CMS and who directed my volunteer fund-raising activities, were keeping the pressure on the Democratic National Committee. Both had been quoted as saying that money from the gay and lesbian community would be withheld if the current administration course wasn't corrected. They had both been major fund-raisers and contributors to the Clinton/Gore campaign and they had a network of wealthy contributors who would heed their advice. The DNC itself was getting calls from large contributors who threatened to withdraw their support.

A week after my *Nightline* appearance, David Wilhelm telephoned, asking for a meeting in Los Angeles. As chair of the DNC, he still had direct access to the administration, although it lessened as time passed because he was not operating out of the White House. His job was to create and sustain a vital, financially sound, victorious Democratic Party. To achieve that, he had to keep intact the broad coalition that had made that victory for the party a reality. Our anger over the segregation statement made his job harder, and he wanted to direct it away from the party.

We met on April 1 at the Century Plaza Hotel. It was late in the day and we sat in chairs in the lobby. It was a conspicuous place, and knowing I was still persona non grata with the White House, I asked Wilhelm if he would be more comfortable talking to me elsewhere. After all, there were a number of people, including his close Chicago ally Rahm Emanuel, who would be less than thrilled to know that we were meeting. He said no. He was representing the party, not the White House.

He was blunt. "David, I know you are upset with the events of the last several weeks but the President is still committed to signing an executive order. You have to give him some room to build credibility with Nunn and the military."

"I am a practical person," I answered. "I understand politics and the need to be flexible. But there is a difference between being politically astute and giving credence to arguments that are simply amoral. For Christ's sake, David, Nunn supported Wallace in 1968 and 1972. Why are we allowing him to appear in public as a reasonable man?"

"I can't control Nunn and neither can the White House. We have to work with him in the Senate. He's powerful."

"*You* might have to do that—I understand—but we don't. Maybe the White House can't attack him directly, but it can use the power of the office to present an alternative view and to isolate his policies. Nunn couldn't operate anywhere near as effectively if we'd handled the military better from the beginning. What he's saying about us is outrageous, and it is being left unanswered not only by the President but by the Democratic leadership in Congress. Where is Mitchell? Where is Gephardt?"

Wilhelm wasn't giving. "David, you have to face it. People are afraid of this issue. It could hurt them politically and they're acting accordingly."

"I understand that but we need people of courage. Where would we be today if people had remained silent in the civil rights movement? This is not an issue to be addressed only when it's politically convenient. People are dying. They're losing their jobs, they're the victims of witch-hunts, they're committing suicide. We desperately need courageous moral leadership. We need your help."

"I see the President often. I promise you that your concerns will be heard directly by him. Just give us some room."

"Of course we will. But not at the price of our freedom." And then, because it still festered, I asked, "Please, when you talk to the President be sure he knows that I tried to reach him and that I did not lie. I *was* warned not to go on *Nightline*. I have enough problems without having him believe that I lied on the program."

Wilhelm asked me to make sure to tell Hochberg and Barrer we had met. Fair enough. I thanked him; he had risked some political capital to see me. A couple of people who knew us both stopped to chat. They'd hit the phones the moment they left us. It was a juicy nugget to pass along: Wilhelm right there talking with Mixner.

He promised to call soon with feedback from the President. I felt a lot of respect for him after the meeting. He really did want to build bridges. Unfortunately, the feedback never came.

Not long afterward William Waybourn of the Victory Fund telephoned to tell me the President was going to meet with lesbian and gay leaders in the White House on April 16 to hear their concerns before the Washington march a week later. This was a genuinely historic moment. Never before had a President of the United States met with a group of leaders from our community. With this one stroke he had reminded us of the importance of having him in the White House.

For years I had dreamed of such a meeting and that I would be part of it. I was not. My appearance on *Nightline* wiped that out. In case I hadn't received the message, a *Wall Street Journal* profile of Rahm Emanuel that ran two months later spelled it out.

> *Mr. Emanuel has already left a lot of Democrats licking their wounds. One is David Mixner, who raised more than $1 million for Mr. Clinton's campaign last year but was left out when the President invited a group of gay leaders into the Oval Office. The reason: After Mr. Mixner complained that the President was waffling on his commitment to reverse the ban on homosexuals in the military, Mr. Emanuel froze him out.*

"He unjustly criticized the President," Mr. Emanuel says. "If somebody criticizes the President, then I think they are persona non grata."

I sat alone in my West Hollywood house the day of the meeting. Despite my best efforts, I was feeling sorry for myself. But I knew this day signified progress and I was also hungry to hear what happened. William Waybourn called.

"It was great from start to finish," he said. "We sat down in two rows with him sitting in the center. Almost the first words out of his mouth were that he intended to sign the executive order lifting the ban on July fifteenth as promised."

"Thank God. I feel years younger hearing that."

"Not only that, he is convinced that Congress will not overturn the order and he is on the verge of convincing Colin Powell to support it. He didn't want any of us to tell about this outside the Oval Office."

"Does he really believe that Powell will be with us?"

"That's what he said."

Whatever the President believed when he told this to the meeting, we were never to see the general waver in his opposition to the order. But that day it sounded promising. We wanted to believe it too.

"What else was said?"

"He said he was concerned about political backlash against the administration and gays and lesbians but he realized that this was a risk worth taking. He was adamant that ending discrimination against anyone was essential."

"He's always good when it comes to basic discrimination," I acknowledged. "That's when he is at his most eloquent."

"Are you okay, David?" Waybourn asked. "I know it was rough for you not being there."

I reassured him. "I have no regrets," I said.

Tom Stoddard and Torie Osborn called with similar reports; we really were back on track with the executive order. The President had been unequivocal about signing it. That was a tremendous relief. Given all the problems in and outside the White House and July 15 only three months off, we hadn't let ourselves expect this.

The meeting had led off a week of activity that would culminate in the March on Washington. This was the community's third march on the city and it promised to be the largest. The debate over how the President should respond to it had been endless. The organizers felt that he should address the marchers from the stage. Those of us who were politically involved felt that at the least he should make a video to welcome them to Washington. I still believed that the approach I had laid out in my memo to Stephanopoulos was the right one—that he should not appear at the march but that it was symbolically important that he be there in the White House when it moved past. In fact, he really ought to have held last week's meeting on the morning of the march. That was an opportunity lost.

But the White House staff made up its own mind, decided to get the President out of town during the march, and quickly arranged a visit to Boston. Not that he was alone in fleeing Washington. Senators and House members suddenly remembered pressing engagements back home. Some long-time supporters of the community stayed in Washington, spoke at the rallies, and marched with their constituents from back home. But overall, there probably were more elected officials in Washington when the British invaded it in 1814 than there were on this April day.

I left Los Angeles for Washington a few days beforehand in a plane filled with freedom marchers. There were so many hundreds of thousands of us on the streets of the capital that for these few brief days we experienced the oddity of finding ourselves in the majority. For a little while we had the gift of knowing what it would be like to not have to hide. It was a wonderful feeling. Every once in a while a tourist would huddle his children closer to his side to protect them from us, but incidents like that were rare. Nothing ever really happened to diminish our joyousness.

Every gay and lesbian organization in the country held receptions, dances, parties, and exhibits that weekend to celebrate our community. The prestigious National Press Club, in association with the National Lesbian and Gay Journalists, had invited me to be the keynote speaker at their Friday luncheon. I was nervous because many of Washington's top correspondents would be in the room and the speech was to be carried on C-SPAN over the next several days. But it went extremely well, and there was a standing ovation and a lively question period afterward. Before I spoke I was taken to a side room to autograph a photograph, which would be hung on the Press Club wall with pictures of everyone who has spoken before the club over the years. I'd like to go back there someday and see it. I think I hang between the Dalai Lama and Robert Dole.

Saturday provided us with two highly emotional moments. The National Gay and Lesbian Victory Fund had organized a luncheon to "honor our own." Once again we returned to the Hilton ballroom. We paid tribute to more than sixty openly gay and lesbian elected and appointed officials from all over the country. White House political adviser James Carville spoke at the luncheon, and he managed never to mention the words "homosexual" and "gay" and "lesbian." Carville and I always kept our distance from each other. We both respected the other's talents and skills but I think we knew we would clash over the gay and lesbian issue. Finally came the moment that had brought us together. As their names and offices were announced, one by one the men and women we were honoring ascended the stage and faced the packed ballroom. Before long the stage overflowed. They spilled over into the ballroom and still they kept coming. For those of us who less than a decade before could count the number of open homosexuals in office on the fingers of one hand, the sight was stunning.

That night, the Campaign for Military Service held a fund-raiser at the Ritz-Carlton. All around the room were active duty personnel and veterans, many of them in uniform. Tom Stoddard had asked me to say a few words to the gathering before the dinner. I spoke of the courage of our veterans and how they had inspired us to greatness. I mentioned some of their names. Someone in the crowd shouted out another name. I said, "Call out their names! Everyone, call them out! They deserve to be remembered by us here." The room turned into a roll call of those brave souls who had borne the brunt of the battle—name after name after name. We fell into silence when it was over. I saw David Geffen standing over to the side, visibly moved. He was not alone.

In many ways, Geffen made much of that evening possible. He was one of the first to come forward with desperately needed funds to finance the Campaign for Military Service. Not only did he contribute generously, he used his access to the White House to advocate on behalf of our active duty gay and lesbian military personnel. Since coming out, his generosity has been responsible for the survival and the growth of numerous organizations. It is ironic that the more generous he became, the more people pressed him to give. In those instances where he declined, there were some who criticized him for not being more forthcoming with his funds. It is a baffling lack of gratitude. I know of no single individual in the community who has been more generous not only with his money but with his resources.

The march was triumphant. We started from Constitution Avenue, and as we passed the White House, the conscience of our movement, AIDS activist Larry Kramer, stepped in front of the procession and led us in chanting "Where is Bill?" I looked over at the handsome building and felt its emptiness. What a difference it would have made if the President had been inside! Back in 1969 Nixon had said proudly that he was watching football when the antiwar march passed by. I had hoped for more today. I was saddened that Clinton had fled town.

I love my country. When we turned the corner onto Pennsylvania Avenue and I saw the Capitol at the end, I knew it all over again. Nothing is more powerful than the freedom to march on your government to express your grievances. This was the heart of being an American. We were exercising that right today.

We went up Pennsylvania Avenue. Thousands upon thousands lined the street, cheering and weeping. People held signs for the marchers to see. I saw one elderly woman, bent with age, who was clearly not able to march herself; but as she steadied herself against a lamppost with one hand, she held up a sign with the other. "I love my gay grandson very much. Thank you!" it read.

Six hours after the march began, people were still pouring into the Mall. I was a speaker at the rally, among many in a long program of speeches and music and entertainment. The crowd was so vast that it stretched as far as our eyes could see. There was a message from the President, received politely. Torie Osborn managed an end run around the stage managers who were trying to stay in control and took Larry Kramer up on the stage to speak. Larry has been a controversial figure in the community, barraging us and the straight world and elected officials with his outcries and writings and angry calls to action around the issue of AIDS. I happen to believe he has performed a valuable service. His hard line not only brought more from the government, his passionate rhetoric made it impossible for any of us to forget our duty. There were moments when I grew weary of fighting. Then I'd see Larry in action and I knew we had to go on.

This was to be a memorable weekend for me for another reason—one I had not anticipated. David Ifshin, a long-time mutual friend of the President's and mine, had offered to arrange an escorted tour through the newly opened United States Holocaust Memorial Museum. David had been instrumental in raising funds for the museum and helping with congressional allocations. I went there the day after the march. He and museum official Ralph Grunwald took me through. I was speechless at what I saw and what I learned.

One room was especially shattering. It laid out the extent of the information available to Americans in the 1930s—the early stages of the Holocaust, when the Nazis were building to the ultimate horror—and our country's reaction to that information. I read the headlines that told of the emerging murder of the Jews. I saw the story of the ship *St. Louis*, packed with Jewish refugees from Nazism, as it was turned away from our shores. I saw the deadly evidence of the Roosevelt administration's unwillingness to face what was going on and to act on it. I asked how the Jewish community here had acted as the terrible news became known, and how they had approached the Roosevelt administration. Some had wanted to work quietly behind the scenes. Others fought for a public confrontation of Roosevelt's failure to respond while the horror built into the millions.

It was an all-too-familiar scenario if you were living through the years of AIDS—but in the terrible message of that room I found comfort in my determination to continue speaking out. If we were going to continue to die of AIDS, we were not going to do it "behind the scenes." This country would know that we were here, and that even in our dying we fought gallantly.

That first time at the museum, I thought of my lost brothers and I remembered those books about the Holocaust I had read during the months in Connecticut after Peter's death, and how the astonishing stories of the survivors had helped me to heal. I do not think I realized the depth of the seed that was planted that day; but I was to come back to the Holocaust Museum many, many times later, and it was to become a pivotal part of my life.

After the march, the real world of CMS and the ban took over again. Tom Stoddard had brought together a remarkable staff of bright young lawyers, lesbian and gay veterans, and young students to fight to lift the ban. Chai Feldblum was our legal wizard, a charismatic, intense young woman who is one of the foremost legal scholars in the country. She had clerked for Justice Harry Blackmun and was now teaching at the Georgetown University Law School. Chai was Tom's right hand on the legal aspects of the ban, contacts with the administration, and networking with key legislative leaders. We were trying to do just what the administration had urged us to. From the very beginning the two of them attempted to find their counterparts within the administration so they could coordinate their efforts. But as CMS raised money and set up its first-rate staff, the administration never attempted to coordinate our needs with theirs. Chai outlined media, legal, grassroots, and advocacy as the four areas in which we needed consistent input if we were to be effective. We kept seeking information, strategy, and guidance. None was forthcoming. We'd deal with a staffer one day, and the next day a new one would tell us something completely different. The only consistent element was the absolute reassurance by the White House that the President was going to lift the ban.

As Chai described it, the administration "had punted the ball to the Secretary of Defense and then sat back and waited." Defense Secretary Aspin had kept a very low profile since his memo was leaked in late January. We knew that putting this issue in the hands of Aspin, his staff, and the Joint Chiefs was really going to hurt us. Defense was not friendly territory. Steve Herbits, a high-ranking Seagram's executive who had once worked in Defense, opened a few doors for Chai. But as she said, "Every time I move within this government, I feel that I am being taken in through the back door."

In March and April, Senate Armed Services Committee Chairman Sam Nunn held his infamous hearings on gays and lesbians in the military. Nunn had no intention of making these hearings fair ones. He had an agenda: to set the tone of the debate and to put the administration seriously on the defensive. The committee had asked CMS to suggest witnesses but this was window dressing to preserve the illusion of fairness. Nunn was joined in this public gay-bashing by his fellow Republicans John McCain of Arizona, Coats of Indiana, and Thurmond of South Carolina. They were just as venomous as Nunn.

The administration exerted very little leverage with the Democratic congressional leadership to ensure that we would be treated fairly. Majority Leader George Mitchell was nervous about taking a strong stand because of what he perceived as a lack of support from the White House. We were left to face this contemporary version of McCarthyism on our own. We even had to fight, often unsuccessfully, to have our witnesses treated with respect and dignity.

The full press was in attendance. At the witness table were half a dozen of our finest gay and lesbian military personnel, including Margarethe Cammermeyer, Tracy Thorne, and Keith Meinhold. They came in uniform to confront not only their accusers but the nation with their proud determination to serve their country. They never had a chance.

The senators brought forth every homosexual stereotype and scare tactic. They spoke of uncontrollable sexual urges, of straight service members in jeopardy in the showers, of the imminence of molestation.

Thurmond leaned over the podium and urged the witnesses to seek psychiatric help because they were mentally unfit. They did not flinch but they were helpless against the invective.

The more I watched the hearings on my television set, the angrier I got. Finally I grabbed a phone, called a White House staffer I knew, and expressed my horror at the lynch mob conducting the hearing. "You guys have got to *do* something," I said, trying to keep myself under control. "We're getting creamed on the Hill. Why isn't Mitchell exerting leadership? What the hell is going on here?"

"Dave, take it easy. We're doing the best we can."

"No, you are not. You know and I know that these hearings are going to make it impossible for the President to have maneuvering room."

"It's a Senate matter and we have to work with Nunn on other issues."

I had to really check my temper at that. It seemed to be a mantra among Washington insiders. David Wilhelm had said the identical thing. As I saw it, this was no more than a way to relieve themselves of responsibility for the very hot potato no one wanted to handle.

"I am not asking you to ram your ship into an iceberg, but how about some good, old-fashioned coordination? A team captain? Hell, how about just having a team on the field?"

"David," said the White House man in a patient voice, "you have been dealing with this issue for twenty years. You know what we are dealing with here. None of these career-building staffers want to make their mark on the 'queer desk.' No one wants to be in charge of this issue. They keep telling me that it's at the Pentagon and the President is waiting for their report."

I hung up the phone and slumped back in my office chair. I knew what he said was true.

There was worse to come. On a rare weekend at home that May I was sitting in my big overstuffed chair doing one of my favorite things in the world: reading the Sunday newspapers. When I can, I save Sunday mornings for me. I put on religious music, go through the papers, meditate, and read books. This morning I had a Forester Sisters album of religious hymns playing on the stereo. My cats were lying nearby. It was utterly peaceful. The phone rang and it was Tom.

I could tell by his voice that something had happened. "Have you seen the Boston newspapers?" he asked.

"Believe it or not, they don't deliver Boston papers in Los Angeles, Tom. What's going on?"

"Barney Frank had an interview in which he says he would support a version of lifting the ban that would limit our free speech on base, but would make 'off-base' conduct off-limits to the military."

This was my first introduction to "Don't Ask, Don't Tell" and I couldn't believe my ears. It meant an entirely different set of different standards for homosexuals than were applied to straight service members.

"You're joking."

"No. I am serious. He said that any knowledge of homosexuality on base would be grounds for dismissal. Off base, we could have freedom."

"Jesus, Tom, has he talked to you about this? You two have had a good friendship. Did he call anyone?"

"Nope. But this certainly hurts our efforts to totally lift the ban. It sets one standard for us and another for the straights. I have a call in to him, but once Barney makes up his mind no one can change it. Trust me, I know."

I knew it too. For the first time I acknowledged we were in real trouble. I had no idea whether Frank had spoken to the White House but I knew he was the consummate insider. He would not have said what he did without White House approval.

I had known Barney Frank for a number of years. He is without question one of the most brilliant people in Congress. No one can debate with the bulldog tenacity of Barney. He is assured, even self-righteous, about his beliefs and is willing to fight for them without compromise. He is a passionate and articulate defender of the system. Since coming out of the closet he has been more determined than ever to have the approval of the Democratic liberal establishment. It seems clear to me that he decided the way to be most effective was being a powerful insider. In many ways, he was right. Having access to the corridors of power can have more of an impact than a thousand marches. In other ways, it has put him at frequent odds with an emerging, anxious homosexual civil rights movement.

At times, our struggle and actions outside the Beltway have definitely made Barney's job more difficult. None of us had been spared his angry calls telling us everything we were doing was wrong. There never is dialogue with Barney, just plain orders—or else an angry tirade about our failures as a movement. He sees a single way, a single road only. He hasn't the temperament to strategize by taking a diversity of approaches and shaping them into a single powerful force.

In the movement, he is the Lone Ranger. When gays and lesbians in California were bitterly opposing Governor Deukmajian's appointment of Republican Congressperson Dan Lungren to be Attorney General of

California because of his anti-gay record, Barney, without letting any of
us know, wrote a warm letter about his "congressional colleague" that
undercut our efforts to stop the nomination.

We all have our jobs to do in this movement and Congressperson
Frank has chosen the path that he believes is the most effective. He
decides what issues matter most to him, and plays an establishment role
to insure that he gets his way on them. If that means backing some other
choices that don't conform to his basic liberalism, so be it. The Lundgren support is an example.

By its very nature, Barney's road is not compatible with a grassroots
effort. But I deeply believe that by becoming a team player in the establishment he is invaluable to our struggle. No one understands Congress
better than Barney Frank. There is no doubt in my mind that he will go
down in history as one of the most effective and powerful of all congressional leaders. Despite our differences, he is a source of great pride to
many of us in the community.

That said, his interview in the Boston paper caused us untold problems. The blatant meanness of the Nunn hearings had increased our
fund-raising momentum. We were bringing in new coalition allies.
Frank set up doubts all over the place. He did return Tom Stoddard's
call and they arranged for Barney to attend the next weekly staff meeting
of CMS. He said there that he had been misquoted and would be holding a press conference to clarify his views. But he refused to let anyone
from CMS attend the conference, and at it he went even further than he
had in the interview, basically coming down in favor of the initial version
of "Don't Ask, Don't Tell" being pushed by Sam Nunn.

It made our efforts for a total lifting of the ban infinitely harder.
Members of Congress from the Midwest and border states who were key
undecided votes started to distance themselves from us. They saw Barney as the spokesperson for the movement. If he wasn't willing to support this, how could we expect them to? He had single-handedly stopped
his own community's momentum in its tracks. And as I realized the
moment I read the interview, his advocacy for this position in all likelihood had White House support.

Under the leadership of Fred and Tom and Chai, we pulled ourselves
together. We still had a battle to wage. Our effective Washington advocate, Tom Sheridan, helped us prepare a memo, to be circulated within
the community and the administration, outlining what we considered the
essential elements in the President's proposal. Anything less would be

considered a deal-breaker. Chai continued to meet with Pentagon officials. Tom's and her contact in the White House was Stephanopoulos. They made sure that all of them knew our bottom-line position. Chai made it very clear to administration members that we would rather lose in the Senate and continue the old policy than have the President of the United States endorse a 1940 policy in 1993 by dressing it up differently. This way the President would not be required to defend an unacceptable policy and the blame would be the Senate's. Chai reported that White House officials were "shocked" by the suggestion.

In early June I traveled to Boston. General Colin Powell had been invited to receive an honorary degree from Harvard University. I found it hard to believe Harvard had decided to honor a man who had become a spokesperson for discrimination against homosexuals. The last months had seen Powell repeatedly play into the worse fears an uninformed public had about us. He was quoted in *U.S. News and World Report* as saying: "[We] will be under constant pressure to show equality to a community whose mores we don't understand. . . ."

It sounded as if the general believed that Americans who didn't fit the mold had no right to Constitutional guarantees of freedom if they made other Americans uncomfortable. If that were the criterion for equal rights, then Powell as an African-American would never have had the opportunity to become chairman of the Joint Chiefs. Now he had had the opportunity to rise to greatness by opening the door of freedom to millions of his country's citizens and he failed to do so. More than any single individual, he made the President's decision difficult. He gave comfort to the bigots.

The Boston and Harvard gay and lesbian communities had been working hard to organize a protest. They were validly concerned about not showing disrespect to an African-American of great achievement, but they wanted to demonstrate that the honor was not appropriate at this time. They asked me to attend. The university, very wisely, worked closely with the community and us to avoid miscommunication or unwanted incidents. It was decided that when General Powell received his degree, those who were opposed would stand silently in protest.

The ceremonies were held in Harvard Yard in the bright June sunshine. Many of the gay and lesbian graduates and their supporters had tied pink balloons to their chairs and they waved over the heads of the throng and lent a festive air to the scene. Harvard was a liberal place and I was eager to see the extent of support we would find here. As it proved, not very much. As the general was presented with his degree, the crowd roared its approval. No more than a few dozen people stood.

Powell was brief and gracious in his remarks. Reading between the lines we found some hope in his presentation. He did compare our struggle to that of women and of African-Americans breaking into the military. Most importantly to us, he said, ". . . once the decision [on the ban] is made, we will faithfully execute it to the best of our ability." This was surely an opening to the President if he chose to hear it. I thought the President should accept Powell's statement at face value, call him to the White House, and move on the executive order. The White House never reacted.

We were in deep trouble. Our theme at CMS shifted from "Lift the Ban" to "No Compromise." By the end of June we were fighting the inevitable, although we were still fighting. One hundred religious leaders from all faiths sent a letter to President Clinton on June 28 saying: "We urge you to stand by your principles. It is immoral for the nation's largest employer to discriminate. It is immoral for the government to force people to lie. . . . We know from personal experience that there is a price for leadership on this issue. We also know there is a greater price to the nation for failure to meet very basic human rights. . . . We urge you to offer this principled leadership."

Tom, Chai, and the CMS team worked night and day to stem the tide that was surrendering us to the mob. Chai quietly worked with her contacts in the Defense Department to have them at least meet our minimum standards. At the end of June, Jamie Gorelick called Chai to a meeting in the Defense Department and basically described the "Don't Ask, Don't Tell" policy to her as a possible option. An option. Did that mean nothing was yet fixed in stone? We started working our contacts at the White House. Only our faith in the President's word kept us going.

Tom and Chai spoke with Stephanopoulos to let him know that such a policy would be a living disaster. George was noncommittal. He said he would get back to them. He didn't. Instead we kept reading carefully orchestrated leaks in *The Washington Post* from the Department of Defense. We were being outmaneuvered in the press and we had to take action. We conferred, and then Chai and Tom called *The New York Times* and briefed Eric Schmitt about the emerging policy. The *Times* story motivated Stephanopoulos to call back at last. He was in a fury. He had no interest in discussing the policy. What he had in mind were threats. He said that CMS had "acted inappropriately and access to the White House was now cut off." There would be no meetings to discuss this policy with the gay and lesbian community. Finis.

Chai saw no indication he cared in the least that the Pentagon had been placing stories in the paper on a daily basis. What she did feel was that the call was his way of not having to face us just before, in her words, "selling us down the river."

Throughout the first two weeks of July, it was clear what was going to happen. No one from the White House would return our calls. On July 14 *The Washington Post* stated that "Don't Ask, Don't Tell" was going to be the President's policy. Still no word from the White House. They left us twisting in the wind. We felt utterly powerless. In her book *On the Edge: The Clinton Presidency*, writer and reporter Elizabeth Drew has given one of the few descriptions of the last days of the decision-making inside the White House. Drew describes a meeting held on the night of July 14 in which Vice President Gore had a rare argument with the President.

> *At a meeting on Wednesday night, July 14, in the President's study in the residence, the issue was argued bitterly. Gore insisted that the President shouldn't compromise, that it was a matter of principle. The President should just lift the ban, Gore argued, even though he was sure to be overridden by the Congress. Aspin argued for accepting the compromise, saying it was as far as the Chiefs would go.*

On July 15 I had a call from Stephanopoulos at last. "We are still drafting the policy," he said, "and I feel that you will be pleasantly surprised. The President and I hope you will know that he did his best and that you will support the policy." He did not outline the policy except to say that what was being reported was reasonably accurate. He indicated that over the weekend the White House would be including new language that would ensure our protection.

As I listened, I wondered if he really thought we were all fools. Or maybe he had gotten so used to being a spin doctor for White House policy that he had lost contact with how people felt when they heard him. He was feeding me a line of bullshit. I knew it and he knew it. Why couldn't he be direct, treat me with respect and not insult my intelligence? In our brief conversation I informed him that I would not be able to support anything approaching a "Don't Ask, Don't Tell" policy, and that I did not think they had "done their best." With an edge in his voice, he said, "David, we have done everything we can. We can do no more. This issue is dead." The CMS team got their calls from him the same day. I never heard from the President.

On July 19, Clinton announced his policy. Elizabeth Drew described the scene:

. . . the President announced his new policy in a speech at the National Defense University at Fort McNair, across the Potomac. Speaking to a sea of uniforms, and with an array of flags behind him, Clinton spoke somberly. . . . He was virtually begging for the military's approval: "I'm here because I respect you." He didn't look like a Commander in Chief.

CHAPTER EIGHTEEN

We Are Not Afraid . . .

I SAT with Jeremy and Tony as the President finished his speech. We couldn't bear to look at each other. It didn't matter that we had known almost certainly what was coming. The reality was still stunning.

I told them I needed to think. I had to have a clear head before I talked to anyone. I took a long walk and I then went to the sundeck on the top of my house. It was hard to journey past the pain. Slowly, very slowly, I grasped the enormity of what had just happened. I knew what my path had to be; that hadn't changed. Toward freedom and a cure. I would use what little access I had to show that we would not take this sitting down.

When I went back to the office downstairs, there were basically two kinds of messages: a few that said the President had done the best he could—mostly, but not all, from straight politicians; and the rest from people in a state of outrage and pain—mostly, but not all, gay. I talked to Tom and Chai and Fred at CMS. They had assessed the speech as I had.

The entire staff of CMS felt as though a good friend had died and some were in tears.

I called William Waybourn of the Victory Fund and Tim McFeeley of HRCF and their reactions were the same. Without exception, those who had been most involved in this battle felt betrayed. Tim wanted HRCF to display its contempt for the new policy publicly, and decided that he and a few other members would be arrested in front of the White House. It was a spontaneous impulse of outrage and there was no effort to include others.

The President's decision was the lead story in most of the media. Editorial reaction was mixed. Some papers strongly hinted that Clinton had failed in his effort to integrate gays and lesbians in the military. Others praised him for doing the best he could, given the military's opposition. The community's press was uniformly outraged.

I accepted an invitation to be a guest on *Good Morning America* at four the next morning Los Angeles time; and I shared our sense of betrayal and strongly criticized the President's policy. And I turned in my time of need, as I so often did, to the Reverend Troy Perry. I had long been scheduled to speak at the International Conference of Metropolitan Community Churches in Phoenix. Would Troy be willing to let me use the occasion of the speech as a forum to respond to the President's message? "Take whatever time you need," he said. "Use it to tell them how we feel!"

As with the last time I had spoken in the sanctuary in Dallas, I wrote down what I wanted to say. This too was not a time to allow for misquotation. Then I flew to Phoenix. I listened to the sermon and then to a young African-American delegate from Houston as she stood and sang the song that singer Holly Near had turned into the gay and lesbian anthem: "We are a gentle loving people who are fighting for our lives . . ."

Reverend Perry mounted the altar. My pastor, Reverend Nancy Wilson, was onstage to give me support, as Troy introduced me and said a prayer.

I began by saying that God is about truth as well as love, and I delivered my response to the President's "Don't Ask, Don't Tell" policy. I spoke of the pain of a community betrayed. I said, "Quite simply, the President of the United States has failed to keep his promise." I warned the delegates that the White House would be telling us how much they had done. I said that the President by his actions had failed to take his place in history as a president of courage. I spoke of the victories that we had won in this battle, of our long struggle, of the more than a dozen firebombed churches of MCC and how the parishioners had rebuilt a future out of their ashes. I reminded them all of the painful journey of our coming out. I once again praised the courage of our veterans and active duty personnel who would suffer the most from this issue. Then I reminded the crowd of our obligation to continue the battle no matter how weary or discouraged we felt: "We will not pass this pain on to the next generation of lesbians and gays. We will not leave this decade without our freedom. . . . We will not be silent gays and lesbians. We will be fighting lesbians and gays. And most of all, Mr. President, we will be free. . . . That, Mr. President, is our promise to you."

As I finished the Reverend Wilson held me tight and kept me strong. I had said what I needed to say.

That afternoon I returned to Los Angeles and started consulting with the leadership of the community about where to go from here. Tim McFeeley and some HRCF staffers had already conducted their symbolic protest and been arrested for refusing to move from the front of the White House. The CMS staff was thinking similarly and called to ask whether I would join them. I brooded over what this would accomplish. It was certainly not going to change the President's mind. But then I reconsidered. I could see two reasons to protest. The first was as an act of conscience. Not to practice the Quaker tradition of giving witness against injustice was out of the question. What had happened was of a magnitude that required people of good conscience to take a stand.

Second, the straight community and many in the gay and lesbian community initially did not realize what a disaster this new policy was for us. People wanted to believe in their hearts that the President had done his best. He had only been in office half a year or so, and they wanted to cling to the enthusiasm they had felt at his inauguration. In addition, outside the community many wished the issue of homosexuality was simply not so prominent. Who needed it this early in the new administration? It wasn't that they were bigots. They didn't feel like taking a stand for homosexual rights and they couldn't see why it should be a priority on the national agenda. They wanted the whole thing to disappear so the President could get on with "real" issues.

By being arrested, we would send them a powerful message that this policy was a serious mistake. Neither the White House nor anyone else would be able to sweep this new policy under the rug. So I called and said I would join them but that it was important to do it right. I also wanted to be sure that we had representation from the West Coast. We set a day for a week away.

ANGLE, which had been the first lesbian and gay group in the country to support Bill Clinton, wrote him a blistering letter condemning his policy and agreed to send members to participate in the protest. Patricia Ireland, the charismatic leader of the National Organization for Women, volunteered to have NOW handle the logistics of the protest, train the newcomers in the philosophy and tactics of civil disobedience, and be arrested herself. I traveled from California with ANGLE participants Diane Abbitt, Roberta Bennett, and civil rights attorney John Duran. Tony Leonhardt and Jeremy came along too. Tony was going to be arrested for the first time in his life. Jeremy, to his dismay, was selected as our point person outside the jail.

On Thursday, July 29, the entire CMS team gathered together to break bread one final time and to honor the leadership of Tom Stoddard. It was a bittersweet evening. We had become family as well as friends. Bob Shrum and Marylouise Oates joined us. They had stood by our side unflinchingly, even though they risked the wrath of the White House by supporting us. We laughed and we cried through the toasts and the memories and the resolve not to give up.

At ten the next morning everyone reported to the national headquarters of NOW to prepare for our arrest. A number of uniformed veterans joined us. Alice Cohan of NOW gave us a brisk, thorough course in the philosophy and tactics of civil disobedience. She described nonviolent actions ranging from Gandhi to Martin Luther King, Jr., and made sure we understood the seriousness of what we were about to do. She used role-playing to prepare us for hecklers; some of us shouted epithets like "Faggot!" and "Queers!" and worse at the others. We were pushed and shoved. We learned how to react nonviolently to verbal and physical assaults. We practiced old civil rights hymns like "We Shall Not Be Moved" as one way to respond to the anger. She also gave us a detailed account of the arrest procedure and told us we could choose whether to be led to the patrol wagons or be carried to them by the police.

Before we wrapped up our training, Alice went around the room and asked each of us to tell why we had decided to join this action. Jeff Matchan had devoted his life to the military from the day he entered the Air Force Academy, but left the Air Force as a captain when he decided he could no longer live a lie. He saw his arrest as a symbol to insure that no other service people would have to experience the pain he had felt when he had to give up the career he loved. Tony Leonhardt talked about a lifetime of fear about his gayness, and about the thousands of hours he had devoted to the election of Clinton in order to obtain his freedom. This would be the first time he had fought back. The Reverend

Mel White of MCC spoke with difficulty of his years of writing speeches for Pat Robertson and Jerry Falwell, ministers themselves, and how this arrest was both an atonement for those years and a message to his old compatriots in the religious right.

A deep sense of purpose arose from the intimacy of this sharing. As our small march, perhaps a hundred in all, made its way to Lafayette Park across from the White House, our lesbian and gay veterans led the way. They held up American flags and the rainbow flag of our movement and they wore their medals proudly. Camera crews and reporters crowded around us in the park and Patricia Ireland spoke eloquently about the reason for our act. Then we crossed the street to the front of the White House. I could see some of my colleagues and political "allies" looking at us from the windows to watch the arrests. I knew that with this action I was never again likely to enter its gates. I felt an overwhelming sense of loss.

We stood quietly for a while, then sang all the great familiar songs: "We Shall Overcome," "We Are Gentle, Angry People," "We Will Not Be Moved." Police vehicles moved in front of the White House. Across the street, hundreds had gathered to cheer us on. The lead officer of the Park Police repeated a warning to disperse three times. A person who said he was from Act Up kept screaming into my ear that I was Clinton's lapdog until I thought my eardrum would burst. (He disappeared as soon as the arrests began.) Tony and Jeff were right behind me. Jeremy was across the street taking photographs in case there were any problems.

It was very hot and humid. Roberta and Diane were handcuffed and put into the back of a police van. Patricia Ireland, William Waybourn, and Mel White stepped proudly forward, singing aloud as the handcuffs were placed on their wrists. John and Tony and Jeff walked calmly to the van. Then it was my turn. This was what the press had been waiting for: this well-known FOB—"Friend of Bill's"—to be arrested outside the President's house. The cameras whirred as I was handcuffed. I had forgotten they take away your belt and shoelaces, and for a moment all I could think of was my pants dropping in front of all the cameras.

There were separate vans for the men and the women. A tough-looking, rather sour policeman led me over to join my friends. As he helped me inside, I said, "Sir, I have a favor to ask of you." He barked, "What?" I felt a little silly but I asked him nonetheless, "When we pull out from in front of the White House, could you use the siren just once? I want those inside to hear the sound of our pain." Rough and tough he may have been but mean he wasn't. "Sure thing," he answered. "You people have guts."

It was sweltering inside the van. Some of those arrested were HIV-positive and I was worried about their health. We sat there, hands cuffed behind our backs, until the arrests were completed. Appropriately, a veteran in uniform was the last one in. He had sat down on the sidewalk in order to be carried off to jail. As our van drove off the siren sounded. We cheered.

The vans pulled up in front of the Park Police station in Southeast Washington. One by one we were led out and taken inside. The officer behind the counter asked us our names and then we were put in holding cells until we could be officially booked—the women in one cell, the men in another. Our cell was small, perhaps six feet by ten, cinder blocks on all sides except for a huge metal door with a tiny opening through which we could peer into the booking room. There was a bench on one side but we were packed in so tightly that it was hard to sit. But our spirits were high. John Duran kept us laughing and singing for the several hours that we stood, waiting, with our hands cuffed behind our backs.

We discovered that we could communicate with the women in the next cell through the vent in the ceiling if we stood on the bench and shouted into it. Diane and Roberta and I kept yelling messages back and forth to each other, repeating bad lines from tenth-rate prisoner movies like "What will you do for a cigarette, babe?"

But despite the good spirits it got very uncomfortable, and each time the door swung open, each of us hoped that he would be the next one booked. One by one we were taken out of the cell, our cuffs removed, and then brought into the main room of the station. I had been through all this before, but it felt different this time. This was not how I envisioned spending my time in the Clinton presidency—having my mug shot taken in a police station. I thought of what the shot must look like, the numbers across my chest. The flash went off.

At one of the desks they filled out the arrest reports. One of the questions asked us whether we went "by any other names." John Duran, our jailhouse cheerleader, couldn't help himself, started laughing, and said, "Well, sometimes I have been called 'Mary' by my friends." It broke us up. Finally we could pay our bail and leave. (The bail would be turned into a fine, so we would not have to make a court appearance.) I came out into the bright sunlight and felt like a free man again. Literally free. This too was what "free" meant. But as I walked to the nearest subway station I knew that today my world had changed. I had closed off a part of it for good.

During the next couple of days, several friends called from within the

White House to report how furious people there were about my setting up my arrest. One of the angry ones called too. "In front of the White House!" he shouted. "How could you?"

"It is my house too," I said coldly.

Perhaps naively, I was amazed at the intensity of the White House's reaction. But there are those I will always respect for not bowing to peer pressure and cutting off contact with me. This small number includes Undersecretary of State Tim Wirth and his wife Wren. I was lying in my hotel room, worn out, soon after I was released from jail, when the telephone rang. It was Tim and Wren. They invited me to join them at the State Department for lunch on Monday in the exclusive Secretary's dining room. I said, "You know that I was arrested in front of the White House, don't you?"

"Yes. So?"

"Well, given that I'm on the shit list, maybe we should meet in a less visible spot than the Secretary's dining room. The White House is not going to be thrilled at your escorting me to lunch."

"David, we are not dumb," said Wren. "We know politics. You are our friend. We have always been proud of you and proud to be seen with you. It will be at the State Department, period."

Wren was waiting for me in the lobby when I arrived at the State Department building in Foggy Bottom. She gave me a great big greeting and took me up to the top floor and into the formal dining room where we were to meet Tim. As we walked across the room I literally heard the silence. The eyes followed us to Tim's table. My arrest had been in all of the Washington newspapers; they all knew who I was. They watched presidential appointee Tim Wirth greet me enthusiastically and take me over to get our salads. He wanted to know all about the arrests and what it was like to go to jail, and Wren couldn't get enough of the details. When we finished lunch, I said my good-byes to Tim and Wren escorted me back downstairs to catch a cab. As we passed through the security area, a military officer passed close to me and said as he moved on, "Thank you, Mr. Mixner." It never stopped.

I don't think Tim and Wren can ever imagine how much that act of kindness meant to me. I did not see much of that kind of generosity—or courage—from other straight friends in the administration.

That was a day with cheer in it and there was more to come in the afternoon. Patsy called to tell me she had been having some problems with her teenage daughters, my nieces. Julia and Elizabeth were upset because they felt their parents should have let them come east and be arrested with their uncle. Patsy and Michael had reached an agreement with them that once they were eighteen, they could be arrested with their uncle anytime they wanted. I liked that. If my nieces were willing to get arrested, then there was hope for the future. Political access and power don't bring you acts of love like this.

The next morning in my hotel, as the door of the elevator opened, George Stephanopoulos stepped out as I was waiting to go in. He was so startled that we almost bumped into each other. It took me a second but I said, "Hello, George, how are you?"

"Fine, David, good to see you out of jail."

"Well, George, it is good to be out of jail."

With that he moved on. I could see the others waiting to catch the elevator scratching their heads. As for me, I felt anger. This was the man who said that I would find something to support in the new policy. At the least, I thought he owed me more courtesy than that.

There was to be one final act in this battle. Until now, the President had had the power to integrate homosexuals into the military by a simple executive order. All it required was his signature. But under the new compromise he had agreed to, Congress would now pass legislation that would take that authority away from the President and "codify" the "Don't Ask, Don't Tell" policy into law. To repeal the policy from now on would require an act of Congress. Congress began to process Senate Bill 1298, which would make the "Don't Ask, Don't Tell" policy the law of the land. The President and the Democratic leadership had all agreed to support it. Our path to freedom in the future would be all the harder.

Our CMS legal counsel Chai Feldblum was determined that there be a debate and a vote in the Congress. The gay and lesbian community deserved a roll call vote on so substantive a matter. Chai believed that a vote like this would show the skeptics the strong support we had in Congress for lifting the ban, and would also vividly demonstrate to the community who its allies were in a time of crisis. She wanted to prove that if the White House had made the courageous choice to lift the ban, we would have had a shot at winning in the Senate.

Chai organized a group of freshman senators, led by dynamic Barbara Boxer of California, to submit an amendment to SB 1298. The amendment, if passed, would gut the legislation, and thereby override the new policy and return the power to determine the status of homosexuals in the military to the President and his advisers. By the mere act of submitting the amendment, a debate and vote would be forced on the reluctant senators.

But the White House congressional operation, the President's staff that works on congressional matters, decided to continue to support the "compromise." It went all out to defeat the amendment proposed by the Senate freshmen. Very systematically it called senators and asked them not to vote for the amendment. Senator Nunn's forces got into action too, submitting a string of amendments making it even easier for the military to dismiss homosexuals under the new policy. In direct contrast to its vigorous actions on Boxer, the White House made little effort to defeat the Nunn amendments. All it wanted was to see the legislation passed and this disastrous debate over and done.

So here we were once again, not only fighting well-known gay-bashers like Senator Nunn but also our own president and the entire Democratic leadership in Congress. Majority Leader George Mitchell, who had been so weak and vacillating in the early days of the debate, showed real enthusiasm for lining up votes for the "Don't Ask, Don't Tell" policy.

As Mitchell was out collecting votes against the Boxer Amendment from his fellow Democrats in the Senate, I was making numerous calls and personal visits to senators in an effort to gain votes for it. On September 9 we got our debate and roll call vote. To our amazement, the Senate's three most decorated veterans—Charles Robb of Virginia, Senator Robert Kerrey of Nebraska, and Senator John Kerry of Massachusetts—stood up and passionately supported the Boxer Amendment. Both Robb and Robert Kerrey were up for reelection in their traditionally conservative states in 1994, yet they were undaunted. Vietnam veteran Robert Kerrey took the floor.

> This is not an act [the vote to support Boxer] based upon some desire to put together, as I said, a coalition. That does not show up on an opinion poll. It never does. We cannot afford to allow any of our personnel policies, whether it is in the Congress or in the military, to be guided by intolerant behavior, whether that intolerant behavior is religious or otherwise.
>
> I believe it is time for the military to change its policies. I acknowledge that it is a traumatic change. I suspect that time will show it is not as traumatic as we, or at least some, are saying it is going to be. It is time for the military to change. And those Americans who want to serve their country, those Americans who say their sexual orientation is homosexual and want to serve their country, if they can satisfy all other requirements, if they meet all other standards, we should allow them to serve.

The honor, courage, and years of military service that these senators brought to the debate was offset by its opponents, who constantly reminded us that the President supported this new policy. Senator Strom Thurmond started it off.

> *Homosexual acts or the propensity to commit those acts are detrimental—I repeat—detrimental to an effective, efficient military. For that reason, we have formulated the legislation now before the Senate today. It is noteworthy that the Secretary of Defense's working group and advisers came to a very similar conclusion after their own studies and deliberations.*

Right-wing Senator Phil Gramm of Texas once again used the President's endorsement of the compromise against us:

> *The senator from California would have us strike that workable policy and give this issue back to the President. There is no evidence that the President wants the issue back. There is no evidence that the President is unhappy with what the Armed Forces Committee did. . . . I do not think we ought to put this ball back in the President's court. I do not think the President has asked for it back. I am not aware of an official White House position in support of this amendment.*

Finally, Dan Coats, the floor leader against us, summed up their arguments.

> *So the question we face today is a simple one. Do we not trust President Clinton, Secretary Aspin, and General Powell to honorably carry out the policy that they arrived at after so much soul-searching and debate?*

At last came the roll call vote that the gay and lesbian community had sought. The results were exactly what we had expected. We felt vindicated. Thirty-three senators voted for the Boxer Amendment. We had garnered enough votes to support the President on a veto if he had dared to take on Senator Nunn. In fact, if the President had stood strong, some of the eighteen liberal and moderate senators who voted against us (such as Rockefeller, Packwood, Kohl, Wofford, Specter, and Mitchell) would probably have supported us. It was even possible there would have been enough votes to win outright.

But there wasn't much reward in vindication. It was impossible not to think "if only" this time, discovering that we had had a good chance of winning this battle if only we had a leader willing to go the route, to fight in the spirit of Truman and Kennedy.

On October 8 the Names Project brought the panels of the AIDS Quilt Los Angeles area to the Pacific Design Center in West Hollywood. This monument to our dead has always overwhelmed me. Every time I have the opportunity, I attend an unveiling of the Quilt. It is a sacred and honored creation. The organizers asked if I would attend the unveiling and read the names of some of my friends on the Quilt. I opened my journal and went down the list of over two hundred names of my friends who had died of AIDS. How could I pick those I wanted to honor that night? How could I choose among them?

In 1987 volunteers in San Francisco led by activist Clive Jones had originated the idea of an AIDS Quilt. They modeled it after quilt-making in the pioneer days of the Old West, where neighbors would use the making of a quilt as a way to create and maintain a community. For the AIDS community, it became a way to share our grief and to remember those we loved who died. Each three-by-six-foot panel, created by family or friends, memorialized the one they lost. When I first witnessed the Quilt at the March on Washington in 1987, it took up a stretch of the Mall between the Capitol and the Washington Monument about the length of two football fields. Today, sadly, it would stretch all the way from the Capitol to the Lincoln Memorial and it would still be pushed for space.

I entered the ultra-modern Pacific Design Center and registered for my participation in the opening ceremony. The unveiling began and it was my turn to read the names of my friends. As I stood at the microphone in the cavernous space, the names ricocheted from one wall to the other, pounding the absences into my head. When I reached Peter's name, I could barely say it.

Shaken, I walked away from the podium to pay respect to our dead represented on the panels. I couldn't manage it. I needed to sit down. I found a chair in a corner, and saw that unknowingly, I had seated myself in front of Peter's panel. It was hung together with the panels of several other close friends we had lost. I tried to remember times we had been happy. I could not. All I could think of was the terrible waste to have lost all this talent and love. A kind young man brought me some tissues and gently wiped my eyes. "It's okay, Mr. Mixner," he said. "We all feel the same pain."

Then I was able to remember Peter. I thought about his courage. He did not surrender to his disease—he fought it with all his heart. He was gone now. I had to give voice not only to him but all my other friends who had died. Those of us who are left just had to work harder, and speak more forcefully, to give their valiant struggles value and purpose. Their voices could only be silenced if I failed to continue to speak up and do battle. I arose from the chair, squared my shoulders, and walked out of the building, ready to go on.

Less than two weeks later I received a call from Presidential Assistant Marsha Scott at the White House. Marsha and I had met in the Clinton/ Gore campaign and became close friends. She and the President had known each other since Marsha was nineteen, in Arkansas. Because of that friendship and the access it created, her power was greater than her position as Presidential Assistant for White House Correspondence would suggest. Marsha was in Los Angeles, and she asked if I was willing to have lunch with her at Hugo's on October 19.

This was my first contact with anyone directly in the White House since being arrested. My curiosity was aroused and I could hardly wait. Marsha was one of those White House staffers whose absolute loyalty to the President was matched by a strong support of lesbian and gay rights. She had come to this commitment through personal friends—she had lost several of them to AIDS—and out of her work with the community in the campaign.

Marsha got right to the point. She was distressed and dismayed that the President and I were not speaking. She felt our friendship of more than twenty years had been seriously damaged by the disagreement over the policy around the military. She wanted to know if I would be willing to visit the President if he was agreeable to it. "He is greatly saddened by the tension between the two of you," she said.

I have trusted her over the years but I honestly did not know if I could trust her about the President's feelings.

"I miss him too, Marsha," I said at last.

"You two can be very stubborn when you dig in your heels. You're so much alike in many ways."

I said I would love to see him, but there were qualifications. "I can't do it if it is interpreted as endorsing the military policy. I have to have the same freedom to disagree with the President that I see others have. Our movement for civil rights must come first."

Marsha had no argument with that. "I understand," she said, and I believed her. "But, David, this is a twenty-year friendship and I want to make an effort to heal the rift. It's not only good for the two of you personally but also for the presidency and the community. There's too much work to be done."

"I am willing. I'm as unhappy about the rift between us as you are. But where do we go from here?"

"Would you be willing to write him a note and tell him that?"

I was taken aback by her request. Tell him I would like to heal the rift? It could certainly not be a letter of apology; I would not do that. It was one of those moments where you have to make a quick decision and can only pray you make the correct one. I wasn't sure I understood the request for the note. I didn't know how I really felt about the whole idea. I took a deep breath and agreed. "Of course," I said. If on reflection I changed my mind, I would be frank with her.

Back home I sat and considered what was happening. I knew I was still angry and hurt by what Clinton had done. Why should I meet with him? I still believed he had betrayed us. Then I thought about it all from where he sat. He too must have had to come to terms with why he should want to meet with me. I was sure he felt betrayed by my arrest. I also realized he must have been thinking of those millions of gay and lesbian votes in key states like California and New York and the need to mend fences with the community.

Well, I had my reasons too. It was in both our interests to open up communication again, his political, mine for the movement. We would be using each other. But putting aside the military issue, there was so much work still to be done, and to be done with this President. I had to get over my anger. I knew the feeling between the two of us would never be the same, but that no longer mattered. I walked around the room composing the words I wanted to say to him and then I sent the letter to Marsha to be hand-delivered to him.

Dear Mr. President:

This past year has been a long and difficult one. We would both have desired different results for our efforts.

The news that you are willing to meet and discuss ways to put the past behind us and to move forward was encouraging and meant a great deal to me. There is so much yet to be done and I still deeply believe in the vision you articulated for the gay and lesbian community. If we can build a cooperative spirit, reasonable expectations, and first-rate communication, our goal of a discrimination-free America has a chance.

I know that we both would welcome the opportunity for private conversation to enable us to move forward.

We can, of course, both enthusiastically agree that we are very fortunate indeed to have Marsha Scott as a friend.

My sincere best wishes.

In peace,

David B. Mixner

Once it was in the mail I decided not to worry about it. If I had a response, I would regard it as progress. If I didn't hear anything, it would be an indication I should remove whatever expectations I had.

In fact, several weeks went by without an answer, but I thought this understandable given the extreme burdens of the office. In early December I came east to give a speech at Brown University at the request of Marylouise Oates's son, Michael Palmer, who was a student there and who is like a nephew to me; and I took advantage of being there to go on to Washington for the anniversary dinner of the National Gay and Lesbian Task Force. I checked into the hotel about noon and was taking a quick nap when the phone rang.

"This is the President's office. The President would like to meet with you in the Oval Office at 6:30 this evening. Are you available?"

I woke up fast. "Yes, of course I am available."

"Expect about a fifteen-minute meeting and leave enough time in case he runs late."

I thought about the sensitive issue of the press. If I entered through the northwest gate, the odds were that I'd be recognized. I wanted this meeting to work, and publicity might hamper that.

"Which gate do you want me to enter?" I asked. "I don't mind using the southwest gate if that would keep our meeting more private." Here I was, volunteering to use the equivalent of the back door of the White House. That was a switch.

"No, please, we would like you to enter the northwest gate. That will be just fine. Now, if you'll give me your Social Security number and birth date . . ."

I arrived at the White House a little early. The winter night had already settled over Washington so the exterior lighting had been turned on. I always thought it at its most beautiful when it was bathed in light like this.

At the northwest gate, I showed my identification and started walking up the driveway. A couple of reporters recognized me. "Hey, Mixner," they called out, "we thought you were banned from here. What's going on?" I shouted back, "I'm delivering a pizza. This is what it has come to." One reporter said, "I think I'll wait around until you come out and see if there's anything to report." I grinned at him. "What makes you think they're going to let me out of here?"

The White House military escort held open the door and ushered me into the reception area of the West Wing. A young assistant saw me and said, "God, is it good to see you here!" That was nice. Then Marsha Scott came out and greeted me. I thought she seemed proud that she had been able to arrange this meeting. The President was running a little late, she said, so we chatted until we were told it was time. As we came into the office of the President's assistants, a photographer showed up. That, I knew, was a good sign.

Then the door to the Oval Office opened and Marsha motioned me toward it. I thought: I am about to see my long-time friend in this setting that so powerfully symbolizes the office itself: the presidency of the United States. I found myself suddenly very nervous. Just inside the door was Vice President Gore. He shook my hand. "I've just finished a meeting with the President, but I wanted to wait and say hello to you. It's good to see you back here, Dave."

The President came around from behind his desk and welcomed me with his usual bear hug. He looked like the same Bill Clinton, yet he didn't—the Oval Office made him different. Behind the desk was the credenza with the photographs of family and friends that was so often the backdrop for his speeches to the nation. Gore said, "I'm going to let you two guys have some privacy," and left.

The President motioned to me to sit at a chair beside the desk, took off his jacket, leaned way back in his chair, and put his feet on the desk. He grinned at me. "So, how's it going for you, David?" he asked.

It was an awkward moment. I didn't quite know how to begin speaking with a friend who was the President. I had no idea what we were supposed to *do* in this meeting. All those years in our shared past had vanished into the distance. He was not the friend on the beach, or the struggling young man at Oxford, or the person who had spoken so eloquently of his vision during the campaign. He was one thing only—the President of the United States.

"Mr. President, may I begin . . ." The formality of the salutation reinforced that feeling of remoteness. I asked, "Would you mind moving a little closer? This is difficult for me and you seem so far away."

Clinton lowered his feet and sat forward in his chair.

"Go ahead, David," he said. I thought I sensed some relief that I was talking first.

"There is something I have to say and I want you to hear it directly from me. You know that I have had some serious disagreements with your policy on gays and lesbians in the military."

He seemed a little ill at ease now. He turned it away with a bit of humor. "Marsha wanted me to present you with a pair of handcuffs from your arrest."

I laughed. "Please know that I understand that you feel you gave us your best and that you feel you moved us forward," I went on. "We just have to agree to disagree on that. But I want you to know that despite differences at times, sometimes angry differences, I don't want anyone else sitting in that chair. I want you in that chair behind this desk."

He was visibly moved. I was too; I truly meant what I said. Somehow, we were both feeling each other's pain of the last year.

"That means a great deal to me, David. I have to say that I believe that I did everything I could. I believe deeply that I took a hit on this issue. Trust me, I have no doubt that you don't agree with that." He broke into his famous smile. "Hell, David, it probably helps in some quarters having you publicly disagree with me."

We were no longer tense with each other. "Well, maybe we can coordinate it a little better so I don't have to go to jail in order to be of that kind of service."

But I needed to be serious now. "Mr. President, just finishing my thought. Having you as president has moved this community forward in a historic way—money for AIDS, appointments to public service, removing barriers to discrimination in many civilian agencies. We are very grateful. Everything that you have done for us can be proceeded with the phrase 'for the first time in history . . .' "

I saw he was pleased that I remembered what he had done for us. He was fighting hard for the Ryan White apportionment legislation that would dramatically increase funding for the care of people with AIDS.

"We have made a lot of progress, haven't we?"

"Yes, sir, we have. You have your mission and it is a massive one—to govern and change a nation. It has to be overwhelming and lonely at times." He nodded. "I also have my mission too. Mr. President, I sit here only by the luck of history. I want no appointment, I desire no perks, and I am not here to spend the night at the White House. I am here because I have the opportunity to talk to the President of the United States about our struggle for freedom and the need to find a cure for AIDS. For me to do otherwise would dishonor those who have died and no longer have a voice."

He picked up on this right away. This was a safer area for him than the controversy of the military policy. His body relaxed. He was eager to show me his commitment to the battle against AIDS.

"You know," he said, "it took me a little while to understand the power of symbolism in this job. Sometimes when you are unable to successfully complete legislation, it is important to let people know that you care and understand their problems. I think I'm beginning to do both, David. We are going to get the Ryan White bill passed. We are stopping most of the damaging Helms amendments and we're starting to get some support from moderate Republicans."

"Mr. President, there is still much more to be done. So many of my friends are dying. We need you to fight for us. We need you to serve as our voice to the nation to express the horror of this epidemic. The community needs to know that you care. We *have* to find a cure. Too many are dying."

He responded by talking about two movies he had just seen in the White House screening room. "You know, David, I think the movie *Philadelphia* has done more to educate America about this disease than all of the position papers. And *Schindler's List*—God, was that a powerful movie—showed us where unchecked intolerance leads a nation. They were both incredibly powerful films—the kind that people need to see."

"I agree, Mr. President. They were astounding. I am living both of them. I have lost well over two hundred friends to AIDS and my community is living its own holocaust. At the same time, we are being denied our rights and people are attempting to use us as political pawns in their effort to achieve power. None of us can afford to remain silent. That is the worse crime of all—to see wrong and not to correct it. That's what came home to me so overwhelmingly when I recently visited the Holocaust Museum here."

"That place is sacred ground, David. The message in that building none of us should forget." He talked about his own visit there and how drained it had left him.

A presidential aide came in and Clinton motioned him away. He wanted more time with me. We talked about the gay and lesbian non-discrimination legislation pending before Congress and I urged him to consider publicly endorsing it to enhance its chances of passage. I also spoke of my deep reservations about the slow pace that AIDS Czar Kristine Gebbe was demonstrating in mobilizing the resources of the government to fight AIDS. The President had kept his campaign pledge to appoint an AIDS czar, but I believed Gebbe to be weak and ineffectual. Finally, I asked him to move quickly in making new appointments of gays and lesbians to governmental positions. There was no time to go into any of this in-depth; and as the clock moved to the hour mark, the frustrated White House staff sent in Marsha Scott to end the meeting and return the President to his schedule. He and I and Marsha wound up relaxed and laughing, old friends together. The President asked about Patsy, Michael, and the girls. We joked about friends. Then Marsha gave me a wink and rolled her eyes. It was time for me to leave.

"Mr. President, thank you for your willingness to meet," I said. "It has meant a great deal to me."

"I am glad we met, David. I know and understand that at times we will have different responsibilities, visions, and tasks. I accept that."

"The press saw me come in here. What do you want me to say going out? I have no problem saying it was a private meeting or just 'no comment' if that's what you want me to do."

"David, just say two old friends met to discuss issues that we both greatly care about."

We said good-bye. I walked down the driveway of the White House still mulling over whether I had made the right decision to come. Reestablishing contact with a close friend felt good, but there is no question that it was awkward for us both. It had been a bittersweet encounter. We were talking again. There was some hope that we would be able to work together. Maybe through this rebuilding of a personal relationship our community might have a greater opportunity to save more lives, to broaden our freedom. I recognized that for me the hope and the idealism were gone. That was certain. There was only an acknowledgment of agreeing to disagree. I believe there was a real respect for each of our different paths—his to govern a nation and mine to fight with others for our freedom. But this meeting was not a healing. What was accomplished was only an understanding that we would be on opposite sides at times, and we would try not to make it personal.

Still, I felt I had done the best job I could for my community. That was what was most important of all.

CHAPTER NINETEEN
Moving On

In the time since that meeting in the White House, there have been some rocky roads and some high ones. The President's relationship with me, and mine with him, tends to be casual and not confrontational. He calls from time to time and our conversations range from the personal to the specific. I have been invited numerous times to White House briefings, Christmas receptions, and other social occasions. There have been times when the administration's willingness to take a principled stand on issues of deep concern to our community has raised our spirits and incurred our admiration. There have also been occasions when its actions have frustrated and angered us—when expedience rather than conviction has governed its decision. The first year and a half after our White House meeting was often a difficult one. Then real progress was made. But if we who are gay and lesbian have learned anything at all from experience, it is not to count on *anything* until we see it before our eyes. We have been betrayed too often, and we know it will happen again.

The midterm congressional elections in 1994 were of special concern to the gay and lesbian community. The preachers of hate were out in full force, tapping into a nation of citizens insecure about their jobs, the stability of their families, the safety of their communities, and vulnerable to sloganeering and the appeal of simplistic solutions for complex problems. In times like that, constituencies that have had to fight for equity and freedom are always vulnerable to the attacks of extremists. African-Americans, women, immigrants, homosexuals—all become convenient targets for scaremongering and slander.

These crucial midterm elections posed a moral dilemma for the community. The temptation was to match their venom with our own. But we had been the recipient of that kind of behavior and knew the real costs to us as a society. Meeting our political responsibilities meant celebrating and supporting those candidates who reached beyond political calculation to understand our struggle. The election of 1994 presented two extraordinary examples of elected officials who were able to hear our cry—Senator Charles Robb and Senator Robert Kerrey. We had an obligation to commit our full resources to supporting them in their bid for reelection, and to show the world that we stood by our friends.

If these fine and courageous men lost, our political foes would use their defeats to proclaim the risk of supporting our struggle. On the other hand, if they won, it would help lay to rest the myth that to associate with us was dangerous. Both men entered the election season under violent attack for having supported gays and lesbians in the military.

Robb's opponent in the Virginia senatorial race was Oliver North, who had the enthusiastic, well-funded backing of right-wing political and religious extremists. Robb might have seemed an unusual person to have as our champion. His knowledge of our issues was minimal. He simply knew we weren't being treated fairly and that was unacceptable to him. But he was the kind of man who sought out the facts when he realized he didn't know something. He spoke to an ANGLE breakfast in Los Angeles to raise funds for his campaign. There were more than two hundred potential donors in the room and at one point someone asked him about his failure to understand an issue important to us. He smiled and shook his head. "Come on, gang, give me a break," he said. "I'm new to all this. Give me time to learn about you. It can't be done overnight." The crowd broke into applause. Candor like this was refreshing.

Robb's wife, Lynda Bird, was the daughter of Lyndon Johnson, and she was passionate about winning this race against Ollie North. It was as if she were campaigning not only for her husband but for her father's social programs. In October the Robb campaign held a fund-raiser at the

LBJ ranch in Johnson City, Texas. A number of us from the community came in support of Robb. We drove through the Texas hill country and along a road bordered by the Pedernales River, passing the grave of President Johnson on the way to the ranch house. Lady Bird Johnson, one of my favorite first ladies, was there to greet us at the door, charming and gracious. The ranch had been the setting of so many events the country had seen on television that I felt as if I had been there before.

The gathering looked like a freeze-frame photograph of a changing Democratic Party. The old stewards of the traditionally conservative Texas Democratic Party turned out in force for Lady Bird's son-in-law. Mingling with them were blacks, women, and gays, guests who had come to ensure that the former President's tradition of fairness and equality be kept alive. Recalling his macho presence, Fred Hochberg said to me, "Wonder what LBJ would think about having openly gay men at his ranch?" Robb knew. When I told him about Fred's comment, he said instantly, "President Johnson would have given you an especially warm welcome. He was the champion of the underdog. He hated folks being treated unfairly."

So did Robb. He was uncompromisingly principled. As *The Washington Post* reported in a story headlined "Robb Hitches Campaign to Gay Rights":

> *U.S. Sen. Charles S. Robb addressed one of the country's most influential gay political organizations yesterday and gave his strongest endorsement ever of homosexual rights, saying he will speak out on the issue even if it jeopardizes his reelection campaign.*
>
> *The Virginia Democrat condemned the "fundamental unfairness" of anti-gay discrimination and called efforts to end it "the last frontier of the true civil rights struggle." He promised that "we're going to get it right in the very near future."*

It was an act of great political courage—a traditional conservative Democrat in a conservative state in a Republican year, and in a tough reelection race, putting his career on the line for the freedom of gays and lesbians.

Equally important was the reelection of Senator Robert Kerrey of Nebraska. His Republican opponent repeatedly used Kerrey's powerful Senate speech for the Boxer Amendment against him. Here too we were being tested in a state that was conservative and rural. We did everything we could do to assist in this race and others. When election night arrived, and the conservative tide swept the Republicans into control of

Congress and launched the Gingrich revolution, our community was the exception. Over 60 percent of our candidates won. Robb and Kerrey won their races with comfortable margins. We defeated the two anti-gay initiatives on the ballot, even in Idaho where the Republican sweep was massive. As William Waybourn of the Victory Fund observed, "It hurt more being a Democrat this year than it did being gay or lesbian."

The Holocaust Museum has haunted me ever since I visited it. I am not Jewish and I was never taught about the Jewish people or their history. I had absolutely no exposure in my schools or church to the Jewish experience or the Holocaust. My first awareness came when at the age of fourteen, I went to Philadelphia on a school-sponsored field trip to see the movie *Exodus* at the big new Cinerama. I was fascinated and moved by how, out of the most devastating tragedy, the survivors rose from the ashes to create the nation of Israel. I wanted to know more. I began to read about the history of that time. Over the years, the Jewish community became a role model for me as a gay man. Its ability in the face of annihilation to surge forward, to create and build, has been an inspiration. After I came out of the closet, I examined its community institutions and political outreach, and the way its people learned to be self-reliant while becoming a crucial part of the social fabric of the larger world. I did my best to replicate their success in the gay and lesbian community. When the darkness of AIDS descended on our homes, once again I turned to the history of the Jews' survival after the Holocaust for inspiration and knowledge. When I retreated to Connecticut after Peter's death, I read accounts by the survivors, seeking wisdom and strength from their journey through the Nazi reign of terror.

The bond I felt through all those years was deepened after my visit to the museum. I grew certain that this institution was a place from which our community could draw strength and to which we could offer our own talents and support. By doing so, we would create a greater understanding between the Jewish community and ours. This sacred museum leaves no visitor untouched by the horror of a nation crazed with intolerance and hate. I believed we as a community had a responsibility to this monument.

My old friends David and Gayle Ifshin arranged for me to have breakfast with Miles Lerman, the chairman of the museum. Miles is a dedicated and passionate advocate for the museum. He hails from Vineland, New Jersey, near my hometown, and the rapport between us was instant and deep. We discovered that our lives had been driven by the same motivation—a passionate antipathy to bigotry and injustice. Miles described the museum's capacity and mission to teach future generations exactly where hatred leads.

As he spoke of the enormous numbers of school children who pour through it each year and told me about its work, I realized that here was an opportunity for us to do so much at the same time: to build coalitions with the Jewish community, to make our own contribution to this monument against intolerance, to highlight our community's history, and, in a personal way, to express my gratitude for the guidance and inspiration the Jewish community has given me over the years.

I said to Miles, "I would like to attempt to have the gay and lesbian community raise a million dollars, over a five-year period, for the museum."

All he could say was *"What?"*

"Miles," I said, "a million dollars. And please understand that it comes with no strings—no conditions or political agendas attached. We should do our part in educating the young about the dangers of intolerance. The museum has already included the gay and lesbian community's history of this period in the exhibition. Now it is our turn to meet our responsibilities."

Miles took my hand. "I know how much your community is going through right now," he said. "You are fighting for your rights and your lives at the same time. This offer is one of the most moving offers we have ever received. I know that in each dollar there is far more value than what the money represents. I thank you."

"I appreciate that understanding more than you will ever know, Miles. Let this be the beginning of building a bridge of understanding between our two communities."

We set to work. Roberta Bennett, passionate about the project, assumed the leadership of the museum's Gay and Lesbian Project. In meetings with historian and museum consultant Klaus Mueller we discovered a startling fact. When the camps were liberated in 1945, most of the homosexual survivors were *rearrested* by the Allies and jailed again for several years! Knowing this, we realized we had to create an endowment on top of our unconditional pledge specifically to continue the museum's work studying the history of gays and lesbians in the Holocaust. The project committee decided to raise an additional half a million dollars for the endowment. While we were working on this, Miles Lerman was gaining the approval of the board of directors for the gift and the endowment. There was not a single dissenting vote.

In May of 1995 leaders from the gay and lesbian and Jewish communities met in the home of David and Gayle Ifshin in Potomac, Maryland, to discuss how to honor those who had died before us. Cultural and political conservatives like David Keene of the American Conservative Union and former adviser to President Nixon Leonard Garment mingled with Roberta Bennett and HRCF's Hillary Rosen. The White House had sent Marsha Scott, Paul Richards, and John Emerson in recognition of the power that was in the room. Miles and I spoke briefly, not only of our fund-raising project but of our hope that this gathering, in and of itself, signified a new beginning of people working together.

Recalling this evening, E. J. Dionne wrote in *The Washington Post*:

> *Above all, he is fighting for a spirit represented by his movement's gesture on behalf of the Holocaust Museum. Arguments about values and culture are inevitable in a democracy. So are arguments about what government's role should be in safeguarding minorities. But Mixner is right when he says that there shouldn't be any doubt about "basic equality, basic protection" for gays and lesbians, and no justification for "hatred and bigotry." Down that road lies the calamity that the Holocaust Museum warns us against.*

By that time—mid-1995—the relationship between the Clinton administration and the gay and lesbian community had deteriorated badly. It was clear to everyone, except perhaps the President and his staff, that the "Don't Ask, Don't Tell" policy was a disaster. The facts speak for themselves. Dismissals of homosexuals from the military increased at an even greater rate than before the new policy. The Service Members Legal Defense Network, an organization dedicated to assisting gay and lesbian service members and protecting their legal rights, has monitored the policy. In its most recent report, released on February 27, 1995, their researchers found a 17 percent increase in discharges over the previous year. The report documents continuing witch-hunts on military bases, destroyed careers, heightened fear, and the absence of any efforts by the Pentagon to stop such tactics. Compounding this was the Department of Justice's insistence on fighting on the side of the military in appeals of cases we had won in the lower courts. There was a clear thrust on the part of the administration to defend the new policy.

The tensions between us were made worse by a case before the Supreme Court. In the 1992 elections Colorado voters narrowly passed an initiative called Amendment 2 that would repeal all civil rights laws that local communities had passed to protect the rights of gays and lesbians. Cities such as Aspen and Denver that had passed legislation to prevent discrimination against homosexuals would no longer be able to enforce those ordinances. The community immediately appealed the constitutionality of Amendment 2 and the Colorado Supreme Court declared it unconstitutional. The State of Colorado then appealed to the United States Supreme Court to reinstate the amendment and the Court agreed to hear the case. A number of us were asked to urge the administration to file an amicus curiae brief on our behalf. We lobbied hard to persuade the Justice Department to file the brief, and found ourselves in another pass-the-buck situation. Justice would tell us that the White House political division was making the decision and the White House would tell us that it was entirely in the hands of Justice and Attorney General Janet Reno.

For a while we were receiving encouraging indications that the administration would indeed be filing on our behalf, so when, in early June, Reno announced that she would not be filing any briefs regarding Amendment 2, we were appalled. The community was ready to walk away from the alliance with the administration altogether. There had been too many disappointments from President Clinton.

As all this was unfolding, Marsha Scott grew increasingly concerned about the fallout. Her experience in the 1992 California campaign had convinced her that if the community stayed home in 1996, the President would be in serious trouble in the large electoral states. Marsha and I talked periodically through those months about the collapse of communication between the community and the administration. We knew that something had to be done, or the alliance that had been built in 1992 would come crashing down.

Marsha used her access to the President to outline the extent of the damage. She strongly suggested there was a need for an official liaison to the community that could improve communication, rebuild some shattered bridges, and—ideally—minimize or avoid future problems. The firestorm around the Colorado decision made it clear this would need to be implemented immediately or there would be no hope of repairing the rupture.

I knew who that liaison should be: Marsha Scott. There would be some fallout from the community because she was straight, but she was the perfect choice. And most importantly, she had access to the President, she understood the importance of the community politically, and she knew most of the players.

In early June she took on the position, and it marked a turning point in the relationship between the community and the President. If there had been any doubt about the urgency of her role, it vanished in a grotesque incident on June 12. Marsha had arranged for gay and lesbian elected officials from all over the country to come to Washington to be briefed by the administration and attend a reception with the Vice President in the Old Executive Office Building. At the end of the day, sixty of these officials arrived at the EOB for the reception. By the time they came to the gate to clear security, all the White House guards had donned bright blue rubber gloves because of their fear of AIDS.

I fully believe that no one inside knew the guards were engaging in such behavior, but I also believe that none of the guards felt that this behavior would cause any risk to their jobs. Marsha grabbed me as I arrived. "We have a serious problem and we need to talk *now*."

Although her smile never left her face so the guests wouldn't notice, I knew it was serious.

"Jesus, Marsha, what now? We don't need a new problem."

"The White House guards wore bright blue rubber gloves when the elected officials arrived at the gate tonight."

"Oh, my God! This is trouble—big trouble."

"David, no one inside knew that it was happening."

"I believe that," I said, "but it's still going to hit the press big-time. Has anyone briefed the Vice President before he speaks?"

Marsha had taken care of that. She had also gotten people inside the White House to do some quick damage control and to make sure it didn't happen again.

As I circulated through the reception, all people were talking about was the glove fiasco. Vice President Gore arrived and spoke well, saying how honored he was to have them as guests of the White House. Then he said, loud and clear, "I want to be sure to take time to shake all of your hands." He left the podium and did just that. As he came to me, he whispered, "David, I am really sorry this happened to these incredible people."

The glove incident was Marsha's introduction to the nature of the problems she had to face. She launched into the process at once. A few days later the President himself wrote a personal letter of apology to all the invited guests and ordered special training for the guards to avoid future incidents.

Marsha got to work cleaning up two years of neglect. Three days into the job it was clear that she was going to deliver on the long-promised, never implemented Presidential AIDS Advisory Panel and that ANGLE member and AIDS activist Dr. Scott Hitt was going to be appointed the chair. She worked hard with Hitt to insure that it would be more than symbolic. It met for the first time in July and issued a series of recommendations for the President to act on before the end of the year. One of those recommendations was for him to convene a National Conference on AIDS and to deliver a televised address to the nation at the conference. Marsha and Scott followed up, working on the White House staff and urging them to implement all the recommendations.

In record time, the White House delivered on the conference. The National Conference on AIDS opened on December 6, with two hundred participants. In the morning breakout sessions, they prepared questions for the President, who was to attend the afternoon session. They were wide-ranging and probing: budget issues, Medicare protection, funding, condoms, sex education, and other important concerns.

CNN and C-SPAN covered the afternoon session live. I wasn't sure how the participants would respond when the President entered but they gave him a standing ovation. He spoke very effectively about a cure being an urgent national priority, of ending discrimination, educating the public. He stunned the audience when he openly spoke about the necessity of fighting homophobia. He listed his accomplishments, including the Office of National AIDS Policy in the White House, the establishment of the Presidential Advisory Council on HIV and AIDS, increased funding for housing for people with AIDS by 46 percent, increased funding for research and care by 30 percent, increased funding for the Ryan White Act by 108 percent, and the dramatic acceleration of the approval process for promising AIDS drugs. He was on point, powerful, and passionate.

Then, for two full hours, he answered questions and listened as the AIDS community told him very explicitly what the administration needed to do. We had turned a corner. Marsha Scott had begun to put us back on track with the administration.

She was not finished turning things around. HRCF had been pushing hard for the President to endorse the national gay and lesbian civil rights legislation called the Employment Non-Discrimination Act (ENDA). Until her appointment, the community had gotten nowhere in its efforts to get the White House to respond. We met with her at Scott and Alex's house in the fall of 1995 when she was in California and she told us it was an uphill battle. She did not expect an endorsement to be forthcoming. But we kept on pushing from the outside and Marsha from within, and at the beginning of 1996 it all paid off. Clinton became the first sitting president in the history of the country to endorse a piece of gay and lesbian civil rights legislation. We were continuing to make history and to mend fences. The community and the President were beginning to work together again. With these initial steps, we were again beginning to feel hopeful.

But hope does not mean taking anything for granted. As I finish this book, within a few days comes the welcome word of the Supreme Court declaring the Colorado law unconstitutional, yet the White House takes a stand against same-sex marriages. It seems clear yet again that whenever principle comes up against political advantage, the community I am part of and which I love will continue to find itself at risk.

It is an extraordinarily heroic community. Our suffering has not defeated us—it has galvanized us and strengthened our resolve to be free. We have so many talents, so much intelligence, love, and courage to bring to this troubled nation. If it embraces us, it will be a stronger and more beautiful place. But until that time of freedom arrives, we have no choice but to continue through nonviolent action to fight vigorously for what is right. No community is more determined than this one to come out of the darkness and seize the protection and freedom guaranteed to it by the Constitution of the United States of America.

ACKNOWLEDGMENTS

Writing a memoir is a difficult task. At times it is hard to remember certain dates and events while at the same time vividly recollecting others. I was fortunate to have many journals, tons of old files, all my old calendars, and especially good friends to assist in re-creating my journey. Even more importantly, as I struggled to give words to the more difficult moments in my life, I had wonderful and loving support from family and friends. There are some to whom it is essential that I express my deep thanks.

First and foremost, thanks to Todd Shuster of Zachery/Shuster. It was Todd who first urged me to write this memoir and gave me the confidence to begin. Without him, this book would never have existed. He has been there as an agent, manager, critic, and devoted friend. His partner Lane Zachery assisted in the initial editing and served as an invaluable sounding board and critic. Her insights and comments were on target.

My sister Patsy has read every word of this book time and time again.

She has tracked down information, given me emotional support when I came to tough personal issues, and assisted in the editing. Her principles were a guide for me to be vigilant, honest, and accurate. She is my best friend, and I have valued her all through this process—and through my life.

Jeremy Bernard has been equally important. He is like a brother to me and I can't imagine working on any project without him. He has devoted hundreds of hours to working with me on this book. His belief in the importance of this project served as a daily inspiration. His own recollections of the Clinton years have been invaluable. I will always be grateful that he is part of the "family."

I was fortunate to have the best of two editors. My initial editor, Rob Weisbach, gave me the confidence and daily direction to write the first drafts. His belief that this book would matter to all people motivated me to continue in times of self-doubt.

Rob left to pursue other career opportunities and at a critical moment my new Bantam editor, Ann Harris, entered my life. She is, quite simply, extraordinary. Her pages upon pages of notes, her hard work and dedication and commitment to excellence, often left me breathless. I have never experienced such professionalism, dedication, and hard work. I can only wish that every first-time author should have the good fortune to have Ann Harris as his or her editor.

In fact, the whole Bantam Books team has been remarkable. Bantam president Irwyn Applebaum has believed in this project with a conviction that has overwhelmed me. The strong direction and advice of consummate professional Barb Burg has been a source of constant reassurance. Bantam has earned my respect and gratitude.

Of course, I thank my family—not only for their faith in the book but for being forced to live with all my antics for so many years. My parents, Ben and Mary Mixner, have given me the gift of love, strong values, and solid principles. I am sad my mother is no longer with us—she would have loved this project. My brother Melvin deserves a special medal for having to endure the name of Mixner turning up in his local newspapers attached to numerous controversial issues. His wife Donna and their children Brad and Monique have also been loving and supportive over the years.

My brother-in-law Michael Annison, one of the world's most patient men, has been a saint. My nieces Elizabeth and Julia have loved me unconditionally and inspired me to work to make the world a better place.

Special thanks must go to Marylouise Oates and Bob Shrum for their faith in me, their invaluable advice, and for their huge phone bills from daily calls to make sure the writing was going well. No one could have better friends.

I don't know what I would have done in the final stages of this book without the emotional and loving support of Patrick Marston. His presence in my life has greatly enriched it and makes me look forward to the future.

Finally, thanks to those friends who have assisted me in many ways in preparing this book. Special thanks must go to Dr. Scott Hitt and Alex Koleszar for reading rough drafts and offering detailed comments. I am grateful to my friends Herb Hamsher, Judith Light, Robert Desiderio, Jonathan Stoller, Jeff Trammell, Cory O'Conner, David Ifshin, Dennis Bailey, Jeff Marcus, Eric Karpeles, Michael Sell, Chris Easton, Kevin Cassidy, and William Waybourn, who have read all or parts of the drafts and offered valuable insights.

I thank those who helped me recollect events. In the antiwar sections, John O'Sullivan, Don and Judy Green, John Shattuck, Sam Brown, Tony Podesta, Anne Wexler, David Hawk, Joan Libby, and numerous others offered valuable information.

I am especially grateful for the advice and support of Tom Stoddard, Fred Hochberg, Chai Feldblum, Andrew Barrer, Sheila Kuehl, Tracy Thorne, Tony Leonhardt, Craig Dougherty, Jeff Matchan, Torie Osborn, Larry Weghorst, Larry Sprenger, Jeff Gibson, Diane Abbitt, Roberta Bennett, Sky Johnson, Craig Bugbee, Cameron Cox, Scott Allyn, Roberta Achtenberg, Mary Morgan, Reverend Nancy Wilson, Reverend Troy Perry, Steve and Kathleen Unger, Bill and Kim Wardlaw.

My life has been enriched with friends who have made this book possible, including Ed Gould, Chuck Holmes, Terry Bean, Michael Bento, Howard Bragman, David Davis, Richard DuPaix, Chris Hershey, Susan Van Horn, Kevin James, Steve Lachs, Michael Ruvo, Doug Lowery, Steve Nuskiewicz, Dan Pallotta, Skip Paul, Sky Johnson, Van Fletcher, Robert Sertner, Steve Tyler, David von Storch, Randy Mc-Whorter, Rick Ellsasser, John Duran, David Wexler, David Beckerman, Preston Phillips, Chuck Forthofer, Trip Wilmot, Tom Henderson, Nancy Moleda, Joy Tomchin, Lynn Greer, Jean O'Leary, Jeff Applegate, Dan Bassett, Kevin Conroy, Philip Mercado, and Bill Huggins.

Special thanks to three friends and professional allies, Kathy Murphy, Phil Cavanaugh, and Tom Reed.

I owe thanks to my three cats, Geraldine, Yeats, and Sheeba, for their patience with my hectic writing schedule that took quality time away from them.

Finally, out of the more than two hundred and fifty friends who have died of AIDS I especially want to remember Peter Scott, Mark Coleman, Kip Ohman, David Quarles, Sheldon Andelson, Dan Bradley, Colin Higgins, Tim Furlong, Neal Tipton, Carl Ripsburger, Randy Klose, and Rob Eichberg.

Index